Essays on the History of Economics

The history of economics is littered with concepts characterized by the multiple ways in which they can be approached and formulated. In essence, this is the thing which makes the history of economic thought so interesting and important.

This volume examines four key subjects in the history of economics: Adam Smith's concept of the division of labour; whether "recent" developments in economic thought are yet worthy of serious examination; the varying approaches to the history of economic thought embodied in textbooks; and the legacy of Thorstein Veblen as an economic theorist.

The caliber of the authors of this book makes it stand out from the crowd and as such this work will be a valuable and interesting tool for all those economists wise enough to thoroughly study their discipline's history as well as its here and now.

Warren J. Samuels is Professor Emeritus of Economics, Michigan State University, USA. Among his many other books, he is also co-editor of *The History of Economic Thought: A Reader*, also available from Routledge.

Willie Henderson is Professor of Continuing Education and Director of the Centre for Lifelong Learning, University of Birmingham, UK. Other books written by Henderson include *Economics as Literature*, also published by Routledge.

Kirk D. Johnson is Assistant Professor of Economics, Wesley College, USA.

Marianne Johnson is Assistant Professor of Economics, University of Wisconsin-Oshkosh, USA.

Routledge Studies in the History of Economics

Essays on the History of Economics

Warren J. Samuels,
Willie Henderson,
Kirk D. Johnson and
Marianne Johnson

LONDON AND NEW YORK

First published 2004
by Routledge
11 New Fetter Lane, London EC4P 4EE

Simultaneously published in the USA and Canada
by Routledge
29 West 35th Street, New York, NY 10001

Routledge is an imprint of the Taylor & Francis Group

© 2004 Warren J. Samuels, Willie Henderson, Kirk D. Johnson and
Marianne Johnson

Typeset in Galliard by Taylor & Francis Books Ltd
Printed and bound in Great Britain by Antony Rowe Ltd
Chippenham, Wiltshire

British Library Cataloguing in Publication Data
A catalogue record for this book is available from the British Library

Library of Congress Cataloging in Publication Data
A catalog record for this book has been requested

ISBN 0–415–70006–X

This volume is dedicated to Sylvia Samuels. It is published in the year we celebrate our fiftieth wedding anniversary. She is to be honored for her support of my work and her unfailing support and hospitality to my students.

Contents

Tables

Contributors

Willie Henderson is Professor of Continuing Education and Director of the Centre for Lifelong Learning at the University of Birmingham, UK. He has written on the language of economics and economics as literature, and is working on women economists and economic educators in the nineteenth century, and on the textual analysis of the *Wealth of Nations*.

Kirk D. Johnson is Assistant Professor of Economics at Wesley College, Dover, Delaware. He specializes in history of economic thought and in economic history.

Marianne Johnson is Assistant Professor of Economics at the University of Wisconsin-Oshkosh. She specializes in history of economic thought and in public economics. Previous work includes the American Economy Series on Early American Economic Thought with Pickering and Chatto. She has written on interpretations of Knut Wicksell, voting and the development of public choice, and is working on issues in early American economic thought.

Warren J. Samuels is Professor Emeritus of Economics at Michigan State University. He specializes in history of economic thought, methodology, and law and economics. He is working on the use of the concept of the invisible hand.

Introduction

Warren J. Samuels

Over the years I have written essays on several fundamental concepts in economics. These include cost, coercion, property, rent, the legal–economic nexus, the problem of order, and distribution. Each of these concepts is characterized by the multiple ways it can be approached and formulated. Because no one formulation can deal with all the issues engendered by each concept, this multiplicity is perennial. Also important is the fact that even if, in some sense, these concepts can be treated as referring to something given and transcendent, they are, as we use them, socially constructed tools of analysis (and of policy).

In this volume, several colleagues and I examine four subjects in the history of economic thought, each of which involves fundamental topics. The subjects are identified by their respective chapter titles.

In the chapter on Adam Smith's concept of the division of labor, written with Willie Henderson, we do not consider the concept in the manner so important to Smith and to later economists, namely, the several domains of the division of labor and its good and bad consequences. Instead we consider the sources—the etiology—of the division of labor. Smith, it is most widely known, attributed the division of labor to a propensity to truck, barter and exchange. It remains an open question as to what Smith meant by using all three of these terms. Smith is also known for attributing the propensity itself to the faculties of reason and language.

It turns out, first, that the principal explanation—the division of labor as a function of the propensity to exchange, itself a function of the faculties of reason and language—is not the only explanation provided by Smith. No less than four alternative accounts may readily be found in Smith's writings. One has to do with individuals taking advantage of opportunities open to them. Another has to do with behavior relating to the commercial stage of society. Still another involves the nature of human nature. And the fourth has to do with the individual's quest for social recognition and moral approbation.

It also turns out that this multiplicity of accounts involves numerous interpretive problems. These include: whether certain factors are causal or limiting; conflicting analyses of the relation between exchange and the division of labor; economic versus non-economic foundations of economic development; the relation of commercial society and the division of labor; the respective roles of nature and nurture, of nature and man, of nature and God, and of God and man; problems of definition; whether differences between people are the cause or the effect of the division of labor; and whether words are instruments of inquiry or definitions of reality.

All of the foregoing suggests a much more complicated and recursive model constituting the etiology of the division of labor. It also suggests how important are the non-economic parts of Smith's total system of social science for the economic parts.

It further turns out that Smith had a particular notion of the role of philosophy (= science). That role was not to ascertain truth if one couldn't but to set minds at rest. He applies that role to his own work, saying that even he

> while … endeavouring to represent all philosophical systems as mere inventions of the imagination, to connect together the otherwise disjointed and discordant phenomena of nature, ha[d] insensibly been drawn in, to make use of language expressing the connecting principles of this one, as if they were the real chains which Nature makes use of to bind together her several operations.
>
> (Smith 1980: 105, IV.76)

This view of Smith's is consonant, we point out, with a variety of postmodern developments. Moreover, if Smith can apply his theory to his own work, so can we. In the third part of the chapter we explore the significance, in view of his conception of the role of philosophy, of his use of the propensity and the faculties in the explanation of the origins of the division of labor—a sixth formulation of the etiology of the division of labor.

The result is an affirmation of language as tools, the identification of numerous problems of language, and the nature of the social construction of concepts and theories. I shall return to this point later.

In the chapter on the problem of considering recent economic thought, Kirk Johnson, Marianne Johnson and I consider the probative value of the argument against doing so made by Joseph Dorfman. Dorfman based his argument on two lines of reasoning: that sufficient time had to elapse for the acquisition of available data necessary for adequate description and the development of proper perspective.

In principle Dorfman's argument makes sense. The problem, we show, is that it is impossible to achieve.

The first part of the chapter follows the presentation of Dorfman's argument. It examines the issues and problems involved in avoiding the undertaking of recent economic thought. These issues and problems arise in connection with the meaning of recency and of history and the absence of an independent test; the teaching of economic theory through the history of economic thought; the history of economic thought as a means of gaining knowledge; the loss of contemporary knowledge as the price of gaining perspective; the absence of any necessary correction of selective perception or bias; the lessened need for recency in some approaches to the history of economic thought; the history of economic thought as what has survived; the necessity for limits to coverage; the inevitable production of the history of economic thought by non-historians; the problem of new publications; the practice of social construction in light of futurity; the possibility of multiple stories; inevitable incompleteness and selectivity; and the pressure for recency—together with an account of arm's length dealing as more important than the passage of time.

It turns out that these issues and problems necessarily arise in the social construction of the history of economic thought. That history does not write itself. It is written by people with their own agendas and their own motivations, and is influenced by Whiggish and presentist orientations—agendas, motivations and orientations that are not always consciously held.

The second part of the chapter inquires as to how recency (relative to date of publication) is treated in the relevant literature. That literature includes, first, the history-of-economic-thought textbooks and other history-of-economic-thought materials, and second, materials not specifically history of economic thought. We find only two cases of textbook authors making major design changes in their treatment of recency over editions; that many authors do not discuss the problem, though numerous authors do explicitly consider it; that many textbooks have no or very negligible coverage of recent materials, that many textbooks have some coverage, and that many have extensive coverage; non-textbook coverage is mixed, some largely stopping short of the contemporary period and some covering the recent period, with some intentionally interpreting recent materials; and some critiques of earlier work use recent work and some publications are intended to be critiques of recent work. Also considered are readers in the history of economic thought, a sample of personal citations for eleven post-World War II economists, the journal literature, and materials not specifically history of economic thought. These considerations of the treatment of the problem of recency reinforce the conclusions of the first part, namely, that undertaking and reporting on the study of recent economic thought is inevitable.

The third chapter, written with Kirk Johnson and Marianne Johnson, examines the prefaces, introductions, epilogues and concluding chapters in textbooks in the history of economic thought. These materials often address questions of historiography. They tell the reader why the author wrote what he or she did and in the way they did. They also often discuss the question, where does all this history of economic thought leave us? This chapter examines what the authors of history-of-economic-thought textbooks have to say about the history of economic thought.

The range of historiographic topics and associated issues that the textbook authors elect to mention is lengthy. Altogether these topics help to identify the design strategy employed by the authors in writing their books. (Inasmuch as the textbooks each tell a story of the history of economic thought, each has a story line, plot or design strategy.) These topics also constitute the historiographic fundamentals of work in the history of economic thought; serious work in the field must deal with them willy-nilly.

The most basic and inescapable design topics include the determination of the intended audience, marketing considerations, when in history the story is to begin, whether the story will be told in terms of individuals, schools or ideas, and which representative individuals will be included. Further basic insights into authorial strategy are given by what authors say about the benefits of studying the history of economic thought.

There are numerous other modes of doing history of economic thought, each mode requiring further selectivity of design. These topics include: a focus on theory or ideas or both; the attitude to be taken in regard to hegemonic mainstream theory; whether the story being told is one of the definition of reality, system of belief, or set of tools; whether the story is told in terms of one or another mode of thought; whether attention is given to the sociology of economics; the origin *vis-à-vis* later use of theories and ideas; whether the story is eclectic or organized around a single principle; the divisions of the subject matter of economics; the attitude to be taken in relation to antiquarianism, error and serious study; coverage of major and/or minor figures; conservative and liberal economists; and classical versus modern theory. Of these topics, the first two are given the most explicit treatment, the third is important but rarely dealt with explicitly, and the others significant enough to be raised by authors.

Much more basic, however, are authorial attitudes toward topics of the substance of the history of economic thought. These topics include: attitudes toward progress in economics; aspects of the history of economic thought and of the dynamics of theoretical change; the problem of presentism; the problem of relativism; the sources of economic ideas and theories, including internalism and externalism; and methodological considerations.

The fourth chapter takes on the twin charges that institutional economists are against theory and, further, have produced no theory. The charges are rebutted using the theories of Thorstein Veblen as an example. The point is not whether his theories are true or preferable to other theories but whether Veblen was anti-theoretical and whether his work is theoretical.

The procedure is as follows. We first consider the nature of theory *per se* with a passing glance at the roles of theory. We show, *inter alia*, the various forms that theory in general can take. We next consider neoclassical theory, showing, in part, the various forms that its theory takes. Finally, we consider Veblen as a theorist, examining the nature of his theories, his treatment as a theorist, and the array of Veblen's theories, classified as to subject; altogether, the various forms that his theory takes. (This paper was originally prepared for the Veblen Conference, Bevagna, Italy, 22–23 November 2003, which, because of infirmities, I was unable to attend. I am indebted to Professor Mino Vianello for the invitation and his understanding.)

The chapters in this volume thus address some of the most fundamental questions confronting the sub-discipline of the history of economic thought. These are:

- What is history? What is the definition of what we do?
- What is language? How are we to understand what we say?

- What is theory? How does theory serve as a means of explicating our interpretation of the world to others?

These questions are approached by considering four subjects, each of which is important on its own grounds:

- The origins of the division of labor—a fundamental concept for Adam Smith and economics since Smith.
- The impact of how historians of economic thought and others treat recent economic thought on how history is practiced and the development of the discipline.
- The impact of what authors of history-of-economic-thought say about historiographic subjects and issues, and the positions they take, on how their sub-discipline works and its relations to other economists.
- The diverse nature of theory in neoclassical and institutional economics and the nature of each as theoretical disciplines.

Pervading the four chapters is attention to aspects and problems of language in economics, and (as raised earlier in connection with chapter 1) questions of the nature and social function of belief.

The four chapters provide contributions to the answers to the fundamental questions by others, and our comments, arguments and conclusions. What emerges, not surprisingly, is that the questions can be posed in different ways and that, however the questions are worded, the answers are multiple. This brings us to a set of themes also ubiquitous in these chapters, namely, the social construction of the economy, economics, and the history of economic thought, and the resultant multiplicity and necessity of choice. It is simply not true that one and only one story can be told on any subject of substance.

The chapters in this volume suggest additional fundamental considerations, with questions that go beyond the result of an affirmation of language as tools, the identification of numerous problems of language, and the nature of the social construction of concepts and theories, questions that apply to but go beyond the history of economic thought.

The result is also a caution about the grounds on which we accept propositions–whether they be the elements of Smith's etiology, the design strategy for textbooks or the theories of neoclassical and Veblenian economics. There may be no grounds or the grounds may lack solid substance. If the Smith–Shackle reasoning is correct, then acceptance is driven by the need to assuage the imagination, to set our minds at rest. But if our caution is correct, on what grounds do we accept the Smith–Shackle reasoning as correct? Karl Popper has a name for the propositions: they are conjectures in a process of inquiry.

Vilfredo Pareto described another process: the process of deploying propositions (he called them "derivations"; James Harvey Robinson called them "rationalizations"; still others, superstition, ideology, myths and signs) that either lack substance or require consideration together with other propositions but are deployed alone in order to manipulate political psychology in a world of fraud and force.

One of the historiographic issues that arises in Chapters 1 and 3 especially concerns the tension between economic thought as definition of reality, system of belief, and set of tools. A quarter of a century ago I sought to provide an understanding of Thurman Arnold's recognition of the symbolic construction of social reality. The article began by asking

> What do the lawyer and economist do upon discovering that the king has no clothes? Economics and law are existential disciplines. Both confront directly the reality of radical indeterminacy: human society is an artifact, subject to revision, reformed (deliberatively and non-deliberatively) through the processes of living and interacting. The future is indeterminate because it is in part created through the very effort to comprehend and control it. What, then, does the law-economics scholar do upon ascertaining that social awareness—including both economic study and the practice of law in all its ramifications—largely deals with symbols which, while socially functional, lack substance?
>
> (Samuels 1992c: 277)

No wonder cynicism and skepticism, as well as force and fraud, flourish—the irony of which is further need and compulsion to set minds at rest.

The argument need not be taken to such an extreme position. But if one accepts something like the statement, propositions will be accepted on the basis of what makes sense, but what determines what makes sense, and is "making sense" not setting one's mind at rest?

One thing that textbook authors generally fail to do is to examine subtle interpretive problems, including rival interpretations and choosing from among them. (Textbooks in economic theory rarely discuss in depth the criteria of theory choice.) Doing so might be an important function of such texts—as suggested by authors who propose that training the mind is an important function of or benefit from studying the history of economic thought. If John R. Hicks is correct that no one theory can answer all our questions, then perhaps there is room for multiple theories of capital, of cost, and so on, each devoted to inquiring into different questions. As it stands, most economists seem compelled to believe that only one correct theory of capital or of cost, etc. can exist and then adopt their favorite one—all the while using it as a tool or element of design strategy. Historians of economic thought can enrich economic theory by educating future economists along the lines of theoretical pluralism—for the reason just given and for other reasons. That economic theorists impoverish their work, often with the support of historians of economic thought, testifies to the importance of the sociology of economics as an historiographic topic and thereby of the relevance of the Smith–Veblen theory of status emulation, the grounds of which need to be established.

One final point. The studies comprising these four chapters demonstrate that meaningful history-of-economic-thought work cannot often be undertaken without serious methodological, ontological, epistemological and historiographic components.

I would like to acknowledge the depth of my obligations to my co-authors, Willie Henderson, Marianne Johnson and Kirk Johnson. From Willie I have learned much, the existence of which was novel to me. Coincidentally sharing the same surname but personally unrelated, Marianne and Kirk also shared several of my classes and were my last doctoral candidates at Michigan State University. Like my students before them, they have been teaching me. The contributions of all three scholars to these chapters have been substantial.

I am indebted to Roger Backhouse, Jerry Evensky, John and Katherine Giles, Andrea Salanti and Jeff Young for help in tracking down fugitive citations.

1 The etiology of Adam Smith's division of labor

Alternative accounts and Smith's methodology applied to them

Willie Henderson and Warren J. Samuels

Introduction

This chapter examines two questions: What is Adam Smith's explanation for the origin of the division of labor? What is the ontological and epistemological nature of his explanation? It turns out that the conventional explanation is not only deeper than is customarily acknowledged but is accompanied by no less than four alternative explanations. Of the total of five, three are singularly or predominantly "economic" in nature, and two are clearly non-economic. That Smith would provide non-economic answers to a question to which an economic answer(s) is given should be no surprise, inasmuch as his is a synoptic and synthetic system of social-science analysis (Samuels 1977; Skinner 1979); the economics-laden *Wealth of Nations* is inseparable from the other spheres of life and from his other works. What may be surprising to some scholars[1] is a still further explanation that fits Smith's own understanding of what he as a philosopher was doing. This sixth explanation emphasizes both mind-satisfying belief and truth, but especially the former. For Smith, the purpose or rationale of social-science analysis was very different from, or more complicated than, that voiced by present-day economists.

A seemingly simple issue—the origin, or etiology, of the division of labor—is thus shown to be extremely complex and to raise serious questions about Smith's overall project and by extension how we reason and how we do economics.

The chapter starts with the division of labor *per se*. The discussion then turns to the principal account of the origin of the division of labor, centering on the propensity to truck, barter and exchange and the faculties of reason and speech (hereinafter the propensity and the faculties, respectively). Next, the four alternative explanations found in Smith's work are examined. Finally, an interpretation is given of what he was doing in proposing and grounding the division of labor that is based on his own account of what people like him are doing as philosophers or scientists—an interpretation that encompasses the fourth of the alternative explanations. Since the fourth interpretation, as given by Smith, applies to people other than philosophers or scientists, its applicability to him implies that to Smith philosophers and scientists are no different in their mental processes (even if more highly trained) than ordinary folk—a point made by him in connection with philosopher and porters (see below).[2] An appendix, prepared by Willie Henderson, further examines Smith's procedure in his writing on the propensity to truck, barter and exchange in Book I, Chapter II.

The division of labor and its manifold consequences, not surprisingly, are given enormous attention in the Smithian literature. As for its etiology, one group of history-of-economic-thought texts and other writings makes no mention of the propensity in relation to the division of labor, and another group notes it only in passing. Some writings that do mention the propensity ignore the questions of *its* origin in the faculties and its nature and status as knowledge; there is precious little elaborate discussion, largely (when mentioned at all) only in relation to its role as the basis of the division of labor. Indeed, some authors start with the division of labor as a given, discussing it as an important fact; other authors treat it as a necessary condition. Several authors have treated the propensity more or less extensively, and they agree on some matters and disagree on others. A few authors do not accept the propensity story uncritically. Throughout the relevant literature, what is not said is sometimes more interesting than what is said. In any event, one-sided interpretations of what Smith wrote likely will be misleading and incomplete. The division of labor is certainly important to Smith as the preeminent cause of the growth of the wealth of nations. The basic analysis of the principal account has been canonized in economics. But his texts are amenable to other accounts. All accounts have been variously interpreted—and his several texts and the variegated interpretations have provided a richer, if more complex, analysis than the simple canonical model. (On interpretation, see Gerrard 1993; on canonization and decanonization, see Brown 1993; Samuels 2001b.) Smith himself partly diagnoses the situation when he writes:

> Different authors gave different systems both of natural and moral philosophy. But the arguments by which they supported those different systems, far from being always demonstrations, were frequently at best but very slender probabilities, and sometimes mere sophisms, which had no other foundation but the inaccuracy and ambiguity of common language.
>
> (Smith 1976b: 27-28, I.ii.3)

The division of labor

Adam Smith was concerned with both the origins and the consequences of the division of labor. Economists' interests in the division of labor have been influenced by generations of varied interpretations of Smith, interpretations influenced by the evolution of economic theory.

The central argument of the *Wealth of Nations* is predicated on the division of labor. Given a conception of wealth as consisting of things which either directly or indirectly contribute to human well-being, the argument is that the growth of wealth is due to the division of labor, through specialization, engendering greater productivity. The power of the division of labor is limited, conditioned, caused or enhanced[3] by the extent of the market, the use of money in lieu of barter, free trade both domestic and international, the technical skills and motivation of labor, the proportion of productive to unproductive labor, and the accumulation of capital. As will be seen later, another condition is a sufficiently developed institution of property; still another is that economic agents are sufficiently equipped with a capacity for language and trade.

Another way of putting this, at least in part, is that Smith's and indeed all of classical economics is a model or paradigm founded on the concept of capital and on decisions regarding the allocation of total capital stock. The elements of this model include the following: Saving leads to capital formation. The deployment of capital leads to the organization for production, though one could say that the organization for production leads to business saving (retained earnings), capital formation and the deployment of capital. The production of commodities is by means of commodities, i.e., capital goods. Output is a function of capital stock and capital stock must necessarily be on hand prior to production. Decisions regarding the allocation of total capital stock between uses govern resource allocation, growth and distribution. The allocative decisions are between fixed and circulating capital, the wages-fund approach to wage-rate determination, and capital setting labor in motion versus capital saving labor, the role of the capitalist class being to provide the means of subsistence to the working class through the organization for production and the conduct of production.

The problem of causal order arises throughout both the foregoing and this essay. For example, Rothbard applauds Jean-Baptiste Say for making investment more crucial than its division *per se* (Rothbard 1995b: 23). Roll argues that accumulation of capital must precede the division of labor (Roll 1946: 176). All this and more (extent of the market, use of money, etc.) govern the division of labor. But the opposite is also true: if investment and accumulation of capital must precede—and in that respect, if no other be more important than—the allocation of capital and the division of labor, it is also true that productivity gains from the division of labor facilitate investment and the accumulation of capital. We shall see that recursive relationships, ones that manifest cumulative causation, such that A→B and B←A, or AÖB, pervade Smith's work. One example is the mutually reinforcing relation between growth and the division of labor (e.g., Taylor 1960: 97; Dome 1994: 6); another, in Marxist language, is that multiple divisions of labor are both cause and consequence of superstructural (especially legal and political) relations. Still another is what Fiori (2001: 436ff) calls Smith's dualities, such as that involving natural and market price.

Each of the concepts utilized in Smith's account can be amplified, raising such matters as the rate of capital accumulation, limits to returns to scale, productive versus nonproductive labor, the working of the price mechanism in regard to relative values/prices, mechanization, capital setting labor in motion versus capital saving labor, the institutions of money supply, the role of "surplus" in exchange, different forms of the division of labor and specialization, self-interest versus benevolence, and so on. This story, fully elaborated, is the heart of Smith's program for economic growth, the more-or-less proximate basis of much post-Smithian economics, and a cause of conflicting interpretations of Smith's analyses. A very different but not mutually exclusive story has the division of labor being the basis of social order, constituting a social bond. Such a story is found in Emile Durkheim's *Division of Labor in Society* (1933) and arises below. Most attention in the history-of-economic-thought textbooks and other writings is given to Smith's pin-making example, types of the division of labor, and the gains and losses consequent to the division of labor.[4]

Attention is also given to the theory of human nature said by Smith to relate to the division of labor. The principal obvious elements of human nature are the propensities to better one's condition and to truck, barter and exchange. These promote "the natural progress of a nation towards wealth and prosperity" (Smith 1976b: 674, IV.ix.28). These are conventionally understood to be causal, hence etiological, factors; they may also be considered to be limiting conditions, such as with the extent of the market, etc. The two propensities are also frequently joined: the propensity to truck, barter and exchange in the service of bettering one's condition—a formulation close to the first alternative explanation, as is the formulation that the "inclination to trade … is but one expression of … self-interested behavior" (Rima 1978: 70).

The propensity to better one's condition is, for Smith, not without exception, though the exceptions are not sufficiently strong and widespread as to make a "sensible impression" (Smith 1976b: 469, IV.ii.41) on the rate of progress, i.e., employment, wealth and prosperity (see Sandelin *et al.* 2002: 29 for details). This raises the interesting problems of who determines what is condition bettering and of circularity. Among the exceptions are drunkenness and gluttony (both addictions) as well as prodigality (unusual time preference, i.e., a dysfunctional inter-temporal trade-off between present and future consumption possibilities). Smith does several things: He defines condition bettering in terms of wealth and prosperity. He identifies certain behaviors as exceptions, on the one hand substituting his own preferences for those of economic actors and, on the other hand, giving effect to and thereby demonstrating the economic role of the Impartial Spectator's formulation of correct behavior. This raises questions as to the universality and equal-intensivity of the propensity to better one's condition and of capital accumulation (Barber, forthcoming) and as to the circularity of any argument dependent upon the definition of condition bettering.

The propensity to truck, barter and exchange is central to the principal account, or at least its simple and conventional form.

The principal account

The propensity and the faculties

The first chapter of Book I of the *Wealth of Nations*, entitled "Of the Division of Labour," establishes the key position of the division of labor in Smith's argument. In the very next chapter, "Of the Principle which gives Occasion to the Division of Labour," Smith attributes it to a "certain propensity":

> This division of labour, from which so many advantages are derived, is not originally the effect of any human wisdom, which foresees and intends that general opulence to which it gives occasion. It is the necessary, though very slow and gradual, consequence of a certain propensity in human nature which has in view no such extensive utility: the propensity to truck, barter, and exchange one thing for another.
>
> (Smith 1976b: 25, I.ii.1)

This propensity has been the conventional explanation for the division of labor. It is, at least, the simple version of his principal explanation. Smith reiterates it two paragraphs later, saying "it is this same trucking disposition which originally gives occasion to the division of labour" (Smith 1976b: 27, I.ii.3).

Smith next considers the origin of the propensity:

> Whether this propensity be one of those original principles in human nature,[5] of which no further account can be given; or whether, as seems more probable, it is the necessary consequence of the faculties of reason and speech, it belongs not to our present subject to enquire.
>
> (Smith 1976b: 25, I.ii.2)[6]

Alas, Smith nowhere indicates what we are to understand by "those original principles in human nature," or how "the faculties of reason and speech" relate thereto.[7] And a certain tension is apparent, involving the principle of unintended and unforeseen consequences: Smith identifies both the non-deliberative—"has in view no such extensive utility"—and the deliberative—"faculties of reason and speech." But this is, as we shall see, not the only conundrum. In any event, the factor "faculties of reason and speech" also serves as a basis of the fourth alternative account.

Smith continues, in the same, very long second paragraph, to assert that "It [the propensity] is common to all men, and to be found in no other race of animals, which seem to know neither this nor any other species of contracts." As for man, who "has almost constant occasion for the help of his brethren," he cannot "expect it from their benevolence only," and "will be more likely to prevail if he can interest their self-love in his favour, and shew them that it is for their own advantage to do for him what he requires of them." This leads, a few lines later, to the famous passage, "It is not from the benevolence of the butcher, the brewer, or the baker, that we expect our dinner, but from their regard to their own interest. We address themselves, not to their humanity, but to their self-love, and never talk to them of our own necessities but of their advantages" (Smith 1976b: 25–27, I.ii.2). (Notice, again, the emphasis on the deliberative.)

He commences the next, third paragraph—the chapter has only five paragraphs—with the reiteration that, motivated by self-interest, "it is this same trucking disposition which originally gives occasion to the division of labour." After a discussion of examples, Smith concludes the paragraph with the following line of reasoning:

> And thus the certainty of being able to exchange all that surplus part of the produce of his own labour, which is over and above his own consumption, for such parts of the produce of other men's labour as he may have occasion for, encourages every man to apply himself to a particular occupation, and to cultivate and bring to perfection whatever talent or genius he may possess for that particular species of business.
>
> (Smith 1976b: 27–28, I.ii.3)

For present purposes we need not consider that such is only one aspect of the division of labor (the individual one, the others being within manufacturing plants and within the economy as a whole); that this takes place in whatever occupation in which a person finds himself; or, for the moment, that this statement also helps form the basis of the first alternative account, and that "differences of natural talents," as Smith put it, are less than we think, the "differences between the most dissimilar characters, between a philosopher and a common street porter," for example, seeming "to arise not so much from nature, as from habit, custom, and education"—points made here (Smith 1976b: 28–29, I.ii.4) and/or elsewhere. We need only note that Smith concludes this paragraph with the reiteration of the importance of "the disposition to truck, barter, and exchange," for without it, with each person performing all the duties of production, the benefits of different talents, enhanced by specialization, would not be achieved. The argument is further reiterated in the final, fifth paragraph, wherein he argues that wanting "the power or disposition to barter and exchange," men are less able to "contribute to the better accommodation and conveniency of the species" (Smith 1976b: 30, I.ii.5). Notice that Smith uses both "propensity" and "disposition" and, moreover, introduces the idea of "the *power* to barter and exchange"—without further elaboration.

Smith also took up the question of the origin of the propensity in his lectures on jurisprudence. The matter is also discussed in one of the fragments of his work now in the literature. These form the basis of two of the alternative accounts and will be discussed below. In any event, in the lectures Smith is reported to have said:

This bartering and trucking spirit is the cause of the separation of trades and the improvements in arts. A savage who supports himself by hunting, having made some more arrows than he had occasion for, gives them in a present to some of his companions, who in return given him some of the venison they have catched; and he at last finding that by making arrows and giving them to his neighbour, as he happens to make them better than ordinary, he can get more venison than by his own hunting, he lays it aside … and becomes an arrow-maker.

(Smith 1978: 348)

[As the labor is divided among the people n]o human prudence is requisite to make this division. … [I]f things be allowed to take their naturall course there is no danger that any branch of trade should be either over or under stocked with hands.[8] … The certainty of disposing of the surplus produce of his labour in this way is what enabled men to separate into different trades of every sort.

(Smith 1978: 351)

What Smith would have replied to an editor who identified and asked him about all these accounts, would be—in this matter as in many others—of enormous interest and help. Like most other people, Smith was susceptible to jargon, mystification, selective reification of universals, ambiguity, and other problems of language.

At any rate, the principal account for some is limited to the propensity; for others the propensity is grounded in the faculties of reason and speech; for some the problem of etiology is irrelevant.

It should go without saying that the problem of the origins of language has received attention in the centuries since Smith wrote. For example, one theory is that language evolved from a gestural system to the spoken word, with signed language, complete with grammar and syntax and punctuated with grunts and other vocalizations (see Corballis 2003). The circumstances likely included hunting, dividing, exchanging, and so on.

One further matter should be noted. Smith's principal account, centering on the principle and the faculties, enters into the controversy over the meaning of Friedrich von Hayek's theory of spontaneous order. One version of the theory juxtaposes non-deliberative to deliberative decision making and emphasizes the former: "Indeed, for Adam Smith," according to one account which readily uses his language:

the observable division of labour is not "originally the effect of any human wisdom, which foresees and intends the general opulence to which it gives occasion. It is the necessary, though very slow and gradual, consequence of a certain propensity in human nature which has in view no such extensive utility: the propensity to truck, barter and exchange one thing for another."

(Nadeau 1998: 479, quoting Smith 1976b: 25, I.ii.1)

A more eclectic account both concurs with the unintended and unforeseen consequences theme, due to interaction and aggregation of individual decision making, and elevates the role of deliberative decision making, for present purposes emphasizing that the role of the faculties of reason and speech necessarily involves deliberative decision making (Samuels 1999b). The latter view also considers the division of labor itself a matter of methodological collectivism, not methodological individualism (Nadeau 1998).

The matter of definition

Several terms used by Smith warrant close examination as to meaning. It would be nice if dictionary definitions could help resolve theoretical ambiguities, such as the meaning of "truck, barter and exchange." Alas, that is not the case.

(A) The following is based on the *Oxford English Dictionary* (1971 Compact edition).

Barter is defined in terms of (1) The act or practice of trafficking by exchange of commodities; truck. (2) Exchange; interchange. (3) Goods to be bartered or traded in by each party. (4) The computation of the quantity or value of one commodity, to be given for a known quantity or value of another commodity.

Exchange is defined in terms of (1) Reciprocal giving and receiving. (2) A mutual grant of equal interests, the one in consideration of the other. (3) [The same as (1)]. (4) A species of mercantile transactions. (5) Bill of Exchange. (6) Sense of change, of substitution. Also: (1) To dispose of by exchange or barter. (2) [The same as (1)].

Truck/trucking is defined in terms of (1) Trading by exchange of commodities; barter. (2) Payment of wages otherwise than in money. (3) Traffic, intercourse, communication, dealings. (4) Commodities for barter. Also: (1) To exchange, to give in exchange. (2) To exchange (commodities) for profit; to acquire by barter. (3) To dispose of by barter. (4) To barter away. (5) To trade by exchange. (6) To bargain or negotiate, especially in underhand or improper way. (7) To pay otherwise than in money.

Each word is defined essentially synonymous with or in terms of Smith's other two terms, implying that the reiteration is intended for the purpose of emphasis (Muller (1993: 69) exemplifies the interpretation of the three terms as synonyms; most authors ignore the matter).

Faculty is rendered in terms of the power of doing anything; a personal quality or disposition; general executive ability; one of the several powers of the mind, variously enumerated; pecuniary ability, means, resources, possession, property; kind of ability; that in which anyone is skilled; conferred power, authority, privilege; a dispensation, license; and so on.

Propensity is explicated in terms of inclination, disposition, tendency or bent, as to some physical condition or action; tendency to move in some particular direction.

Disposition is reckoned in terms of the arrangement of affairs for the accomplishment of a purpose; ordering, control, management; natural tendency or bent of the mind; a frame of mind or feeling; mood, humour; physical constitution, nature or permanent condition; physical aptitude, tendency or inclination; aptness or capacity for doing something; normal or natural condition. The word is used, accordingly, in contexts of both deliberative and non-deliberative condition and/or action.

The words *propensity* and *disposition* seem, accordingly, to be essentially synonymous. Yes, but. Yes, because the one seems to imply the other; but, because of the deliberative and non-deliberative elements of action. Smith says, as we have seen, "This division of labour … is not originally the effect of any human wisdom." Smith may be moving textually to a discourse in which deliberation and reason is given more importance. Alas, the textual evidence is ambiguous.

(B) Recourse has also been made to Samuel Johnson's *Dictionary of the English Language* (1755), using modernized spelling.[9]

Propensity is defined as inclination; disposition to any thing good or bad.

Truck is rendered in terms of exchange, giving in exchange, traffic by exchange, to give one commodity for another. Also, by implication, a wheeled device used to haul (Johnson notes what carries a cannon and trucklebed, a bed with wheels).

Barter is explicated as to trick in traffic; to traffic by exchanging one commodity for another, in opposition to purchasing with money; to give anything in exchange for something else; sometimes the thing given in exchange. *Bartery* is given as exchange of commodities. From French *barat*, which relates to craft and fraud, hence a possible bad connotation.

Exchange is defined in these terms: to give or quit one thing for the sake of gaining another; to give and take reciprocally; the thing given in exchange; traffic by permutation; the form or act of transferring, properly by bills or notes; the balance of the money of different nations; the thing given in return for something received; the thing received in return for something given; the place where the merchants meet to negotiate their affairs, place of sale.

Faculty is rendered in terms of the power of doing any thing; ability whether corporal or intellectual; powers of the mind, imagination, reason, memory; a power or ability to perform any action natural, vital, and animal; a knack, habitual excellence; dexterity; quality; disposition or habit of good or ill; power; authority; privilege; right to do any thing; etc.

Again, the three words are defined in terms of each other, encouraging their treatment as synonyms.

Given the foregoing, and short of further contextual deconstruction, the three definitions seem to cast no conclusively dispositive light on either the epistemological meaning and/or ontological status of a "propensity to truck, barter, and exchange." No helpful differences in nuance are present either among the three terms or between propensity and disposition.

It is possible to distinguish truck from the other terms on the basis of humanity's ability to use its knowledge of nature and reason to reduce the trans-action costs associated with making exchanges. As for barter, since bartering is associated with the direct exchange of goods for consumption, to barter involves the process of determining the respective values of the goods in question. I am trying to trick, or persuade you into valuing a good in the way that benefits me, and you likewise, and out of this process we finally come to an agreement on what valuations we are willing to accept. Hence barter may refer to our ability to make valuations. Exchange appears to be associated with the final act of transfer-ring ownership of the goods in questions. This is the final volitional act that would not be possible were it not for the ability (truck) and willingness (barter) of both parties to come to an agreement. Clearly, reason could be associated with the first and speech with the second of the three elements of the propensity.[10] But, while it is possible to distinguish the three elements of the propensity in that manner, to our knowledge, no evidence exists that Smith in fact made these distinctions. Thus, the content of the propensity remains unclear; but so also does its ontological and epistemological status.

One further definitional matter remains, the difference between a general propensity to truck, barter and exchange that is part of human nature and a propensity to exchange something particular that one has for something partic-ular that one does not have. Consider again Smith's formulation:

> This division of labour … is the necessary, though very slow and gradual, consequence of a certain propensity in human nature which has in view no such extensive utility: the propensity to truck, barter, and exchange one thing for another.
>
> (Smith 1976b: 25, I.ii.1)

This speaks of a general propensity in human nature. Compare Governor Pownall:

> Before a man can have the propensity to barter, he must have acquired somewhat, which he does not want himself, and must feel, that there is something which he does want, that another person has in his way acquired.
>
> (Pownall 1776: 4)

This speaks of a particular desire, hence propensity, to engage in barter. The former lacks an immediate object of acquisition; the latter, while enabled or facilitated by the former, is motivated not by it but by the desire for a particular immediate object of acquisition. The former is a general propensity; the latter is behavior actuated by a desire for a particular object. Actually, this matter is not only definitional; it exemplifies a more general tension in Smith's work itself, that between final causes and proximate causes, representative of his analysis operating on two levels, that of general propensities and that of particular behaviors. But that need not detain us.

Diverse treatment of etiology

The general problem of the etiology of the division of labor is not universally raised and the problem of the treatment of the propensity and the faculties in particular is itself given varying treatments.

Raising the question of etiology and attributing the genesis of the division of labor to the propensity to truck, barter and exchange is common (Fusfeld 1966: 29; Ingram 1888: 94; Lekachman 1959: 88; Neff 1946: 89 (cf. 93); 1950: 102, 103; Rima 1978: 76–77; 1986: 77; 1991: 91; Sandelin *et al.* 2002: 29; Schumpeter 1954: 187; Spiegel 1971: 246; 1983: 246, 1991: 246; Staley 1989: 44).

Although the questions of etiology and the grounding of the propensity in the faculties have received their greatest attention recently, neither was absent earlier; the relation of the faculties to the propensity was identified by Bell (1967: 154).

Still, a substantial literature exists that ignores the problem of the source of the division of labor and thereby discusses neither the propensity nor the faculties of reason and speech (Backhouse 1985, 1988, 2002; Blaug 1985a, 1997; Canterbery 1987, 1995; Ekelund and Hébert 1975, 1983, 1990; Heilbroner 1972; Landreth and Colander 1994; Oser 1963; Oser and Blanchfield 1975; Oser and Brue 1994; Rima 1991).

In addition, not everyone stresses the centrality and importance of the division of labor. Murray Rothbard, no fan of Smith, writes that:

> for Smith the division of labour took on swollen and gigantic importance, putting into the shade such crucial matters as capital accumulation and the growth of technological knowledge. As Schumpeter has pointed out, never for any economist before or since did the division of labour assume such a position of commanding importance.
>
> (Rothbard 1995a: vol. I, p. 441)

The implication is that one could assemble a model, say, incorporating the factors identified in the section above entitled "The division of labor," and relate the factors to each other in a recursive way (cumulative causation, over determination); one of them would be the division of labor as both a determined and determining variable. In such a recursive model the difference between the extent of the market, etc. limiting or causing the division of labor (the form or structure taken by the division of labor) would be unimportant. But this ability to model does not in and of itself address or solve the problem of the etiology of the division of labor, apropos of either Smith or actual economies.

Rothbard is also critical of Smith's idea of the propensity to truck, barter and exchange as the source of the division of labor. He adopts, in effect, the first alternative account, saying that:

> The older and truer perception of the motive power for specialization and exchange was simply that each party to an exchange (which is necessarily two-party and two-commodity) benefits (or at least expects to benefit) from the exchange; otherwise the trade would not take place. But Smith unfortunately shifts the main focus from mutual benefit to an alleged irrational and innate "propensity to truck, barter and exchange", as if human beings were lemmings determined by forces external to their own chosen purposes.
>
> (Rothbard 1995a: vol. I, pp. 441–442)

Rothbard attributes this position to Smith's having chosen the erroneous egalitarian position that rejects innate differences in natural talents and abilities (1995a: vol. I, p. 442). Rothbard's account raises at least three issues: one as to rival claims as to *true* explanation; a second as to the absence of demonstration of truth, only mere assertion; and the third as to the relative roles of non-deliberative propensities and of deliberative self-choice.

The claim of "an alleged irrational and innate 'propensity to truck, barter and exchange', as if human beings were lemmings determined by forces external to their own chosen purposes" (Rothbard 1995a: vol. I, p. 442), is a difficult position. Individuals are influenced by external forces in choosing their purposes, preferences, and means. One external force is the price mechanism; and one must deal with Hayek's notion of spontaneous order and his principle of unintended and unforeseen consequences. If some of Hayek's disciples overemphasize the nondeliberative, Rothbard, no Hayek disciple, seems here to over-emphasize the deliberative (see Samuels 1999b).

Rothbard is not alone in criticizing Smith. Guy Routh, a critic of Smith from the left, refers to Smith's attribution of the division of labor to the propensity as a bit of "phoney anthropology" (Routh 1989: 86). This criticism can be understood as relating to either or both of Smith's penchant for hypothetical, conjectural history and his use of a proposition as a connecting principle. If we read Routh correctly, he uses Smith's language—"it is this same trucking disposition which originally gives occasion to the division of labour"—to implicitly emphasize "originally" and not necessarily a continued status of equal importance.

Several writers argue that Smith's grounding of the division of labor in the propensity is nonetheless no guarantee of the division of labor. For one thing, the division of labor is limited by a narrow extent of the market, the failure to use money, the failure to adopt free trade, constrained accumulation of capital, and so on, all part of Smith's model. Such is the position of A.K. Dasgupta (1985: 22). Roll claims that Smith over-generalizes his reasoning into a universal principle, saying:

> Adam Smith was guilty of making the characteristics of the society of his own day valid for all time; he regarded as a natural human motive and made into a universal principle of explanation a feature of the contemporaneous social

order which was historically conditioned. But Smith's purpose was propagandist.

(Roll 1946: 162)

The latter point brings us close to part of the second further account offered below.

Glenn Hueckel suggests that, following Jeffrey Young:

> Smith's empiricist epistemology would seem ... to preclude any discussion of universal principles of behavior. But, Smith gets around this difficulty by his premise of certain immutable elements of human nature ... [o]ne of which, of course, is the propensity to truck and barter.
>
> (Hueckel to Samuels, 22 December 2000)

The question of a universal principle of behavior stands alone; but as suggested several paragraphs above, the propensity is but one factor in a model and its success in generating the division of labor is conditioned by other factors.

Donald Winch makes a number of pertinent statements. One is that the adverse effects of the division of labor "posed one of the main problems to be tackled by the wise legislator" (1996: 59), thereby introducing a particular, further deliberative element. Another is an important formulation of the relation of the faculty to the propensity: "With language comes the unique human capacity to persuade others to collaborate in satisfying wants, allowing them to make use of that famous propensity to truck and barter which Smith employs to account for the origins of the division of labour" (Winch 1996: 70). The propensity is not the consequence of the faculty in a causal sense; the faculty only allows use of the independently existing propensity, the exercise of the faculty is the condition permitting the propensity to come to fruition. The reference to a "unique human capacity to persuade" suggests a connection with the fourth alternative account.

Geoffrey Hodgson argues, "the division of labor is a necessary but not a sufficient condition for exchange in a meaningful sense" (Hodgson 2003a). This brings us to a conflict over the relation of exchange and the division of labor to be considered shortly. That conflict aside, the same point again applies: the division of labor (and exchange) is but one factor in a model.

Nor has the etiology of the propensity to truck, barter and exchange deriving from the faculties of reason and speech escaped criticism. Governor Pownall, for example, criticized Smith on that account because he, Pownall, held that the propensity derived from the way nature has formed mankind—in effect, the third alternative account. Pownall writes that

> It is not in the voluntary desires, much less the capricious 'propensity to barter' that this first principle of community resides; it is not a consequence of the reason and speech actuating this propensity it is interwoven with the

essence of our nature, and is there in the profess of, and as part of that nature.

(Pownall 1776: 5; see also Lewis 2000: 277ff)

Apropos of the conflict between interpretations of deliberate and nondeliberate, Pownall is on the side of the latter. Pownall also held that the division of labor derived from differences in natural ability, and that the division of labor was the cause rather than the consequence of the propensity to exchange. Conflicts between accounts need not be sought out; they are logical and inevitable. More immediately relevant is a conflict involving the specific relation of exchange and the division of labor.

Allen Oakley, in a discussion of economic agency in economy and society, commences the pertinent discussion with Smith's distinction of humankind from other animals, and the need for cooperative behavior. He quotes Smith about the individual "man constantly standing in need of the assistance of others," and how the individual goes about procuring their help. "Such inter-agent relations," Oakley says about Smith, "are predominantly functionally oriented," and have to do with the "operational implementation of production and … exchange, and are of a largely anonymous and distant nature as a result" (Oakley 1994: 78). This is accomplished, according to Smith, by appealing to others' self-love. Oakley argues, therefore, "that something more than an innate 'propensity' [to truck, barter, and exchange] is involved in the development of the specialization phenomenon" (Oakley 1994: 79). In exploring that "something more" Oakley touches on elements of several of the alternative accounts.

But what is that "something more"? Oakley quotes Smith's statement in the *Wealth of Nations* that the propensity seems more probably the necessary consequence of the faculties of reason and speech than an original principle of human nature. Oakley then becomes one of the very few who proceed further and critique Smith's argument, saying that

> once human reason is allowed to prevail, the logic of the emergence of specialization cannot be summed up by merely arguing that it arose as a "necessary consequence" of the existence of this propensity. It is more appropriate to attribute specialization to applied reason: that is, to the coincidence and mutual enforcement of the practical realization that concentration upon one specific line of production improves agent productivity, and thus leaves a surplus over personal needs, with the recognition that exchange by means of mutually advantageous bargaining with others is possible. These are learned manifestations of that very "reason and ingenuity" which … Smith cited as lifting humans out of the animal world, and thus do not require the evocation of any particular innate "propensities" at all. Indeed, his own illustrative examples suggest that specialization comes with the progressive realization by human agents of just such a coincidence (WN, p. 27; cf. LJ(A), p. 348). Most importantly, once the specialization of labour becomes established, individual agents are socialized into it as one

of the many institutions which they inherit and with which they cooperate in their own interest and thereby reproduce for future generations.

(Oakley 1994: 79–80)

Oakley thus goes from the human mind and its faculty of reason to learned behavior, socialization, and a social character to what is going on. The mind uses reason and ingenuity to realize both that, and how, specialization (and thus dexterity and speed of operations) increases productivity, and thence to further develop it in order to still further better their condition. Deliberative and non-deliberative elements coexist. Division of labor carries specialization further through mechanization. But, suggests Oakley, the effectiveness of the division of labor in thus raising productivity does not depend on post-production bartering, leading him to question the causal role of the propensity to truck, barter, and exchange. Oakley concludes, therefore, that: "Quite clearly, the so-called propensity, whatever its origin and status as a human trait, is not a necessary condition for the emergence of the division of labour, even though it is for trade specialization" (Oakley 1994: 80). Oakley thus concurs with Meek and Skinner that "the division of labour properly so-called only exists where there is specialization both in terms of area of employment and process of manufacture," a characteristic only of Smith's fourth "commercial" stage (Oakley 1994: 80).

Like several other writers, Oakley interprets the propensity as economic-system, or economic-stage, specific.

Conflict no. 1: exchange and the division of labor

Smith argues, in part, that the propensity to truck, barter and exchange is the proximate cause of the division of labor. He can be read, and sometimes has been interpreted, as saying that exchange *per se* is the cause of the division of labor. (Or one can have the propensity to exchange lead to both the division of labor and exchange.) Others have argued the opposite, that exchange is the consequence, not the cause, of the division of labor. A variant interpretation of the former position is that exchange leads to an extension of the division of labor. Another interpretation is that exchange is a condition of the division of labor, more or less like the wide extent of the market, or that exchange is a limit *vis-à-vis* the cause of the division of labor. Many if not all of these differences can be eliminated by considering both exchange, or a propensity to exchange, and the division of labor as parts of a system of general interdependence, cumulative causation, over-determination or recursive relationships.

Part of the reconciliation somewhat, but only somewhat, parallels the afore-mentioned difference between a general propensity to truck, barter and exchange that is part of human nature and a propensity to exchange something particular that one has for something particular that one does not have, which is in part a matter of final and proximate causes. If exchange can lead to division of labor, and with it greater prosperity, the division of labor, under the condition of greater prosperity, can lead to greater exchange—which can lead to greater division of labor. So exchange can lead to an extension of an "original" division of labor (Smith 1976b: 27, I.ii.3), and division of labor can lead to an extension of "original" exchange. In this generalizing formulation, the *propensity* to exchange seems to drop out but it is at least possible to say that the propensity is reinforced by experience under extended division of labor. On the other hand, the difference between final and proximate causes collapses within a model of cumulative causation.

A sample of the literature will help illustrate the multiplicity of interpretations.

As has been seen, much literature holds that Smith's argument is that the division of labor is a consequence of the propensity to exchange. One recently published history-of-economic-thought textbook reads: "The inclination to bargain and exchange is the ultimate cause of the division of labour" (Sandelin *et al.* 2002: 30). As Bowden (1981: 49) puts it, "only with *trade* can people specialize"; and Fusfeld (1972: 38) says, "exchange gives rise to specialization and division of labor."

But others have held that the propensity to exchange is a consequence of the division of labor. This could be included, as above, in a recursive model of cumulative causation in which the propensity leads to division of labor and division of labor reinforces the propensity. In any event, Roll argues that "Smith reverses the true logical and historical process by making division of labor depend upon the propensity to exchange, which he regards as one of the principal motives of human conduct. There can be little doubt that on this point Smith confused cause and effect" (Roll 1940: 156; Roll 1946: 154 deletes "reverses the true logical and historical process" and retains "confused cause and effect."). Others have expressed a variety of views:

Gray and Thompson (1980: 113) hold that "division of labour postulates exchange later" and that the division of labour has as "its inevitable concomitant, the subsequent exchange of products."

Blaug (1962: 39) suggests that it is the opportunity to exchange that leads to the division of labor—a view approximating the first alternative account.

Scott's account (and those of others) of these topics makes it clear that the existence of factors limiting the possibility of exchange and thus the division of labor (e.g., the extent of the market) means that increased exchange leads to the extension of the division of labor (Scott 1933: 70–72).

Muller has the propensity lead to the division of labor: "The first principle in Smith's systematic chain of explanation was the uniquely human propensity to exchange goods in search of self-interest. The second principle was the division of labor" (Muller 1993: 68). Muller also writes that "The division of labor is made possible by the ability of men to *exchange* their labor or the products of their labor"—anticipating the first alternative account—and that "the propensity to satisfy self-interest through exchange" sets and keeps the market in motion (Muller 1993: 69, emphasis in original). He also implies that for both Smith and Marx commercial society is based on the division of labor, despite their different moral judgments thereon (Muller 1993: 183). This elevates the discussion from the level of one factor causing another, or vice versa, to the level of the system—say, of cumulative causation—in which both factors operate.

Hodgson suggests that for Smith, competition among traders favored the "relatively more intelligent and cunning" in an evolutionary process in which "natural selection favored those with the greatest mental capacities. Positive feedback led to … an enlarged brain and a highly developed intelligence as a result" (Hodgson, forthcoming). This may be interpreted as exchange leading to an extension of the faculties of reason and speech, bringing the latter into the recursive model as well.

Young follows Skinner in concluding that Smith, even before he left for France in 1764, had "attained a sophisticated grasp of the interdependence of economic phenomena" (Young, forthcoming, p. 5). This view sets the stage for the recursive model. The problem is that Smith, the Physiocrats and most schools of economic thought have emphasized the interconnectedness or interdependence of economic phenomena—only to then stress some principle endowed with one-way causation.

Hueckel quotes Jeffrey Young that "Since Smithian individuals learn from empirical experience they could not know about the benefits of the division of labour before they had first experienced the division of labour itself" (Glenn Hueckel to Warren Samuels, 22 December 2000; from Young 1997: 59).

Notwithstanding the recursive model, the literature is replete with conflicting formulations of the relation of exchange and division of labor. Also in conflict are different meanings of "principle," though most authors do not specify the meaning they intend.

Paradox no. 1: the division of labor—bond or separation?

Successful production and exchange require cooperation; the division of labor and competition, for example, are each modes of both cooperation and individuality, or individualism. The relevant literature thus manifests two different types of consequences of the division of labor and with them a paradox. One consequence is that the division of labor leads to social bonds—though some would say that the division of labor requires social bonds in order to work. The second consequence is that the division of labor loosens social bonds and renders individuals separate. Some would say that the division of labor requires social bonds in order to work; the question is, which ones? The paradox is that the division of labor both creates (and reinforces) bonds and weakens if not destroys bonds and enhances individualism and idiosyncracy. The division of labor is a dual socialization process. Inasmuch as cooperation (through bonds) and individualism are both characteristics of modern economies, it is presumptuous to either lay down some rule or judge with putative conclusiveness some balance between the two.

The foregoing arises in the relevant, Smithian literature in a number of ways.

Apropos of the construction of bonds: Ranadive (1977, in Wood 1984: vol. II, p. 252) raises the question whether self-love, or self-interest, a source of exchange activity, is a culturally produced phenomenon rather than an originally natural one (conflicting with the third alternative account). A possible variant is to treat self-love as natural and the specific identifications of self-interest as cultural and situational. In any event, the bond is socially produced and at risk. West (1969, in Wood 1984: vol. I, p. 364) says that the propensity to truck, barter and exchange leads to social intercourse—and, presumably, social bonds. Levy (1992b: 69) suggests that, in Smith's view, Providence has formed a moral sense, instincts of sex and self-preservation, and the propensity, which leads to a contractual society, i.e., one with bonds. Kalyvas and Katznelson (2001: 552) interpret Smith's theory of speech and rhetoric as dealing with elements of the process of social integration through the struggle for moral approbation and social recognition—as part of their explication of the fourth alternative account. But this is approbation and recognition of the individual. Social bonds are between individuals. Hence tension between bonding and individualism, complicated by bonding helping form individual identities. Fusfeld (1966: 29) has interdependence leading to social bonds, as a mode of cooperation. The standard account, of course, is that of Emile Durkheim (1933), who combines the economic efficiency analysis of the *Wealth of Nations* and the solidarity analysis of the *Theory of Moral Sentiments*, including tension between bond creation and bond destruction (separation) through the division of labor. Bond destruction is correlative to bond creation in the process of working out the conflict between continuity and change of bonds.

Apropos of greater individualism and separateness, Lewis (2000: 273) says Smith envisioned extensive division of labor through market exchange as a means to overcome entrenched dominance and servile dependency. Yet exchange obliged people to attend to the interests of others in order to satisfy their own needs, compelling trade-offs between the propensity to dominate and the propensity to exchange (Lewis 2000: 284).

Individualism and separateness are thus relative to the need to cooperate (on the necessity of cooperation, see, e.g., Bell 1967: 154; Ferguson 1938: 61; Neff 1946: 93). Of course, Smith bases some or much of his discussion on how the individual "stands at all times in need of the co-operation and assistance of great multitudes, ... almost constant occasion for the help of his brethren" (Smith 1976b: 26, I.ii.2; see Biggart 2002: 12).

Roll (1946: 16) suggests that changes in the distribution of power, i.e., of social structure, break old social bonds and replace them with new ones. In any event, individuals are, because of the division of labor, no longer independent of each other (Roll 1946: 153, 176). Presumably this means that changes in economic stage—apropos of the second alternative account—and changes in the division of labor involve changes in social bonds and the context and meaning of individualism. The division of labor, one may interpret, both creates and destroys social bonds. Further, apropos of changes in economic stage for Smith, Finkelstein and Thimm (1973: 114) recall how the emergence of capitalism involved the destruction of traditional social bonds (eventually engendering the opposition of the Romantics), implying that within capitalism changes of the division of labor do likewise. Similarly with globalization: the changing division of labor both destroys and creates social bonds and the values to which they relate (Hansen 2002). (Apropos of the structures of opportunity and of sacrifice, see Warschauer 2002 (in part as to whether internet technology isolates or brings people together—relative to prior technology); apropos of the structure of industrial power, including the hegemonic organizational power of "those who plan and control the manufacturing process," see Groenewegen 1987: 901, see also 902; and Melman 1975).

Economists conventionally ignore the socialization of the individual. Not, however, Frank Knight. Notes from his course on the history of economic thought in the Fall of 1933 record him saying "What Smith meant by 'division of labor' is the *socialization* of economic life" (Ostrander 2004). Such a view amounts to an emphasis on what is here called the stage theory, the second alternative account.

Relating to some or much of the foregoing is the matter of teleology. As if the end of efficient resource allocation is given by nature, one reads that efficient resource allocation *requires* the division of labor (Niehans 1990: 63) and similarly that specialization *necessitates* exchange (Staley 1989: 44). Thus Smith is said to hold that human drives are adopted in light of their ultimate end, the ends of human actors (Khalil 2000a: 388), and that human happiness is the Final Cause in Smith's system (Hill 2001).

Consider the treatment of the division of labor by Smith's contemporary, Adam Ferguson, in *An Essay on the History of Civil Society*. The fourth part thereof is entitled "Of Consequences that result from the Advancement of Civil and Commercial Arts," and Section I, "Of the Separation of the Arts and Professions." That is Ferguson's term for occupational division of labor. He argues that greater material wealth requires the separation of tasks: "By the separation of arts and professions, the sources of wealth are laid open; every species of material is wrought up to the greatest perfection, and every commodity is produced in the greatest abundance" (Ferguson 1966 [1767]: 181). Ferguson takes up only the necessity of the division of labor for increasing the wealth of nations. He does not consider how it comes about. The closest, perhaps, that one can come to that is an implicit argument from teleology: the anticipated consequence engenders the development. But this is an argument seemingly quite at variance from his theme of social arrangements that are a result of human action but not of human design.

Paradox no. 2: non-economic foundations of economic development

Perhaps the deepest paradox, ultimately irony, is that some or much of the foregoing amounts to a non-economic theory of economic development. Socialization of the individual is critical for the economic system; not just any socialization, but one propitious to commercial society. The division of labor and economic development are a function, too, of any number of geographical, biological, and other non-economic circumstances (Biggart 2002: 55). The division of labor itself, according to both the principal account and the fourth alternative account, is a function of language. Language (and many other factors) can be seen as a cause, a background condition, or a limiting factor, or even one aspect of a process of which another (relevant) one is exchange itself; the modeling possibilities are multiple. Alternative account number 2 provides a deeply social, or socioeconomic, or cultural foundation; and alternative account number 3 a possible, if (by modern standards) radical, transcendental foundation; both are conventionally non-economic.

The paradox may dissolve into irony when two points are realized. First, "non-economic" and "economic" comprise a taxonomy dependent upon definitions and modeling strategy. Second, whatever one calls the "non-economic," it is part of Smith's total synoptic and synthetic system of social science; both the economic and the non-economic are part of his larger system. Why irony? Because later economics ostensibly in the image of Smith generally (but by no means always) excluded from the discipline what is here called the non-economic and was so important to Smith.

Conflict no. 2: commercial society and division of labor

Is commercial society a function of the division of labor, or is the division of labor a function of commercial society? Before moving on to the alternative accounts, it will be useful to consider this conflict of formulations. As with conflict no. 1, the present conflict poses the question of causal order. Certainly the division of labor enables a commercial society to exist and prosper, but so too can one say that the existence of a commercial society enables the division of labor to exist and proliferate. The difference is a matter of perspective; one perspective makes the division of labor primary; the other makes commercial society primary. Each has its uses; but each is clearly a matter of selective perception. As earlier discussions have shown, actual economies are recursive, a matter of cumulative causation. The conflict does raise the question, however, of the stage-specific nature, grounds and justification of Smith's overall argument. For example, Hunt (1992: 71) writes, "the extent of the division of labor was [for Smith] governed" in part by a particular circumstance: "there had to be a well-developed market, or a commercial exchange economy, in order for extensive specialization to take place." And Blaug notes that different sectors of the economy afford lesser or greater scope for specialization and the division of labor (Blaug 1997: 35).

Four alternative accounts

The account that relates the division of labor to the propensity (or disposition) to truck, barter and exchange, and the latter to the faculties of reason and speech, is not the only account discernible in the *Wealth of Nations* and found in the literature. No less than four such alternative accounts can be identified.

Alternative account no. 1: opportunity and advantage

In the *Wealth of Nations*, Smith explicitly argues that the opportunity, power and certainty of the advantages to be had from exchange leads to exchange and thence to the division of labor:

> the certainty of being able to exchange all that surplus part of the produce of his own labor, which is over and above his own consumption, for such parts of the produce of other men's labour as he may have occasion for, encourages every man to apply himself to a particular occupation, and to cultivate and bring to perfection whatever talent or genius he may possess for that particular species of business.
>
> (Smith 1976b: 28, I.ii.3)

Both more clearly and more tersely, he writes, "it is the power of exchanging that gives occasion to the division of labour" (Smith 1976b: 31, I.iii.1; Neff 1946: 93 quotes this without further amplification).

Also, one of the fragments of Smith's work now in the literature suggests an account different from the faculties–propensity one. Here Smith writes, "it is the power of exchange which gives occasion to the division of labour" (and then discusses the "extent of that power," i.e., "the extent of the market" (Meek and Skinner 1977: 51)). This suggests that neither the propensity to truck, barter and exchange nor the faculties of reason and speech either alone or together generate the division of labor. The division of labor arises "naturally," one can almost hear Smith say, from opportunities to make more money, thereby to better one's condition.[11] (Of course, taking advantage of an opportunity requires the ability to see that it is an opportunity, so nature has given us the capacity by virtue of our endowment with "the faculties of reason and speech" to seize the opportunity—imagination extends the reach of reason beyond the obvious.) The implicit relevant model may be either different, more material and less overwhelmingly psychological, or one which combines material and psychological elements.

We remain at the mercy of Smith's usual practice of presenting his views on a subject in bits and pieces rather than together in a clear and complete manner. Smith had a propensity to invoke propensities, powers, faculties, etc. of the mind as suited his immediate purpose, a habit, as it were, of raising only those aspects of something he felt necessary or useful for the discussion at hand. It is always possible, of course, that Smith changed his mind. A different view will be presented in the following pages.

One can treat this formulation as an expansion or further explication of the propensity argument; one can also treat it as an implicit condition or limitation, such as with the extent of the market. But one can also treat the foregoing as an independent account—description and/or explanation—of the etiology of the division of labor—and such is indeed found in the literature (Blaug 1962: 39; 1985a: 37; 1997: 35; Hunt 1992: 71). A propensity to exchange is one thing; decisions over individual trades are quite another. Unless opportunity, power and certainty are present neither capital accumulation nor exchange nor further division of labor will take place.[12] The opportunities argument is nothing if not situational, but that is true of all accounts.

Among the varying formulations that trace the division of labor not to the propensity *per se* but to behavior taking advantage of opportunity and seeking advantage are the following:

Muller (1993: 69, 70, 72) first writes of exchange and opportunity to exchange and then says, "Self-interest, then, channeled by the market, leads to the division of labor." Two decades earlier, Finkelstein and Thimm (1973: 50) write of the division of labor being driven by self-interest.

Rima (1991: 91) speaks of the propensity's "inclination to trade" being "but one expression of self-interested behavior."

McConnell (1943: 69) states the underlying motivation of the economic man: "the average man seeks his own economic self-interest, that to secure wealth with the least effort is his chief motivating force and because of this he seeks the cheapest market in which to buy and the dearest in which to sell"—a line of reasoning that pervades Smith's chapters on the division of labor.

Lekachman (1959: 87–88) similarly quotes Smith on finding "the most advantageous employment for whatever capital he can command" (Smith 1976b: 454, IV.ii.4). Thus Dasgupta (1985: 22) relates the division of labor to productivity: productivity is a function of the division of labor but anticipated productivity shapes capital accumulation and the division of labor—again, the recursive model.

Fusfeld (1966: 29; 1972: 38) argues that basing the division of labor (specialization) on a propensity to trade is "an old-fashioned view." The modern economist, he maintains, traces specialization to increases in productivity and earnings.

Rothbard, we have seen, criticizes Smith for giving the division of labor a "swollen and gigantic importance" and attributing it to "an alleged irrational and innate" propensity. "The older and truer perception," he writes, is that each party expects to gain from an exchange; his focus is self-interest and mutual benefit, i.e., opportunity and advantage (Rothbard 1995a: 441–442).

Canterbery (1980: 51; 1987: 47) similarly traces the division of labor to decisions by workers and others to make money.

Skousen (2001: 19) considers the division of labor "a superior management technique."

Khalil does not examine the set of division of labor–propensity–faculties connections but he does provide a somewhat different and suggestive formulation of the surrounding ideas. He says that "when agents truck and barter, they are exclusively motivated by the extra gain" (Khalil 2000b: 55); that "The drive to improve one's condition is a healthy occupation and, in fact, defines what it means to be alive" (2000b: 56); and that the "ambitious desire of a higher station

... is not motivated by the utility which one may gain from the admired person. It rather stems from the love of perfection, which the admired seems to approximate" (Khalil 2000b: 57). It is not clear just what such might mean for a definition of human nature, but Khalil's analysis brings into play the more conventionally understood Smithian theme of status emulation that is taken up below.

A different but related aspect is provided by Aykut Kibritcioglu's (2002) identification of learning by doing as a factor alongside economies of scale in Smith's overall growth model and treatment of the division of labor.

In short, the first alternative account proposes that people seek to better their condition and advance their self-interests in buying, selling and organizing production. In taking advantage of opportunities and seeking their own advantage, they tend to act in ways that lead to specialization and the division of labor. No deeper etiology is deemed necessary.[13] The power of exchanging, anticipated advantage and opportunity is sufficient.

Alternative account no. 2: stage theory

Smith believed that the economy evolved through a sequence of stages. The stages are characterized in terms of their respective systems and structures of property and government. Transformation from one stage to another is marked by fundamental changes in property and government, the erosion of traditional forms of power and status, and the eventual collapse of old hierarchies (Kalyvas and Katznelson 2001: 565).

The stages are also marked by stage-specific behavior patterns. These behaviors may be seen as accompanying, constitutive of, or caused by their respective stages. The same is true of the system of property and government that marks each state.

In this context, Smith is readily seen to be making two arguments.[14] The first has to do with the division of labor with which he is primarily concerned being specific to the stage of commercial society. The second has to do with the distribution of power represented and given effect by the particular system and structure of property and government in commercial society. If the former seems somewhat pedestrian (though it is not), the latter is decidedly not. The latter penetrates to systemic fundamentals; and if largely ignored by later mainstream economists, it was not ignored by Smith. Indeed, the fact that he is so explicit—much more so than about the former, though it pervades the *Wealth of Nations*—makes him seem more radical than he is—and he is radical enough for his day (consider the major changes in effective property rights and in the control and use of government entailed in his criticism of Mercantilism).

Once again, the substance of the second alternative account can be comprehended as either an implicit condition or a limitation, e.g., before the extent of the market can matter there must be a market (system of markets) and antecedent thereto a commercial system. But one can also treat it as an independent account—description and/or explanation—of the etiology of the division of labor—and such is indeed rarely found in the literature.

One can proceed from the individual or from the system. But the individual is, at least in part, a function of the system, and the system—the society and its division of labor—is a function, in part, of how individuals, and which individuals, seek opportunity and advantage. The first alternative account takes place on the stage contemplated by the second alternative account. The two accounts can be treated as rivals or in combination in a recursive model.

The first argument, that the division of labor with which he is primarily concerned is specific to the stage of commercial society, amounts to assuming a particular system. (The reader will notice the language, "with which he is primarily concerned." The division of labor was present in earlier stages; it evolved.) In that system, the particular set of recursive and over-determined relationships of cumulative causation is established. If there is a conflict between saying that the division of labor is a function of exchange and that exchange is a function of the division of labor, it is because the commercial system manifests widespread and increasing exchange *and* division of labor. Which of the two one chooses to emphasize is a matter of perspective. Both are aspects of the system in that stage.

So far the discussion concerns the division of labor in general and its stage-specificity in relation to commercial society. The behavior that leads to the division of labor is specific to commercial society. People's self-interests and how they seek to better their condition, say, by taking advantage of opportunities and seeking their own advantage, are commercial-system specific. So too is the stage-driven division of labor. In this context, the propensity and the faculties are outside the model.

Pocock writes,

> A crucial step in the emergence of Scottish social theory is, of course, that elusive phenomenon, the advent of the four stages scheme of history. The progression from hunter to farmer, to merchant offered not only an account of increasing plenty, but a series of stages of increasing division of labour, bringing about in their turn an increasingly complex organisation of both society and personality.
>
> (Pocock 1983: 242)

Pocock thus sidesteps both the propensity and the human nature accounts; his is a more empirical and non-metaphysical account. With the ascendance of commercial society comes a new structure of political, economic and social power and a newly predominant form of behavior, *homo economicus.*

In one sense, the market becomes the newly dominant mode of organization and control; though, in another sense, there is no such thing as "the market," only actual markets as a function of and giving effect to the structure of power—including that exercised through control of government—that forms and operates through them. And individuals adopt the ethic and logic of rational acquisition (Kalyvas and Katznelson 2001: 573–575).

The second argument, that the distribution of power is represented and given effect by the particular system and structure of property and government in commercial society, deals with the ownership of property, initial and growing inequality, the role of civil government in relation to property, and the conflict between those who have and those who have not. It also deals with who makes decisions about the accumulation and use (allocation) of capital, the valuing of labor as a commodity, notions of economic liberty, and thus the division of labor and the path of economic growth. Perhaps most interestingly, this second argument considers an additional propensity, the propensity to dominate.

This particular coin has two sides. On the one hand, commercial society has its system of power, dominance and dependency. On the other hand, Smith favors competitive exchange, compelling people to attend to the interests of others in order to satisfy their own interests. Lewis (2000: 273) correctly says that Smith envisioned extensive division of labor through market exchange to be a means of overcoming entrenched dominance and servile dependency— within that system. Lewis's formulation is that the propensity to exchange will counter and at least modify the effects of the propensity to dominate (Lewis 2000: 284, 288 and passim).

But the propensity to dominate is widespread and powerful. It influences legal policy generating labor markets, a subject on which Smith had much to say (Samuels 1983).

Let there be neither obfuscation nor mistake. Commercial society is a system and structure of power. Commercial society did not emerge in a harmonious and peaceful manner. Commercial society was a product of gradual—sometimes violent and not so gradual—extirpation of the social formations (Marx's term) that preceded it. This involved a prolonged contest over the control and use of government; it involved, from the viewpoint of the beneficiaries of the old regime, robbery. It involved coercive state action on behalf of the beneficiaries of what became the new regime. As one writer put it, there was "The Iron Fist Behind the Invisible Hand" (Carson 2002; Carson is writing about what he calls "corporate capitalism as a state-guaranteed system of privilege" (subtitle)). For Smith, the development of the institution of property and the distinction between those who have and those who have not, leads to civil government, and only thence to the markets of commercial society and to the division of labor.

Exchange is an exchange of property rights. Property and other rights are not given by nature. They are a result of government—of who uses government to protect their interests as property (Samuels and Mercuro 1999). The continuously changing structure of such rights influences the formation and structure of markets; it also influences the division of labor. The category or primitive term "division of labor" relates to the similar term "commercial society." The specific division of labor and both commercial society writ large and the specific commercial society are deeply influenced by control of government in continually changing rights. Property is a matter of power, including social structure, as both dependent variable (consequence) and independent variable (cause)—the recursive system again. When one thinks of rights as factors of production (Coase 1960: 44), the argument readily converts to what most economists consider "economic" terms and thereby the connection with the division of labor is unavoidable.

Smith is extraordinarily candid about these matters. So much so that economists, including historians of economic thought, have not known what to make of what he says. Power, coercion, and the control of government, not to mention class conflict, are not the typical topics of economics. Here is what Smith wrote:

> Men may live together in society with some tolerable degree of security, though there is no civil magistrate to protect them from the injustice of those passions. But avarice and ambition in the rich, in the poor the hatred of labour and the love of present ease and enjoyment, are the passions which prompt to invade property, passions much more steady in their operation, and much more universal in their influence. Wherever there is great property there is great inequality. For one very rich man there must be at least five hundred poor, and the affluence of the few supposes the indigence of the many. The affluence of the rich excites the indignation of the poor, who are often both driven by want, and prompted by envy, to invade his possessions. It is only under the shelter of the civil magistrate that the owner of that valuable property, which is acquired by the labour of many years, or perhaps of many successive generations, can sleep a single night in security. He is at all times surrounded by unknown enemies, whom, though he never provoked, he can never appease, and from whose injustice he can be protected only by the powerful arm of the civil magistrate continually held up to chastise it. The acquisition of valuable and extensive property, therefore, necessarily requires the establishment of civil government. Where there is no property, or at least none that exceeds the value of two or three days' labour, civil government is not so necessary.
>
> Civil government supposes a certain subordination. But as the necessity of civil government gradually grows up with the acquisition of valuable property, so the principal causes which naturally introduce subordination gradually grow up with the growth of that valuable property.
>
> (Smith 1976b: 709–710, V.i.b.2)

It is in the age of shepherds, in the second period of society, that the inequality of fortune first begins to take place, and introduces among men a degree of authority and subordination which could not possibly exist before. It thereby introduces some degree of that civil government which is indispensably necessary for its own preservation: and it seems to do this naturally, and even independent of the consideration of that necessity. The consideration of that necessity comes no doubt afterwards to contribute very much to maintain and secure that authority and subordination. The rich, in particular, are necessarily interested to support that order of things which can alone secure them in the possession of their own advantages. Men of inferior wealth combine to defend those of superior wealth in the possession of their property, in order that men of superior wealth may combine to defend them in the possession of theirs. All the inferior shepherds and herdsmen feel that the security of their own herds and flocks depends upon the security of those of the great shepherd or herdsman; that the maintenance of their lesser authority depends upon that of his greater authority, and that upon their subordination to him depends his power of keeping their inferiors in subordination to them. They constitute a sort of little nobility, who feel themselves interested to defend the property and to support the authority of their own little sovereign in order that he may be able to defend their property and to support their authority. Civil government, so far as it is instituted for the security of property, is in reality instituted for the defence of the rich against the poor, or of those who have some property against those who have none at all.

(Smith 1976b: 715, V.i.b.12)

The theme of the last sentence of this last quotation is no random idea of Smith's. It is found in several places in the *Lectures on Jurisprudence*. The editors of the Oxford edition added the following footnote at this point:

Cf. LJ (B) 20, ed. Cannan 15: 'The appropriation of herds and flocks, which introduced an inequality of fortune, was that which first gave rise to regular government. Till there be property there can be no government, the very end of which is to secure wealth, and to defend the rich from the poor.' LJ (A) iv.21 states that 'the age of shepherds is that where government first commences. Property makes it absolutely necessary.' A similar point is made at iv.7 and Smith added at iv.22–3 that 'Laws and government may be considered in this and indeed in every case as a combination of the rich to oppress the poor, and preserve to themselves the inequality of the goods which would otherwise be soon destroyed by the attacks of the poor, who if not hindered by the government would soon reduce the others to an equality with themselves by open violence.' Cf. also LJ (B) 11, ed. Cannan 8: 'Property and civil government very much depend on one another. The preservation of property and the inequality of possession first formed it, and the state of property must always vary with the form of government.'

(Smith 1976b: 715 n. 21, V.i.b.12)

Werhane writes that

Smith envisions the development of property, labor, land, and civil society as commencing with the distinction between those who have property and those who do not, a distinction that gives rise to the necessity of government. In turn, the development of markets, the valuing of labor as a commodity, and the notion of economic liberty evolve from the institution of property. Subsequently, these phenomena lead to the division and specialization of labor and thus economic growth.

(Werhane 1991: 68)

It is not just any interests that are protected as rights and it is not just any division of labor that arises. It is the interests of those who control government and the division of labor that is engendered by, *inter alia*, the structure and distribution of rights thus created (see Melman 1975; Seidman 1973). It is not only someone like Marx who illustrates de Jouvenel's dictum that history "is in essence a battle of dominant wills, fighting in every way they can for the material which is common to everything they construct: the human labor force" (de Jouvenel 1962: 177). Smith, as well as Marx, understood "that labour—the shaping and reshaping of nature and of oneself, under circumstances given from the past—is what constitutes human being (or human beings), and history is the story of how that labour has played out" (Peter G. Stillman, HES list, 13 October 2002; hes@eh.net) in an economy that, whatever else can be said about it, is a system of power (Samuels 1973).

Except for some of their historical digressions and illustrations, the *Wealth of Nations* and the *Lectures on Jurisprudence* reflect the situation that Smith is writing within, and assumes: a commercial stage. (It is not intended by this to say that the past is irrelevant to Smith; his knowledge of the past is a source of his understanding of his present, not a digression.) The division of labor, in the view of the second alternative account, is derivative of the existence of this stage; what is said about the first alternative account, as to the power of exchanging, anticipated advantage and opportunity, in this view, is itself derivative of the existence of commercial society. Moreover, the division of labor is specific to and gives effect to the structure of power, which in turn is a function of legal rights, the existence of which is influenced by those with control over government.

Muller raises the question of the institutional condition under which the propensity to truck, barter and exchange comes to fruition. He writes:

> Smith believed that, though this propensity [to exchange] was innate in human nature, its influence on economic relations had come about slowly, gradually, unintentionally, and as yet imperfectly. As market exchange became the basis of economic life, society reached the stage where 'Every man … lives by exchanging, or becomes in some measure a merchant, and the society itself grows to be what is properly a commercial society.'
>
> (Muller 1993: 69–70; *WN*, I.iv.1)

This is one possible dimension of either the social nature or conditional status of the propensity in operation.

Alternative account no. 3: the nature and source of human nature

The third alternative account is ontologically and epistemologically of a very different character. This account maintains that human nature, behind which is the role of nature and/or of God, constitutes the final cause of the more proximate causes that lead to the division of labor.

That this alternative account surfaces should be no surprise. The eighteenth century was arguably the first period when naturalism (in various forms) captivated inquiring minds, while supernaturalism continued (also in various forms). Smith himself had his analytical feet in several different modes of thought, namely, supernaturalism, naturalism, empiricism, utilitarianism (= pragmatism), historicism, rationalism, and so on.

Most expressions of this account are limited, and go back only to the propensity to exchange or, more rarely, the faculties of reason and speech. In this account's fullest form, the division of labor is due, in sequence, to the propensity, the faculties, the motives constituting human nature, and the action(s) of nature (or of God through nature) in forming or designing human nature. The usual language is something like Smith's own: "Nature endowed man." Smith erects his economic theory, in part, on very slender assumptions about human nature; nowhere elaborating the topic in detail.

Part of Scottish methodology was to explore "natural causes." One problem—others will be raised below—is that if some A is used as a natural cause to explain some B, both are or may be within nature and the model gives effect, in part, to selective perception. Another part of Scottish methodology was to make assumptions about human nature, Providence, and the relation of Providence to human nature, assumptions that fill the space or affirm connections where evidence is absent, unavailable, even problematic (Poovey 1998: xxi).

As to the motives and/or features of such an endowed human nature, the array is both considerable and formidable. Included are the propensity to trade, the faculties of reason and speech, the desire to better one's condition, prudence, etc.; and they may be modeled in various ways. Modeled, that is, until "no further account can be given"—as in the statement already quoted, "Whether this propensity be one of those original principles in human nature, of which no further account can be given; or whether, as seems more probable, it is the necessary consequence of the faculties of reason and speech, it belongs not to our present subject to enquire" (Smith 1976b: 25, I.ii.2)—where analysis ceases with either the propensity or the faculties, ceases except in the attribution to nature.

For example, Waterman (1998: 8) stipulates, from Smith, "*two fundamental, biological laws of nature*" and "two fundamental, *psychological* laws of nature." The first two, in Smith's words, are "men … naturally multiply in proportion to the means of their subsistence" and "land … produces a greater quantity of food than what is sufficient to maintain all the labour necessary for bringing it to market." The second two are the "propensity to truck and barter" and the "natural effort of every man to better his condition." A hint of another, domination ("love to domineer"), follows two pages later.

Roll (1946: 152; unchanged through his several editions) identified six motives that, for Smith, "naturally actuate" human conduct: "self-love, sympathy, the desire to be free, a sense of propriety, a habit of labor, and the propensity to truck, barter and exchange one thing for another."

Kevin Quinn would include glory and honor-seeking, vengeance, religious fanaticism, etc. (HES list, 13 October 2002; hes@eh.net). Sumitra Shah includes sympathy, envy, need for approbation, and the desire to better oneself, and thinks "it would be difficult to reduce it [human nature] to one overriding sentiment" (HES list, 15 October 2002; hes@eh.net). Hugo Cerqueira specifies "benevolence, compassion, generosity and other passions" (HES list, 17 October 2002; hes@eh.net). Tony Brewer would include both self-sacrificing behavior and domination, stressing that condition-bettering for the purpose of being noticed and admired by others (see below) has "(proximate) aims and behaviour" dependent on "context and change over time" (HES list, 14 October 2002; hes@eh.net), a position applauded by Tiziano Raffaelli (HES list, 15 October 2002; hes@eh.net). As for change, Michael Perelman stresses that behaviour in pre-commercial societies is "quite different from the behavior in a commercial society" (HES list, 14 October 2002; hes@eh.net).

As already indicated, several problems, well known to specialists, arise here. One is the reliance on selective perception to identify a "natural cause" of something arguably also *de natura*. Second is the multiplicity of meanings of "natural" used by Smith. Third is further ambiguity in the relation between nature and God. Fourth is the circumstantial character of the "natural"—in regard to Smith's stages. Fifth is the non-universal realization of that which is deemed "natural." Sixth is the significance of the role of conditions or limitations.

The seventh problem is the naturalistic fallacy of equating the arrangements of one's own society with nature, or, as we have already quoted from Roll, "making the characteristics of the society of his own day valid for all time" and regarding "as a natural human motive" and making into "a universal principle of explanation a feature of the contemporaneous social order which was historically conditioned" (Roll 1946: 162)—as well as diverse among peoples.

An eighth problem encompasses several of the preceding, namely, the situation that scholars in different disciplines have been unable to choose unequivocally from among different theories of human nature, each of which has several variants (see, e.g., Stevenson and Haberman 1998).

Another problem has to do with the meaning of "innate" when used to argue, for example, that self-interest is innate. One commentator asks, "Is it that in Smith there is a true innate human nature, just waiting to be let free by the expansion of the scope of market economies? (If so, that suggests that economies with limited or constricted markets can modify human nature?)" (Peter G. Stillman, HES list, 13 October 2002; hes@eh.net).

A further, compound problem is whether there is a pattern in nature and if so, what is its relationship to patterns in society (e.g., Fitzgibbons 1995: 87 and passim). This problem relates to more mundane ones, e.g., the unequal division of land in relation to institutionalized coercion and incentives to work (Perlman and McCann 1998: 181), egalitarianism in general (Lekachman 1959: 88); and, *inter alia*, the absence of analysis of the relations, or connections (see below), between general (natural) patterns and structures *and* the position of particular individuals.

Still another compound problem involves the selective perception of the respective domains of mankind and of nature, of nature and of God, and of mankind and of God. An alternative formulation of the first would consider mankind and mankind's works as part of nature. Apropos of mankind and God, if God has sovereignty, not only is there nothing left for man, the denial of human agency seems to negate both human responsibility and morality, and if God has determined everything important, we have no way of knowing whether that view is correct and no way of explaining why one person believes in the negation of human agency while another does not (based on Menand 2001: 218, see also 247).[15]

One aspect of the relation of mankind and God raises the question of the specific role of God. One view has God design and set up the world, thereafter the world runs on its own with God remaining passive and outside the system. Another view adds to the designer role a God who is active in the world. So far as we can recall, although such may be implicit in certain statements, we have not found any claims that God manipulates either the division of labor or the allocation of resources. This and related matters are, however, beyond the scope of this chapter.

A different compound problem involves the treatment of government. Many authors consider government *sui generis*, even outside the economic system, whereas some authors consider government to be one institution among others, as part of the system. This is more than a modeling problem; it is laden with ideology, especially with regard to the ontological nature of the economic system.

A final problem arises from the use of ambiguous relative statements, a practice of which Smith was a master—illustrated by "The differences between the most dissimilar characters … seems to arise not so much from nature, as from habit, custom, and education." The next subsection has a number of further examples.

Several of the foregoing problems relate to two further interpretive conflicts.

Conflicts no. 3: nature versus nurture; and no. 4: differences between people:—effect versus cause of division of labor

Smith held that the propensity to exchange, motivated by self-interest, gives rise to the division of labor. The certainty of exchange, he writes, "encourages every man to apply himself to a particular occupation, and to cultivate and bring to perfection whatever talent or genius he may possess for that particular species of business" (Smith 1976b: 28, I.ii.3). This gives rise to the question whether the talents thus cultivated and deployed are due to natural endowments or to socialization, the perennial conflict between nature and nurture. In Smith's view, differences in natural talent exist but are less than people think:

> The difference of natural talents in different men is, in reality, much less than we are aware of; and the very different genius which appears to distinguish men of different professions, when grown up to maturity, is not upon many occasions so much the cause as the effect of the division of labour. The difference between the most dissimilar characters, between a philosopher and a common street porter, for example, seems to arise not so much from nature as from habit, custom, and education. When they came into the world, and for the first six or eight years of their existence, they were perhaps very much alike, and neither their parents nor playfellows could perceive any remarkable difference. About that age, or soon after, they come to be employed in very different occupations. The difference of talents comes then to be taken notice of, and widens by degrees, till at last the vanity of the philosopher is willing to acknowledge scarce any resemblance. But without the disposition to truck, barter, and exchange, every man must have procured to himself every necessary and conveniency of life which he wanted. All must have had the same duties to perform, and the same work to do, and there could have been no such difference of employment as could alone give occasion to any great difference of talents.
>
> (Smith 1976b: 28–29, I.ii.4)

The key is that differences "arise not so much from nature, as from habit, custom, and education." Nature is relevant but not as much as nurture—habit, custom, and education. Throughout history, this issue has engendered conflicting views as between changing human nature and changing institutions. In the relevant Smithian literature, that conflict does not often directly arise. The conflict between nature and nurture does. So also does the related conflict, whether differences between people are the effect or the cause of the division of labor. Emphasizing nurture over nature (but not totally excluding the latter) with regard to talent, Smith also, even more strongly, emphasized talents as the effect, not the cause, of the division of labor, i.e., to acquired talents over natural talents—here, too, nurture over nature.

Smith, however, also gave a different view. In the *Wealth of Nations*, he writes of "the natural aristocracy of the country" (Smith 1976b: 707, V.i.a.41)—though he may here be using "natural" in a different sense. In his *Theory of Moral Sentiments*, in the chapter "Of the influence and authority of the general Rules of Morality, and that they are justly regarded as the Laws of the Deity," Smith seems to reject the idea that people are pretty much alike: "The coarse clay of which the bulk of mankind are formed, cannot be wrought up to such perfection"—but nonetheless emphasizes the role of social control through moral rules:

> There is scarce any man, however, who by discipline, education, and example, may not be so impressed with a regard to general rules, as to act upon almost every occasion with tolerable decency, and through the whole of his life to avoid any considerable degree of blame.
>
> (Smith 1976a: 162–163, III.5.1)

Here, nature and nurture are more amenable to serious consideration. Smith has posited that nature seems to contribute more than nurture for the differences between philosophers and porters, but nurture remains powerful.

Smith switches from human nature *per se* to social contexts once the division of labor is under way, moving away from nature to custom, or nurture, or some combination. This is a move that Hutcheson had already contemplated: "When we have these natural senses antecedently, custom may make us capable of extending our views further" (Hutcheson, "An Inquiry concerning the Original of our Ideas of Beauty and Virtue ..." (1725), in Kemp-Smith 1964: 89).

Cannan wrote of Smith, "He rejects the idea that its [the division of labor] first origin can have been caused by a sense of the advantage which results from it, because he thinks that the advantage is due, not to the difference of natural talents between individuals, but to the difference of acquired talents" (Cannan 1917: 44; the difference, for Smith, between artisans and philosophers is developed by Fiori 2001: 434–436).

Gide and Rist say that Smith "definitely affirms that it is human activity and not natural forces which produces the mass of commodities consumed every year. Without the former's directing energy the latter would for ever remain useless and fruitless" (Gide and Rist 1948 [1913]: 56–57).

Schumpeter, after commenting that only Smith "put such a burden on the division of labor" that "it is practically the only factor in economic progress" and attributing it to the propensity to truck, says that it "appears and grows as an entirely impersonal force" (Schumpeter 1954: 187–188).

Neff emphasizes relatively equal natural talents and the role of nurture (Neff 1946: 92ff and passim; 1950: 100ff).

Blaug's Reader's Guide to the *Wealth of Nations*, through the first four editions but not in the fifth, includes the statement, "The characteristic 18th-century faith in the powerful influence of nurture as against nature explains why Smith neglects to cite the accommodation of different natural aptitudes as one of the advantages of the division of labor" (Blaug 1962: 39–40).

Spiegel summarizes Smith's position thus: "Differences in human abilities are often not so much the cause as the effect of the division of labor"; "This point of view ... emphasized nurture rather than nature as the determinant of human differences"; and "the division of labor ... is not derived from any native inequality of men" (Spiegel 1971: 246; the position is unchanged in subsequent editions).

Sandelin *et al.* cover the propensity, that "different individuals are quite similar to begin with," and nature not as important as nurture, amplifying (qualifying?) the latter by saying, "However the inclination to truck, barter and exchange results in a specialization of people which reinforces the original differences" (Sandelin *et al.* 2002: 30).

Hunt emphasizes nurture as the sources of differences (Hunt 1979: 56; 1992: 77).

Not every commentator accepts Smith's position on these two issues or interprets Smith's position in the same way (e.g., both Plato and Aristotle grounded the division of labor in differences of natural talents).

Pownall rejects both of Smith's themes, arguing instead that nature, in the form of natural ability, was the origin of both the propensity to exchange and the division of labor, and that the propensity to exchange was driven by, not the result of, differences in the natural talents of individuals. Calling the division of labor the "first principle of community," Pownall says that it is not due to "voluntary desires, much less the capricious 'propensity to barter,'" nor is it "a consequence of the reason and speech actuating this propensity," rather "it is interwoven with the essence of our nature, and is there in the profess of, and as part of that nature" (Pownall 1776: 5). It is differences in talents and capacities, produced and acquired assets, and wants, that leads to trade. As seen above, Pownall seems to mean by the "propensity to barter" not a principle of human nature but the desire for something that activates exchange, "seeking something which he does want" (Pownall 1776: 4).

Rothbard says that Smith "took an egalitarian-environmentalist position, still dominant today in neoclassical economics, holding that all men are uniform and equal, and therefore that differences in labor or occupations can only be the *result* rather than a cause of the system of division of labor" (Rothbard 1995a: 442; 2000). Mises, of whom Rothbard is a disciple, felt that the division of labor was the result of unequal abilities, unequal distribution of opportunity, experience of cooperative action, and the necessity of joint action (Mises 1949: 157).

Birner interprets Durkheim as saying in the *Theory of Moral Sentiments* that "sympathy is based on the similarity of human beings" and in the *Wealth of Nations* that "The division of labor ... presupposes that humans are different" (Birner, in Birner *et al.* 2002: 26).

Some of the issues raised in these conflicts involve empirical questions. Other issues are a matter of modeling an arguably recursive world. Still others involve problems of language. Some are matters of ideology, providing acceptable definitions of reality and mobilizing and manipulating political psychology.

Conflict no. 5: language or definition of reality?

The question arises whether naturalism—or, for that matter, supernaturalism—is a mode of language or a definition of reality. The question deals with the issue of whether what is involved is the exercise of rhetoric or the articulation of truth. Although it is more evident (to the modern mentality) in connection with the third alternative account, it also applies to the first and second alternative accounts. Although people may believe and articulate them, i.e., take them as truth, each may simply be an agreeable exercise of rhetoric. Comin (2002: 107ff and passim) contrasts the views on language between Thomas Reid and Adam Smith, the former said to emphasize the epistemological and the latter the psychological perspective. Also, economic formalism, like legal formalism (analytical jurisprudence), treats concepts as referring to something given and transcendent, immutable and determinate, "treating what were merely tools of analysis as though they named actual entities" (Menand 2001: 223)—the ubiquitous problem being that different people identify the concepts differently (Samuels 2001a).

This consideration brings us to the fourth alternative account and then to the account derivative from Smith's methodology.

Alternative account no. 4: rhetoric in the service of social recognition and moral approbation

The most recently developed account of Smith's analysis of the basis of the division of labor is not unrelated to some elements of the principal account and the first three alternative accounts, such as the faculties of reason and speech, bettering one's condition, and the impact of stage theory. These elements can be combined into a model: people seek to better their condition; the form and mode that condition-bettering takes is channeled by the current stage; and reason and speech are deployed in aid thereof. But such a model takes us only so far; the fourth alternative account goes further.

The fourth alternative account holds that the universal motivation is for moral approbation and social recognition. Smith is very clear on this, saying that this motivation is the source of status emulation and condition-bettering:

> From whence, then, arises that emulation which runs through all the different ranks of men, and what are the advantages which we propose by that great purpose of human life which we call bettering our condition? To be observed, to be attended to, to be taken notice of with sympathy, complacency, and approbation, are all the advantages which we can propose to derive from it. It is the vanity, not the ease, or the pleasure, which interests us. But vanity is always founded upon the belief of our being the object of attention and approbation.
>
> (Smith 1976a: 50, I.iii.2.1)

The quest for moral approbation and social recognition is a, if not the, mechanism of social integration (set of bonds). Self-interest itself is grounded in a deeper, more essential drive for social recognition and moral admiration. Rhetoric is used in aid of recognition and approval, i.e., as a means of persuasion.

It may or may not be the case that, for Smith, self-interest has no other etiology than its natural or Providential source—an original principle of human nature.

Smith does not analyze this in depth; it is, nonetheless, the major premise of his economics. The precise relationship of self-interest to moral approbation and social recognition is uncertain. It may well be the case that what Smith and the rest of us perceive as self-interest is undertaken through a consciousness more or less specific to the commercial stage. The present analysis, it should be clear, does not turn on the specifics of the relationships among the elements of human nature. Also, just as the institution of property has to be distinguished from particular property rights, self-interest in general has to be distinguished from the particular forms taken by self-interest.

Smith's emphasis on persuasion can be seen as a precursor of Deirdre McCloskey's view that all language, including that comprising economic analysis, is—or can be comprehended and analyzed as—rhetoric for the purpose of persuasion (McCloskey 1998).

Smith's emphasis on persuasion is unquestionably important for his understanding of the etiology of the propensity to truck, barter and exchange. In both sets of *Lectures on Jurisprudence* he is reported to have said something like the following. The notes on his 1762–1763 lectures report him saying that

> If we should enquire into the principle in the human mind on which this disposition of trucking is founded, it is clearly the naturall [*sic*] inclination every one has to persuade. … Men always endeavour to persuade others to be of their opinion even when the matter is of no consequence to them. … And in this manner every one is practicing oratory on others thro [*sic*] the whole of his life.
>
> (Smith 1978: 352)[16]

The notes dated 1766 recount much the same story. The "disposition to barter and exchange the surplus of ones [*sic*] labour for that of other people" is

> by no means founded upon different genius and talents. It is doubtfull [*sic*] if there be any such difference at all; at least it is far less than we are aware of. Genius is more the effect of the division of labour than the latter is of it. … Thus … different genius is not the foundation of this disposition to barter, which is the cause of the division of labour. The real foundation of it is that principle to perswade [*sic*] which so much prevails in human nature.
>
> (Smith 1978: 493; see also Meek and Skinner 1977: 41)

The questions arise: why are people motivated to persuade others? and what does it have to do with the propensity to exchange?

A significant and growing literature has grown up during the last decade or so that examines economics as rhetoric and literature subject to the procedures and insights of literary criticism, hermeneutics, rhetoric, linguistics, discourse analysis, structuralism, and so on, some of which has dealt with the writings of Adam Smith (for example, Brown 1994; Rubinstein 2000; Shapiro 1993; see also Henderson *et al.* 1993; Henderson 1995; more generally, see Shell 1978;

Mirowski 1994; Samuels 1990a; 1993b). The point of the fourth alternative account goes beyond rhetoricity *per se*, i.e., the rhetoricity of Smith's work as an object of analysis. It maintains that at their deepest levels, Smith's own social and economic theories *include* the quest of moral approbation and social recognition through rhetoric as persuasion. The division of labor, in this view, is not simply the result of the faculties of reason and speech operating through the propensity to truck, barter and exchange. It is the result of reason and speech deployed for the specific purposes of moral approbation and social recognition. The chain of causation[17] has been lengthened:

> desire for moral approbation and social recognition→faculties of reason and speech→propensity to truck, barter, and exchange→successful prosperity→recognition and approval [→reenforcement of desire for moral approbation and social recognition]

Such is the core of recent work from which has arisen the fourth alternative account. An alternative formulation would read, in part "Desire to be the object of sympathy of others→bettering one's own condition" (Matt Forstater, HES list, 17 October 2002; hes@eh.net).

David Levy has been one of the first to use linguistics to get deeper into and interpret Smith's ideas. For example, in one piece, Levy maintains that, for Smith, "being human is the same as using language. Reason and speech are primitives for him," that "trade and language are two aspects of the same process," and that "language is a background condition for human choice" (Levy 1997: 672). The argument of his paper, perhaps largely a brilliant conjecture, goes further: the development of language is influenced by rational-choice considerations, e.g., to minimize transaction costs in making trades. In another article, Levy links trade and language, and suggests a further link between cooperation and language. He also proposes that Smith followed a 'katallactic' approach, not a Crusoe one (Levy 1999a; 1999b). In another paper, Levy connected the development of language and the metrics of style in Smith; for Smith the effectiveness of a sentence is inverse with length, i.e., more efficient (Levy and Diamond 1994; also on the economics of language, see Rubinstein 2000). In yet another paper, he identifies in Smith a combination of two important points. One is that property rights block grabbing and make trade sensible. Second, the more complex and subtle point is that language is a prerequisite for trade, as a constraint upon grabbing, through mutual approbation leading to mutual respect for ownership, part of the mutual development of language and the brain (Levy 1992a). In a companion paper, he interprets Smith's naturalism to include Providence having formed a moral sense, instincts of sex and self-preservation, and the propensity to truck, barter and exchange (Levy 1992b).

Perhaps the earliest instance of the fourth alternative account, in its articulation of, if not emphasis on, rhetoric and persuasion, was published by Napoleoni in 1975. Napoleoni recounts Smith's tracing the origin of the division of labor to "a propensity to exchange and barter" as presented in the

Wealth of Nations. Napoleoni also says that "It is by virtue of this propensity that men enter into a structure of social relationships which, through specialization, leads to ever greater exchanges of surplus products" (Napoleoni 1975: 33). Napoleoni goes further, to the faculties of reason and speech. "The *Lectures*, however," he notes, "consider an even more basic question, even if only by implication, *viz.*: on what is the propensity to exchange based?" After quoting the *Wealth of Nations* about an original principle in human nature or a necessary consequence of the faculties of reason and speech, Napoleoni says that in the *Lectures on Jurisprudence* Smith

> had been more explicit, and affirmed that "the real foundation of the tendency to exchange is found in the fact that there is an inherent need in man 'to persuade'". It is from this natural—and therefore inevitable—propensity for spiritual commerce, for the exchange of ideas, that Smith makes spring the tendency to trade and the exchange of material riches. Thus, commercial advantage is based upon a "method" that men had originally cultivated for the exchange of products of reason. What the *Wealth of Nations* had put forward as merely the more likely reason for exchange, the *Lectures* asserted as a certainty: the propensity to exchange material wealth (and therefore the division of labour on [*sic*] which is based on it) is not an original principle in human nature, but is "the necessary consequence of the faculties of reason and speech".
>
> (Napoleoni 1975: 33)[18]

The argument is more or less slightly amplified in the next paragraph:

> The *Lectures* specify that this process whereby wealth is increased through the spread of exchange has its roots in man's natural *rationality*, or rather that man, in so far as he is endowed with reason communicable through speech, can fully realize his nature only if he allows all his activities to be governed by the rule of communication and exchange.
>
> (Napoleoni 1975: 34)

Patricia Werhane's approach is something of a combination of the principle account and the first and fourth alternative accounts. She treats the propensity as "an illustration of the intersection of self-interest and social interest" and explicates the intersection in at least three more or less different, but mutually exclusive, ways. The propensity is one of human nature but so too "Our natural desire to cooperate motivates us to barter with other individuals while at the same time appealing to their self-interest in the exchange" (Werhane 1991: 93–94). "In the *WN* the social passions reappear entwined with the selfish passions in the form of our natural desire to truck, to barter and exchange, and our wish to be admired or approved of" (Werhane 1991: 109). And

Smith finds that the division of labor is a "natural consequence" of our affection for, and need of, the assistance of others. The "propensity to truck, barter and exchange" arises from the social passions and interests and is in our self-interest as well, because by trading our surpluses or the produce of our labor, we are thereby able to increase our own advantages while cooperating with others. Thus the division of labor is natural; it derives from the social passions; and it is beneficial to ourselves and to society.

(Werhane 1991: 137)

An elaborated core of the fourth alternative account is found in articles by Lewis (2000) and by Kalyvas and Katznelson (2001), who go far beyond Napoleoni.[19]

Lewis, in part utilizing work by Michael Perelman, relates Smith's concept of persuasion to both the propensity to exchange and the propensity to dominate. "Smith's interest in the division of labour," says Lewis, "extended well beyond the creation of wealth. He saw an extensive division of labour through a system of market exchange as a means to overcome entrenched systems of dominance and servile dependency" (Lewis 2000: 273). This is accomplished through "the human need for recognition," which can be accomplished "through the pursuit of wealth in a market system in a way that can constrain the propensity to dominate" (2000: 275). The argument is essentially similar to that of Taussig, whose pithy expression of it was "Better that we should have Napoleons of industry than the blood-guilty Napoleons of history" (Taussig 1989 [1915]: 129).

Using the *Lectures on Jurisprudence*, Lewis concludes that "Smith employs a general concept of persuasion to explain the connection between the faculties of reason and speech and the propensity to exchange" (2000: 280). Lewis quotes Smith, in part,

The offering of a shilling, which to us appears to have so plain and simple a meaning, is in reality offering an argument to persuade one to do so and so as it is for his interest. Men always endeavour to persuade others to be of their opinion even when the matter is of no consequence to them. ... And in this manner everyone is practicing oratory on others thro the whole of his life.
(2000: 280, quoting the lectures of 1762–1763; Smith 1978: 352—and those of 1766 to the same effect)

Noting that Smith identified three types of persuasion—begging, exchanging and convincing—Lewis, having established the ubiquity of persuasion, then establishes that, for Smith, "The common element in each form of persuasion is the attempt to elicit the attention and approval of others" (2000: 281). Not only is the propensity to persuade for Smith "a more basic or original principle than the propensity to exchange," successful approval gains recognition and approval for being right. Indeed, for Smith, the connection between persuasion and approval is so close that they can hardly be distinguished from each other: "To approve of another man's opinions is to adopt those opinions, and to adopt them is to approve of them. If the same arguments which convince you convince me likewise, I necessarily approve of your conviction; and if they do not, I necessarily disapprove of it: neither can I possibly conceive that I should do the one without the other."

(Lewis 2000: 282, quoting Smith 1976a: 17, I.i.3.2)

Moreover, again quoting Smith, "The desire of being believed, the desire of persuading, of leading and directing other people, seems to be one of the strongest of all our natural desires. It is, perhaps, the instinct upon which is founded the faculty of speech, the characteristical faculty of human nature" (Lewis 2000: 283, quoting Smith 1976a: 336, VII.iv.25; Smith concludes the paragraph saying, "Great ambition, the desire of real superiority, of leading and directing, seems to be altogether peculiar to man, and speech is the great instrument of ambition, of real superiority, of leading and directing the judgments and conduct of other people.").

"[T]he desire of persuading, of leading and directing other people … is, perhaps, the instinct upon which is founded the faculty of speech." The chain of causation has been revised:

> desire for moral approbation and social recognition→desire of persuading, of leading and directing other people→faculties of reason and speech→propensity to truck, barter, and exchange→successful prosperity→recognition and approval [→reenforcement of desire for moral approbation and social recognition]

Lewis thus concludes that for Smith "the propensity to persuade … is the foundation of the propensity to exchange" (Lewis 2000: 283) and its foundation is the desire for moral approbation and social recognition.

The recognition, Lewis continues, "is important in and of itself" and the different human talents, developed as a result of the division of labor, "become essential elements of each person's sense of self" (Lewis 2000: 283, quoting Smith 1976b, I.ii.5: "The difference of talents comes then to be taken notice of, and widens by degrees, till at last the vanity of the philosopher is willing to acknowledge scarce any resemblance.").

Again building on Perelman, Lewis's next points are that "wealth itself can become an alternative to domination" and that "the process of bartering and exchanging offers a new sphere for recognition from others." Therefore, "because exchange is a means of creating wealth, it can, to some extent, induce those who love domination to pursue wealth instead" and "It is the search for this form of recognition and approval that, according to Smith, accounts for the strength of the propensity to persuade" (Lewis 2000: 288–289).

The larger prospect addressed by Lewis on behalf of Smith is that of Taussig, that "the instinct of domination" can, by "capitalistic institutions, through the very desire for wealth" be "turned into channels of general service." "The instinct of domination is not necessarily ferocious or predatory; it may be satis-fied by the achievements of peace as well as of war" (Taussig 1989 [1915]: 128–129). The problems, of course, are, *inter alia*, first, that the Napoleons of history tend to accompany the Napoleons of industry, e.g., imperialism and, second, that apropos of capitalism (commercial society) the more devious and cunning have an advantage, hence the creation of the Napoleons of industry to begin with.

The more immediate, if narrower, prospect advanced by Lewis on behalf of Smith is that the division of labor is ultimately due to the universal motivation for moral approbation and social recognition operating through the desire to persuade, itself operating through the faculties of reason and speech.

Apropos of the other accounts, we intuit here a general model of how the propensity to exchange leads to the division of labor, driven immediately by the power of exchange engendered by advantage and opportunity, especially driven in the stage of commercial society to take the form of wealth seeking, all driven by the motivation for moral approbation and social recognition, the last oper-ating through the exercise of the rhetoric of persuasion enabled by the faculties of reason and speech. In short, the division of labor is the ultimate consequence of the motivation for moral approbation and social recognition—in a model of psychology that is said to be the design and creation of Providence.

Lewis's interest is principally in the *substitution of exchange for domination* in a world driven by the desire for moral approbation and social recognition, and the use of rhetoric to that end; the ultimate eventuality of the division of labor follows, but it is not his central focus. Kalyvas and Katznelson (2001) make much the same argument but their interest is principally in what they see in Smith as the desire for moral approbation and social recognition and the use of rhetoric to that end, not the substitution of exchange for domination, and the division of labor. It is because of that desire that in commercial society exchange substitutes for domination and, further down the causal chain, the propensity to exchange leads to the division of labor. Where Lewis built on Perelman's anal-ysis of Smith on dependence, i.e., power relations (see also Samuels 1973; 1977), Kalyvas and Katznelson build on Griswold's theme, "Life in a market society is an ongoing exercise in rhetoric" (Griswold 1999: 297), adding that individuals are driven by the desire for moral approbation and social recognition and that that desire is the ultimate etiology of the division of labor. They ques-tion Smith's recusal, that

> Whether this propensity be one of those original principles in human nature, of which no further account can be given; or whether, as seems more probable, it is the necessary consequence of the faculties of reason and speech, *it belongs not to our present subject to enquire.*
>
> (Smith 1976b: 25, I.ii.2; emphasis added)

People seek approbation and recognition. The content of what is given approbation and recognition varies but ultimately serves the drive for social esteem and praise. That drive is "a universal, transhistorical, motivation for human action, the main torque by which societies achieve cohesion and continuity" (Kalyvas and Katznelson 2001: 553).

Instead of the principal account's story of the division of labor leading to a set of social bonds, Kalyvas and Katznelson trace the causation back to the desire for desire for moral approbation and social recognition. The propensity to exchange that directly generates the division of labor is due to the exercise of speech and rhetoric in a struggle for moral approbation and social recognition. Smith's theory of moral approbation and social recognition drives sympathy—the ability to sympathize—and status emulation as well as market activity (Kalyvas and Katznelson 2001: 553ff).

Kalyvas and Katznelson's analysis at bottom is much the same as Lewis's: the role of rhetoric in the service of persuasion, in order to achieve moral approbation and social recognition and the quest for moral approbation and social recognition through the accumulation of wealth (Kalyvas and Katznelson 2001: 554ff).

They claim that by his recusal, Smith facilitated "the conventional understanding that he endorsed an economically reductionist interpretation of human nature" (Kalyvas and Katznelson 2001: 568)—and an equally economically reductionist account of the division of labor (due to the propensity to exchange, not the faculties of reason and speech, and certainly not their explanation). Given the place of the division of labor in the *Wealth of Nations*, this is a major indictment indeed. In grounding this criticism, Kalyvas and Katznelson present the quotations from the *Theory of Moral Sentiments*, p. 336 ("[T]he desire of persuading") and the *Lectures on Jurisprudence*, p. 352 ("The offering of a shilling"), given above. Their explanation is that the "foundation for Smith's political economy is not the natural drive to exchange," it is, rather, "the struggle for recognition and the search for social approval"—ultimately our vanity driven by our "desire to be esteemed by peers and [the] community" (Kalyvas and Katznelson 2001: 571).

In their view, Smith, effectively escaping an economically reductionist interpretation, thus grounded "self-interest in the deeper, more essential, drive for mutual recognition and social admiration" (Kalyvas and Katznelson 2001: 575 n. 98). To that they add the individual's self-constitution, the formation of moral rules and social order, and the recursive relationship between individual and social order—all again driven by the quest for moral approbation and social recognition (Kalyvas and Katznelson 2001: 577–579 and passim).

So rhetoric, specifically rhetoric in aid of moral approbation and social recognition, is, in effect, the origin of the division of labor. Lewis's and Kalyvas and Katznelson's accounts are derived through combining what Smith had to say on the etiology of the division of labor with his ideas on moral approbation and social recognition and on rhetoric. The faculties of reason and speech are thus placed in a larger model—longer causal chain, or longer set of connections—

and thereby instrumental in the role of persuasion in the quest for moral approbation and social recognition. Implicit is success reinforcing both the desire for
moral approbation and social recognition and the stage- and system-specific
content of the means thereto. In the following section, we further combine the
foregoing with what Smith had to say about the function of science and philosophy, and arguably about religion as well. In other words, we shall inquire as to
the applicability of the fourth alternative account to Smith himself and thereby
into the ontological and epistemological status of his theories.

Smith's methodology: a further account

One has to be struck by the role that Smith assigns to rhetoric (language/talk)
in economic and general life.

As part of his discussion of education in Book V of the *Wealth of Nations*,
Smith introduces his reader to the task of natural and moral philosophy and to
how the performance of this task is undertaken. Natural phenomena "excite the
wonder" of mankind and "call forth the curiosity of mankind to enquire into
their causes." The phenomena were first examined through religion:

> Superstition first attempted to satisfy this curiosity by referring all those
> wonderful appearances to the immediate agency of the gods. Philosophy after-
> wards endeavoured to account for them, from more familiar causes, or from
> such as mankind were better acquainted with, than the agency of the gods.
>
> (Smith 1976b: 767, V.i.f.24)

> Mankind also sought to generate "reputable rules and maxims for the
> conduct of human life" and, eventually, to "connect them together by one
> or more general principles, from which they were all deducible, like effects
> from their natural causes." The "beauty of a systematical arrangement of
> different observations connected by a few common principles" was seen
> initially in efforts "towards a system of natural philosophy" and was eventu-
> ally applied not only to the maxims of prudence and morality but to "moral
> philosophy," which is his name for the "science which pretends to investi-
> gate and explain those connecting principles" of social existence
>
> (Smith 1976b: 768–769, V.i.f.25).

Smith goes on to note:

> Different authors gave different systems both of natural and moral philos-
> ophy. But the arguments by which they supported those different systems,
> far from being always demonstr tions, were frequently at best but very
> slender probabilities, and sometimes mere sophisms, which had no other
> foundation but the inaccuracy and ambiguity of common language.
>
> (Smith 1976b: 769, V.i.f.26; this language may apply to Smith himself,
> not least in regard to the propensity)

He continues with a critique of metaphysics, physics and ontology. He emphasizes the roles of casuistry and the corruption of ideas in the service of various schools of natural and moral philosophy. He lauds the efforts of some universities to escape casuistry, subtlety and sophistry in favor of what he considers improvements in philosophy (= science), though noting the continued hold of established modes of doing philosophy (Smith 1976b: 770ff, V.i.f.28ff).

Smith gives a condensed but pointed account of his theory of philosophy (= science) in his *History of Astronomy*. Smith says there that man is in a state of wonder and awe when confronting his world. Man needs to make sense of this, and it is philosophy that provides

> the science of the connecting principles of nature. ... Philosophy, by representing the invisible chains which bind together all these disjointed objects, endeavours to introduce order into this chaos of jarring and discordant appearances, to allay this tumult of the imagination, and to restore it, when it surveys the great revolutions of the universe, to that tone of tranquility and composure, which is both most agreeable in itself, and most suitable to its nature.
>
> (Smith 1980: 45–46)

It is the function of "all the different systems of nature" to endeavour "to sooth the imagination, and to render the theatre of nature a more coherent, and therefore a more magnificent spectacle, than otherwise it would have appeared to be" (1980: 46); "the repose and tranquility of the imagination is the ultimate end of philosophy ... to allay this confusion ... and to introduce harmony and order into the mind's conception" (1980: 61).

This is true of physical nature—astronomy—and natural philosophy and it is true of moral philosophy, including political economy. Smith would have understood the economist, Umberto Ricci, who once referred to general equilibrium analysis as "a joy to the imagination" (quoted in Bini 2003). Philosophy/science needs to establish the connecting principles with which to provide descriptions and explanations that "allay the tumult of the imagination" by introducing order into chaos. In the *History* Smith surveys the religious origins of such a philosophy, using, for example, the term "invisible hand of Jupiter" to explain the irregular events of nature (1980: 49). In time, philosophy comes into existence to explain the chain that "subsists betwixt ... disjointed phaenomena" (1980: 50). Even this development has to be explained and Smith uses the same method of analysis, saying that "Wonder ... is the first principle which prompts mankind to the study of Philosophy, of that science which pretends to lay open the concealed connections that unite the various appearances of nature" (1980: 51).

Smith readily uses first principles as postulates to explain what he believes may be said to ensue from them, i.e., to establish his connecting principles. It is Smith's manner of speculating or hypothesizing as to causation and/or condition, of establishing a generalization beyond data or possible data, of constructing the elements of a chain of reasoning and a model or paradigm covering the experience under discussion.

Smith surely was aware that different first principles, like different definitions, could be used for different purposes, are socially constructed and not derived from reality, and are tools. Smith seems to think that what makes sense to *him* is therefore the principle, therefore the definition of reality that assuages his own mind and likely will assuage the minds of his readers, and that identification of first principles, perhaps with a modicum of discussion is sufficient. But the identity of first (and successive) principles, again like definitions, is ultimately a matter of which theory of an object should be made a first principle (or ensconced in its definition).

First principles are formed in the context of problems taking shape in our minds, problems that point to experience and/or data of certain kinds, which in turn suggest propositions posing explanations. Today these are considered either assumptions and/or hypotheses (conjectures). They permit some degree of coherence and confidence by helping provide a connection that enables a manageable explanatory framework or chain.

The creation of first principles is one form that his procedure takes; another is the creation of conjectural history. Smith's treatment of the propensity to truck, barter and exchange to explain or ground the division of labor is an example. His invocation of the faculties of reason and speech to explain or ground the propensity itself is another. Still another is his assertion of the drive of every man to better his condition to explain the form or direction taken by self-interest. His stories include putative examples of conjectural psychology, anthropology and history.[20]

Smith's own approach to theorizing can be applied to his own work, with results that are interesting and important, results pertaining both to Smith and to present-day theorizing. Smith effectively poses the question: what type of answer is desired or acceptable? Smith's answer is that type of answer that sets minds at rest. In his words, the answer that allays the tumult of the imagination and soothes the imagination. Such an answer renders nature a more coherent and therefore, and especially, a more magnificent spectacle. Philosophy (= science) proceeds by developing a pleasing, persuasive story.

Smith is an honest and candid scholar; he may be wrong about something but he is not disingenuous. Perhaps the most dramatic example is his statement, quoted earlier, that "Civil government, so far as it is instituted for the security of property, is in reality instituted for the defence of the rich against the poor, or of those who have some property against those who have none at all" (Smith 1976b: 715, V.i.b.12). Smith does not deny his own rhetoricity. For him, it is natural, not artificial, to stipulate in advance, as it were, what he is doing (Aune 2001: 42; cf. Ziliak, forthcoming). It is possible to claim, with reason, that "there is even more to learn from an interesting mind than its owner wished to teach us" (Stigler 1982: 108, writing about Smith) and then to impute to him what we are actually only projecting. But here we need to neither impute nor project his methodological procedure; he himself tells his reader what it is.

What, then, is Smith's procedure?

First, as already seen, its aim is to set minds at rest. He remedies the discomfort of the imagination through the creativity of the imagination.[21] He endeavors to provide a persuasive story, one constructed with a few simple principles, and is systematically comprehensive, consistent with the relevant familiar observations and preconceptions of common life, comfortable and beautiful, reflecting the harmony and elegance of the design in nature while reasonably free from burdensome philosophical abstractions (Brubaker 2001: 5). Smith takes the same position as Shackle:

> Insight into the thing in being of which we form a part, whether we attend chiefly to its non-human or its human aspect, cannot consist in a knowledge of its nature or meaning in an ultimate sense. All we can seek is consistency, coherence, order. The question for the scientist is what thought-scheme will best provide him with a sense of that order and coherence, a sense of some permanence, repetitiveness and universality in the structure or texture of the scheme of things, a sense even of that one-ness and simplicity which, if he can assure himself of its presence, will carry consistency and order to their highest expression. Religion, science and art have all of them this aim in common. The difference between them lies in the different emphases in their modes of search. ...
>
> The chief service rendered by a theory is the setting of minds at rest. ... Theory serves deep needs of the human spirit: it subordinates nature to man, imposes a beautiful simplicity on the unbearable multiplicity of fact, gives comfort in the face of the unknown and unexperienced, stops the teasing of mystery and doubt which, though salutary and life-preserving, is uncomfortable, so that we seek by theory to sort out the justified from the unjustified fear. Theories by their nature and purpose, their role of administering to a "good state of mind", are things to be held and cherished.
>
> (Shackle 1967: 286, 288–289)

Smith's view of science contemplates an activity principally aimed at reconciling people emotionally with the world, not necessarily at theoretically or empirically apprehending it. The goal is not so much to disclose the truth about the world—though it is that, if possible—as to soothe the imagination (Denis 2001: 75, 79).

Second, his procedure may resemble, and indeed may in part overlap with, present-day ontology and philosophy of science in their quest for truth, even Truth.[22] But Smith is not necessarily, perhaps only in part, interested in truth; he is unwilling to wait to judge theories by their truth or probability (Schliesser 2002: ch. 4); alternatively, he ranks truth along with setting minds at rest and is willing to settle for the latter (which may well best describe modern practice). Smith is principally interested in language, theories, hypotheses and the like as tools of inquiry (Schliesser 2002: ch. 4), not only definitions of reality. His use of premises, first principles, and conjectural psychology, anthropology and history is as tools. Smith's procedure is much more akin to that of religion than of modern science—though even that statement must be qualified by reference to Shackle's position. Belief is, or may be, more important than fact. The test is not that of any formulation of modern positivism; the test is plausibility as he understands it (Evensky 2001: 22; Smith's story is not about Truth but about imagining the truth and the standard of a good story is its persuasiveness, p. 48). Stated in conjunction with Smith's Deism and the argument from design, the point is, "For Smith, then, inquiry is not about Truth—what is the deity's design—it is about imagination: what we believe that design it" (Evensky 1998: 469). Belief is more important than fact for two reasons: first, belief will set minds at rest, soothe the imagination, in the absence of fact; and second, justified true fact is hard to come by. Even if truth be preferred to mere belief, belief is quantitatively more important than truth because unequivocal truth is so difficult to achieve.

In these respects Smith anticipated the view of the members of the Metaphysical Club "that ideas are not 'out there' waiting to be discovered, but are tools ... that people devise to cope with the world in which they find themselves" and that "Scientific and religious beliefs ... are only tools for decision making" (Menand 2001: xi, 145). Smith therefore might well have agreed that Herbert "Spencer's mistake was to treat the concepts of science, which are merely tools of inquiry, as though they were realities of nature ... imput[ing] cosmic reality to what are just conceptual inferences—just words" and promoting "prejudices that masqueraded as timeless truths" (Menand 2001: 210, 67).

These ideas are fairly commonplace, if still controversial, today. John Sutton thus can quote both the British philosopher Roger Scruton, "A human loves an explanation, and if a good one is not available, a bad one will be confabulated. We see patterns where there are none, and plan our actions around them," and the economic high-theorist Trygve Haavelmo, "it is not to be forgotten that the [explanations we offer] are all our own artificial inventions in search of an understanding of real life; they are not hidden truths to be discovered" (Sutton 2000: vii, 16).

Smith, in *Astronomy*, can be interpreted as claiming not to be concerned with truth—or necessarily more with belief than with truth. But this position engenders several questions. What of the truth of his argument? Is his argument intended to be "soothing"? Does he claim to believe the argument or is he describing the views of others? Is his argument self-referential, or reflexive? What, if anything, can be labeled truth?

In any event, Smith's position here is a corollary to Hume's argument that we do not perceive external objects directly, only through and as mediated by the mind; the object perceived is in the mind.

But Smith is concerned with truth, with ontology and epistemology, with the ontological and epistemological standing of his assertion of "a certain propensity in human nature ... the propensity to truck, barter, and exchange one thing for another" and other principles. Several possibilities, by no means mutually exclusive, exist:

- A proposition or postulate constituting an element in a systematic arrangement of propositions, serving as a conjectural definition of the relevant world, in effect an hypothesis.
- A deduced element in a chain of reasoning.
- A premise in a logical sequence of reasoning.
- An empirical observation.
- An empirical generalization.
- An element of a model of final versus efficient causes.
- Instead of a definition of reality relating to human nature, a methodological construct, perhaps an element in a model or paradigm, serving as an analytical, stochastic tool in a larger organon of inquiry.

If the analysis centering on psychic balm leaves the ontological and epistemological status of Smith's arguments and explanations hanging, so too does the analysis centering on truth.

It may well be, however, that what Smith describes is akin to the usual notion of truth as a matter of what satisfies a community of scholars, or simply a group of people, but also to Peirce's view of the pragmatic production of knowledge: "the action of thought is excited by the irritation of doubt, and ceases when belief is attained, so that the production of belief is the sole function of thought" (Peirce 1957: 36). Substitute "awe and wonder" for "irritation of doubt" (perhaps one needs only to add, not subtract) and consider that attained belief sets minds at rest—allays the tumult of the imagination—and one has Smith. Moreover, these beliefs, once widely enough accepted as justifiably true, become part of the status emulation process of society, and thereby become conventional in the quest for respectability and reputability, i.e., social recognition and moral approval. Finally, since the propositions that become truth are likely to be conjectural, and are recognized as such by Smith, it is no surprise that they typically are hedged in his work by the use of such terms as "perhaps" and "seem" (Henderson, n.d.)

Some of the foregoing reduces to, or includes, something like the adoption of a conjecture as a working assumption with the intention of seeing how far it helps his chain as suggested by its reception by others. He possibly would have expected some readers to be uninterested in the matter, others to resist his assumption, and still others to accept his conjecture by virtue of his assertion of it. (It is possible, too, that God is similarly assumed.)

Third, Smith's practice resembles ideas of Freud and Pareto. Freud found that people believe or act as if they believe in the omnipotence of thoughts, or of words. They believe or act as if they believed that words alone can have an effect on the world. Paul writes, "The basis of this attitude is the narcissistic overvaluation of one's own psyche and one's power to determine events. In at least part of the mind, the reality principle is rejected as too great a narcissistic blow" (Paul 1991: 273; that undoubtedly is true of certain people, e.g., some of those with deep feelings of inferiority—but prayer, for example, can be simply wishful thinking or psychic balm). Pareto identified certain beliefs as rationalizations[23] or myths that are essentially metaphysical and aprioristic assertions, allegations, and speculations that have no foundation (no possible foundation) in fact; they are imaginary principles (Samuels 1974a: 34 and passim). Menand (2001: 212) writes (apropos of Chauncey Wright) of the "fetishization of words" and that "concepts ... [are] the means, and not the ends, of inquiry." Menand himself writes of the "idolatry of ideas" and the "idolatry of concepts," such as "the danger of principle" (Menand 2001: 374, 425).

One application of the omnipotence of words is the practice of politicians and public-relations specialists of making statements in order to finesse problems or manipulate political psychology by assuaging their auditors' minds even though the statements misrepresent actual policy. Here language is a tool not of truth but of illusion, dissimulation and obfuscation.

Fourth, Smith anticipates a number of modern writers, indeed postmodernism (said with due regard to Smith having his feet in several different modes of thought). A two-century-long "tradition" from Smith and Kant through Wittgenstein and Shackle can be identified in which the description of science and other endeavors involves belief rather than truth. Smith anticipates (in both his theory and his practice) the ideas of the later Wittgenstein, in which he rejects the correspondence-with-reality theory of language—that science is the mirror of nature—and affirms language as tools of expression and inquiry (Wittgenstein 1958)—as means of projection, not necessarily of correspondence. Smith anticipates Popper insofar as he treats first principles and conjectural anthropology, psychology and history as conjectures in Popper's sense—albeit without Popper's correlative process of refutation (Popper 1965)—that is, as a thought experiment, an investigative tool, a tool isolating a number of manageable variables. Smith anticipates Boulding's theory in which he affirms that what counts is not some imposed reality but our image of putative reality (Boulding 1956). Smith approximates Peirce's concept of abduction, combining abstract formulations that lead him to concrete examples and generating (or illustrating) examples that enable him to formulate abstract accounts. But throughout he composes stories hopefully amenable to the psyche. Smith anticipates Kuhn's approach to science, namely, social constructivism, non-material criteria of evaluation, and so on—implicitly challenging the descriptive accuracy of traditional ontology and epistemology (Kuhn 1962). More traditionally, Smith's procedure could be interpreted as a rudimentary covering-law approach, accounting for a particular observed phenomenon by subsuming it under a general law or hypothesis—here accounting for division of labor by the propensity and for the propensity by the faculties, or else by the desire for moral approval and social recognition. Finally, Smith anticipates Pierre Bourdieu's concept of habitus, a body of principles that generates and organizes practices and representations, deeply internalized and persistent mental schemes that frame and organize thought, schemes that conceptualize and help reproduce social arrangements (paraphrased from Christian Smith 2000).

An example that the foregoing is a sensible view of Smith is provided by the high theorist, Robert Dorfman, in a piece explicating the significance of Gerard Debreu's work. Dorfman argues that Smith's formulation of the invisible hand in the *Wealth of Nations* "has served as the unifying principle of economics" (Dorfman 1997: 399). On it was predicated the attack on mercantilism. But it was, says Dorfman, a "conjecture," and "a long sequence of economists struggled to confirm it, or, at least, to ascertain the kind of economy for which it could be confirmed" (1997: 400). Dorfman further states that "while Professor Debreu established that under his conditions the invisible hand could work effectively, he did not show that it would" (1997: 401). Establishing the conditions under which a conclusion is valid is different from Popperian falsificationism regarding statements applicable to actual economies (or their generalized abstract formulation). But the idea of conjecture and testing is common to both (the tests are different)—and Dorfman clearly treats Smith as proclaiming a conjecture ("Smith proclaimed his conjecture" (1997: 400)), a tool of analysis.

What is the nature of Smith's anticipation (along the immediately preceding lines)? His position is postmodernist in that he does not present a normative argument for the foregoing. His argument, rather, centers on how philosophy (= science) is actually done willy nilly, like it or not. Smith's description and practice may not differ from modern practice.

It is possible that Smith postulated the propensity in order to help complete his model, his system of connections that he offered to make sense of the world and to allay awe and wonder and to set minds at rest. This postulate was not taken out of the air; it was not, or not entirely, a metaphysical assertion. He seems to have felt that he could ground it in mankind's faculty of reason and speech. The propensity is, in effect, offered as a conjecture or hypothesis—as is the model as a whole. This also applies to his postulate that the propensity itself is grounded in the faculties of reason and speech. (Evensky suggests that "it is a hypothesis, but it is not a metaphysical assertion, it is an empirical one. It is derived from what he sees" (Evensky to Samuels, 15 December 2000)). It further applies to the application of his argument in *Astronomy* to his own work.

Fifth, although Smith emphasizes the role of connecting principles and identifies some of them, he only negligibly explores the causal connections between them. As Raphael (1997: 48; Khalil 2000a makes a similar point) says, Smith "shows curiously little interest in connecting this trait [the propensity] with his basic psychological and sociological analysis." Assumptions about human nature and Providence filled the gaps where evidence is unavailable; final terms of explanation are couched in terms of a purposeful or engendering Nature or God. The neglect is due to lack of information—confirmed truth is not possible—and to his emphasis on setting minds at rest. Relatedly, Fiori (2001: 430 and passim) emphasizes Smith's use of first principles, etc. to point to a "hidden organized structure to which observable events referred," an invisible order that is impenetrable by our senses. If identifying connecting principles assuages the imagination, then no more is needed. If the connecting principles belong to the invisible order, then no more can be done. The result is that Smith's principles, as persuasive as they may be, are conjectural ex cathedra assertions. If the combination of "conjectural" and "ex cathedra" seems awkward together, it reflects the predicament Smith has left for us.

One problem is that the principles, postulates and propensities are used by Smith to play explanatory and setting-minds-at-rest roles for which they are imperfectly and inconclusively suited. Neither their content nor their connections with their consequents are spelled out. As Evensky writes, "Reading the words for independent meaning is to read the meaning out of Smith. His purpose was the flow of the story. The words were chosen to carry that flow. Their meaning cannot be appreciated outside that flow. As you write: '[T]he story is not in the details but in the overall paradigm, the general Smithian paradigm.' I agree" (Evensky to Samuels, 15 December 2000).

How each term led to the next—how the faculties of reason and speech led to the propensity to exchange and the latter to the division of labor—was left largely explicitly unexplained (though see the first and second alternative accounts), perhaps because Smith saw the process as historically contingent, perhaps because he adopted the term as hypothetical, or because he had nothing to say, or all three. The invocation of Nature or God may have been serious or else a stopgap metaphor for what he did not know (bringing into play the third alternative account). Or else he assumed that his readers knew of his *Astronomy* argument and knew the methodological context of his statements. His account of an important topic is typically fragmented. Each part is limited to his immediate purposes while a unified, full story is presented nowhere.

One aspect of the foregoing (and the following) concerns whether Smith is trying to soothe the imagination by using ad hoc explanations to fill in gaps or whether he is trying to fill in the gaps by using the imagination to generate the invisible connecting principles. Imagination, in other words, is both a more or less pathological condition and a resource. This is, for modern interpreters, a matter of interpretation and thus problematic. For example, some interpreters perceive the Deity performing an active role. Other interpreters see the Deity as "merely" (in comparison) enabling Smith to reinforce his sense of a coherent, designed order.

The general problem extends to Smith's putative Deism. Consider his statement:

> This reverence is still further enhanced by an opinion which is first impressed by nature, and afterwards confirmed by reasoning and philosophy, that those important rules of morality are the commands and laws of the Deity, who will finally reward the obedient, and punish the transgressors of their duty.
>
> (Smith 1976a: 163, III.5.2)

This statement can be read as affirming the role of a benevolent Deity. It can also be read as affirming merely that the existence of Deity is a matter of "opinion," and that the confirmation by reasoning and philosophy is only a matter of psychic balm, of setting minds at rest. The topic is the rules of morality, here said to be "the commands and laws of the Deity," but which can be read as the formulation of moral rules through the operation of the God-given principles of approbation and disapprobation, through the operation of the Impartial Spectator, i.e., a matter of human social construction. Providence has provided the principles, not the rules. As for the Deity (though the subject is beyond present concern), Smith speaks of God sometimes having designed and set up the world and then only observing it, and other times thereafter being active in the world. And then there is the problem of the relative scope of action by God and by man, respectively.

A correlative difficulty is that Smith is not clear as to how he determines what behavior is due to learned custom and habit and what has natural or divine origin or what belief is laudable because it sets minds at rest and what because it is true. To the extent that Smith is a philosophical realist—which may not be much—he is subject to the same problem as are realists in general: even if everyone were a realist, they would still disagree as to the substantive content of reality. Given a putative reality of custom and habit, nature and Providence—which is nowhere demonstrated—behavior would be attributed to difference sources by different people.

Smith lauds Newton's system and principles. They are so impressive, so persuasive—"an immense chain of the most important and sublime truths"—that, he writes,

> even we, while we have been endeavouring to represent all philosophical systems as mere inventions of the imagination, to connect together the otherwise disjointed and discordant phenomena of nature, have insensibly been drawn in, to make use of language expressing the connecting principles of this one, *as if they were the real chains* which Nature makes use of to bind together her several operations. Can we wonder then, that it should have gained the general and complete approbation of mankind, and that it should be considered, not as an attempt to connect in the imagination the phenomena of the Heavens, but as the greatest discovery that ever was made by man, the discovery of an immense chain of the most important and sublime truths, all closely connected together, by one capital fact, of the reality of which we have daily experience.
>
> (Smith 1980: 105, IV.76; italics added)

Statements of expressive language of connecting principles are juxtaposed to real chains; mere inventions of the imagination are juxtaposed to a transcendent reality. Impressive as Newton's system and principles may be, how gravity works, how mass attracts at a distance, is not explained (Fiori (2001: 432) quotes Newton: "I have not been able to discover the cause of those properties of gravity from the phenomena"); nor is much explained in Smith's overall account(s) of the etiology of the division of labor.[24]

Likewise, Menand (2001: 124), after noting that for Darwin "Natural selection was only a hypothesis," says that "since Darwin did not know the science of genetics, he was unable even to explain how characteristics get passed on."

Smith's confident tone suggests that he thought that he had achieved close-to-true explanations all the while asserting his belief and emphasizing that his was an invention of the imagination to allay the tumult of the imagination (Schliesser 2002: ch. 4).

Let us reconsider the last indented quotation from Smith. There are either two arguments, or only one argument with two parts, or two interpretations, being made here. One argument is that language lulls one into talking *as if* the philosophical system in question is true—how easy it is to be deluded. The other argument is that it is possible to conclude, on whatever grounds may satisfy us, that a particular system or theory is or should be given approbation as truth. Deconstructing Smith's language, he can be read as using the language of setting minds at rest *or* the language of reality and the truth about reality. But a third interpretation with two parts is possible: One part is that for Smith language can be and very often is used to set minds at rest, lulling or deluding our minds into thinking that such language does correctly explain reality and constitutes truth when it does not. The second part is that the language of a philosophical system, a theory, can correctly explain reality and constitute truth. Schliesser (2002: ch. 4) stresses the alternative of the language of reality and of truth, yet renders convincing the third alternative, leaving the choice of emphasis on its terms an empirical or an interpretive matter. Schliesser's solution only rescues the category of truth; it does not negate the view that setting minds at rest is given greater if not predominant weight in *Astronomy*.

Still to be noted is that, in the last indented quotation above, Smith is describing the reality of how people approach the world-reality around them. The reality of inquiry is different from the reality studied by inquiry; the former is comprised of second-order statements and the latter by first-order statements. For Smith, the truth of the reality of inquiry is that people are compelled to settle for belief when they might prefer truth as to the reality studied by inquiry. They are compelled to settle for belief because they lack sufficient knowledge to reach truth; moreover, their psychology requires something, so, as a psychic balm to soothe their imagination, they readily either settle for belief or accept belief as truth.

On the basis of the foregoing reasoning, we stress the third interpretation. This interpretation is also driven by his failure to provide support for his connecting terms. It fits in well with the other elements of Smith's methodology. The methodology of setting minds at rest can readily be coupled with the quest to know reality even if the latter is so frequently frustrated that philosophers and scientists must settle for allaying the tumult of the imagination—and the manipulation of political psychology.

Smith may have thought, in part, that he was uncovering underlying "real" structures and causes. Hueckel believes that the propensity to exchange was both believed and postulated by Smith to help complete his analysis. But the propensity was not seen by Smith to be part of psychological reality; it was principally a hypothetical-conjectural hypothesis, i.e., part of a hypothesis about human psychology but not psychological reality (Glenn Hueckel to Warren Samuels, 22 December 2000). Reality versus hypothesis is parallel to truth versus tool, and while Smith may (or may not) have been thinking in terms of the reality of the propensity, its meaning was a tool and hypothesis. He surely understood that he and others could not know the ontological status of the conjectural theoretical systems he generated (Poovey 1998: 274; Denis, forthcoming). The system, and the order it represents, is something in which we believe, not something we know by means of evidence and reason (Denis, forthcoming). Smith does not deny some role to the natural world in the production of human knowledge, but he does underscore the role of interpretation; the natural world does not impose itself on us directly, only through social filters.

The method of the Scottish Enlightenment was in part to infer causes from phenomena and thereby to establish a cause (or causes) by which the phenomenon could be explained. How far back one goes, or feels one must go, depends on what is necessary to allay the imagination. Such connecting principles, if they are to please the mind, must be "familiar to all mankind" (Smith 1980: 46); the faculties of reason and speech are more familiar, ergo more pleasing, than the propensity to truck, barter and exchange (on some points in this paragraph, see Montes 2001). Jerry Evensky comments as follows on this point:

> Both terms, propensity and disposition, are contingent/tentative terms. They reflect the actual invisibility of the principles Smith is trying to represent. Imagination is contingent and presenting it should be done with humility. He is not presenting knowledge. He doesn't know that there is such a propensity. Its very existence is conjecture and so to claim to know whether the source is nature or nurture would be to layer conjecture on conjecture. He needs the first conjecture, that there is such a propensity, for the sake of his story. He believes that there is such a propensity because it seems consistent with his observation of human nature. But it is simply an assumption. He leaves further speculation as to its origin behind because, unlike his friend Hume, he really doesn't get into the epistemology and ontology of his assumptions. He just assumes what seems to him reasonable based on his observations of human nature and goes on.
>
> (Jerry Evensky to Warren Samuels, 15 December 2000)

Apropos of Smith's statement, already quoted, that

> The desire of being believed, the desire of persuading, of leading and directing other people, seems to be one of the strongest of all our natural

desires. It is, perhaps, the instinct upon which is founded the faculty of speech, the characteristical faculty of human nature. ... Great ambition, the desire of real superiority, of leading and directing, seems to be altogether peculiar to man, and speech is the great instrument of ambition, of real superiority, of leading and directing the judgments and conduct of other people.

(Smith 1976a: 336, VII.iv.25)

Evensky writes that

the words "seems to be," "perhaps," and, again, "seems to be"are contingent/tentative modifiers. Smith is simply asserting a premise based on observation. He doesn't discuss epistemological meaning and/or ontological status of the issue at hand. It may interest him, but it's not his primary interest and he doesn't want to get drawn into pages of analysis on these subjects. He's really a very straightforward guy. I think his response to your piece would be:

Dear friend, you explore some very interesting questions very richly, but we're asking different questions because we're looking at the world in different ways. [Handing you his collected works] These works represent the way I see the world given what I've seen of the world and what I 'see' in its history. The terms I use are the best I can find to describe what I 'see.' They *seem* reasonable to me. Please don't try to deconstruct my vision. Listen to my full story: Look at how I model the human process, follow along with my explanation of the course of human history based on my model, then decide if you find it persuasive. I'm not interested in debating the epistemological meaning and/or ontological status of my premises. I'm interested in whether the model seems to offer a plausible representation of the invisible connecting principles that give rise to the unfolding human events that we observe.

(Evensky to Samuels, 15 December 2000)

Sixth, Smith was aware that persuasive principles could be useful tools (useful to the wielder):

You will be more likely to persuade, if you describe the great system of public police which procures these advantages, if you explain the connexions and dependencies of its several parts, their mutual subordination to one another, and their general subserviency to the happiness of the society; if you show how this system might be introduced into his own country, what it is that hinders it from taking place there at present, how those obstructions might be removed, and all the several wheels of the machine of government be made to move with more harmony and smoothness, without grating upon one another, or mutually retarding one another's motions. It is scarce possible that a man should listen to a discourse of this kind, and not feel himself animated to some degree of public spirit.

(Smith 1976a: 186, IV.i.11)

These principles can be used to manipulate perception and definition of reality and sentiment and to mobilize and manipulate political psychology and power (as Pareto stressed; Samuels 1974a). The so-called principle may be a figure of speech, for example, the invisible hand, and as such quite vague,[25] and anti-politics may operate as politics (Menand 2001: 13, 16).

Seventh, we must consider the fact that Smith did not expressly discuss the etiology of the division of labor in the terms of his *History of Astronomy* argument that we apply to him. Indeed, Smith nowhere raises these terms in regard to any of his own theorizing. Two reasons come immediately to mind; we offer them as conjectures. First, he avoids repetition of the arguments of all of his works—especially his books on the moral sentiments and the wealth of nations and his lectures on jurisprudence, which three subjects he considered to be parts of his general system, but also his essays on philosophical subjects. The people with whom he would discuss his works (having also already discussed his ideas with them), knew what was involved and did not need to be reminded. Second, Smith, along with Hutcheson and Hume, to mention only two other people, shared a mentality that, it seems to us, was comfortable with indeterminacy and open-endedness. The critics of Hutcheson, Hume and Smith, on the other hand, sought closure and determinacy, whether in their religion or in their philosophy. Such people would not be comfortable with a setting-minds-at-rest view, for it would signify the utilitarian or instrumental status of their beliefs and call into question the ontological foundations of those beliefs. This difference in psychology characterizes readers of this chapter (in their own writings and in their reactions to this chapter); we would be surprised if he did not encounter a comparable pair of reactions. Accordingly, he chose not to remind them, or not too overtly.

Finally, Smith, it seems likely, would have candidly acknowledged that his own motivation in working out and publishing his ideas was social recognition and moral approbation. He desired to soothe the imagination, he gave effect to a love of system or order, he sought pleasure in using his mind to get to the bottom of things, he desired to contribute something useful to the improvement of mankind, and he sought status, fame, even immortal glory (paraphrasing Schliesser 2002: 58).

Smith may or may not have been that candid. But, as Raphael says,

> Smith would say of his own system of economic what he says of the Newtonian system of astronomy. It is sounder than its predecessors but it is still a theoretical system, a product of the imagination, not a description of 'real chains which Nature makes use of to bind together her several operations'. … these are all products of the imagination which help us to

connect observable facts but are not themselves facts or realities that might be observable or otherwise knowable.

(1997: 100)

Conclusion

(1) We are not interested in the truth or falsity of Smith's account of the propensity to truck, barter, and exchange. We are interested in making sense of it.

(2) Adam Smith, like most of his readers and interpreters, i.e., like most later economists, was more interested in the consequences—both good and bad—than the origins of the division of labor. Consistent with the methodology set out in *The History of Astronomy*, however, he did offer certain principles or propositions as the relevant connecting principles.

(3) Not one but five theories of the etiology of the division of labor can be identified in Smith's work. The principal account involves the propensity and the faculties. The alternative accounts involve the logic of taking advantage of opportunity, behavior during the commercial stage, the nature of human nature, and rhetoric in the service of social recognition and moral approbation.

The five theories are not necessarily all mutually exclusive but they are different. They can be combined into a recursive model (or models). The factors that they embody can be modeled as a cause, a background condition, or a limiting factor, or even one aspect of a process of which another (relevant) one is exchange itself; the modeling possibilities are multiple.

Smith seems to have emphasized the propensity to truck, barter and exchange and the faculties of reason and speech but there are others: the desire for moral approbation and social recognition and the desire of persuading, of leading and directing other people. The pursuit of self-interest and of bettering one's condition is, he felt, largely conducted as a means to those latter ends; even exchange, reason and speech are conducted with status emulation in mind.

(4) Applying Smith's own methodology to his own work yields a further explanation or understanding of his ideas on the etiology of the division of labor.

Smith combines two positions, the skeptic and the realist. He is interested, of course, in the possibility of arriving at, or nearing, justified truth. His interest is in truth and reality but it is also about "mere" belief. He provides no criteria of truth, implying it rests on agreement—hardly conclusive. Perhaps a summary of his overall position is this: seek truth, don't expect to find it, treat your findings as belief, and avoid delusion.

Smith's objective is to at least set minds at rest.

Smith is interested in truth, but he knows that it is difficult to attain, and human practice leads him to emphasize setting minds at rest and the delusory role of language or system. He seemingly would like to rank truth above setting minds at rest, but he finds it both experientially compelling and useful to rank truth below setting minds at rest; truth is not as quantitatively important as belief. In the actual world, as contrasted with an ideal world in which truth is readily attainable, Smith is principally interested in language, theories, hypotheses and like subjects as tools of inquiry, not conclusive definitions of reality.

Smith's practice assumes that people believe or act as if they believe in the omnipotence of thoughts, or of words, and in beliefs that are essentially metaphysical and aprioristic assertions, allegations, and speculations that have no foundation (or possible foundation) in fact; they are imaginary, albeit well-sounding and well-intentioned principles.

Smith affirms language as tools of expression and inquiry, principles as conjectures or hypotheses, the role of images as a putative reality, and principles as modes of organizing inquiry, i.e., social constructivism (Samuels 1993b), while holding in necessary abeyance the correspondence theory of truth and language, and truth itself.

Smith emphasizes the role of connecting principles and identifies some of them, but he only negligibly explores the causal connections between them.

Finally, it seems likely that Smith would have candidly acknowledged that his own motivation in working out and publishing his ideas was social recognition and moral approbation. He desired to soothe the imagination, he gave effect to a love of system or order, he sought pleasure in using his mind to get to the bottom of things, he desired to contribute something useful to the improvement of mankind, and he sought status, fame, even immortal glory—a quest in which he was eminently successful.

(5) We take the position that the story is both in the details and in the overall paradigm, the general Smithian paradigm. We have both spelled out and summarized the details. But what is the paradigm?

Self-construction and self-improvement, not least through commerce, albeit with tensions between reason and self-interest (prudential calculation) and between perceived self-interest and Smith's Impartial Spectator, were parts of the belief system of the Scottish Enlightenment. Smith envisioned every person to be engaged in a quest to better their condition; this is a driving force in the *Wealth of Nations*—and leads to the growth of wealth. Smith also envisioned every person to be engaged in a quest to look better in both the eyes of others and their own eyes—and to warrant such approbation; this is a driving force in the *Theory of Moral Sentiments*—and leads to the formation of moral rules. The two quests are not only related—greater wealth engenders greater respect—they are two aspects of a theme latent in Smith's work: the material and moral improvement of mankind. The transformation of the economy into an orderly and productive system paralleled the transformation of the individual into an orderly and productive person.[26]

(6) Perhaps every aspect of the origin of the division of labor found in Smith's writings has been given multiple interpretations. Much of this multiplicity of interpretation is ignored by the textbook literature, which largely ignores the existence of subtle and deep interpretive issues, on the division of labor and

many other matters, especially his account of philosophy (= science) in the *Astronomy*.

One source of conflict is that of context: whether the propensity is to be contemplated in an individualist or social context. Economists conventionally address the division of labor in terms of individual actions. Sociologists, especially those influenced by Durkheim, trace the causes of the division of labor to social structure and related factors (Trigilia 2002: 79; see also Perelman 1989, on Smith and dependent social relations). Smith does both, especially with regard to moral approbation and social recognition.

Consideration of such conflicts often leads to more complete, if more complex and less determinate, recursive models.

Probably not all conflicts can be so reconciled (if that is the appropriate term). Conflicts in Smith's ideas exist over whether moral rules are due directly to God or only indirectly (socially constructed, through the principles of approbation and disapprobation, implanted by Providence operating through nature), whether Smith disparages religion (including Christianity) or whether his system is inherently theological (compare Waterman 1998 and Hill 2001 with Minowitz 1993), whether the capacity for reason and speech is an original principle of human nature or evolves through Smith's stages, whether spontaneous order is a function of individual action or whether individual action is constrained from interfering with spontaneous order (Maitre 2000), and whether the propensities of human nature exist independently of our knowledge of them or whether what counts is our use of certain linguistic formulations to allay the imagination (paraphrasing Skinner 1979: 16), and so on. These conflicts seem to compel taking a position favoring or giving effect to (through the hermeneutic circle) one or another of the paradigms that Smith combined. Such would set our minds at rest at the price, one thinks, of rendering his system more coherent and more internally consistent than it arguably really was.

(7) The meaning we adduce to the propensity, the faculties, and so on, therefore, is at least in part, perhaps a very large part, a function of what we take to be Smith's epistemological program. It also depends on how we combine and/or interpret the many partial and incomplete formulations of the various postulates and connections that Smith used in explicating and discussing various different matters. Thus, the propensity can be an original principle of human nature or derivative of the faculties of reason and speech, and the faculty of speech itself may be founded on the natural desire to be believed, to persuade, to lead and to direct other people.[27]

Smith is concerned with both belief and truth, ontology and epistemology; both can contribute to the setting of minds at rest. Numerous points are at issue on which conflicting positions can be taken. Not least is the ontological and epistemological standing of Smith's assertion of "a certain propensity in human nature ... the propensity to truck, barter, and exchange one thing for another" and other principles. Several possibilities, by no means mutually exclusive, exist as to the propensity:

- A proposition or postulate constituting an element in a systematic arrangement of propositions, serving as a conjectural definition of the relevant world, in effect an hypothesis.
- A deduced element in a chain of reasoning.
- A premise in a logical sequence of reasoning.
- An empirical observation.
- An empirical generalization.
- An element of a model of final versus efficient causes.
- Instead of a definition of reality as to human nature, a methodological construct, perhaps an element in a model or paradigm, serving as an analytical, stochastic tool in a larger organon of inquiry.

But also,

- Instead of a direct or indirect affirmation of a particular definition of reality as a matter of truth, a statement aimed at setting minds at rest, a psychic balm.

Especially unclear was whether, in different relevant contexts, Smith intended to introduce differences of meaning as between individual and social, between rational and customary/learned behavior, whether the propensity is the first term in a string of logic, a first principle, or a seriously thought-out element in a theory of human nature, and so on. Apropos of the last, was he engaged in discerning a logical exercise or meaning? Did he believe he was dealing with psychological reality itself or with a hypothetical-conjectural construction to be taken as a problematic representation and then used in a conjectural logical sequence? Was the propensity both a descriptive proposition and a rhetorical-logical term?

Smith discusses, more often only mentions, various aspects of a topic, without laying the topic out in detail. He typically does not make further explicit use of a proposition. This is true of his use of the invisible hand in the *Wealth of Nations*; it is also true of the propensity to truck, barter, and exchange. Perhaps no further use of it was necessary, but the degree of his commitment is called into question. Perhaps it is only a temporary rhetorical move, intended to ground the next element in a chain of reasoning, perhaps only to obfuscate the fact that he has nothing further or more substantive to say. Arguably the *most* question-begging rhetorical device used by Smith was the word "natural."

One example will illustrate a further problem of applying Smith's analysis. One of his reasons for emphasizing reason and language is the need to enlist through persuasion the cooperation of others. In a world of conflict and cooperation, one can interpret Smith's approach to politics, i.e., to the state, in a comparable manner: the necessity of cooperation requires politics, not only trade, as a mode of persuasion and action. As one legal philosopher expresses it, politics is explicable because "the satisfaction of human desires, material and moral and intellectual, requires the cooperation of other human beings, but life with other human beings frustrates the satisfaction of desires by producing conflict over scarce goods." Politics is thus a means of solving the question of "how our collective lives ought to be arranged, to secure the goods that are necessary and to achieve the goods that make us happy and enable us to flourish" (Berkowitz 2000: 44). If the faculties of reason and speech are the basis of the propensity to truck, barter and trade, they are also the basis of politics; alternatively, politics and commerce are two domains in which the faculties of reason and speech are put to use, and for much the same reason.

(8) We reiterate that Smith's own approach to theorizing can be applied to his own work, with results that are interesting and important and pertain both to Smith and to present-day theorists. Smith effectively poses the question, what type of answer is desired or acceptable? Smith's answer is, first, that type of answer that sets minds at rest. In his words, the answer that allays the tumult of the imagination and soothes the imagination. Such an answer renders nature a more coherent and therefore, and especially, a more magnificent spectacle. Here, the visible division of labor is traced back to one or another invisible principle (Fiori 2001). Smith's second answer is that his own motivation was social recognition and moral approbation—a venture, as we have already said, in which he was eminently successful.

(9) This chapter both shows the richness of and raises serious questions about Smith's project, largely by assembling his themes pertinent to the problem of the origin of the division of labor. Uncertainty remains, but all of his themes must somehow be reckoned with.

Notes

The authors are indebted to Y.S. Brenner, Jerry Evensky, Glenn Hueckel, Sebastian Mitchell, Leonidas Montes, Spencer Pack and Eric Schliesser for comments on earlier drafts; to Lauren Brubaker, Andy Denis, David Levy, Eric Schliesser and David Wetzell for various materials and discussions; and to Kirk D. Johnson, Elias Khalil and Larry Moss for assistance. The authors apologize for any mischaracterization of a text, especially having emphasized that such readings are subject to selective perception.

1   Different parts of the analysis have been identified and/or stressed by various authors.

2   All that said, the authors are not claiming to identify what Adam Smith "really meant" in the sense of what he would say after reading this chapter, because the modern mode of thought is so different from his. Per contra, the importance of rhetoric *à la* Deirdre McCloskey, and the importance of the psychic balm function, *à la* George Shackle, suggest how close we might be, or how not so different Smith would clearly be on several fundamental points.

Our purpose here is *not* that of Smith as to either seeking moral approbation and social recognition or setting minds at rest. It is, rather, to identify "true" (meaning accurate description and/or correct explanation) answers to the two questions identified at the beginning of this essay.

3   The differences between these terms, and their significance, are not further examined here. One writer, Satoko Nakano-Matsushima (2001), has added to the list of limiting or causal factors. He argues, apropos of Mandeville but presumably appli-

cable to Smith, that the pliability of desires allows for a greater degree of coordination between agents, with the result being a more developed division of labor across the economy as a whole. Also, the idea of status emulation as an engine of growth and mode of social order—perhaps for that reason, certainly for others—is prominent in the account of emulation theory in Guidi (1999), who emphasizes evolution in the meaning of emulation, and in both the fourth alternative account and the further account propounded below.

4   The last topic involves some irony. Although Smith is not a marginalist, in the sense of giving explicit attention to marginal costs and marginal benefits, he does identify both the productivity gains from the division of labor and the costs thereof to the workers. This recognition alone would serve to compromise the harmonistic nuances found in the *Wealth of Nations* and, even more so, attributed to him by certain devotees. See Sandelin *et al.* 2002: 30–31. Further irony involves the juxtaposition of the mind-numbing effects of the division of labor, perceived by Smith, to the theory of the mind, or of human nature, involved in Smith's explanations of the etiology of the division of labor and to his more or less explicit analysis of the distribution of sacrifice (cost; worker deprivation) as a function of power structure subsumed in his stage theory (see Dasgupta 1985: 70; and later in this chapter). A still further irony—or, in the sense used below, paradox—involves the claim that "Division of labor comes into existence spontaneously without the necessity of human wisdom, planning or intervention" (Rima 1967: 66, attributing the division of labor to the propensity) in juxtaposition to Smith's grounding of the propensity in the faculties of reason and speech. Individuals and subgroups do make deliberative decisions as to the division of labor (in its various forms) but not all of the division of labor is so determined; some is due to the principle of unintended and unforeseen consequences.

5   The phrase "original principles of human nature" is one used by Hume. The influence of Hume's thought in chapter 2 is profound. While we do not think it necessary to deal with this at any length in this essay (except in connection with the third alternative account, and then in a limited way), Smith's use of the phrase introduces both the question of sources (other than in Smith's own writing) but more significantly, with respect to interpretation, the question of (implied) audience. The question of audience is relevant to the question of interpretation, e.g., with respect to an intellectual context that allowed Smith, as it allows any writer, to assume certain knowledge rather than spell it out—as in all his references to existing notions of human nature in the chapter (language/reason/benevolence/self-love or self-interest). What is given for a target audience and what is new? This understanding of audience would allow one to at least gloss Smith's "bits and pieces" approach to articulating his argument.

6   This equivocation is an exception to Smith's inclination not to say he does not know the cause, or origin, of something; doing so would compromise or negate what is discussed below as the soothing role.

7   Griswold commences with a short account of the division of labor resulting "without anyone's intending it" from the propensity and goes on to Smith's "intriguing query" about the propensity being an original principle of human nature or a necessary consequence of the faculties of reason and speech. Griswold then says of Smith that "Nowhere in the extant *corpus* does he work this out explicitly." After noting that the query leads up to the famous passage about addressing ourselves to the self-love rather than the benevolence of others, Griswold says, in a nod in the direction of Smith's notion of language and persuasion, "Life in a market society is an ongoing exercise in rhetoric" (Griswold 1999: 297).

8   According to Smith it is this flow into different professions that gives rise to the different talents of men, not the different natural talents that give rise to the flow: "The difference of natural talents in different men is, in reality, much less than we are aware of; and the very different genius which appears to distinguish men of different professions, when grown up to maturity, is not upon many occasions so much the

cause, as the effect of the division of labour. The difference between the most dissimilar characters, between a philosopher and a common street porter, for example, seems to arise not so much from nature, as from habit, custom, and education" (Smith 1976b: 28–29). As described in chapter 1, we may turn out very differently, but we are all molded from the same "coarse clay" (Smith 1976a: 162).

9   This discussion was facilitated by Leonidas Montes.

10 This paragraph is due to David L. Wetzell.

11 This can also be intuited from Smith's explanation of international trade, e.g., "Whether the advantages which one country has over another, be natural or acquired, is in this respect of no consequence. As long as the one country has these advantages, and the other wants them, it will always be more advantageous for the latter, rather to buy of the former than to make" (Smith 1976: IV.ii.15).

12 In the Keynesian system, for example, capital-goods investment will be forthcoming only if the marginal efficiency of capital is higher enough than the rate of interest. Accordingly, even though business decision makers want to have greater profits, and to accumulate to that end, they will do so only if conditions are propitious.

13 The situation is similar to one version of a Marshallian demand curve. A downward-sloping demand curve need not be grounded in/derived from a curve of diminishing marginal utility. All that is needed is the principle of substitution: people tend to substitute the cheaper for the dearer.

14 Spencer Pack communicated a different pair of objectives:

> We also now know from the Jurisprudence Lectures, that Smith was well aware that the working out of the propensity to truck and barter was keenly modified and structured by the stage of society—be it hunting, shepherding, farming or commercial; it depends upon different societal institutions. But Smith is careful to slough over that point here, because against the ancients, he wants to show how commercial society is natural, and that it is based precisely on that part of human nature that distinguishes us from the brutes. Therefore, for Smith characters formed by the division of labor are in a sense natural, as opposed to slavery, which is not natural.
>
> (Pack to Warren Samuels, 10 December 2000)

15 The problem exists whether or not God is present. Menand summarizes Locke, in part, as combining (1) the mind as a blank slate, written on by experience, with "no innate ideas, no mental contents that just automatically come with having minds" and (2) "the belief that societies are composed of autonomous individuals who establish governments in order to protect their natural rights" (Menand 2001: 244). Menand comments, "By making everything inside us determined by something outside us, these philosophers [Locke and other empiricists] denied the possibility of human agency, and thus removed the foundation for morality" (2001: 247). Apropos of God, "Squaring this enterprise with moral principles understood by most Americans to derive from divine revelation and to depend on the existence of a faculty of free will in human beings was a tricky business" (2001: 258).

16 Meek and Skinner (1977: 39) summarize this and other ideas as follows: " 'the disposition of trucking' is founded on 'the natural inclination everyone has to persuade'. Men, the argument runs, 'always endeavour to persuade others to be of their opinion', and thus acquire 'a certain dexterity and address … in managing of men'. The activity of bartering, in which they 'address themselves to the self-interest of the person', is the result of their endeavours to do this 'managing of men' in the simplest and most effective manner." This emphasis on "the managing of men" is both prescient and suggestive of the importance of power in Smithan economics.

17 The search for ultimate or first causes has several problems: first, the tendency to infinite regression; second, confusion through treating terms—serving as tools of

inquiry—as though they are real things; third, singling out one element from a set of elements as if it was the essential one; fourth, treating one element of an over deter-mined pair as if it were the decisive element. See, for example, Menand 2001: 279, 329, 339, 330.

18 One has to weigh the relative credence to be given to student notes *vis-à-vis* an author's own text.

19 Y.S. Brenner found the attitude in his Ghanaian students, who

> had no difficulty whatsoever in accepting the idea that God or nature endowed mankind with the kind of self-interest that Smith combined in the *Moral Sentiments* and in *The Wealth of Nations*. For them the people who wanted to be respected by others had to build a larger house and for this they needed money. Hence the pursuit of wealth was a direct corollary to the pursuit of public esteem. The propensity to truck, barter and exchange was for them a natural (logical) off-shoot of the pursuit of wealth which needed no further explanation. It was taken for granted that people see that the division of labour increases their ability to gain profit and hence they will have this propensity to truck, barter and exchange.
>
> (Brenner to Samuels, November 2000)

20 Marianne Johnson points out that Pownall also used conjectural history—his own—to reach different conclusions (Johnson 2002: 8). Conjectural history, etc., is just that—conjecture, i.e., hypothesis.

21 One writer claims that "Capitalism, in the view of Smith, was not an artificial construct of the human imagination ..." Charles Anderson, HES list, 13 October 2002; hes@eh.net.

22 The quest for truth is a legitimate, if illusive, goal in itself. It is also the core of the defense of academic freedom. Both yield tension with instrumentalism. But, as Menand (2001: 431) says of the constitutional law of free speech, "It makes the value of an idea not its correspondence to a preexisting reality or a metaphysical truth, but simply the difference it makes in the life of the group."

23 Pareto used the term "derivation"; the comparable term "rationalization" comes from Robinson 1921.

24 Speaking of Smith's intermediate drives, e.g., the sexual drive, Khalil argues that "Smith did not provide an account of how the drives are connected to their far-reaching, invisible beneficial ends" (Khalil 2000a: 373).

25 "[T]he general principle behind the invisible hand was left rather vague" (Stiglitz 1991: 2 n. 2).

26 The foregoing was suggested to Warren Samuels in reading Guelzo 2000.

27 There seems to be a powerful association between rhetoric and substantive economic life that has become a feature of capitalistic development. This is presumably true of all economic systems but especially noticeable in capitalism, due in part to the faster and more complex pace of socioeconomic change. The development of the economy influences the development of language—not just advertising rhetoric but entire specialist ways of talking that reflect in part the specialization produced by the division of labor and the stylized talk within particular institutions, such as central banks. This may well be a necessary connection given speech. Either way, and even if there are complexities and problems, it is impressive that Smith notices this central location of rhetoric within the market economy.

Appendix
How does Smith achieve a synthesis in writing?
Evidence from his analysis of the propensity to truck, barter and exchange

Willie Henderson[1]

What is striking about Chapter II of Book I of the *Wealth of Nations* is that the format and content of the argument are very similar to (say) arguments presented by David Hume in both the *Treatise* and the *Inquiry*. Start with human nature; link human nature to all aspects of human behavior; compare, using examples, human nature to animal nature, looking at similarities and differences, and reach conclusions about human relations and human institutions. With respect to Hume's work, his conclusions concern property, justice and morality. With respect to Smith's second chapter the conclusions relate to the respective role of benevolence and self-interest, contracts, class structure, genius and the impact of the division of labor. So in exploring the implications of the human propensity to "truck, barter and exchange," is it possible to look at processes in the text to reach conclusions about Smith's writing as a combination of the familiar and new? Can we look at the product and reach conclusions about the writing process? Can we, in any sense, watch Smith writing?

In a general sense, the form of Smith's argument, i.e. its structure and moves, is one that would have been familiar to an educated eighteenth-century reader. Whilst there are some advantages in interpretation in isolating Smith's chapter, by close reading, a richer investigation would be that of interpretation based upon sources. Or, to put the problem another way, Smith's chapter is an outcome of a longer eighteenth-century discussion of the relationship between human nature and the economy. This is, of course, what is implied by synthesis. To Hume, as a model for a form of argument, we can add texts by Mandeville and Hutcheson, for example, and, no doubt, many others.

It is a long-established commonplace in studies of Smith that the *Wealth of Nations* is a work of synthesis (Stewart 1980 [1794]: 320; Roll 1942: 148; Schumpeter 1954: 18; Skinner 1979). In this view, the work finds its strength not in the originality of the many principles expounded within it, but in the way that the various parts are brought together into a relationship with each other, and, though this is not often stated quite so clearly, with Smith's target reader. In other words, the strength of the text is to be found in its composition, its rhetoric and also in its familiarity (Schumpeter 1954). Much scholarly attention has been given to the synthesis of theoretical ideas, but comparatively little has been given to Smith's writing as writing. One exception is Brown's reading of Smith's works in which the issue of intertextuality is a basis for the analysis (Brown 1994: 3, 5).

There has been discussion, also, of Smith's writing as evidencing plagiarism—a charge that ignores Schumpeter's caveat, that "no charge of plagiarism can be made against Smith or on his behalf against others" (Rashid 1990; 1992; Rothbard 1995a: 435; Schumpeter 1954: 185).[2] Although Rashid's charge of plagiarism was challenged, robustly, (Ahiakpor 1992) the initial debate was confused.[3] It needed a clearer understanding that ideas can be borrowed without incurring the charge of plagiarism, but words cannot be borrowed in the same way. Paraphrases, saying the same thing but in different ways, are part of the writing process and distinguished from plagiarism by the fact that different words, and altered purposes, are involved; i.e., there are issues of context and objectives. In addition, issues of plagiarism have to do with words internal to one text in relation to words internal to another. Matters outside the text such as biographical information are irrelevant. Evidence is primarily textual (though there are, in modern-day discussions, issues of intent). Ahiakpor implicitly understood this point when he called for detailed textual exemplification from Rashid, a request that does not seem to have been met (Ahiakpor 1992: 171).

Ahiakpor's defense of Smith with respect to the charge of plagiarism continued in his response to Rothbard's views, published later, on Smith's plagiarism. Ahiakpor quotes, in support of his skepticism, "Cannan's view of Smith's acknowledgements" (Ahiakpor 1999: 380). But, despite this defense, detailed analysis of Smith's writing, in relation to possible sources, is still required. Furthermore, an acceptable analysis would need to accommodate old and new rhetoric. From classical rhetoric the notion of "transformative imitation" (*imitatio*) may be relevant. From the modern, "intertextuality," the location of texts in the spirit of a particular time, is also relevant when considering Smith or any other author's writing. This approach accepts, as does that of Dooley, that the continuity of discussion is significant: "As Smith followed Hutchison, so Hutchison followed those that went before him" (Dooley 2003: 1).

Whilst there has been much written on Smith's work as a work of (economic) synthesis, the question of how Smith achieved this synthesis in writing has tended to have been sidestepped. Can we trace out how this synthesis is achieved in writing? Can we establish a sense of what is given in the text and what is new? This is a bigger question and it is within this context that the question "What are we to make of Smith's propensity?" is to be addressed.

In what follows, close attention is given to Smith's writing in the second chapter of Book I of the *Wealth of Nations*. The evidence is not thematic but based upon the comparison of passages with earlier writers. We are still interpreting and the attention is still focused on "truck, barter and exchange," but the attempt is to dig over Smith's sources and so understand Smith's argument as an eighteenth-century argument, complete with characteristic moves and common lexical elements, that he then bends to his own uses. The article does not always present, essentially, new ideas, for it restates some already established links between Smith's text and those of other writers, e.g. in the annotations provided in the Glasgow Edition of the *Wealth of Nations*. The paper does not re-produce influences already noted if there is nothing to add. Rather it illustrates, at the level of a given chapter, paragraph or phrase, the sense in which Smith's writing is a synthesis.

The wider literature and Chapter II

Chapter II has rarely been subjected to close analysis, and, as far as I can establish, nor to any sustained studies of relationships with other texts. The Glasgow Edition of the *Wealth of Nations* sets out sources in the footnotes and comments on them. These do not cover all aspects of Smith's sources for the chapter. How could they? A basic insight of intertextuality is that all texts are made up, knowingly or unknowingly, of shreds of other texts—and although the comments are extensive, there is always more that can be said. Furthermore, Smith's notion of the origins of the propensity to truck, barter and exchange is not given a lot of analytical attention in the secondary literature, whilst other details in the chapter (e.g. Smith's controversial notion of genius) have been given some attention.

Survey of written work in the history of economic thought, on the propensities, has not yielded much in terms of detailed analysis—the treatment has been variable—and this has promoted new work (such as chapter 1, to which this is an appendix). Rothbard, for example, is critical of Smith's notion of propensities (Rothbard locates motivation for exchange in the fact that each party benefits) and provides, essentially, an ahistorical account: "But Smith unfortunately shifts the main focus from mutual benefit to an allegedly irrational and innate 'propensity to truck, barter and exchange', as if humans beings were lemmings determined by forces external to their chosen purposes" (Rothbard 1995a: 441–442). This and explanations like it (see chapter 1 of this volume), overlook the fact that Smith was operating, as we shall see, within an established discourse structure. Evensky, who has made detailed analyses of several of Smith's strategic chapters, has not paid, as far as I can establish, detailed attention to Book I, Chapter II. In a recent paper, however, he has shown the role of Chapter II in the development of Smith's fuller "moral philosophical vision." Essentially Evensky illustrates how Smith develops "a compelling story" about social evolution based upon the division of labor and its consequences over time for productivity, inventiveness and social and economic divisions (Evensky 2003: 6–9). This "compelling story" is composed partly of elements found in the works of earlier writers.

The reading that is presented here is built around the question "How does Smith achieve a synthesis in writing?" It is not a search for origins as such—even although some parallel passages are established—but a means of illustrating an approach to understanding Smith's writing that goes beyond simple categorization in terms of this or that source.

An analysis based primarily upon some of Hume's writing

Smith's text:

> Whether this propensity be one of those original principles in human nature, of which no further account can be given; or whether, as seems more probable, it be the necessary consequence of the faculties of reason or speech, it belongs not to our present subject to inquire.
>
> (*WN*, I.ii.2)

Hume's text:

> Its effects are every where conspicuous; but as to its causes, they are mostly unknown, and must be resolv'd into *original* qualities of human nature, which I pretend not to explain. Nothing is more requisite for a true philosopher, than to restrain the intemperate desire for searching into causes, and having establish'd any doctrine upon a sufficient number of experiments, rest contented with that, when he sees a farther examination would lead him in to obscure and uncertain speculations. In that case his enquiry wou'd be much better employ'd in examining the effects than the causes of his principle.
>
> (*Treatise*, p. 13)

And elsewhere:

> We must … glean up our experiments in this science from a cautious observation of human life, and take them as they appear in the common course of the world, by men's behaviour in company, in affairs, and in their pleasures.
>
> (*Treatise*, p. xxiii)

So what we have in Chapter II is a form of argument that follows Hume in the sense that human nature is a given. We do not know why it is the way it is: that part of nature is shrouded in darkness, as it were. It is foolish to speculate, that is not the road to knowledge. Focus on the consequences of human nature, for these can be discovered experimentally through observation and experience. Notice too that not only is the form of argument similar to that of Hume, so too is a detail of the language: "original qualities of human nature" (Hume); "original principles of human nature" (Smith, though the phrase used to translate Grotius in a recent modern translation is "the first principles of nature" (Grotius 1964 [1625]) so that although the investigation of the synthesis here is limited, it must be understood as yet more complex); "they are mostly unknown"; "no further account can be given" (Smith, though this is closer in phrasing to Hutcheson); "I pretend not to explain" (Hume); "it belongs not to our present subject to inquire" (Smith). This insight does more: it places the idea of unintended consequences in a philosophical context. If the consequences were intended there has to be some thing or someone (God) who intends: this sort of investigation is ruled out by Hume's method. It is pointless to speculate, for such speculations are not based upon observation and experience. Another implication of the unintended consequences is that human society progresses as human needs develop, i.e. that there is a human propensity for action in the world. The text signals, here and elsewhere, through notions of unintended consequences, an evolutionary approach to society. Hume, of course, in the *Treatise*, saw justice, arising out of common adjustments to self-love, as "advantageous to the public; tho' it be not intended for that purpose by the inventors" (*Treatise*, p. 529). Unintended consequences abound, they are part of a wider discourse.

This progressive discovery of human possibilities, and of what is advantageous and what is not, is also in line with the natural law tradition as initiated much earlier by Grotius and expounded by Pufendorf (Buckle 1991: 67). It is also in keeping with Adam Ferguson: "Man, like other animals, has certain instinctive propensities, which, prior to the perception of pleasure or pain, or prior to the experience of what is pernicious or useful, lead him to perform many functions of nature relative to himself and his fellow creatures" (Ferguson 1966 [1767]: 10–11).[4] Hutcheson too talks about "propensity" in relation to "those 'springs of action' which do not presuppose antecedent opinions of good or evil in their objects" (Jensen 1971: 12). Smith also held (*WN*, p. 540) that humans exhibit "a natural effort which every man is continually making to better his own condition." He does not use the term propensity for this potentially powerful "natural effort" but it is clearly meant to be such (see chapter 1 of this volume). The phrase "natural disposition" is how Smith refers in the *Lectures on Jurisprudence* to what later becomes "propensity" in the *Wealth of Nations* (*LJ*, vi, 44). Statements about propensities and dispositions are part of a wider discursive practice.

It would seem that in writing this passage, Smith had Hume's recommendation for the experimental (scientific) study of society in mind. That he does not specifically say so is probably partly due to eighteenth-century convention and partly due to his understanding of his target audience. Smith assumes that his intended reader has knowledge of current philosophical discussions. This is taken as a given. Of course, it is possible to dig much deeper. For a deeper understanding of Smith's "propensity," there is always Aquinas and the notion of "natural inclination" to turn to. A target audience for his published work is, accordingly, people that would have some knowledge of Hume and of relevant writings prior to Hume, such as Hutcheson, Locke, and Grotius, and so on, back to medieval conceptions of the natural law. But Smith tells us none of this directly: *imitatio* suggests that "the structure and language of an old text may help introduce radically new ideas" (Leff 1997: 201, 203). Some of this will be in the *Zeitgeist*. Some of this will be derived from the general intellectual character of the times (*Zeitgeist*) rather than simply from particular texts. If we accept the idea of intertextuality, two related texts (say) may contain common elements derived from an ongoing intellectual conversation informed by the general climate of opinion and by common assumptions and vocabularies.

Smith's text:

> as seems more probably, it be the necessary consequence of reason and speech.
>
> (*WN*, I.ii.2)

Hume's text:

> Men are superior to beasts principally by the superiority of their reason; and they are the degrees of the same faculty, which set such an infinite difference between one man and another.
>
> (*Treatise*, p. 610)

Grotius's text:

> The mature man in fact has ... an impelling desire for society, for the gratification of which he alone among animals possesses a special instrument, speech.
>
> (Grotius 1964 [1625] (*DJBP*): Prol. 7)

The emphasis of the second part of the quote from Hume is mine. Given how Smith develops his text, it is significant that, as will be seen later, he does not share Hume's view in this respect. Hume influenced Smith's thought, though this does not mean that Smith swallowed Hume's ideas whole. Smith's argument is original in many respects, and that also needs to be kept in mind. That Grotius identifies the social significance of speech and its consequence, a desire for social order, underscores Smith's concerns, as do the views of Hutcheson, about the sociability of human nature. Smith's "reason" suggests that as progress takes place, instinct ("propensity") gives way to reason for this too is part of human nature. Linking the propensity to speech stresses that the propensity be linked to sociability. The word is loaded, of course—especially when combined with trade and the property that trade implies—with, for example, notions in Grotius and Locke concerning (self-) "Preservation" and hence acting according to our nature and following the dictates of self-love (Buckle 1991, passim). This strengthens the role of the propensity with respect to self-interest.

Smith's text:

> Two greyhounds in running down the same hare, have sometimes the appearance of acting in some sort of concert. Each turns her towards his

companion, or endeavours to intercept her when his companion turns her towards himself. This, however, is not the effect of any contract, but of the accidental concurrence of their passions in the same object at that particular time.

(*WN*, I.ii.2)

Hume's text:

An old greyhound will trust the more fatiguing part of the chace to the younger, and will place himself so as to meet the hare in her doubles; nor are the conjectures, which he forms on this occasion, found in any thing but his observation and experience.

(*ECHU*, section ix, p. 83)

Pufendorf's text:

From this state it follows that man should recognize and worship his Author, and marvel at all His works; and also pass his life in a very different manner from the brutes. Hence this state is contrasted with the life and condition of the brutes.

(*De Officio*, II.2.1)

The Glasgow Edition makes no mention of this link between Smith and Hume at this point. Again, the form and content of the argument are close to that of Hume though the context is different. Both writers appreciate the need for exemplifications that will make issues clear for the reader. Both settle on the hunting of hares with greyhounds. Smith writes in terms of the accidental concurrence of the passion of each dog.[5] Hume writes in terms of the experience and observation of the "old" dog: ultimately Hume did not use reason as a distinctive attribute of humans. Hume does not accept any sharp distinction between the human and animal in this respect (Buckle 2001: 231). That two greyhounds and a hare are chosen for the exemplification suggests, not simply that the example would have been understood by the target readers, but that Smith had Hume in mind when writing this section. The dog in both cases is male and the hunted animal female. It is likely that the dog in the chase would be male and that the female for the hare is suggested by the need to contrast the pronouns. But then again, the sexual imagery may be culturally telling. Smith's point is one about "contract." This evidence would suggest that Smith knew Hume's writings in detail and that in thinking about the relationship between economics and human nature, he would turn, in his writing, to Hume.

It is not suggested that the quote from Pufendorf is directly relevant. It does however illustrate that the contrast between human nature and brutish nature is fundamental, even if in some later discussion, animal and human nature share some elements. Pufendorf builds his ideas upon Grotius, and so a cumulative discussion becomes part of intellectual life. Economy is organized, and social, and fundamentally linked to human nature. It is useful to keep in mind that, according to Buckle, the Scottish Enlightenment read Locke as having a significant relationship with the thinking of Grotius and Pufendorf and that Hutcheson's predecessor at Glasgow, Gershom Carmichael, worked Pufendorf into Scottish moral philosophy (Buckle 1991: 193). Hutcheson himself tells us as much, referring, in his *Short Introduction to Moral Philosophy*, to his sources in the ideas of Cicero, Aristotle, Pufendorf and Carmichael (Dooley 2003: 2). Given Smith's early biography, it is not surprising that he synthesized his own thinking through exploration of earlier writers whose acquaintance he made by studying at Glasgow. Smith benefited accordingly from these teachings in an already synthesized form.

Smith's text:

> Each turns her towards his companion, or endeavours to intercept her when his companion turns her towards himself. This is, however, not the effect of any contract, but of the accidental concurrence of their passions in the same object at that particular time.
>
> (*WN*, i.ii.2)

Hume's text:

> Thus animals have little or no sense of virtue and vice; they quickly lose sight of the relations of blood; and are incapable of that of right or property.
>
> (*Treatise*, p. 326)

Hume's text:

> And that all contracts and promises ought carefully to be fulfilled, in order to secure mutual trust and confidence, by which the general *interest* of mankind is so much promoted?
>
> Examine the writers on the laws of nature; and you will always find, that, whatever principles they set out with, they are sure to terminate here at last, and to assign, as the ultimate reason for every rule that they establish, the convenience and necessities of mankind.
>
> (*ECPM*, p. 195)

Smith is of the same opinion as Hume concerning "right or property." His context is the propensity to "truck, barter and exchange." When exchanges take place, essentially what are exchanged are property rights. But in the example of the greyhound and the hare, the chase is instinctual, it is not based upon discussion and bargaining, there is no operating propensity based upon reason and speech, though the notion of experience is not necessarily ruled out. In this context, contract is about agreements to exchange, either implicit or explicit. The links are between property and contract, i.e. between creating, exchanging and maintaining. Smith's animals are also (largely) Hume's animals, as we might expect, though Smith's poor are not Hume's poor. Smith terminates his chapter with the bringing together of difference and specializations for the benefit of society as a whole. The overall structure of Smith's chapter is in conformity with a style of argument shared with others, especially Hume. The context of his writing includes some of the sustained intellectual arguments of his day and with respect to his reader, he takes this as a given.

Smith's text:

> Nobody ever saw one animal by its gestures and natural cries signify to another, this is mine, that yours; I am willing to give this for that.
>
> (*WN*, I.ii.2)

Hume's text:

> What other reason, indeed, could writers ever give, why this must be *mine* and that *yours*; since uninstructed nature, surely never made any such distinction.
>
> (*ECPM*, p. 195)

Again, although the sentence and the context are not identical, there is a close affinity between what Smith writes and what Hume writes. Smith's words could be seen as a (very loose) paraphrase of Hume's, though this is a view that requires some justification. In both, the reader is expected to agree with what is on offer. This expectation is carried in the opening phrases: "Nobody ever saw" (Smith) and "What other reason indeed, could writers ever give" (Hume). Smith's use of "mine" and "yours" (located centrally in both sentences) and the setting of his animal episode in what is, in effect, "uninstructed nature" ("gestures and natural cries") suggest, again, that at this point in his writing, he had Hume in mind. Even if the relationship between this sample of Smith and the sample from Hume is not a directly corresponding one (though I think that it is), this would still be information relevant to understanding the way or ways in which Smith achieves synthesis in his writing. Smith's sentence is not strictly a paraphrase of Hume—it is certainly not plagiarism—but it is close both in meaning and in structure. Both are drawing upon juridical vocabulary and distinctions made, concerning "meum and teum," in Roman Law, the system to which Scottish thinkers turned to "fill in the gaps in their own law" (Herman 2001: 84). Smith writes out similar ideas to Hume—as a man of his time—but the ideas are transformed, characteristically for this chapter, into dramatic narrative.

An analysis based upon some of Mandeville's writing

Mandeville's influence on the *Wealth of Nations,* and on Smith's understanding of the division of labor has long been recognized. We know that Smith came to

Mandeville through Hutcheson and Hume and directly by his own reading. It is also recognized that "one of the most famous passages of the *Wealth of Nations* that about the labourer's coat is largely a paraphrase of the *Fable*" (Kaye, in Mandeville 1924: cxxxv). The phrase, "the division of labour" given pride of place in the opening sentence of Chapter II, is Mandeville's (Kaye, in Mandeville 1924: cxxxv). Hume had also talked of the "partition of employments" and Hutcheson, earlier, had referred to the idea—again this topic was one that was part of an ongoing discussion (Herman 2001: 200). Dooley traces origins in the work of Petty and in Plato's *Republic* (Dooley 2003: 3). It is significant that Kaye uses the term "paraphrase" even though he makes no analysis of its linguistic elements. What else is there around that suggests Smith had Mandeville in mind as he wrote?

Smith's text:

> It is the necessary, though very slow and gradual consequence of a certain propensity in human nature which has in view no such extensive utility; the propensity to truck, barter and exchange one thing for another.
>
> (*WN*, I.ii.1)

Mandeville's text:

> Cleo. But it is a great while, before that Nature can be rightly understood; and it is the Work of Ages to find out the true Use of the Passions, and to raise a Politician, that can make every Frailty of the members, add Strength to the whole Body, and by dexterous Management turn *private Vices into public Benefits*. It is the necessary, though very slow and gradual consequence of a certain propensity in human nature ...
>
> (*Sixth Dialogue*, 1924 [1732]: vol. ii, p. 319)

An aim is to show how Smith's second chapter is constructed as an eighteenth-century argument. Smith does not share Mandeville's views on "Management." But he shares the notion that establishing the outcome of human nature is a slow process. It is "the Work of Ages to find out the true Use of the Passions" (Mandeville). Smith's statement is "It is the necessary consequence, though very slow and gradual." Elsewhere Mandeville demonstrates the evolutionary significance of "Experience" (Mandeville 1924 [1732]: 171). Smith has not identified the exchanging of goods and services as a "passion" but rather as an orientation, a "propensity," though any distinction between a "passion" and a "propensity" is not explicitly made. However it may be implicit in the reference to "reason and speech." For Hume, reason is a means of achieving ends that "passions" set. A propensity, linked to reason and speech, would not have the force of passion but would rather be a means of channelling "passion" into productive activity, by reason and discussion. The coexistence of "Deliberative and non-deliberative elements," with respect to motivation in Smith, is an aspect noted by Oakley (Oakley 1994: 79–80; see also chapter 1 of this volume). Hume's views, in attenuated form, can be traced back through Hutcheson and even to Aristotle (Buckle 1991: 63). This is what it is to write as a contribution to a developing analysis.

It is, nonetheless, the "Work of Ages" before that propensity is manifest in highly specialized economic activity. In this sense Smith echoes Mandeville's notion of historical evolution and in this sense too, Mandeville inspired Smith, an insight, with respect to the division of labor, supported by Dugald Stewart (Kaye, in Mandeville 1924: cxxxv). He also seems to share Mandeville's view that "What belongs to our Nature, all Men may justly be said to have actually or virtually in them at their Birth" (Mandeville, *Third Dialogue*, 1924 [1732]: 121). But he does not seem to share Mandeville's view that "All Passions and Instinct in general were given to all Animals for some wise End," for Smith writes that human nature "has in view no such extensive utility" and, as someone interested in Hume's philosophy, Smith is unlikely to make any arguments about the origin of human nature. So whilst there are some things that are the same and said in related ways, with respect to Mandeville's writing, other elements are carefully avoided. Smith (elsewhere) acknowledges Mandeville as having "original" ideas (*EPS*, p. 250).

Smith's texts:

> But man has almost constant occasion for the help of his brethren, and it is vain for him to expect it from their benevolence only.

> It is not from the benevolence of the butcher, the brewer, or the baker, that we expect our dinner, but from their regard to their own interest. We address ourselves not to their humanity but to their self-love; and never talk to them of our necessities but of their advantages.
>
> (*WN*, I.ii.2)

Mandeville's text:

> (On money)
>   How to get the Services perform'd by others, when we have Occasion for them, is the grand and almost constant Sollicitude in Life of every individual Person. To expect, that others should serve us for nothing, is unreasonable; therefore all Commerce, that Men can have together, must be a continual bartering of one thing for another. The Seller who transfers the Property of a Thing, has his own Interest as much at Heart as the Buyer who purchases the Property; and, if you want or like a thing, the Owner of it, whatever Stock or Provision he may have of the same, or how greatly soever you stand in need of it, will never part with it, but for a Consideration, which he likes better, than he does the thing you want.

Which way shall I persuade a Man to serve me, when the Service, I can repay him in, is such that he does not want or care for?

(*Sixth Dialogue*, 1924 [1732]: vol. ii, p. 349)

The two extracts from Smith and the longer extract from Mandeville are set in different contexts but Mandeville rehearses the issues—in a different context from Smith—which Smith treats in his famous aphorism. Smith did not arrive at his aphorism without effort. An earlier reference is less dramatic:

When you apply to a brewer or butcher for beer or for beef, you do not explain to him how much you stand in need of these, but how much it would be your [*sic*] interest to allow you to have them for a certain price. You do not address his humanity but his self-love.

(*LJ*, vi, 46)

Revisions made for publication in the *Wealth of Nations* successfully add to the dramatic force of the statement. It is transformed from a commonplace to an aphorism. Note also that Smith is concerned about what Hutcheson called "springs to action" but Smith assumes pre-existing knowledge: the term "benevolence" is not explained but taken as given, or already understood.

Whilst there are common themes in the two authors, there is, here, neither common language nor common context. Both share the notion however that there is a power to persuade, located in self-interest. Both, interestingly, are written from the point of view of the agent and not of the social critic.[6] Smith's aphorism is, in words, entirely his own but if we were to treat it fully we could trace a line of development back through Hutcheson to Shaftesbury. Shaftesbury, according to Miller, conceptualized "a balance of selfish and benevolent feelings within human nature" such that, quoting Shaftesbury, "the private interest and good of everyone … works towards the general good" (Miller 1995: 49; Shaftesbury 1964: vol. I, pp. 336, 338). Again, the issue of benevolence versus self-love is a concept that is repeatedly reflected upon, prior to the publication of the *Wealth of Nations*. Throughout the eighteenth century "benevolence" versus self-love was part of the discourse and located both within and beyond texts. Smith does not deny benevolence, simply records that it is not a strong enough motive in commercial transactions.

Smith, the storyteller, also borrows from Mandeville. We have already mentioned the laborer's coat from Chapter I. Smith makes use of Mandeville when telling his tale of how the division of labor comes to be established as the norm in a developing community.

Smith's text:

As it is by treaty, by barter and by purchase, that we obtain from one another the greater part of those mutual good offices which we stand in

need of, so it is this same trucking disposition which originally gives occasion to the division of labour. In a tribe of hunters or shepherds a particular
person makes bows and arrows.

(WN, I.ii.3)

Mandeville's text:

> Cleo. Man, as I have hinted before, naturally loves to imitate what he sees
> others do, which is the reason that Savage people all do the same thing:
> This hinders them from meliorating their Condition, though they are
> always wishing for it: But if one will wholly apply himself to making Bows
> and Arrows, whilst another provides Food, a third builds Huts, a fourth
> makes Garments, and a fifth Utensils, they not only become useful to one
> another, but the Callings and Employments themselves will in the same
> Number of Years receive much greater Improvements, than if all had been
> promiscuously follow'd by every one of the Five.
>
> (Mandeville 1924: vol. ii, p. 284)

Smith's passage is too long to reproduce here, besides which it is well known.
The two passages are available in the Glasgow Edition but no analysis is made
there of them (Mandeville's version of the spread of the division of labour is
reproduced in the Glasgow edition at I.ii.3, p. 27, in footnote 8). What is
striking about Smith's narrative episode is that its main dramatic elements are
structured according to Mandeville's text. Smith writes of four people: the
arrow maker, the hut maker, the brazier and the tanner (who makes clothes),
whereas Mandeville writes explicitly of five. The 'food' maker is implied,
however, in Smith's text, for the arrow maker "frequently exchanges" the
arrows "for cattle or venison." The "smith or brazier" is the equivalent of the
one who makes "Utensils." Smith has modeled the five elements of his writing
here directly on Mandeville.

   This insight need not be used to do Smith down: Smith does not use
Mandeville's words, or at least not in the development of the narrative—the
attributes of "the Savage," such as bows and arrows, may well be conventional—nor even Mandeville's theory.[7] The developmental context of the tale is
different from that of Mandeville, in that the analysis is consistently focused
upon propositions that are broadly theoretical. Smith is, again, expanding a
narrative and making it work within the context of a developing and consistently worked argument. Mandeville's context is (initially) that of imitation,
Smith's is that of the propensity ("this same trucking disposition"). Mandeville
opens his passage with: "But if one will." There is no theory grounding this
change, indeed the general principle of imitation acts against it. Smith develops
Mandeville's short six-line illustration into a story of social evolution based on
an operating principle, linked to self-interest—the propensity to truck, barter
and exchange. This is seen even more transparently in the *Lectures on
Jurisprudence* where Smith introduces a short passage, parallel in spirit to the

passage in the *Wealth of Nations*, on "A savage who supports himself by hunting" with "This bartering and trucking spirit is the cause of the separation of trades and the improvements in the arts" (*LJ*, 348, 47). The relationship with Mandeville's example becomes thus more complex as the text in the *Wealth of Nations* is adapted also from Smith's prior writing. The relevant textual process is that of paraphrasing though the results move the (final) new text beyond mere paraphrasing, as there is a theory-based, and extensive, creative element in Smith's writing that is absent from Mandeville's original. Smith's story is placed within a systematic account of socioeconomic development and this systematic element is lacking in Mandeville.

Smith's text:

> The difference of natural talents in different men is, in reality, much less than we are aware of; and the very different genius which appears to distinguish men of different professions, when grown up to maturity, is not upon many occasions so much the cause as the effect of the division of labour.
>
> (*WN*, I.ii.4)

Mandeville's text:

> Human Nature is every where the same: Genius, Wit and Natural Parts are always sharpened by Application, and may be much improv'd in the Practice of the meanest Villany, as they can in the Exercise of Industry or the most Heroic Virtue.
>
> (*An Essay on Charity and Charity Schools*, 1924 [1732]: vol. i, p. 275)

The Glasgow Edition makes no reference to this link between Mandeville's thought and Smith's writing, at this point, but when it is taken together with Mandeville's view on schooling and that the "Brain of a Child, newly born is a Charte Blanche" (Mandeville, *Fourth Dialogue*, 1924 [1732]: 168), then Smith's writing is here, again, synthesizing many elements that would have been familiar to eighteenth-century readers. The two excerpts (above) seem to be saying the same thing in different words; i.e., the themes are similar though the details of the language completely different. The Glasgow Edition at this point in the text points to extensive passages in Hume. The whole passage on nature and nurture is interwoven with ideas from other writers such as Hume.

So what do we make of Smith's "propensity" and can we watch Smith writing?

Smith's "propensity" is located in Humean, and pre-Humean, ideas about human nature and the link between nature and economy. In this sense it is a familiar starting point, a means to get into the matter at hand which is that of setting a framework for the development of society through a cumulative process of experiment and conversation: trucking, bartering and exchanging are social activities aided by speech. It acknowledges Smith's debt to Hume generally and specifically with respect to links between "property" and human nature, essential foundations for specialization and exchange. But the influences on his writing are also multiple. Smith was a man of his time and he was writing in the context of a developing eighteenth-century argument—about links between human nature and economic activity—some of which had already become part of a synthesized, standard body of shared knowledge and were not therefore located in any specific text.

What also emerges, from this analysis, is a sense of how Smith achieved a synthesis in writing. The product, i.e. Chapter II and its outcomes, is unique to Smith, even if strongly influenced by others, and his text is carefully constructed to show how individual specialization and interest are inevitably and usefully bound together as a contribution to the whole. But the process is one in which elements of earlier eighteenth-century thinking, including terminology (lexis), and expectations about moves in the argument (comparisons of human and animal nature), are drawn together to produce a new text. Smith's writing is located in a series of eighteenth-century discussions and any one element in the text may draw from a number of sources—Mandeville, Hutcheson and Hume being the most easily recognizable. A methodological basis for the construction of the chapter is based upon Hume's ideas concerning observation and experience. In other words the chapter is partly constructed around Hume's interpretation of Newtonian methods ("experimentalism," rejection of *a priori* principles and the practice of simplicity in explanation) as applied to the study of human nature and society, an interpretation that Smith also set out for himself (*LRBL*, pp. 145–146; see Buckle 1991: 237; Smith 1983).[8] That this is all packed into two short episodes should not give any cause for concern; Smith's target reader was expected to have recognized the argument. It is a decision made, by the author, between what needs to be said (i.e. about what is new) and what can be taken as given (Coulthard 1994: 4–5). The contrast made between human nature and animal nature, is, textually, informed by Hume, but there is also a smattering of Mandeville and no doubt many others. The location of economic life in human nature is informed by details of the writings of Hume, Hutcheson and Mandeville, but those details are carefully adapted to Smith's purpose. Suggestions of plagiarism, on the evidence supplied here, seem misguided. Even though the evidence presented here is not drawn from areas directly relating to either Rashid's or Rothbard's discussion, the method used here needs to be applied to the episodes referred to in those articles. On the basis of what has been demonstrated here, Ahiakpor's skepticism of Rothbard's claims seems justifiable.

Smith's notion of a "propensity in human nature" is his way of linking to the ongoing eighteenth-century discussion of the ways in which economic life is related to human nature. He does not explicitly say that what is traded is property, i.e. the product of individual human effort. Neither does Smith explicitly say, in his opening moves, that human nature is social, and that there is no state of nature in the sense contrived by Hobbes. There are implications that follow from what he does say. Trade implies others. Speech implies others. Property implies product and producers (others) since such rights are social and based upon constraints. A "propensity to truck, barter and exchange" implies a human nature that is purposive and active in the world and that results, in contradistinction to animals, in patterns of living that are subject to significant change over time. Human society is located in a human energy to transform materials and relationships. And by identifying the link between human nature and economic life, in the way that he does, Smith has a sure foundation (we are talking eighteenth-century) for unintended consequences and for his use of "every man" (i.e., human nature is consistent) as an economic agent, later in his work. Indeed unintended consequences in this view come out as very significant and even if the "invisible hand" is used ironically later in the work, it is still contained within the notion of human nature. Not only that but the invisible hand is textually realized elsewhere in the *Wealth of Nations* by the development of language that removes the actor.

But can we really watch him writing? Well, yes, but only in a very general sense. He is clear about his target reader: from the evidence presented here, the target reader knew something of Hume, Hutcheson, and of Mandeville, for example. He did not need to spell everything out for them: the target reader was already engaged in a conversation about the origins of social and economic life. Was it one target reader or a set of target readers? Smith is consistent in his theoretical arguments, in this chapter, but the argument is shaped by a variety of different means, though narrative predominates. This suggests that he may have had more than one target reader in mind: the message is consistent but the means of achieving it textually are varied by genre, i.e. logical and story-based. The target reader helps an author define the writing and the writing then defines the audience. Actual readers were more or less similar to target reader(s), or struggled to become his target reader, and familiar with the cultural context, and, therefore were unlikely to be surprised by (say) the comparison of human nature and animal nature. Indeed, once human nature was mentioned, the comparison would be expected. If animals are constantly engaged in reproducing the same and humans engaged in change and exchange (i.e. engaged in a set of changing relationships with each other and, so, if the implications of the narrative of the "tribal society" are followed through, with nature) then the eighteenth century would locate such behaviors in human nature. Readers were, like him, aware of other literature and of the discussion of the properties of human nature. Human nature was engaged in a struggle between benevolence and self-interest, but constrained by social possibilities such as "contracts" and social divisions created by education and the division of labor.

He knew his sources and his social and cultural context well and so borrowed, imitated and adapted by responding to his reading. Still and Warton put the idea of all writing in the context of any writer's experience of reading: "[s/he] is a reader of texts (in the broadest sense) before s/he is a creator of texts, and therefore the work of art is inevitably shot through with references, quotations and influences of every kind" (Still and Warton 1990; Jasinski 2001: 323). He also knew how to transform a good workable example when he saw one and this he could even have considered as an exercise of rhetorical imitation. He synthesized from a number of sources, though he did not swallow the arguments whole, and produced a text that was still his own. Hume's greyhound example is close to Smith's but the use to which Smith puts the example goes beyond Hume. The fact that he can incorporate elements of Hutcheson (to whom Mandeville was anathema)—Smith does not deny benevolence, he just points out that in terms of commerce it is not relevant as a motivating passion—with Mandeville attests to his writing skills, and the power of his synthesis. He is likely to have read other writers imaginatively, with his writing project in mind, and to have carefully identified passages—noting them either mentally or mechanically or simply by absorption—that he would draw upon for elaboration. In the passage on the evolution of the division of labor in a tribal society, for example, he has worked out the elements in Mandeville's brief example and translated those same elements into a convincing story of his own, even if modeled on the same moves as made by Mandeville. How he actually did this (i.e. by intuition or by careful plotting) remains unclear (what we know of his redrafting activities suggest plotting, by rewrite, though the differences between the passage in the early draft and in the published work are slight), though the textual outcome is carefully constructed. Either way, he turned a simple illustration into a more significant story in the context of a developing theoretical argument.

Another aspect of synthesis is his ability to paraphrase. Here, however, the notion of paraphrase is not precisely specified. It can be characterized as involving "various types of transformations of expressions into the same language" (Yamamoto 2003). The sentences identified in Smith and in others are not always doing the same kind of work but there are elements in common: repetition of words and phrases being a significant element. We are dealing with more or less, sometimes there are common elements; sometimes the relationship is more remote or elaborated. Sometimes the commonalities are distilled from more than one source. Paraphrasing was of considerable cultural significance in the sixteenth and seventeenth centuries and is likely to have found it way into non-theological writing in the eighteenth century. Its origins are to be found in biblical study but the practise was extended to secular writing. "Paraphrases" were also part of Presbyterian services in Scottish churches. In modern discussion of "paraphrasing," in the context of developing students' capacities to write, the issue of paraphrasing is linked to the avoidance of plagiarism. On the evidence supplied from Book I, Chapter II, there are no grounds for a charge of plagiarism. To understand Smith's writing, as writing, requires a cultural context that is more sophisticated than a simple search for origins.

A significant point about paraphrasing is that readers in the eighteenth century would have been expected to recognize the sources—texts were very long-lived. There would be an element of familiarity even though Smith, as a writer of a didactic text, would have aimed at transforming the target reader's experience. The familiar gives way to the new, and this is what happens in his contrasts between human and animal nature. The ideas are familiar but the use that Smith finally puts them to is radical. His conclusions that invention is the product of the ordinary mind engaged in daily business or that street porters and philosophers differ only in situation and as the result of institutional arrangements and not essentially in nature must have startled.

His second chapter demonstrates many of Smith's qualities as a writer, for not only does Smith use synthesis in his writing, but there is some evidence of different qualities (e.g., he writes as a moralist, a political economist, a logician, and, in this chapter above all, a storyteller. Evensky describes Smith's purpose, in Book I, Chapter II, as that of telling "a compelling story of mankind's evolution" (Evensky 2003: 7). That story was told in ways that reflect the *Zeitgeist* and ways that help transform it. Smith also, then, achieves a synthesis amongst these different forms of writing. That he produces a whole with the reputation of gently leading the reader, by the hand, is a significant rhetorical achievement.

Notes

1　Thanks go to Warren Samuels and Roger Backhouse for comments on an earlier draft.
2　A similar charge was made, in the nineteenth century, against Locke whose philosophy was described as "unoriginal and a mere unacknowledged plagiarism."
3　Rothbard wrote later and claims that Smith "originated nothing that was true, and whatever he originated was wrong; that [Smith] was a shameless plagiarist, acknowledging little or nothing and stealing large chunks, for example, from Cantillon" (Rothbard 1995a: 435).
4　Hutcheson also stressed propensities in human nature to social action.
5　"Passion," as an eighteenth-century notion, suggests a range of phenomena: pain and pleasure, instincts, propensities, emotions and sentiments.
6　Smith can change perspectives as he does elsewhere, according to Ahiakpor, in looking at the whole subject from the point of view of the "statesman or legislator" (Ahiakpor 1999: 370).
7　Elsewhere Smith demonstrates an awareness of the contrasting ways (Mandeville versus Rousseau) of depicting the "life of a savage": "a life either of profound indolence, or of great and astonishing adventures" (*EPS*, p. 251)
8　Buckle also argues that Hume's Newtonianism is over-stated (Buckle 2001).

2 Should history-of-economic-thought textbooks cover "recent" economic thought?

Warren J. Samuels, Kirk D. Johnson and Marianne Johnson

it is too early to treat of the economics of the second half of the nineteenth century in a historical spirit. It must be left to the next generation, or the next generation but one.

(Cannan 1917: 395)

These histories of doctrines and the critical reviews devoted to them are of very unequal value but they are nevertheless attempts at a genuinely scientific treatment of ideas. In a wider sense it would be possible to place here almost our entire literature as almost every author offers surveys and reviews in the field of doctrinal history.

(Schumpeter 1967 [1912]: 7)

the history of economics, like intellectual history in general, is an irrepressible activity.

(Blaug 1991: x)

Introduction

This chapter examines the views and practices of authors of textbooks on the history of economic thought on the *relatively* simple question of whether recent economic thought should be covered in such textbooks.

It is *not* the purpose of this article to treat the problem of doing recent economic thought *normatively*. The objectives are to identify and consider the issues and operative factors involved in the problem of including or excluding recent economic thought, to examine how the problem is handled in the literature of twentieth-century textbooks and other materials, and to conclude what we have learned as a matter of *positive* analysis. The risk that is undertaken is that of mischaracterization of particular texts, always subject to the principle of selective perception.

"Recent," "modern," and "contemporary," the terms used in the relevant literature, are treated here as synonyms, although it should be noted that "contemporary" (as distinct also from "current") is the term seemingly most frequently used in the literature in this matter. "Modern," of course, also is often used to refer to economic thought beginning with Adam Smith.

It is widely, and not inappropriately, held by some historians of economic thought—notably Joseph Dorfman—that recent economic thought is too close in time to the historian to be a proper subject of inquiry. Proximity in time prevents, it is felt, adequate description and/or proper perspective. But what are adequate description and proper perspective? What is the context in which history-of-economic-thought work of various kinds is undertaken? Contemporary economists do economics and their work can be and is reported on and interpreted relative to other work, past and current (Medema and Samuels 1998). By the time recent work becomes past work, historians of thought and others have presumably acquired adequate description and proper perspective. But which description and which perspective, and how are they acquired? Do historians of economic thought practice what some preach? And when they are silent, does practice signify what they would have preached?

Serious consideration of what may at first appear to be obvious—either in support of or in opposition to a Dorfman-like proscription—shows the problem of recency (as we will call it) to involve some of the deepest issues of historiography, and considerable irony as well.

After examining Dorfman's position, we next identify the issues and operative factors. We then examine practice and include further comments on issues identified earlier.

In summary, the conclusion is that the negative view is both too general and unrealistic, and is literally impossible for a discipline to follow. It is impossible for economists to ignore recent economic thought and it is impossible not to deal with it in ways that presume, give effect to, create, and promote some version of the history of economic thought. A wide range of uneven practices exists among historians of economic thought. Practitioners of economics who are not historians of economic thought also undertake considerable interpretation of contemporary economic thought. Attention to recent work is as necessarily incomplete as is attention to past work. The implicit (in a few cases, explicit) periods assumed to constitute the necessary passage of time vary among authors. Pressures exist for authors of textbooks and other writings to cover contemporary work. Overall, for reasons made clear below, attention to recent economic thought is inevitable. It is impossible to abide literally with Dorfman's proscription. Given, however, Hume's injunction that an "ought" cannot be derived from an "is" alone, the fact that many history-of-economic-thought textbooks and other works attend to recent developments is insufficient ground on which to conclude that such *ought* to be done. What is inevitable should, however, both be accepted with good grace and understood deeply.

The position of Joseph Dorfman

In 1959, Joseph Dorfman published the fourth and fifth volumes of his magisterial study, *The Economic Mind in American Civilization*. These concluding volumes covered the period 1918–1933. In the prefatory statement that he called "Final Foreword," Dorfman wrote:

> The present two volumes are a unit which conclude the series of five. They begin with the reconversion of the war economy to a peace-time basis after World War I, and they end with the inauguration of the New Deal. It would be interesting to go on with the story, especially since the subsequent installment seems to suggest the possibilities of drawing strong parallels and contrasts with the initial period of this study, when the colonies were faced with the urgency of meeting the exigencies of survival and progress. I have decided, however, to conclude the project and stop in 1933 out of a deep respect for one of the soundest canons of the historian: namely, that the passage of time is needed for perspective and the fullness of available data for adequate description.
>
> (Dorfman 1959: x)

The Foreword is dated November 1958; Dorfman (1904–1991) was in his middle fifties. When Warren Samuels discussed the matter with him in the early 1970s, he reiterated his position.[1]

Dorfman raised two points in defense of his position. One is the "passage of time needed for perspective," the other is the "fullness of available data for adequate description." The two points are intertwined; consideration of one often involves consideration of the other.

Before taking them up, it will be useful to consider a major recent development in work on the history of economic thought that lends credibility to Dorfman's position, albeit not without irony. The development involves research into the state of economics during the period between the two world wars. Without going into detail, the research supports wholesale revision of the view of historians of economics of the relationships between institutional and neoclassical economists, even suggesting that the dichotomy itself may constitute a misrepresentation, inasmuch as individual economists were much more pluralistic, and the discipline as a whole likewise, than has hitherto been comprehended (see Yonay 1998; Morgan and Rutherford 1998; Samuels 2000; especially the current research program of Malcolm Rutherford). The irony is that no small part of the problem stems from the unduly narrow notion of who was an important institutionalist, or who was doing important institutionalist work, advanced by Dorfman himself. Rutherford and others have shown that Thorstein Veblen, John R. Commons and Wesley C. Mitchell by no means exhaust the answers to those questions.

It also turns out that Dorfman's work on Veblen himself was misleading (see Jorgensen and Jorgensen 1999; Edgell 2001). The defects stem, ironically, from incomplete or inadequate description and the failure to allow sufficient time to elapse for Dorfman to acquire proper perspective (Veblen died in 1929; Dorfman's biography of Veblen was published in 1934).

The answer to the questions of why and how the notion of a more or less rigid separation between institutional and neoclassical work got started and was perpetuated remains to be worked out. Surely it includes the role of history written by members of the eventually hegemonic school. But it gives some measure of support to Dorfman's argument, an argument in terms of necessary adequate description and the passage of sufficient time for that to happen and to gain appropriate perspective. Yet, as Merle Curti is cited below for emphasizing, there is no guarantee that the necessary work will be done and that the self-serving myopia of the hegemonic school will not prevent it from happening or trivialize or neglect it once accomplished. That the matter turns on relatively straightforward interpretive positions is indicated by the importance of recognizing both that neoclassical theory is not the only form that theory can properly take and that institutionalists had their own subjects and forms of theory. Such adequacy of description need not come with the passage of time; it takes a Rutherford or his like. Still, Dorfman has scored important points, some inadvertently.

A comparable example is George Stigler's remark that the Marginal Utility Revolution did not take place in the 1870s but in the 1950s, when economists first widely formulated everyday problems using utility functions in a context of constrained maximization. But people continue to refer to a wide-ranging Marginalist Revolution of the 1870s. Again, adequacy of description and interpretation need not come with the passage of time.

It has been suggested by Mark Perlman that Dorfman's argument has to be understood in one or both of two contexts; whatever the context, however, the argument does stand on its own. First, Merle Curti received the Pulitzer Prize for his *Growth of American Thought* (Curti 1943); Dorfman had been told that he was a candidate after his first two volumes were published. The surmise is that when Dorfman completed his fifth and last volume, he conjectured that an additional volume would not help him receive the award. Second, Dorfman was a believer in progressivism (manifest, for example, in the Wisconsin Idea and the New Deal). His third, fourth and fifth volumes projected a dichotomy between progressive and reactionary attitudes and policies. By the late 1950s, he was disillusioned: economists embraced the Cartesian approach embodied in Paul Samuelson's works, and the Columbia department had not only lost its principal institutionalists but was coming under the sway of George Stigler and Gary Becker. In sum, Dorfman had lost heart and motivation (Perlman to Samuels, 28 August 2002).

In any event, Dorfman's proscription leads to a dilemma: either following or not following Dorfman's proscription will set in motion certain but different path dependencies; the doing of the history of economic thought will influence the development of the subject. "Accurate description" loses much of its meaning.

The passage of time can act as a filtering device and thereby select and thus include and privilege simultaneously as excluding and dispossessing (see the discussion, later in this chapter, regarding Ingrid Rima's first edition). If idea, theory or field X could develop along paths X1, X2 or X3, and if it does develop (or is treated only as if it developed) as X3, X will take on the meaning and nuances of X3 rather than of X1 or X2, which will be forgotten. That part of the field constituted by X1 and X2 will be neglected, trivialized or marginalized, and/or forgotten. Filtering can result from simple forgetfulness, failure to be taught in graduate school, or deliberate exclusion by victorious, hegemonic schools. No assurance can be given that the passage of time will not be accompanied by less rather than more information as to what transpired in the past. We have, for example, learned a great deal about mercantilism, the development of economic ideas, the fecundity of thought, and the connections between economic history and the history of economic thought (without becoming mercantilists) by retaining mercantilism as a viable topic rather than excluding it from study because of certain errors (which, as it turns out, may not have been made) or because no leading professional economist advocates mercantilism today.

Luca Fiorito points out (Fiorito to Samuels, 4 July 2002) that Dorfman himself produced the striking case of path dependency already noted. Dorfman identified Thorstein Veblen, John R. Commons and Wesley C. Mitchell as the founding fathers of institutional economics, leading at least two generations of historians of economic thought (and of institutionalists themselves) along that path. Malcolm Rutherford has convinced many historians of economic thought that the story is more complex; Walton Hamilton, Carleton Parker, John Maurice Clark and Charles H. Cooley, among others, played significant roles.[2]

In one respect, at least, the problem of recency itself is ironic. It is now a commonplace belief that graduate students study *only* recent materials—and only journal articles—in their courses; nothing over, say, four years old need be considered. Presumably anything older is relegated to the history of economic thought. Here recency is approached in a dismissive sort of way compared to Dorfman. Dorfman wanted to enhance historiographical interpretation; modern teachers, to the extent that the commonplace belief is accurate, could not care less about the past.

In a different vein, but to the same conclusion of myopia, Mary Morgan opines that "in 1979, it was a fairly common assumption amongst economists that econometrics had no past, no history, before the 1950s." She finds, instead, that "it was during this early period that the fundamental concepts and notions of the econometric approach were thought out" (Morgan 1990: xi). If only the present counts, how could the past contain anything valuable?

The issue is not whether the historian—after proper passage of time—can understand the past better or more fully than someone who lived in the past. Different people who lived in the past will have different views of the past, and different historians will likewise have different views of the past. The point is that it is likely that those who lived in the past and the historians in the present will differ, not only among themselves but with each other. The lesson of this point is in part that those living in the past will not have the perspective(s) of later historians with the benefit of hindsight and that later historians will not have the local knowledge held by those who lived in and through the past period under study. The lesson, therefore, is also in part that one should not jump to conclusions; one may be caught in a hermeneutic circle. The argument of postmodernists is not, or not necessarily, that one cannot know the truth of the past; the argument is that one should not jump to the conclusion—or give effect to the premise—that what one thinks one knows of the past is the truth.

Issues and problems involved in avoiding recent economic thought

The meaning of "recency"

As already indicated, "recent," "modern," and "contemporary," the terms used in the relevant literature, are treated here as synonyms.

One question that immediately and necessarily arises: what is "recent"? It is not the purpose of this article to suggest an answer to this question. It must be worked out in practice and subsequent discussion will identify details of the diversity of practice. Recency is differently treated by different authors.

Recency is differently defined in various schools of thought in history and historiography, and thereby permits, presumes and conveys a variety of possible modes of understanding. These modes of understanding govern what constitutes "adequate description" and give meaning to "the passage of time."

An obvious point is that "recency" depends upon the date of publication. A book published in 1922 and another published in 1972 will have very different materials constituting "recent (or contemporary) economic thought." This applies in particular to multiple editions of a book running over several decades. "Recency" progresses with time. In the 1940s and even in the 1950s, Keynes's 1936 *General Theory* was recent by Dorfman's rule, but not in the 1980s.

The meaning of "history," as in "history of economic thought"

Another question that immediately and necessarily arises from Dorfman's position is, what is "history" in the history of economic thought? Again it is not the purpose of this article to suggest an answer to this question. There is no unequivocal line differentiating between "history," "current problems," and "contemporary analysis." As time progresses, what is current one year eventually passes into what people in later years consider history. In another respect, the present is history: action in the present makes, or helps to make, history (Sweezy 1953), a matter, a more complex matter, to which we will soon turn. The meaning of "history" must be worked out in practice and subsequent discussion will identify details of the diversity of practice. History is treated differently by different authors, often in conjunction with their treatment of recency.

One common view of history postulates that history is intertemporal in nature and applicability. Recency is therefore a secondary matter. As to the means of addressing history, if the method used to describe the events can be used in future periods by subsequent generations of readers/writers to describe the same phenomena, then that method has a certain validity. Even if the subsequent interpretation differs, such would simply point to a change in the social conditions in which the events and the interpretation are happening rather than the earlier interpretation being wrong. If the method is unusable for future interpreters, then the original analysis and understanding of the events studied may not be revealing.

History, like recency, is differently defined in various schools of thought in the disciplines of history and historiography, and thereby permits, presumes and conveys a variety of possible modes of understanding. These modes of under-standing govern what constitutes "adequate description" and give meaning to "the passage of time." The combination of recency and completeness is, accord-ingly, viewed differently depending upon the perspective of the historian. The following is a brief overview of a range of views, moving from one extreme—everything is history, including future events—to the other—history does not exist until events pre-date the living participants and observers.

History seen as the study of only past events is a fairly recent development. Medieval historians often wrote about the future events and results of a monarch's reign prior to the monarch's coronation. They were well aware of the social power and authority of the printed word, and history came to be defined as all events. Therefore, recency as a separate analytical domain was nonexistent. This is a rare occurrence among economists writing as historians of thought. It is not uncommon among critics of economic systems, who often both cover the past and portend the future. Among these authors are Marx and a series of prescriptive development economists such as W.W. Rostow.

The opposite extreme narrows history to events pre-dating the living and is used extensively by governments and military agencies. The sealing of records until fifty years after the events has resulted in World War II historians receiving a wealth of documentary evidence during the last few years. This view broadens the definition of recency to include the greatest breadth of material. This approach is common among authors of history-of-economic-thought text-books, as will be seen below.

In between are the approaches of Thucydides and Herodotus (see Breisach 1983), in which history is inclusive—all actions put into print. The act of recording an event validates and confirms a particular interpretation that will be subject to further layers of interpretation by readers and subsequent authors. Narratives on current events, once recorded, become part of the interpretive process, history. Avoiding the truncation of knowledge is paramount. Ignoring alternative perspectives is invalid history (see Subrahmanian 1973, Barnes 1979, Salvemini 1939 and Weinsheimer 1993).

No independent test

An obvious problem with the passage-of-time injunction is that no rule or metric exists by which one can unequivocally determine that sufficient, satisfac-tory perspective has emerged. The rule of thumb, judging by the gap between Dorfman's 1933 ending date and 1959 publication date and later reiteration, is about, or at least, a quarter century. This may well be something like what many people have in mind. Something like a generation—though for some people a generation is twenty years and for others, twenty-five years. The idea of a "generation" is socially constructed—a point underscoring discussion below of social construction and circularity to which self-referentiality can be added. For some people, sufficient passage of time is governed by the achievement of their respective desired results. At any rate, as of 2002, when this chapter was written, Dorfman's "rule" would point to roughly 1977 as the relevant cut-off date.

Teaching economic theory through the history of economic thought

One difficulty with Dorfman's position is that present-day ("current") economic theory may be taught through the vehicle of the history of economic thought. The question is rarely raised (but see Negishi 1989: 385) as to the division of labor between the history-of-economic-thought course and other courses, for example, courses in micro, macro and monetary theory: contributions of recent scholars "should still be considered as a part of the contemporary economic theory rather than in the history of economic theory." Some professors have taught this way and at least one author—Mark Blaug—and one type of text—the history of economic *theory*—has such pedagogy in mind. One subordinate but not unimportant problem is that it is rare (or so it seems) for a lecturer or author to stick to their design; they usually go beyond theory *qua* theory—though this judgment depends on the scope of what is recognized as theory. Institutional economics is often accused of being either anti-theory or non-theoretical but history-of-economic-thought textbooks typically (and properly, in our view) have sections or chapters on institutionalist theory.

Teaching theory through the history of economic thought is in part a curricular matter, depending in part on staff interests, i.e., an allocative problem. It is also in part a pedagogical matter. Alfred Marshall, John Maynard Keynes or Paul Samuelson are *talked about* in the history-of-economic-thought course; in the theory course, they are *taught*. It is also a historiographic problem. By "taught" we mean that a subject is defined by the work of one person, e.g., teaching microeconomics by teaching Marshall's version, among others. By "talked about" we mean that the work of a person is summarized and placed in perspective without either going into it in detail or representing it as the definition of a subject. Also, the person and the context in which a theory originated may be "history" and the theory itself may remain currently taught in the theory course. If the work of economist X, or work on topic Y, is no longer taught in the theory class, does that automatically render it a candidate for the history-of-economic-thought course? Perhaps that work should not have been included in the theory course in the first place. Perhaps its current deletion is myopic. But surely it is part of the history of economic thought, if one wants to know what comprised economic thought in the past.

Positions on these questions turn in part on one's judgments on modern developments. It is, in part, these questions and the relevant judgments that Dorfman's rule regarding the passage of time necessary for perspective is intended to help resolve. If neither Keynes nor Rational Expectations are taught in theory classes in 2040 (we are neither predicting nor advocating here; the reader can substitute Friedman and Sraffa, etc.), should they be included in the history-of-economic-thought course? Surely they will be part of the history of economic thought, along with Plato on the division of labor, Aristotle's critique of communism, Petty's theory of Political Arithmetic, Malthus's theory of population, Hawtrey's monetary theory of the trade cycle, and so on.

It is presumably awkward for a history-of-thought text or course to cover materials included in courses dealing with current topics. An old topic or source may be currently relevant, but it would have been awkward in the 1920s to teach *about* Alfred Marshall in the history course when Marshall's economics, more or less amended, was the centerpiece of the theory course. Yet James S. Earley taught an essentially Marshallian graduate microeconomic course at the University of Wisconsin in the 1950s *and* taught about Marshall in his history-of-economic-thought course. The difference, briefly, was that in the theory course he taught the theory and in the history course he taught about the theory. In a different vein, the student who learned about Professor X's work in a history-of-thought course may have felt X was now of historical interest only; and when the same student encountered serious discussion of X's work in a specialized "current" course, some cognitive dissonance may have resulted. The student may learn something from this experience but what does it mean for the passage-of-time rule? At any rate, the treatment of recent work is partly a curricular matter, one of the division between teaching economic theory and/or some sub-field *and* teaching the history of economic thought in different courses.

The treatment of recent work is also partly due to the fact that studies of individual topics do not terminate at either early or specific dates; how recent work is treated therefore functions to define the history of thought for the particular subject matter.

History of economic thought as a means of gaining knowledge

The argument that the writing of history must await fuller, more complete information can be turned on its head. The writing of history, and the critique of that writing, can be a means through which more complete information is gained. The inclusion of contemporary economic thought serves the function of promoting a more historically complete story. Such inclusion is important *per se*; it is also useful in providing different views of the world.

Gain in perspective versus loss of then-contemporary knowledge

Another problem with the passage-of-time injunction about recent work being too close in time to the historian to be a proper subject of inquiry is that with the passage of time the historical activity passes from one generation of practitioners and historians to the next. Whatever gain in perspective is arguably achievable, part of the cost is the loss of then-contemporaneous knowledge with the passing of both the original economists and the old historians. One advantage of contemporary analysis that is lost over time is knowledge of common context. On the one hand, this is aggravated by the myopia of history based on the hegemonic perspective; on the other, ignoring the recent past precludes taking advantage of contemporary local knowledge and therefore aggravates the inability of the present to know the past.[3]

No necessary correction of selective perception or bias

It is not clear that the passage of time coupled with efforts at refinement will suffice to eradicate bias, adjust for selective perception, and establish correct perspective. Not only is there no independent or unequivocal test for correct perspective, neither Joseph Schumpeter's combination of vision and rules of procedure nor Karl Popper's combination of conjectures and refutations, for example, suffice to exclude the influence of ideology, metaphysics, dominant paradigm, and/or hermeneutic problems. No guarantee exists that hindsight will not be myopic.

Lessened need for recency in some approaches to the history of economic thought

Certain understandings of the history of economic thought, certain design strategies, or certain organizing strategies, of either an epistemological and/or ontological nature, may lessen the need to include recent developments (and thereby to update text material through successive editions). Barber (1967), Boucke (1921), Perlman and McCann (1998) and Pribram (1983) each define the history of economic thought in terms of different modes of economic reasoning, different philosophical systems, different modes of understanding, different patristic legacies and traditions—or different paradigmatic understandings of the world. Somewhat similar, but narrower in scope, is the juxtaposition of philosophies found in Werner Stark's *The Ideal Foundations of Economic Thought* (1943) and, broader in scope, Ferdinand Zweig's *Economic Ideas: A Study of Historical Perspectives* (1950). These visions are rendered more complex by additional attention to national traditions. It may be useful to include recent materials to bring illustration up to date, but it is not absolutely essential—or less essential than for a design strategy that presents, and even emphasizes, a chronological sequence.

On the other hand, Wesley Mitchell's *Lecture Notes on Types of Economic Theory* (1949) stresses the conflict between types but covers in depth a wide variety of then-recent (1934–1935) economic theory/thought

The history of economic thought as what has survived

One question pertinent to the question of time both affects adequacy of coverage and constitutes a historiographical problem in its own right. The question is whether histories should cover only what survives—not all books and articles, or people, only those important later on, when the history is being written. An affirmative answer poses further problems. One problem is that it is presentist and Whig history. Indeed, it is not a full history; only a selective history, one viewed from the perspective of what has presently survived and/or is hegemonic. A second problem is circularity. X is defined by x, and x is itself defined by what X is taken to be. Thus, for example, "precursors" tend to become presentist phenomena, acquired by searching for anticipations of modern theory using the lens of contemporary theory—and being tautological with that theory (email from Luca Fiorito to Samuels, 4 July 2002). A third problem is that the work may have initially lacked contemporary relevance. As conditions (within the discipline or in the outside world) change, omissions may be seen and the work may be better received as its relevance becomes recognized. A fourth problem is the possibility that writings are omitted because they were never any good.

In other words, if the entire body of work and output of economists is a set of paths, if the history of that work includes only a few paths, say those that presently survive, such selectivity will influence future work and output, engendering path dependency—selective past and present leading to selective future. For those who are presentist and Whig, or preach what amounts to status emulation, this may pose no problem; for those who seek "adequate description" and those who seek a rich economics, serious problems exist.

Assume that economists, recent and current, are working along lines A, B, C, D and E. Assume further that at some date, sufficiently in the future for historians of economic thought to have acquired "perspective," only lines A and D are continuing. If the historians paint a picture of what has transpired only in terms of A and D, then the economics represented by lines B, C, and E will pass from disciplinary memory and consciousness. History written by survivors, if not also victors, will be written from a certain angle and omit much, especially what is felt to be inconsistent with their work and interests. The picture will be skewed and biased. The surviving lines A and D will have served as a filter, allowing only their ways of doing economics to define historical consciousness of the past and to prescribe the future. The history of economic thought will become a history of survivor lines, a history of the past from the point of view of the surviving lines. *It will not be a complete record of the history of economic thought.* It will tend to be a self-congratulatory paean to the present, the past seen and defined only through a particular prism, a particular story line, a particular point of view.

It may be objected (1) that it is too early to know how certain lines will develop. That cannot prevent meaningful accountings of how they have developed thus far, the issues involved, and so on. Any literature review (say by a non-historian practitioner of any sub-field of economics), if it has serious depth to it, will accomplish the same thing—from the practitioner's point of view.

Or it may be objected (2) that lines that do not develop and survive are of no interest. Of no interest to whom? Lines B, C, and E were presumably of no interest to those undertaking A and D. But *all should be of interest to the histo-*

rian of economic thought—and will be of interest to prospective new devotees of B, C, and E if not also of A and D.

Consider what seems to be a major (more or less) new development in economics; in the past we have had imperfect competition theory, Keynesian economics, rational expectations, transaction cost, quantity theory, game theory, general equilibrium, etc. Generalizing, let a few be designated A, B, and C. Each claims to be the new center of gravity for economics. Each has existed for thirty years. The question is, is each to be interpreted by the historian of economic thought on its own terms—yielding three new centers of gravity? Or is the historian merely to report the existence and claim in each case—discounting the claims as so much puffery, as efforts to manipulate and mobilize disciplinary allegiance? Or should the historian remain silent, until the situation clarifies? And, if so, for how long?

The case can be made that the dominant—certainly a modal—approach to the history of economic thought is the presentist and Whig perspective, for which all of history is a process, but only the theories that survive are valid subjects of study. The process of getting to today is relevant only insofar as it helps us to better understand the dominant ideas of today. Failed theories should disappear from history-of-economic-thought textbooks, but might remain as brief footnotes on what to avoid (the classic admonitions being, "Those failing to understand history are doomed to repeat it" and "from error to truth"). This approach to history, in which only the surviving is valid, may explain some of the hesitancy of history-of-economic-thought authors to address more current material. If a current theory does not survive, its lack of validity may extend to the histories themselves whose authors are unwise enough to include it in their coverage. The best way to avoid this problem is to employ the intellectually respectable view that only what has survived is valuable.

Enormity of materials requires limitation of coverage

At any period in the history of economic thought and increasingly over its history, the range of work done by economists has been enormous. This situation engenders the reasoning that the enormity of the practice of economics requires limitation of coverage. This reasoning has merit as a scarcity argument. As will be seen below, limitation of coverage and correlative selectivity is inevitable. But for whom is the limitation of coverage operative? Any historian of economic thought can allocate their own resources to study whatever interests them. Journal editors and other publishers will then have to compare and weigh relative merits against other submissions. Most important for present purposes, any perceived major limitation of coverage conflicts with Dorfman's argument concerning fullness of coverage, an argument already compromised, as we have seen, by the problem of the vast scope of economics.

A related problem is the limited time available in a history-of-economic-thought course. Most colleges and universities have a one-semester course, and the problem of selection can be overwhelming; it is only marginally less so in a two-semester sequence. Are Smith, Ricardo, Marx, Marshall or Keynes to be omitted or seriously abbreviated in favor of more recent contributions to economic thought? Professorial prioritizing often contributes to inertia in the topics covered in textbooks.

History of economic thought produced by non-historians of economic thought

Non-historian economists write what amount to histories of economic thought that strongly tend to cover recent developments. This is one principal reason that the Dorfman position, whatever its merits, is *impossible* to achieve in practice. It cannot be overemphasized that much ostensible disciplinary memory is constructed out of articles and opening sections of articles that are area reviews, literature surveys, and celebratory affirmations of certain developments and not others. The same is true of companions, dictionaries and encyclopedias, whose overviews and summaries are often presented in historical form and serve as, or are proxies for, histories. Some or much of this covers recent developments, thus constituting the doing of contemporary history; all of it being selective. Dorfman's rule could not preclude specialists in various fields from trying to make sense of recent developments, thereby to survey, summarize and interpret each field, and to do so in ways that amount to creating histories of recent economic thought. One cannot imagine companions, dictionaries and encyclopedias written that paid no attention to recent work on Dorfman's grounds because doing so meant that the stories told were overly preliminary if not precipitous.

These histories are also written in part to position the author's own work in a meaningful light and in part to influence future development. Such efforts may produce particularly singular or one-sided histories but even these nonetheless contribute to the history in the process of being constructed. It may well be that these partial histories are more important, at least to area specialists, than the work of historians of economic thought. In any event, the relevant literature is written by both historians of economic thought and non-historians; and if the former are more interested in the past, the latter are more interested in the future, i.e., the present and future in the process of becoming the past.

The role of a literature review or of dictionaries and anthologies is to define a field. Literature reviews also tend to be oriented to render novel, even awkward, analysis well defined, consonant with the relevant paradigm, targeted, and important *pro tanto*. Most if not all are school- and/or paradigm-specific and in this respect are Whiggish—notwithstanding the effort being made to legitimize innovation and change. Some are conspicuously potted and ceremonial, the intent being to definitively but narrowly define a subject and its history. Efforts to establish the history of early Chicago law and economics readily come to mind (e.g., Kitch 1983; Coase 1993). Steven Medema has described the story thus told as "a narrative … in strictly internalist terms, essentially denying any link to or commonalities with and overtly attempting to distance itself from other legal-economic" movements (Medema 2002: 17). This is an example of Backhouse (2002: 328): "Different schools will construct their own histories, ... while being aware that other stories can be told. The role of the historian is to bring these stories together, correcting and amplifying them where appropriate, showing where they fit into a larger story."

Eric Hobsbawm has emphasized the role played by "inventions of traditions" in the history of political thinking and the formation of "schools" in the history of ideas (Hobsbawm and Ranger 1983). The term is undoubtedly applicable to the history of economic thought, in which, as Kitch's and other accounts of "Chicago" suggest, the construction of coherent traditions to fit one's own purpose has been present. Karl Marx is another good example; he invented a labor theory of value going back to Petty; so also is Keynes, who created a tradition reaching back to the mercantilists in order to bolster his own views on the role of demand and under-consumption (Magnusson 2004).

The case can be made that textbooks in the principles of economics, for use in introductory courses, represent crystallizations of the present state of economic thought. These presentations include recent economic thought and authors undertaking updating revisions regularly make choices from recent work as to both what is important and the specific content thereof in making those revisions. Dorfman's rule could not preclude this mode of selectively recounting, interpreting and assessing recent thought.

With the rise of specialized and highly structured fields of study in economics, students often read the "classics" in their own fields, as well as the contemporary literature. In macroeconomics, for example, the "classics" include the seminal articles on rational expectations theory, many of which are less than twenty-five years old. As already indicated, reading lists may only go back four years or so, severely attenuating student definitions of both the field and the history of economic thought, especially if the course is driven not by the field as a whole but by the professor's own research interests. Field surveys and anthologies often operate as contemporary history of economic thought in a field; in this sense, a graduate field textbook may constitute contemporary history of economic thought. However, Whiggism, presentism, and factionalism within a field are inevitably present and channel the exercise of selectivity.

One may reasonably query: is a literature review history of economic thought? What about an article that critiques a current economic theory? What about an article published immediately following another, either critiquing or pointing out a putative error in the original? What about letters to the editor? Book reviews? Further, is it a problem that history of economic thought takes these forms? In many cases, contemporary history of thought in these forms operates to cast selective luster on certain ideas and methodologies. It can also define a research topic, by identifying points of conflict or tension in the literature that the researcher purports to resolve. Such types of literature make comparisons with other and/or earlier work; they tend to presume and give effect to, and thereby promote, a particular rendering of history, however selective. They are as much a mode of creating as of recording a view of history.

We sense that many, perhaps most, historians of economic thought are dismissive of literature reviews. To the extent that they are dismissive, the attitude may be based on the fact that the authors are not trained and specialized historians of economic thought, that the reviews are narrow, myopic, self-serving, and Whiggish in general. Some of these conditions may be true but need not be; for example, a review can be Whiggish, and in some respects at least probably is, but they need not be; moreover, the author of a literature review faces peer review by other practitioners, implying that the situation is a matter, at least in part, of market structure and not of authorial belief and behavior alone.

John Davis suggests that (greater) reliance on practitioner-written literature reviews may relate to the seemingly systematic elimination of history of economic thought from graduate economics instruction. This is at least an "as if" argument. It concludes that the profession of practitioners has decided to become its own historian through the route of literature reviews, handbooks, encyclopedias and companion volumes (Davis to Samuels, 9 September 2002). On the other hand, our examination of articles in the principal history-of-economic-thought journals did not produce evidence of an increasing interest (at least by editors, i.e., by editors choosing from among submissions) in recent economic thought.

An examination of the programs of the History of Economics Society for the last three years (2000–2002) indicates that papers devoted to recent economic thought comprise, very roughly, between 20 and 25 percent of all papers, in comparison with the 10 percent of total articles in the journals. In 2001, both of the Young Scholars Sessions were almost entirely composed of papers on recent economic thought.

Davis's point may also be considered in the context of other disciplines that have eliminated their own histories as areas of study, such as chemistry and physics. Although they sometimes offer the history of their respective disciplines, it was largely eliminated from their curricula some time ago. One could speculate that the eliminations coincided with, or were caused by, their move into a more unified approach with a mathematical system that removed the perceived need for a systematic study of the disciplinary path. A similar development seems to have begun in political science coupled with an increased desire to move away from the teaching of traditional political theory in a historical manner, as is still largely done in philosophy. Given the shift in emphasis, scarce faculty positions are reallocated away from disciplinary history.

(Some young historians of economic thought, perhaps with a bias against feeling a need for disciplinary approval, question whether historians of economic thought will convince any doubting peers in economics that resources devoted to the field will satisfy their equimarginal principle with this change in research focus. In particular, they feel that the more the lines are blurred between literature reviews by macro/micro/banking/etc. practitioners and work by history-of-economic-thought specialists, the more the lack of specific, new, theoretical contributions on the part of historians of economic thought may make them appear superfluous. They would prefer to be distinguished from this form of history so that peers, chairs and administrations no longer ask questions like, "If you have made no specific contributions other than recent history of economic thought, why would we need you, or your field, when we have a [insert field] economist contributing both to the new body of theory and performing that occasional bit of retrospection?" Arguing about the importance of better understanding the path that brought the discipline to its present point, they sense, has failed to convince anyone in the recent past, and with less differentiation appearing between their work and that of the practitioners (seen as dabblers) they fear the risk of being trivialized. Alas, all this confronts the reality principle.)

The problem of recency in the face of new publications

The problem of recency of publication arises in a much larger domain than work in the history of thought *per se* and does so in a way that, while it does not preclude an author from having a stopping point, does suggest the widespread futility and even fallacy of Dorfman's concern. Consider an innovative article or book on a topic. Should the rule against recency preclude use, interpretation, critique and/or revision of that article or book for a generation? If the passage-of-time requirement were followed, the process of innovation, critique and revision would be stretched out; moreover, a quite different set of developments and developmental paths likely would ensue than if the rule were ignored. Yet how could this happen even if the rule was ostensibly followed? Individuals would read the innovative piece, and even if they followed a ban on publishing pieces on it, they would have absorbed its contribution and thus it would influence their own work. Consider too a comparable situation in the domain of the historian of economic thought. Since, and even in anticipation of, the bicentennial of Adam Smith's *Wealth of Nations* in 1976, over a dozen books and hundreds of articles on perhaps every aspect of Smith's work have been published. Surely, consideration of them could not be delayed a generation in the hope that their significance would become more clear. The fallacy is evident. Unless consideration of new works ensued more or less immediately, there would be no way that their significance could be worked out through use, critique, evaluation and revision. Indeed, Dorfman himself used post-1933 materials to help supplement his interpretive base in his two 1918–1933 volumes (*vide* the references given in his endnotes). Significance does not determine itself.

A correlative example is courses that cover or include recently published materials. Professors teach current theories and new ideas as soon as they are published. This is a mode of their treatment and a contribution to the history of economic thought. The alternative is to ignore them for the proscribed period, hence the passage of empty, untreated time. This is an impossible situation;

their consideration in courses, as well in journal articles and books, is part of the history of economic thought, and part of the process through which new theories and ideas are critiqued and filtered. Finally, how odd it would be if new material could be interpreted, etc. but not material within the proscribed period prior to the publication of the most recent material.

Social construction and futurity

The history of economic thought is in some respects found but it is principally and at its deepest levels made. It is socially constructed in two senses: through the work of the economists reported on and through the work of the historians and non-historians who do the reporting. Social construction is the first of two related points, the other being futurity, namely, that social construction of the past is undertaken with a view to the social construction of the future.

History is the interpretation of the past; the past does not write its own history. The interpretation of the past is controversial; it is contested terrain. The historian brings to work a personal perspective—for example, as to what Adam Smith, Karl Marx, John Maynard Keynes *et al.* "really meant"—and their own paradigm within which history acquires meaning. Historians, as we have seen, are not the only definers of the past. Practitioners of economics themselves also contribute to the creation of disciplinary and sub-disciplinary past (Medema and Samuels 2001). Both historians and practitioners are of two types: nondeliberative believers and deliberative constructors, and both contribute to the construction of the perceived past. The believers are acting upon what they were taught in school, what seems "natural" to them, what they find advantageous, etc.; the constructors know that both the perceived past and the created future are subject to control and they consciously write the history they prefer, e.g., that which will cast luster on and engender the future they want. Stylized interpretations of recent work are constructed—consciously or unconsciously—in order to influence both the field's or sub-field's definition of reality and its future development. Coverage matters, too, as that which is considered anathema, e.g., an alternative explanation, is ruled out of court. Historical treatments of macroeconomics, public choice theory, Austrian economics, institutional economics, law and economics, and the stabilization of price theory readily come to mind.

Postmodernism emphasizes the social construction of both economics and its history, social construction that is both deliberative and nondeliberative in origin. Both sources compromise the corrective qualities of the passage of time. The nondeliberative are by their noncognitive nature only subject to Schumpeterian checks in a limited way, and the deliberative seek to forestall or control such checking.

Constructing the history of economic thought may well be an author's immediate objective. Potted histories of relevant economic thought are constructed and deployed for both substantive and rhetorical purposes. Such histories package and are used to cast luster on particular sets of ideas, for example, to promote those ideas being seen as the whole of which they and others are only parts. Such a history can serve to both define the past and provide paradigmatic perspective and a basis for critique of the work of others. If one goal of economic ideas is the control of policy, then defining the past is a means of controlling the future; i.e., the problem is not that it is too early to know how certain lines will develop but that part of the doing of history-of-economic-thought work is precisely to influence how certain lines *will* develop—to promote some and to inhibit others.

Hindsight may have its own myopia, in part because hindsight is driven by ideas and goals of futurity. Most people are interested most of the time in the future, not the past. Social constructivism is forward-looking; and the past is more instrument than cause in its creation.

Both the past and present are a result of past politics; the future will be the result of present politics. It may well be that historical resources—personnel—are available to the highest bidder; it certainly is the case that ignorance of the uncontrived history of economic thought is a constraint on the ability to critique the contrived versions. Because these activities are current, the coverage of contemporary economics is both inevitable and necessary. The use and arguable misuse of the history of economic thought for ideological purposes or self-interest is not novel. It is both a form of ancestor worship and a form of argument by appeal to authority. In the case of inclusion or exclusion, some price will be paid and some feedback effects will influence development, including individual subjects.

Whose ideas of social construction and futurity will count is largely determined by the structure of social power in the discipline. This structure includes the concentration of the production of academic economists in a dozen or so departments, departments that "play a very big part in forming beliefs about the profession, within the profession" (Paul Wendt, HES list, 11 October 2002; hes@eh.net).

The insider–outsider model of unemployment and disequilibrium wages might be a useful source of sociology-of-science insight as to coverage. Insiders to the discipline (as presently defined) have no motive to act to the benefit of outsiders. Editing boards and referees may serve as insiders to the system, while junior faculty and other types are outsiders seeking insider status. Editing boards have filtering tasks and problems: subscriptions depend on generating readership with an interest set (excepting, perhaps, publications which come with membership in professional associations that all practitioners are expected or required to hold). Early career efforts may define one's ultimate research path (once working in an area, it is easier to stay with it, because of success, one's accumulated human capital, inertia, comfort with the familiar, etc.). Pretending to be an insider, by practicing what everyone else is doing until one actually becomes an insider, prevents and/or delays alternative hypotheses from being developed and thereby represented in the history-of-thought literature. One can influence what everyone else is doing. But peer review enforces what passes for Kuhnian normal (= insider) science. Paul Samuelson's now-classic articles on public goods (1954, 1955) initially were rejected by several major journals because the editors felt that the articles were uninteresting and did not contribute to the body of knowledge on public goods. Gans and Shepherd (2000) report on cases in which articles were rejected—in at least one case, not even sent to referees—that later became classics; including articles that served as the basis of the award of the Nobel Prize.

A cognate social-constructivist problem concerns the relation to mainstream neoclassical economics of economists who look neoclassical in many respects but claim some degree of distance if not departure from neoclassicism. We have in mind such people as Douglass North, Oliver Williamson and Ronald Coase, as well as others working in economic psychology (such as Robert Frank and Tibor Scitovsky) and experimental economics (such as Vernon Smith). How much, if any, is a matter of creating ostensible product differentiation? How much, if any, is a matter of moderating differences in defense of professional status within the hegemonic school? How much, if any, is a matter of exaggerating differences in defense of independent professional status? Can a discipline that distrusts self-answering interview data distinguish between intent and impact? Do we know, three-quarters of a century later, where someone like Frank Albert Fetter stood? Will time help us with our contemporaries? Is it significant that some of the people characterized earlier in this paragraph as (marginally) outside of mainstream neoclassical economics have received the Nobel Prize in Economic Science?

Furthermore, it is the nature of economic research and publication that critique—in the sense of literary criticism, if no other—has numerous roles. Criticism is at the heart of the invisible college of researchers and authors in a field. Criticism is a means by which consensus is worked out. And so on. Critical interpretation and/or evaluation by historians of economic thought can influence the course of their subjects' future work. Interpretation and criticism by others can show an author the various meanings their work can have for others, and authors can react. Interpretation and criticism can generate feedback effects on an author's own sense of what they are doing, on what they do in the future, and so on. Contemporary attention to recent work can influence—can apply torque to—the next round of work. There is no insulation between practitioners and various interpreters, including historians of economic thought. The latter are practitioners, too, and inevitably part of the process they describe, interpret and critique. This influence and its recursive impact is inevitable, part of the process in which a new article or book is evaluated in relation to previous work, an activity that necessarily takes place within either a particular definition of the history of that segment of economic thought or a clash of such definitions.

All of the foregoing—especially the interactive or recursive process—underscores that both historians of economic thought and non-historians who contribute to the definition are willy nilly participant observers in the formation and evolution of economic thought (on which see Dopfer 1998).

The history of economic thought indeed does not write itself. Economists engaged in constructing the history of economic thought—engaged in the construction and promotion of disciplinary memory— generally ask questions the answers to which then become the substance of the history of economic thought. They form the questions and the answers, in the process socially constructing the history of economic thought. The questions are something like these:

1   What did X mean when he wrote Y? What did he really mean?
2   How does X or the work of X fit into economics and/or influence future economics?
3   How did X contribute to the study of economics?
4   What do others believe X meant? Does it matter what X really meant?
5   Do X and X's ideas and theories warrant inclusion in the canon of the history of economic thought, insofar as canonization is provided by historians of economic thought?

Apropos of recent economic thought, any of these questions could be addressed in an interesting fashion, except perhaps the first—the question that can be answered by asking the author. In that case, though the recipient is living, the work is often decades old. Recognition is given to contemporary work through awards, reviews and presentations. Mozart, for example, was popular in his own time, and has served to influence music over time, becoming "classic." Economics recognizes "contemporary" work through awards for articles and overall publishing activity, and the Nobel Prize. In the case of contemporary recognition, the issue arises that the award is not free of influence: the politics of the field or discipline influence who and what works are recognized. The facts of selection and of contests among agendas arise at every turn, though such does not prevent temporary suspension of agendas. At stake is the social construction of the discipline in the future.

Possibility of multiple stories

It would be nice, one supposes—at least it would make doing the history of economic thought easier—if only one story of the past could be told. We would be comfortable with a belief that the past—either the remote or the recent past—had one true, objectively true account. But empirical, historical experience and hermeneutic and other postmodern sources of insight indicate that the object of inquiry can be variously interpreted and that different people view that object from different standpoints. Hence a variety of stories are told—and these differences do not diminish over time.

Consider the following. A great deal of work has been done, especially during the last quarter-century (not to forget much earlier work), on the individual, on institutions, on markets, and on their interaction and overall integration into a meaningful and useful account of economic life. A. Allan Schmid reports that, in regard to his own integrative effort, this work has produced much, perhaps undue, product differentiation. There is, he says, the new institutional economics and transaction cost economics of (Williamson 1985) and (Coase 1998); the historical and comparative institutional analysis of (Greif 1998); the comparative institutional analysis of (Aoki 2001); the theory of regulation of (Boyer 2001); the historical institutionalism of (Powell and DiMaggio 1991); the new economic sociology represented by such people as (Granovetter 2002) and (Fligstein 2001). There are other major themes that do not have a broad label such as the evolutionary perspective of (Hodgson 1993) and (Potts 2000); an emphasis on cognition and behavior such as (Rizzello 1999); the economic history of (North 1990); the methodological work of (Lawson 1997) and (Mirowski 2002); and the theoretical work of (Bromley 1989) and (Samuels 1992a).

(Schmid to Samuels, 20 June 2002)

One could say that each of these authors is attempting to provide their own systematic, integrated account of this complex and variegated domain. Each, however, is also constructing a selective history of what was important, in their view and for their purposes, during the period. Combining them, we have multiple histories of thought, and the basis for analysis as to significance. Again, significance does not determine itself, nor is it determined by ignoring the material in question and waiting like Godot, for perspective.

In the discussion, reported on below, on the history of the AD–AS graph, Susan Feiner made a point that is pertinent here (hes@eh.net, 5 June 2002). Economists like unique determinate results; these they identify with a certain notion of science. They would like for all economists to speak with the same voice, to avoid internal controversy confusing to the public. Multiple results, multiple interpretations and multiple disagreements among experts as to how a theory or a model is to be used seem anathema but have dominated controversies in economics not only in recent decades but for centuries. Economics is well known as a field in which ten experts have twelve different opinions. It is not difficult to conclude that such considerations contribute to a proclivity against including contemporary work.

A discipline that is dominated by the research protocol of unique determinate optimal equilibrium solutions carries that protocol into the study of its own history. This protocol reinforces, indeed may be derived from, one of two mindsets, that which requires determinacy and closure rather than that which is comfortable with ambiguity and open-endedness. What cannot be so treated is excluded. On the other hand, stopping a story a quarter-century or so ago may inevitably mean that the story is unresolved or unconcluded. One reason for concern about recent work is that conflicts are generally unresolved.

The fact that multiple histories of economic thought can be constructed, a fact supported by postmodern insights, renders nugatory the Dorfman-like premise of one correct explanation awaiting fullness of knowledge and the necessary passage of time. The conclusion of impossibility arises again, notwithstanding the discipline's discomfort with, even antagonism to, multiple stories.

Inevitable incompleteness and selectivity

The fact of multiplicity of historical interpretations leads to two other conditions that further negate and render impossible Dorfman's proscription, inevitable incompleteness and selectivity.

The historian defines the reality with which he or she deals. The picture can never be complete as to detail. Even Dorfman's monumental study, noted for its breadth, is inevitably selective. Not only is historical data organized around chosen themes, it is at best a representative sample of themes and individuals as well as movements; much is excluded.

The matter can be appreciated by a simple thought experiment: consider all the journal articles and books published on economic topics during a period. No history-of-economic-thought text can possibly fully describe the totality of how economics was done during the period. No literature survey can possibly encompass all the literature arguably pertinent to a topic. A variety of filters operate to select the literature deemed pertinent to the author. These filters include congruence with dominant paradigm or school, membership in a self-citing school of literature, language, and so on.

The problem is one example of what may be called the X:x problem: if X is reality and x is our evidence of that reality, how do we know whether x is representative of X when all we know of X is x? What about that which has been omitted or neglected?

Another example is the history of economic thought that centers on the major figures—the "stars"—and thereby tells only part of the story.[4] Many textbooks focus on the "great" economists. This is not necessarily wrong but it constitutes incompleteness. There is more to economics during any period than the work of innovators or intellectual giants. Granted that Smith, Ricardo, Marx, Marshall, Keynes and Samuelson are luminaries for good and sufficient reason, they are not the only ones who have contributed to the discipline and comprise its history (see Samuels 1998: xi). With the passage of time these others, who have been the footsoldiers of economics (with reference to Joseph Schumpeter's "review of the troops" (1954: 463)), have been increasingly lost to disciplinary memory; thus, contrary to Dorfman's view, coverage is inversely related to the passage of time. To his credit, Dorfman himself was aware of the problem. As expressed by Murray Rothbard, one of Dorfman's dissertation supervisees, Dorfman

> demonstrated conclusively how important allegedly "lesser" figures are in any movement of ideas. In the first place, the stuff of history is left out by omitting these figures, and history is therefore falsified by selecting and worrying over a few scattered texts to constitute The History of Economic Thought. Second, a large number of the supposedly secondary figures contributed a great deal to the development of thought, in some ways more than the few peak thinkers. Hence, important features of economic thought get omitted, and the developed theory is made paltry and barren as well as lifeless.
>
> (Rothbard 1995a: viii)

(Rothbard also deployed the ideas of Thomas Kuhn in criticizing such neglect.) The same applies to neglect or omission of "lesser" topics.

A further example is the eclipse in Kuhnian "normal science" of multiplicity, that is, of variations of formulation and of approach. This exclusion renders the history of ideas more homogeneous than in fact it has been, both within mainstream or normal science and between normal and heterodox science. The resulting attenuation and finessing of multiplicity obfuscates both the incompleteness and selectivity that also result. Varieties of Kuhnian normal science and of heterodoxy are important for an accurate picture of the actual history of how economics was being done.

Still another example is the total exclusion of a putative part of economics, a matter of the operative scope given to economics. Let $X = A + B$, with X the broadest possible scope of economics; A, the study of the market system; and B, the study of such "sociological" topics as social control, class and other structures, and socialization and acculturation. Or let X again be the broadest possible scope of economics; A, the central problem of resource allocation; and B, the problem of organization and control. Or let X again have the broadest scope of economics; A, the study of pure conceptual a-institutional markets; and B, the study of the institutions that form and operate through actual markets. What "recency" and "coverage" mean substantively will depend on what is included and what is excluded from "economics." Coverage and recency go hand in hand. Both are, in part, a function of the definition of the scope (and method) of economics and the nature and purpose of the particular history of economic thought being undertaken.

Some contributors to the creation of disciplinary memory use their notion of the "mainstream" or of "economics" to rule out of disciplinary bounds what does not comport with their definitions of the mainstream and of economics. Thus a book reviewer may complain that certain work covered in the book under review should not have been included because it was either not central to or in conflict with their conception of the mainstream (equated with economics). This is particularly important in regard to recent work inasmuch as the reviewer's objective is to influence future work ("Why would anyone do such and such since it is not mainstream?" "Since it is not mainstream, why bother with it?").

The problems posed by Dorfman's proscription are ubiquitous. Consider, for example, Merle Curti's position in the first edition of his *The Growth of American Thought* (1943)—in which he calls attention to Dorfman's forthcoming "systematic history of American economic thought" (1943: xv). Curti acknowledges that

> Some may contend that the history of intellectual life in America cannot be written now for the reason that adequate special studies on which a general synthesis must rest have not yet been made. According to one widely held view, efforts to grasp the whole or any part, even in thought, are useless until preliminary inquiries have been completed.

(1943: xvii)

This way of expressing the problem leads to the part–whole predicament, that parts have meaning (only) in terms of the whole of which they are a part, and wholes acquire meaning from the parts that comprise them, and to the thorny issue of precisely when preliminary inquiries have in fact been completed. Curti thus offers his rebuttal to the Dorfman position: His reasoning is that

> In fact, however, monographic studies made without thought about the relations of the special to the general are likely to be arid.
>
> Actually it is not possible ... for specialized research and writing to proceed without some reference to thought, however stray and surreptitious such thought may be, about wider relationships. Since particulars do bear relations to the general, preliminary thought about the problem of these relations, based of course on the knowledge available, can aid in the production of monographs that will be useful as the higher and higher generalizations are reached. To wait until scholars have completed all the requisite special studies is to postpone wider considerations on the assumption that these studies will in fact be completed; such an assumption may or may not be warranted. So to wait is to deprive even particular inquiries of the thought about the problem of the whole, which is available at the present stage in the development of the theme.
>
> The task of writing a social history of American thought ... is a task of such magnitude that the author has no idea that his labors are definitive.
>
> (Curti 1943: xvii)

In his third edition (1964) Curti notes the "possibility and desirability of a drastic reorganization within an essentially different framework." But he finds that "many ideas, approaches, and emphases" in his original edition "have since become popular," so he has only "tried to take into account the new scholarship and fresh points of view" (Curti 1964: viii, ix).

It is of present significance that in each edition Curti carries his story up to the time of his writing. So too, for example, does Ralph Henry Gabriel in the three editions of his *The Course of American Democratic Thought* (1940; 1956; 1986).

Dorfman's proscription makes sense in avoiding premature elevation of an active, brilliant, larger-than-life leader to the status of a "giant." On the other hand, Dorfman's proscription may lead to the ignoring of certain individuals for so long that they are forgotten. There is no escaping this dilemma: either following or not following Dorfman's proscription will set in motion certain different path dependencies; the doing of the history of economic thought will influence the development of the subject. "Accurate description" loses much of its meaning; it is not something found but made through whatever path is re-enforced.

The pressure for recency

Pressure seems to exist to give attention in writing textbooks to recent or contemporary developments. This is so for a number of reasons. One is the sheer intellectual interest in the material. Another is authorial bias and desire to influence future developments. Still another is to respond to perceived student interest, or explicit publisher interest, in relevance; conversely to avoid any sense of antiquarianism. Still another is to continue the telling of a story along presumably obvious lines.

More can be said, for example, about publishers. As David Colander says in regard to the introductory principles course, the history-of-economics course is something of an institution, "which means that it is expected that certain things will be covered in certain ways." He also suggests "a 15% rule which is the degree to which a major book can differ from the others" (hes@eh.net, 2 June 2002). This inertia, as much as the difficulty of covering very much recent material in depth in the conventional history-of-economic-thought textbook, may help explain the preponderance (as we shall see) of limited and selective treatments of recent developments as the standardized presentation. (Actually, the distribution is bimodal, the other mode being no inclusion of contemporary materials. The base is the set of twentieth-century textbooks, but especially present-day texts.) Publishers are very wary of investing in a very different type of textbook in any field.

It may well be less methodological ideology, however, and more pedagogical ideology that is operative: first, both students and professors like examination questions to have unequivocal answers; and professors seem to dislike questions ("According to school A, ...") that suggest economists are basically divided, with the implication that one view may be as good as another. Second, the problem with teaching the history of economic thought, especially in a one-semester course, is the amount of material to cover; expanding into potentially endless contemporary materials is attractive to neither professor nor students. These considerations, too, drive adoption decisions by publishers and professors.

Arm's length dealing more important than passage of time

A requirement of arm's length may be more important than the passage of time and the acquisition of ostensible completeness of information and perspective; indeed, both of the latter may depend on historical work being undertaken at arm's length. Arm's length work should provide greater opportunity for unbiased study. It should facilitate less passivity toward and less honorific treatment of important organizations (such as the Federal Reserve System and International Monetary Fund). Arm's length rules would control history written by in-group personnel from the hegemonic school. It would control overly saccharine, legitimizing, public relations-type history. It would lead to questioning the meaningfulness—or lack of meaning—of words and of claims of scientificity. It would control the exclusion of unsafe, heterodox topics, themes and personnel. It would control the role of status emulation in the discipline.

The passage of time may overcome the sensitivity of certain subjects to perceived and actual criticism; but the passage of time may result in the loss of understanding of what transpired, possibly if not probably more important than certain persons' feelings.[5] It is unfortunate that the records of certain organizations and individuals are available only with long lags. Sensitivity to contemporary issues may skew analysis; but postponement carries its own price.

Another term for "arm's length" is "agnostic," by which is meant here that the historian of economic thought makes great efforts to avoid basing his or her analysis, description and interpretation on their own personal views. Objective history of ideas can be written on people, groups or ideas with which the historian disagrees or agrees. Consider a history of the idea of God written by an atheist, or an essay on religion as social control by the same person, or on the mercantilists or the Physiocrats or neoclassicism by someone who questions their authors' work. Consider an account of Adam Smith's several stories about the origin of the propensity to truck, barter and exchange, or others' stories about the identity and function of Smith's "invisible hand" without being wed to any one story.

The upshot of the foregoing is that even if one were persuaded by Dorfman's proposed proscription, it is impossible to achieve. At worst, it is illusion; at best, it amounts to standing aside and deferring to others. Whether or not historians of economic thought follow Dorfman's proscription different path dependencies will ensue. The doing of the history of economic thought will influence the development of the subject. "Accurate description" and "adequate perspective" lose much of their meaning; they are not found but made through whatever path is engendered.

Treatment of the recency problem

In the literature: results of a survey

It is well and good to speculate normatively about the issues considered above. The positive, empirical question includes how the problem of recency is handled in the literature.[6]

The totality of the preceding analysis may read like a brief against Dorfman's rule, and for Samuels it may well be that. But that analysis may also help explain why so much history-of-economic-thought work has been done for periods that the Dorfman rule would proscribe.

The survey reported on here was conducted principally in the summer of 2002. Included was Samuels' very large collection of twentieth-century history-of-economic-thought textbooks (see Howey 1982 for a list, to 1975, of general histories of economics[7]). These number over about 100, including multiple editions, and include all the major textbooks. Also included in the survey were a variety of other books that seemed to bear on our problem, largely chosen at random. The relative comprehensiveness of the former group contrasts with the relative randomness of the latter group. Although some allusions and references to journal articles are made below, no wide-ranging survey of economics journals was specifically conducted for this project.

Empirical examination of the literature—especially but not solely the history-of-economic-thought textbooks—involves a number of complicating factors. These include coverage, dates of cited materials, early and later editions of a work, level of sophistication (both *per se* and between undergraduate and graduate levels), design strategies—such as history of technical theory *vis-à-vis* humanistic/intellectual history and critical *vis-à-vis* non-critical—and so on. No distinction is made here between texts written for undergraduate and graduate students, though to some extent that distinction parallels that between theory and humanistic/intellectual history. Non-textbook materials include collections of essays on individual figures. An effort has been made to constrain the volume of referenced materials; except for the history-of-economic-thought textbooks, only a rough sample of examples is provided.

The results of our inquiry follow, first with regard to the history-of-economic-thought texts and related materials, and second with regard to other materials. No distinction is drawn between textbooks on the history of economic theory/analysis and those more broadly oriented (philosophical and/or intellectual history, schools not deemed "theoretical," etc.), largely because most authors of the former type execute more broadly than they design. Not all design strategies are equally conducive to emphasis on recent developments, though most if not all have some opportunity to do so; it is always up to the author. This is because the textbooks vary in their degree of theoretical technicality and therefore how much attention to ongoing development of theoretical details is likely. Several books that, strictly speaking, are not textbooks are included because of the relevance of their design strategy. Within each category, the sequence is roughly by date of publication.

Two further preliminary observations may be made. First, the textbooks that do include recent economic thought—excepting those in the 1990s—seem to do so as a reaction to political and economic events in the world, especially World War II and communism and the Cold War. Second, the textbooks that identify the problem of recency do not always include then-recent material, and those that do include recent material do not always identify and discuss the problem; for the latter, perhaps, the matter is not a problem.

The history-of-economic-thought textbooks and other history-of-economic-thought materials

The problem not discussed

Most texts do not explicitly discuss the problem of recency (those not identified in the next subsection). One must intuit the author's position from what is included and excluded, given the date of publication—an exercise that we do not pursue.

Paul Homan's *Contemporary Economic Thought* (1928) is remarkable for its combination of silence and execution. The author does not discuss the problem of recency but, effectively assuming the amenability of contemporary thought for historical analysis, he devotes the book entirely to a critique of contemporary thought. Homan is motivated by his dismay with the diversity, fertility and incompatibility of then-contemporary general economic theory and therefore with what the title of his concluding chapter calls "The Present Impasse." Homan says that the "real point" of the work "lies in the attempt to explain why at a given point in time men engaged in the analysis of approximately the same objective data come to such disparate conclusions" (1928: ix). He seeks to reconsider "the whole framework of thought" and to provide "a critical examination of the assumptions which underlie the disciplines of all social sciences" (1928: ix).

The problem explicitly discussed

Explicit positions on the issue can be found. In each case the position taken will be identified and critiqued.

Erich Roll's first edition of *A History of Economic Thought* (1940) identified its objective as providing only "an introduction to modern theory" (1940: 14), not modern theory itself. This implies less necessity to and opportunity for incremental additions to later editions in order to achieve recency. As for inclusion, the reader is told that "apart from the most outstanding economists of the past, only those have been included whose contributions to economic thought appear to have significance in relation to present-day theory and controversy" (1940: 18). This introduces a presentist view of precursors: past innovations are viewed through the lens of contemporary theory, searching for anticipations of modern theory, indeed being defined in terms of modern theory. The search for precursors is a somewhat stilted task for historians of economic thought; it may not be history-of-economic-thought as such.

John Fred Bell's first edition of 1953 announces that its coverage extends "from antiquity to the present time" and that included are "only those thinkers whose ideas, insights, and teachings have had a substantial influence, directly or indirectly, on the main stream of economic thought"—by which he clearly does not mean orthodox economics alone (Bell 1953: v). Bell's second edition (1967) makes several interesting and partly conflicting claims, one of which seems akin to Rima's initial claim (later in this section). Bell applauds "careful study of the evolutionary growth of economic doctrines." He says both that his book "brings together the most significant scholars and schools whose influence has left permanent imprint on the body of economic doctrines," and that "Attention has been given to less well-known authors and their contributions as well as to the better-known names and their contributions." He also notes, "While it is true that some elements of history never change, it is possible for new interpretations to be placed on events as a result of further research" (Bell 1967: v). The question of recency pervades all this, but is buried, combined with other themes requiring more critical attention, such as the nature, meaning and significance of "evolutionary growth," the relation of significant to less well known, the meaning and status of the survival requirement, and the significance of changing, if not multiple, interpretations.

Edmund Whittaker's *Schools and Streams of Economic Thought* (1960) takes up the question of recency as part of his explanation for writing a successor to his *History of Economic Ideas* (1940), which presented materials on a topical rather than chronological basis but covered, somewhat unevenly, then-recent work. "With the passage of time, interest and emphasis change. The maturing of thought on such matters as employment and cycle theory and economic aggregates has made it both possible and necessary to treat topics and writers neglected or not yet emergent in 1940." Also, the rise of "widespread central-ized economic planning ... calls for some special attention to this subject. Generally, the writings of the past have to be looked upon in terms of new contemporary interests as well as continuing old interests" (1960: vii). Although some of the terminology is the same, Whittaker's argument, or at least his presumption of need for recency, is quite different from Dorfman's. Still, his comparison of 1960 with 1940 comports with Dorfman's sense of time. Ben Seligman's *Main Currents in Modern Economics* (1962) specifically criticized texts that "almost entirely" lacked coverage of contemporary work and called for "an adequate exposition of contemporary aspects of the develop-ment of economic theory which might provide guidelines in unraveling the numerous strands lying about" (1962: xi–xii). An estimated one-third of his book is devoted to the seventeen years of post-war materials.

Although not a history-of-economic-thought work as such, Robert Heilbroner's *The Future as History* (1960) emphasizes relevant themes. Heilbroner argues that neither the future nor the present can be understood from the historic trends that shape them. In part, this means that the future must be seen in a historic context for the events of the future to be meaning-fully understood. Heilbroner believes that historic and social trends in thinking, as well as in science and economics, shape the evolution of the future. Study of both the present and the recent past is, accordingly, necessary.

Mark Blaug's first edition of *Economic Theory in Retrospect* (1962) stated that "My purpose is to teach contemporary economic theory. But contemporary theory wears the scars of yesterday's problems now resolved, yesterday's blunders now corrected, and cannot be fully understood except as a legacy handed down from the past" (1962: ix). Presentism, but more emphasis on practice.

W.E. Kuhn's *The Evolution of Economic Thought* (1963), however, took the opposite position. Arguing against the Keynesian revolution "resulting in the frontiers of economic knowledge being repeatedly pushed back," Kuhn used an argument quite different from Dorfman's writing:

> There is manifest danger that the mid-twentieth-century historian of economic thought becomes so engrossed with the recent macroeconomic exploits that all pre-1930 contributions to economic theory appear to him as only 'prepara-tory' in nature. The author, while prepared to use them as tools, does not rate so highly the analytic advances of the last quarter of a century; much sifting will have to precede the ripening of historical judgment on this epoch.
>
> (Kuhn 1963: vi)

The position is maintained in the second edition (1970). "Passage of time" here correlates with a negative attitude toward the development in question.

The comparison of Kuhn with Seligman is striking. Neither is happy with recent developments. But they differ on what they dislike and on whether the developments that they dislike should be minimized.

In the first edition of Ingrid Rima's *Development of Economic Analysis* (1967) one reads that "The problem of selecting which contributions to include and which to omit becomes more difficult as one approaches the present" (1967: ix). She then says, "After the selections have been made, there is the even more formidable problem of determining the detail with which to review their substance and appraise their significance" (1967: ix–x). This she elaborates by saying, "One can summarize the legacy from the past with far more assurance than one can select for review those aspects of contemporary theory that seem likely to withstand the test of time" (1967: x).

This latter assumes, however, that the only ideas, etc. from the past that should be reported by the historian are those accepted today. If past economists believed, or otherwise entertained favorably, ideas A, B, C, D and E, and if present-day economists accept D, should not the historian of ideas report both that fact and the totality of what was believed in the past—and perhaps explain how the discipline arrived at D? Are we not interested in what past economists believed, quite apart from the present status thereof? Is not part of the story how the discipline got from A through E to D alone, requiring reporting and discussion of the other ideas? We may believe today that price is price, independent of any metaphysical notion of value, and that price is a function of the price mechanism, etc., i.e., at least demand and supply, but the history of economic thought includes the nature and significance of the theories of value that led to the present—some of which are still emphasized by some economists today. Expressed differently, if a filter is at work, is the historian interested only in that which the filter has permitted to pass and not in that upon which the filter operated, and in the filter itself? Rima's view here is close to George Stigler's "from error to truth" approach, less aggressive with regard to the "truth" requirement (though perhaps that is what "withstanding the test of time" becomes) and more aggressive in ruling out of bounds everything hitherto filtered out. It would be in any case a myopic and incomplete view of the history of economic ideas and theories. Fortunately (in our view) she does not follow her own prescription, covering much that has not "withstood the test of time." One wonders if she fully appreciated the implications of her position.

Rima's concern changed in her revised edition of 1972. Indicating that she has increased "the presentation of contemporary theory," making the book "more comprehensive and sophisticated to meet the needs of the more technically oriented user" (1972: ix), she takes up either a different historiographical issue or the same issue from a different angle. She hopes "this revision will also help end the unfortunate schism between the history of economic theory and contemporary theory." This is a schism partly of her own making or re-enforcement. She goes on to suggest that one can master contemporary theory "without any knowledge of what came before." But contemporary theory did not arise out of nothing.

It is ... the product of an on-going intellectual process that seeks, albeit not always successfully, to correct, improve, refine, and add to the analytical tools and concepts which were previously fashioned. Thus there is much about contemporary theory that will never be understood except in retrospect.

(1972: x)

Is this the lesson of "withstanding the test of time"?

William Breit and Roger Ransom's *The Academic Scribblers* (first edition 1971; revised edition 1982) pursued a different line, namely, economic-policy relevance. Their book is an attempt "primarily to capture within the confines of a single volume the most elusive game of all: contemporary economic thought." In support of this view they quote A.W. Coats: "Studies of recent economic thought and policy are especially important because the economists' direct influence has latterly been much greater than in most earlier times" (1971: vii; 1982: ix). They restrict their coverage to American economists and ideas "which have had or are likely to have impact on economic policy" (1982: ix). Thus they declare their purpose: "to study contemporary American economic theorists who have had a policy impact" (1971: vii; 1982: xii). This may or may not have been an acceptable rationale for Dorfman, but theirs is not the conventional history-of-economic-thought textbook.

Takashi Negishi's *History of Economic Theory* (1989) has negligible twentieth-century material: Marshall is the last economist discussed in any depth; only bits on Schumpeter and Keynes are presented. Negishi expresses the position that the contributions of economists such as "Pareto, Wicksell, I. Fisher, Hicks, Samuelson, Mises, Hayek, and Pigou ... should be considered as a part of the contemporary economic theory rather than in the history of economic theory" (1989: 385). Similarly, "Since it is an important part of contemporary economics, a study of the economics of Keynes as such is beyond the scope of this book" (1989: 386). Keynes is brought into the picture only in relation to mercantilism and Schumpeter only in relation to Böhm-Bawerk's theory of equilibrium. Negishi raises the question of when the "present" commences and "history" ceases, at least for now; i.e., the meaning of "history." Negishi's approach treats the history of theory course as the resting place of those no longer included in theory courses. Negishi does make considerable use of twentieth-century exegetical, critical and interpretive literature.

Design changes

Several series of editions have undergone significant if not major change in design strategy, sometimes with and sometimes without the addition of a co-author. Other authors have continued with their earlier design, some have engaged in noteworthy updating, and some have expanded their range of coverage. The first indicates confidence and contentment, though perhaps also inertia and/or the high cost—in terms of time and effort—of major revisions.

The latter two suggest the difficulty of coping with the explosion of diversity—both within individual schools of thought and between them—in the post-war period and the difficulty, too, of reconciling the goal of recency (which would be for many a new goal) with their other goals. Strikingly, every design change has been in the direction of greater attention to recent materials.

Lewis Haney started out with no desire to include contemporary materials but with his third edition made serious attempts to add contemporary materials. In terms of years, the difference is between a gap of some ten years (1900–1911) and a gap of some three years (1946–1949; but see below for inter-country variation).

In the revised (second) edition (1920) of his *History of Economic Thought*, Haney asked the reader to "bear in mind the fact that no attempt is made to cover the period since 1900" and that "mention of developments since 1900 are for the most part designed to be but cursory and tentative" (1920: ix–x); this had been true in the first edition (1911). The three chapters preceding the concluding chapter in the second edition give accounts of the leading schools in the latter part of the nineteenth century in Germany and Italy, England and France, and the United States, respectively.

Haney notes that among his major additions in revising the book were those made to the chapter on the Austrian School, saying, "In the author's judgment, the Austrian School can now be treated in a final way, and it has been his aim so to treat it in this edition" (1920: ix). In retrospect such a judgment—"in a final way"—was premature, supporting Dorfman's position.

The change in design strategy comes in the third edition of 1936, the preface of which commences with the statement, "It has been my endeavor thoroughly to revise the work, and to bring it as nearly down to date as seems wise" (1936: v). He has added three chapters, one on Benthamite utilitarianism, one on Marshallian neoclassicism, and one on institutionalism, the last of which he calls "the most recent movement in American economic thought" (1936: v). This (1936) was also the year of publication of Keynes's *General Theory*; its publication is noted in a footnote. Keynes is principally cited for his "work in mathematical economics," work described as dealing "with results rather than causes" (1936: 700).

In his fourth and enlarged edition of 1949, he offers no specific rationale other than his desire "to bring up to date" his previous accounts so that "the student may find a reasonably adequate account" throughout the book (1949: v). In comparison with the third edition of 1936, he has added five new chapters and added to his previous chapters. The new chapters discuss Wicksell, business-cycle theory, limited-competition theory, Keynes, and general-equilibrium theory. Brief discussions are now found on new welfare economics and econometrics. The succeeding chapters examine developments to World War II: Germany and Austria, Italy, and France and Belgium. For England the period ends with c.1936; for the United States, with 1946. Haney voices his concern that "possibly too much space relatively has been given to recent developments. A hundred years from now," he says, "some things which seem in the present worthy of a chapter may be dismissed with a paragraph. But who among us can yet say which ones?" (Haney 1949: v).

Two further prefatory points made by Haney are worth noting. First, that "Value Economics is being subordinated to price economics." Second, "Particularly dangerous is the specious argument in favor of dealing with theories rather than with theorists. In no field of knowledge is thought so molded by the thinker and his environment as is the case with economics; and it is therefore always desirable to know something about circumstances" (1949: vi). Would the history of the quantity theory look different if only negligible attention were paid to Friedman? How can one do justice to modern quantity theory without much attention to him? Is the question of recency affected by Haney's position?

In the series begun by Harry Landreth and continued in joint authorship with David Colander, the attention given to modern developments gradually expanded with the addition of Colander.

Landreth and Colander's second (1989) and third (1994) editions of *History of Economic Thought* cover "the development of the scope, method, and content of economics from about 1200 to the present" (1989: xix; 1994: xix; Landreth's first edition (1976) covered the period "1500 to the present" (1976: xvi)). In the second edition they indicate that their aim is to make the book "as relevant as possible to individuals interested in current, not past, debates" and that they have allocated "much more space to modern economic theory than usual" (1989: xvi). As for "coverage of modern economic thought," they write in the third edition that they have slightly decreased and simplified the coverage of "modern economic thought" because of "difficulties many professors have in covering so much material in a single term" (1994: xx). They suggest that these chapters can be simply read by students even if not covered in class. It is not clear, however, that the coverage has in fact materially decreased.

Landreth's first edition (1976) had covered a limited and selective array of post-war developments: methods and models, microeconomics and welfare economics, and some macroeconomics after Keynes. In Landreth and Colander's second edition (1989) the coverage of recent developments is greater. Chapter 10 on modern microeconomics runs thirty-three pages and is the most comprehensive. Chapter 11 on modern macroeconomics covers microfoundations, new classical economics, the Lucas critique, and the neo-Keynesians and the New Keynesian responses—all in ten pages. Chapter 12 on modern non-mainstream economics covers radical economics, institutional economics, British and American post-Keynesian economics, Myrdal and Galbraith, public choice, Austrian economics and experimental economics—in twenty-five pages. In their third edition (1994), contrary to their description, somewhat more considerable and wide-ranging attention is given to post-war developments, grouped into diversity with modern heterodoxy (thirty pages), modern microeconomics (thirty-three pages), modern macroeconomics (twelve pages), and econometrics and empirical methods (twenty-five pages). Their fourth edition very much resembles the third, amended by marginal extensions. The general problem (for the textbook literature as a whole) of inevitable limitations of coverage is raised by a reviewer of the fourth edition:

> Part Four deals with economics in the twentieth century with its enormous cast of characters and issues in dispute. This is difficult to cover in a little over 100 pages, and many will feel that their favorite economist has been slighted. The subjects range from Morgenstern and von Neumann to Arrow and Debreu, from Keynesianism to monetarism, from W.C. Mitchell's business cycles to econometrics, from institutionalism to public choice. Joan Robinson gets two paragraphs, Piero Sraffa one.
>
> (Dooley 2002: 5)

Ingrid Rima's first edition (1967) of *Development of Economic Analysis* has negligible post-war material, though much from the 1930s. Her revised edition (1972) increases the amount of post-war material and references, though the coverage is limited and selective. The third edition (1978) has four parts: "Preclassical Economics"; "Classical Economics"; "Marginalism"; and "From Marshall to the Present", the last including material on the old and new welfare economics, and chapters on "Keynesians, Monetarists, and the Reaffirmation of the Neoclassical Tradition," "The Chicago School of Political Economy," and a chapter discussing Galbraith, radical economics, and post-Keynesian economics—some 70 of 490 pages, a much more serious effort at recency. By the fifth edition of 1991, the material is divided into six parts. The first five are "Preclassical Economics" (60 pages); "Classical Economics" (140 pages); "Critics of Classicism" (100 pages); "The Neoclassical Tradition, 1890–1945" (110 pages); and "Dissent from Neoclassicism, 1890–1945" (70 pages). Part VI, "Beyond High Theory" (80 pages) has four chapters, on: econometrics; Keynesians, neo Walrasians and monetarists; the Chicago tradition; and controversies raised by heterodox authors and schools, including neo-institutionalism, radical economics, US and UK post-Keynesian economics, and Austrian economics. That last part is an updating from Part VI of the fourth edition of 1986. From 80 of 560 pages in the fifth edition, post-war economic thought takes up 90 of 570 pages in the sixth edition of 2001, covering much the same material as the fifth edition. Rima has gone from relatively negligible to considerable and wide-ranging—though inevitably limited and selective—contemporary materials, amounting to a design change. (Design change also took place with regard to the initial emphasis on analysis. By the fifth edition (1991), the emphasis is no longer on the development of analysis; it is now a more conventional history-of-economic-thought text encompassing both theory and ideas.)

Alexander Gray and A.E. Thompson's second edition of Gray's textbook (1980) has considerable then-recent material. Gray's first edition of 1931, which ran to 369 pages of text and concluded with the Austrian School, stated that "the economic doctrine of to-day, and probably of yesterday, [should be] expounded in the ordinary text-book, or in the class-room" and "The current account of economic principles ... should reflect and expound the wranglings of the last twenty or thirty years" (1931: 363), thus articulating the Dorfman rule. Gray went on to state, "we are still too near post-Austrian developments to be able properly to assess their value" (1931: 364). Discussing what he identifies as an age of transition, Gray argues, "When there is no dominant school, when theory is in solution and truth may be anywhere, ideas of all kind, mutually contradictory, jostle against each other in the pot in which public opinion is cooked" (Gray 1931: 369)—but ceases his story with the Austrian school. The history of economic thought deals with settled interpretation; the unsettled is the domain of courses on current topics. In his introduction to the second edition, Thompson cites Gray's "argument that we should not write about our contemporaries" and his own departure from Gray's practice on pedagogical grounds (Gray and Thompson 1980: xv).

Thompson added four chapters and eighty pages—XIII. Marshall; XIV. Keynes; XV. Neo-classical Developments; and XVI. Contemporary Economic Controversies. Chapter XV covers, in twelve pages, Wicksell, Robinson and Chamberlin, Veblen, and the neoclassical synthesis. It has two remarkable interpretations. The section on Veblen commences thus: "The neo-classical tradition was wide enough to encompass those who challenged its assumptions and mobilized their criticisms around its central propositions" (Gray and Thompson 1980: 395). The neoclassical synthesis is not that of Samuelson's marriage of neoclassical microeconomics and Keynesian macroeconomics. It is the integration of Marshallian partial equilibrium analysis and Walrasian–Paretian general equilibrium analysis effectuated by Hicks (Gray and Thompson 1980: 398–400). Chapter XVI, forty-nine pages, covers monetarism; Galbraith and Mishan on overconsumption; the ecological debate; neo-Marxist developments; the New Left; and imperialism and domination. Much is omitted but an unusual amount is included. The change in design strategy is evident.

The fifth edition of Jacob Oser's *The Evolution of Economic Thought*, now authored solely by Stanley L. Brue (1994), unlike its predecessors (see above) has considerable post-war coverage, to 1975 and beyond, representing a design change.

No or negligible coverage of recent materials

Many texts and treatises cover almost no recent or contemporary material, given their date of publication. Any recent material covered is very limited and highly selective.

Edwin Cannan's study of the history of production and distribution theory had a closing date of 1848; it was published in 1893, forty-five years later. Stigler's book on the same subjects commenced with Jevons and concluded with Euler's theorem and marginal productivity theory; Stigler carried the story to c.1910 and published in 1948, a lag of around thirty-eight years. Stigler's *Essays in the History of Economics* (1965) includes several essays with some but relatively negligible then-recent materials.

William A. Scott's *The Development of Economics* (1933), with the exception of five pages on Veblen and statistical work in the 1920s, has no then-recent coverage.

John M. Ferguson's *Landmarks of Economic Thought* (1938) has a limited, fifteen-page survey of twentieth-century post-Marshall economists.

Frank A. Neff's *Economic Doctrines* (1946) covered very little of twentieth-century economic thought, examining only Alfred Marshall, John A. Hobson, Thorstein Veblen, and the "isms." The second edition of 1950 added a fourteen-page chapter on Keynes

Terence Hutchison's *A Review of Economic Doctrines, 1870–1929* (1953) was self-consciously limited to deal with "what economists in, say, 1890 took as their 'normal' model" (1953: x). It was a period in which "the development of economics as an academic specialism coincided with a period of *comparatively* stable politico-economic development in the Western world" (1953: vii) in comparison with the "Economics of Disturbance, Instability, and Insecurity" that has provided "so expensive an education" since 1929 (1953: ix). The difference between 1929 and 1953 (last year of coverage and date of publication) comports with Dorfman's rule.

Robert Heilbroner's *The Worldly Philosophers* (first edition, 1953) has no history of economic thought beyond Keynes. Heilbroner is interested in the application of the ideas of the great worldly economists to the present but not in contemporary economic thought. His concluding chapters relate his personal attitudes to the changing modern world.

William Barber's *A History of Economic Thought* (1967) makes no effort at recency, and has no reason to do so. That is because Barber's objective is "to present the properties of four distinct modes of economic reasoning" (1967: 9). These are the classical, the Marxian, the neoclassical and Keynesian modes of reasoning. A much earlier book with a similar objective was O. Fred Boucke's *The Development of Economics*, published in 1921 with an ending date of 1900, consistent with Dorfman's view (he also remarks, "distance does give perspective" (1921: 315)). For Boucke, too, economics also had four systems: for him these were naturalism, utilitarianism, historicism, and "marginalism." Later comparable books centered on competing legacies of more complex or variegated philosophical—epistemological and/or ontological—traditions: Karl Pribram's *A History of Economic Reasoning* (1983) and Mark Perlman and Charles McCann's *The Pillars of Economic Understanding* (1998). A common theme of these two books is the tension between treating the economy as a pure abstract a-institutional conception and as a set of actual arrangements formed and operated through by institutions (power structure). They too had little if any need for recency. Their respective authors, one surmises, intended (and succeeded in writing) more a magisterial treatise than a conventional textbook whose market awaited the next edition. Much the same can be said of Werner Stark's *The Ideal Foundations of Economic Thought* (1943), and Ferdinand Zweig's *Economic Ideas* (1950).

Joseph Finkelstein and Alfred Thimm's *Economists and Society* (1973) presents the history through Keynes, concluding, however, with an unusual chapter entitled "The New Behavioral Economics," covering systems theory, model building, simulation business decision making, and the quality of American life.

Guy Routh's *Origin of Economic Ideas* (first edition, 1975; second edition, 1989), whose purpose is as much, if not more, criticism as instruction, presents negligible material on post-war developments, adding little in the second edition. His design neither leads to nor requires incremental additions for the purpose of recency—though such might be useful to show that systematic problems still exist.

Stephen Stigler's *The History of Statistics* (1986) terminates its study of the measurement of uncertainty in 1900, as does Theodore Porter's *The Rise of Statistical Thinking, 1820–1900* (1986).

Pier Francesco Asso's (2001) study of the spread of Italian economic thought—not strictly a textbook—covers the period 1750–1950, thus stopping short of most of the post-war period.

Gianni Vaggi and Peter Groenewegen's *A Concise History of Economic Thought* (2003) covers the period 1600–1960, also stopping short of most of the post-war period, and is intended to be preparatory to the study of more recent work, interpreting the history of economic thought as a dual division between classical political economy and modern post-1870 developments

Some coverage of recent materials

Many, perhaps most, texts cover some more or less recent material, given their date of publication. Most cover a selective and limited amount; some, a relatively considerable but still selective, and thus limited, amount.

Charles Gide and Charles Rist's celebrated textbook, *A History of Economic Doctrines*, was first published in English in 1915 from a translation of the French edition, and reprinted in 1948. The subtitle announces the authors' intent: "From the Time of the Physiocrats to the Present Day." The overall structure of the history is as follows: I. The Founders; II. The Antagonists; III. Liberalism; IV. The Dissenters (which includes the historical school, state socialism, Marxism, and Christian-influenced doctrines); V. Recent Doctrines, which includes the hedonists, the theory of rent and its applications, the solidarists, and the anarchists. The chapter on "the hedonists" is twenty-seven pages in length (out of a total of 650), is an introduction to the beginnings of modern price theory and also distribution theory, covers the early Austrians, Clark, Walras, Jevons, Edgeworth, Marshall, and others, with a view backward to Gossen and others, and concludes with an account of the criticisms of the hedonistic doctrines. Given, therefore, the date of publication of the French edition from which the translation was made, the impressive and informed high quality of the material, and the relative length of the material, it is equivocal whether the treatment of recent developments—which go back some forty years—is to be designated "some" or "extensive." We opt for the former.

Similarly with John Kells Ingram's earlier *A History of Political Economy* (1888). The structure here is as follows: I. Introductory; II. Ancient Times; III. The Middle Ages; IV. Modern Times: Two First Phases (the first is the period of conflict especially between crown, feudal chiefs and towns; the second, the ascendancy of central temporal power); V. Third Modern Phase: System of Natural Liberty; VI. The Historical School; VII. Conclusion. The chapter on the historical school includes a section on English economic thought. It covers Bagehot, Cairnes, Cliffe Leslie, Rogers and Toynbee, but also Jevons inclusive of his pure theory. The concluding two sections are compact surveys—more like lists—of American and contemporary English economists (the former includes both Walkers and Dunbar; the latter, the Marshalls, Sidgwick, Fawcett and others. The book runs to some 250 pages. The three concluding sections of the chapter on the historical school run to 15, 3 and 2, respectively, or 20 of 250 pages—a higher ratio than Gide and Rist's but less deep.

At the beginning of his discussion of "Contemporary English Economists" Ingram makes two points of interest. First:

> It is no part of our plan to pass judgment on the works of contemporary English authors,—a judgment which could not in general be final, and which would be subject to the imputation of bias in a greater degree than estimates of living writers in foreign countries. But, for the information of the student, some opinion may be expressed which scarcely any competent person would dispute.
>
> (1888: 238)

Ingram here raises two relevant problems, that of adequacy of information and that of bias. Second, in a surprising (given the foregoing point) but brief criticism of Henry Sidgwick, he argues that:

> It cannot be permanently our business to go on amending and limiting the Ricardian doctrines, and asking by what special interpretations of phrases or additional qualifications they may still be admitted to having a certain value. The time for a new construction has arrived; and it is to this, or at least to the study of its conditions, that competent thinkers with the due scientific preparation should not devote themselves.
>
> (Ingram 1888: 239)

Passing over Ingram's recognition of the practice of defending a theory's hard core, one can only remark on Ingram's prescience: Alfred Marshall's *Principles of Economics* was only two years away.

Glenn Hoover's collection, *Twentieth Century Economic Thought* (1950) is both policy and layperson oriented. It carries the story, in essays on twenty topics, through Keynes. Because of its date of publication, Keynes counts as recent economic thought.

Philip Newman's *The Development of Economic Thought* (1952) has chapters on imperfect competition theory, Schumpeter, Commons, and (two) on Keynes. Because of its date of publication, such too counts as recent work.

John Fred Bell's *History of Economic Thought* (1953) devotes about 80 of some 664 pages to Veblen, Mitchell, Commons, Marshall, Keynes, and English, Swedish and American post-Marshallian developments. His second edition,

1967, added new material on various topics, including European and US developments, and a new chapter on mathematical economics; i.e., an effort that, like most of the rest of these textbooks, is necessarily limited and selective but does indicate some effort at recency.

Robert Lekachman's *A History of Economic Ideas* (1959) devotes at least 70 of its 400 pages to "Contemporary Economics." This includes chapters on Keynes, business cycle theories, price theories, the old and new welfare economics, socialist economics, and Schumpeter. Much, though not all, of the contemporary discussion relates to 1930s materials. Either he is avoiding the last twenty years or so, with the noted exceptions, or he is satisfied with a sampling of more recent materials—a situation that applies to most if not all the authors included in this section.

Overton Taylor's (1960) text apologizes for its selective and limited inclusion of then-recent ("modern") work. Included are communism, fascism, democratic socialism and interventionist liberalism; E.H. Chamberlin, J.M. Keynes, and Keynesianism's early days.

Edmund Whittaker's *Schools and Streams of Economic Thought* (1960) has three chapters (of sixteen) that deal in whole or in part with then-recent developments. Chapter 14 includes econometrics and linear programming. Chapter 15 covers Keynes and ideas after Keynes. Chapter 16 examines the problem of authority in society, association and political pluralism, and state economic planning.

Mark Blaug's first edition (1962) of *Economic Theory in Retrospect* has negligible material after Keynes and Hicks-Hansen—notwithstanding his stated intent to teach "contemporary economic theory." The revised edition of 1968 says "As before, the story is carried down to our own times, roughly 1960" (1968: xii). Here one finds much post-war material, especially on activity analysis, economic dynamics, welfare economics, growth models, and technical change—a slight updating beyond 1960. The third edition of 1978 carries and expands the story into the 1970s, to include the Clower-Leijonhufvud disequilibrium interpretation of Keynes, Sraffa, and the reswitching controversy. The fourth edition of 1985, in addition to a chapter on location theory and a revision of the treatment given Keynes, has new material on Paretian welfare economics, monetarism, and new classical economics-rational expectations. The fifth edition of 1997 increases the attention to developments in macroeconomics but makes no increase in coverage; the overall level of recency is increasingly limited and selective. The focus on neoclassical theory is increasingly evident; and the selectivity of its coverage is more than matched by the exclusion of non-neoclassical theory.

Warren Catlin's *The Progress of Economics* (1962) has a topical structure. Some post-war coverage is present but obscured by the design of the volume. No evident intent is shown to cover then-recent economic thought. The same holds for John W. McConnell's *Basic Teachings of the Great Economists* (1943): a topical organization of materials with no attention to recent materials.

W.E. Kuhn's *The Evolution of Economic Thought* (1963) includes negligible and selective recent material, notably four pages covering Hicks, Leontief and Samuelson, and game theory. The second edition (1970) has additional contemporary material, including extensions of Keynesian analysis by Harrod, Domar and Kuznets; recent work in monetary theory by Patinkin, Gurley and Shaw, Tobin, and Friedman, Harry Johnson on international trade theory; and more detail on the isms.

Jacob Oser's *Evolution of Economic Thought* (1963) has one chapter on "mathematical economics," covering econometrics, general equilibrium, indifference curves, and input–output analysis) and another on "modern theories of economic development and growth" (Schumpeter, Baran, Nurkse, Myrdal and Rostow) but very little beyond Chamberlin and Robinson in microeconomics and beyond Keynes in macroeconomics. So, too, the second edition (1970), which strengthens, not updates, earlier treatments. The third edition (1975), co-authored with William C. Blanchfield, adds Friedman; linear programming and game theory; deletes Rostow; and adds a chapter on post-Keynesian economics (Galbraith, Samuelson and Arrow), continuing limited and selective coverage.

Richard Gill's *Evolution of Modern Economics* (1967) goes beyond Keynes in a seven-page "Postscript" covering quantitative and mathematical economics, growth economics and "the issues of the future."

Henry Spiegel's *Growth of Economic Thought* (first edition, 1971) devoted some attention, both scattered and concentrated, to post-war developments, especially chapter 28 on econometrics and related mathematical topics. Pages 642–643 discuss Samuelson. The revised and expanded (second) edition of 1983 and the third edition of 1991 added chapter 29 on increasing diversity in economics. No presently relevant material change was made between the 1983 and 1991 editions. Each edition has especially valuable bibliographical notes (eventually 150 pages), including materials from the post-war period. Otherwise the text is selective, omitting much of the post-war diversity. For example, neither Blaug nor Spiegel discuss post-Keynesian economics.

Phyllis Deane's *The Emergence of Economic Ideas* (1978) goes beyond Keynes only in presenting growth theory.

Vivian Walsh and Harvey Gram, in their *Classical and Neoclassical Theories of General Equilibrium* (1980), have no hesitation in covering post-war developments, though these are not entirely central to their story. The same is true of Roy Weintraub's *General Equilibrium Analysis* (1985), albeit perhaps for different reasons.

A.K. Dasgupta's *Epochs of Economic Theory* (1985) covers developments only through Keynes, though some recent work is cited and an evaluation is given of the status quo.

Jürg Niehans's *A History of Economic Theory* (1990) carries the history to the last quarter of the twentieth century, concentrating on what he considers "classic contributions." Chapters 29–36, out of thirty-seven, covering pages 372–515, out of 562 pages, discuss Frisch, Tinbergen and Leontief; von Neumann; Koopmans; Samuelson; growth theorists; neoclassical monetary theory; Arrow; and monetary theory. These chapters follow three on welfare economics, Keynes and Hicks. Ironically, Niehans, despite his unusually extensive coverage, is somewhat apologetic: "I know that, despite all efforts, the present work is imperfect. The history of economic theory is an immense field, and for each aspect there are specialists, past and present, who know (or have known) more than I shall ever know. If this book has merit, it arises not from completeness but from selectiveness. It raises the question of what contributions to the history of economics deserve to be regarded as classic" (1990: x).

Takuo Dome's *History of Economic Theory* (1994) has limited, highly selective coverage of recent work, presenting Hicks's re-examination, European post-Keynesian economics, and monetary and rational expectations theory.

E. Ray Canterbery's *The Literate Economist* (1995) is about one-sixth on post-war developments, principally post-Keynesian economics, supply-side economics, and Hyman Minsky's financial instability theory.

The very short textbook by Bo Sandelin, Hans-Michael Trautwein and Richard Wundrak, *A Short History of Economic Thought* (2002), is intended to provide a small book (105 pages of text and notes) for courses in which the subject "constitutes only a part of a course" and concentrates "on a few representatives of schools and ideas" (2002: 9). Still, the authors include several pages each on post-war neoclassicism, monetary macroeconomics, and several heterodox schools, as well as on "theories about the development of theories"—Kuhn, Lakatos, and McCloskey.

Extensive coverage of recent materials

Some texts include an extensive amount of then-recent or contemporary work, toward which status two or three of the immediately foregoing works tend.

The final two-thirds of Luigi Cossa's *Guide to the Study of Political Economy* (1880, translated from the second Italian edition of 1878), some 145 pages, is devoted to a survey of the history of economic thought from the ancient world to the beginning of the final quarter of the nineteenth century, i.e., right up to the time of publication. The thirty-five pages of chapter VI are devoted to the nineteenth century, with sections covering England; France; Germany; the Netherlands, Belgium, and Switzerland; and Spain and Portugal. The eighteen pages of chapter VII survey contemporary Italian economic thought. The work of no American economist is covered.

Cossa's 1893 work, *An Introduction to the Study of Political Economy*, is "an English version of what was begun as a third edition of [the earlier] work, though it … finally shaped itself into a completely new book" (1893: v). In it almost 440 pages (of 590) comprise a history of economic thought. Coverage extends to near the end of the nineteenth century; moreover, it has been expanded relative to the earlier work. Chapters IX through XVI cover (with some odd combinations) England; France; Germany; Austria, the Netherlands, Spain and Portugal; Scandinavia, the Slavonic countries, and Hungary; the United States; Italy; and contemporary theories of socialism. Cossa thus responded to his critics who, he says, legitimately complained that in the earlier work he had ignored too many countries, persons and topics. Another criticism, incidentally, was that "There were too many quotations from writers, especially from Italians, not of the first rank" (1893: 4; another criticism was that the earlier work had "too minute an account of various arguments which have from time to time been brought against political economy" (1893: 4)).

Richard Ely wrote extensively on the history of economic thought from at least 1889 through 1931, including sections in all editions of his *Outlines of Economics*. Given the date of publication, significant, if inevitably selective, attention to contemporary economists (US and foreign) and their work was included. Inclusion was extended to the field of the history of economic thought itself. Ely's *The Story of Economics in the United States*, which was published for the first time in 2002, was written over a period of years. The 1931 manuscript, the last one prepared by him and the version published, has several chapters and one thirty-page appendix covering then-contemporary or then-recent work (an account of his work on the history of economic thought is given in the editorial introduction by Warren Samuels (Ely 2002: 2ff)).

Joseph Schumpeter's first major work on the history of economic thought, *Economic Doctrine and Method* (1967 [1912]) has considerable then-recent material, i.e., within a decade or so. His fourth and final chapter, "The Historical School and the Theory of Marginal Utility," covers, first, German and English historicism and an array of methodological and paradigmatic issues in its first twenty-nine pages; and, second, a broad array of marginal utility theorists, going beyond the Austrian school, in twenty-one pages. Thus 50 of 200 pages are given to then-recent work.

Schumpeter's *History of Economic Analysis* (1954) covers, or would have covered, much then-recent economics. One need only look at the plan and partial draft of part V, in which he would have presented "A Sketch of Modern Developments" (1954: 1137). His coverage would still have been selective but highly then-contemporary and broader than theory or analysis.

Paul Homan's *Contemporary Economic Thought* (1928), motivated by his perceptions of the diversity, fertility, fluidity and incompatibility of contemporary economic thought, is aptly titled. Its intensive survey of John Bates Clark, Thorstein Veblen, Alfred Marshall, John A. Hobson and Wesley C. Mitchell by no means exhausted the variety of ways in which economics was done. But putting aside the admitted and inevitable arbitrariness of selection (1928: viii), the coverage as of its date of publication is manifestly contemporary, by Dorfman's or any other reckoning.

Theo Suranyi-Unger's *Economics in the Twentieth Century* (1932), a translation from the original German, not only took up recent work but the author went out of his way to "include the most recent developments of the years 1926–1928" (1932: x). Coverage includes Frank Knight and Maurice Dobb, as well as a wide range of topics in value and price theory and distribution theory; simultaneously the content includes broad and deep treatment of many topics now excluded from economics.

The notes from Wesley Mitchell's course on types of economic theory given in 1934–1935 reveal him to have lectured not only on John R. Commons's *Institutional Economics*, published in 1934, but on the ideas of Frank A. Fetter,

John Davenport, Friedrich von Wieser, Gustav Schmoller, Leon Walras and Gustav Cassel, Thorstein Veblen, and John A. Hobson—a significant and widely representative array of then-recent (by Mitchell's colleague Dorfman's standard) economic thought.

Eric Roll's design for his long-admired textbook was to include a relatively small but nonetheless substantive and increasing amount of then-contemporary economic thought. In the reprinted edition (1940) the twenty-five-page chapter VIII presented price theory as "Modern Economics" and included the various streams of modern thought leading to it plus some companion topics to price theory. The forty-two-page chapter XI of the 1942 second edition covers uncertainty (Knight), equilibrium theory (Hicks, Sraffa, Robinson, Pigou), and the new political economy (Keynes). Chapter X, forty-three pages on the American contribution, is also new but, appropriately, is not labeled "recent" (1942: vii). It starts with "the background," namely, Franklin, Carey, Walker, the AEA imbroglio, and George, continues with "the marginalist school of Clark, Fisher, and Fetter", and concludes with Veblen. The third, 1956 edition continues with the two chapters added in the second edition and adds a chapter on "political economy to-day," covering the economics of underemployment, the statistical contribution, and "towards a new synthesis," which finds increasing coalescence in analytical techniques and increased conceptual synthesis, but also continued controversy. The fourth edition of 1974 contains, in chapters XI and XII, one hundred (of 600) pages on post-war developments, including macroeconomics, monetary and international economics, and the topics of growth, welfare and economic structure. Another chapter deals with the erosion of the "New Political Economy" of the third edition. His prefatory statements (1974: 8) about recent developments underscore his interest in both their inclusion and the problem of the best way of doing so (electing not to proceed under the headings of individual names).

Eduard Heimann's *History of Economic Doctrines* (1945) devotes two of nine chapters and one-quarter of its 240+ pages to twentieth-century work, including the Austrians through Wieser, Mises, Schumpeter and Hayek, Pigou, Wicksell, Hahn, and Keynes, though seemingly understating Marshall's place and omitting much else.

Leo Rogin's *The Meaning and Validity of Economic Theory* was published in 1956 but he had worked on it only into 1947. By any reckoning, the content of his final chapter (no more than half-written then (1956: xv)) on Keynes represented then-contemporary developments (Keynes died in 1946).

Allen Sievers's *Revolution, Evolution, and the Economic Order* (1962) has chapters only on Keynes, Schumpeter, Galbraith, Hansen, and John Maurice Clark. Not strictly a history-of-economic-thought work, in comparing and contrasting their ideas, Sievers nonetheless tells a story somewhat comparable to those whose design is different, and the materials are contemporary as of date of publication.

Claudio Napoleoni's *Economic Thought of the Twentieth Century* (1963) has numerous chapters on subjects whose development in the post-war period is included. The revised edition has an additional chapter by Alessandro Cigno (1972). Attention is devoted to both ideas and individuals.

Daniel Fusfeld's *The Age of the Economist* (first edition, 1966) states its goal in its subtitle (on the paperback cover but not its title page): "The Development of Modern Economic Thought." Following the chapter on Keynes, chapter 10, "Economic Planning," covers planning in the Soviet Union, the theory of planning (von Mises versus Lange), and planning in underdeveloped nations, the latter covering Boecke, Rostow, Myrdal and Prebisch. Chapter 11, "Will Capitalism Survive?," examines in sixteen pages (of 137) other post-war developments and the related literature, including the work of Joseph Schumpeter, John Kenneth Galbraith, Roy Harrod and Evsey Domar, Adolf A. Berle, Jr., and Gardiner C. Means, Sumner Slichter and Solomon Fabricant. The revised edition of 1972 presents a still more elaborate picture of contemporary developments, covering in thirty-five pages (of 178) Schumpeter, automation, Berle and Means, Slichter, Fabricant, Eli Ginsburg, Harrod and Domar, John Maurice Clark, W.W. Rostow, John R. Hicks, Paul A. Samuelson, Milton Friedman, Frank H. Knight, Galbraith, Paul Baran and Paul Sweezy, C. Wright Mills, and Seymour Melman. The third edition of 1977 has both expanded coverage of some previous topics and new sections. The later chapters in the fourth edition of 1982 "were modified to a greater extent" than the chapters on Marxism and neoclassical economics, now "with emphasis on the economic problems of the 1970s, the limitations of economic policy, current economic controversies, and the consequent disorder within economics as a discipline" (1982: preface). Revised and updated chapters on economic planning, the mixed economy, and the contemporary crisis now take up 50 of 150 pages. The same program of revision and updating is carried through in the fifth edition of 1986 (60 of 190 pages); the sixth edition of 1990 (60 of 185 pages); and the seventh edition of 1994 (64 of 180 pages). The eighth edition of 1999 makes major changes. In addition to some changes in earlier chapters, gone are the updating chapters of recent editions; in their place are chapters on women and the economy, World War II and the Cold War, capitalism after World War II, and a half-century of high theory (revision and updating accounts for some 90 of 225 pages). The ninth edition of 2002 adds a chapter on the new economy (and 10 more pages, of 235). The design strategy is clearly one of serious updating.

William Breit and Roger Ransom's *The Academic Scribblers* (first edition, 1971; revised edition, 1982) has as its design the idea of contemporary policy relevance. Seven of their twelve subjects are essentially pre-war (Marshall, Veblen, Pigou, Chamberlin, Keynes and Simons—all both background for and directly relevant to post-war problems of policy. One subject spans the pre- and post-war periods: Knight. The other five are primarily post-war: Hansen, Samuelson, Lerner, Galbraith and Friedman (as it turned out, the last four of these five are included in the eleven subjects of the quantitative analysis presented below).

Robert Ekelund and Robert Hébert's first edition of their *A History of Economic Theory and Method* (1975) has very limited post-war materials, covering Galbraith (and Veblen) and Friedman in fifteen pages, plus some historiography. Their second edition of 1983 has relatively negligible post-war coverage, including Friedman and monetarism, Galbraith, public choice theory, including Lindahl and Wicksell, and bureaucracy; and "the new political economy of regulation", e.g., Stigler and Friedland, Averch and Johnson, rent-seeking theory, capture theory, and the Chicago School. These total almost thirty-five pages; they devote only 150 of 540 pages to the entire twentieth century. In their third edition, 1990, recent developments in macroeconomics, Austrian economics, mathematical and empirical economics, and microeconomics are added. The chapter on public choice and regulation is slightly updated; two pages on Schumpeter are also added. The fourth edition, 1997, does not make major additions. From the beginning to the fourth edition the authors have updated somewhat limitedly and selectively but relatively effectively, given their objectives—though overall without a change in design.

The first edition (1976) of E. Ray Canterbery's *The Making of Economics* had about four and a half of fourteen chapters and the second edition (1980) had at least five and a half of fifteen chapters on post-war economics. The second edition's topics include Bastard Keynesians and the monetarists, Veblen and Galbraith, the new radical economics, economic crises, stagflation and the post-Keynesians, and further aspects of a paradigmatic vision. The third edition (1987) is also devoted to a wide range of post-war economic thought—at least one-half the book: largely chapters 8–17 of eighteen, and pages 143–364 of 372. The emphasis taken in his preface is clearly on carrying the story to the present day of his writing.

T.J. Kastelein *et al.*'s collection, *25 Years of Economic Theory: Retrospect and Prospect* (1976) deals with the recent history of several fields (consumer demand, macroeconomics, international trade, rationality, management science, and information theory) with a view to the future, but clearly violating Dorfman's rule with regard to the recent past.

Sidney Weintraub's edited collection, *Modern Economic Thought* (1977), not strictly speaking a textbook, presents twenty-seven intensive and extensive surveys of post-war economic topics. The principal topics (and number of essays) are Keynesianism (3), equilibrium systems (4), microeconomics (3), money (4), growth (3), and distribution theory (2). Other single-essay special topics are welfare economics, ideology, population, technology, international economics, development economics, and radical economics.

E.K. Hunt's *History of Economic Thought* presents an increasing amount of post-war material. The first edition (1979) had three of nineteen chapters, some 60 of 460 pages, and the second edition (1992) had four of nineteen chapters, and 120 of 640 pages, devoted to post-war economic thought. The latter's four chapters covered Sraffa, diversity within orthodoxy, institutionalism and post-Keynesianism, and the revival of critical political economy. The "updated second edition" (2002) continues but does not make much further effort at expansion. Some of the historical sketches and most of the contemporary material was changed; for example, discussions of such topics as the Soviet Union and the Cold War have been either omitted or rewritten fairly extensively. The history of ideas *per se* was changed very little. (Hunt's *Property and Prophets* (updated seventh edition, 2003) devotes two of its fourteen pages to the post-World War II period into the 1990s. This work is considered in more detail in chapter 3 of this volume.)

Elbert Bowden's *Economic Evolution* (1981), which is both idea- and issue-oriented, has extensive coverage of then-contemporary economic ideas. Much of it is macroeconomics—monetarism, post-Keynesianism, rational expectations, supply side economics—but aspects of international economics, business power, energy and pollution, and conflicting economic systems are presented, though in much less of a history-of-economic-thought manner.

Charles Staley's *A History of Economic Thought from Aristotle to Arrow* (1989) devotes two of twenty-one chapters and 24 of 264 pages to post-war developments, covering macroeconomics, econometrics and microeconomics.

Ernesto Screpanti and Stefano Zamagni devote one-third of their *Outline of the History of Economic Thought* (1993) to an extensive coverage of post-war economic theory, covering major topics in three sections entitled "Contemporary Economic Theory I, II, III."

Mark Skousen's *The Making of Modern Economics* (2001), perhaps the most overtly conservatively ideological of the textbooks in the US field, has four chapters on modern economics, covering Samuelson, Friedman, Schumpeter, and "the triumph of market economics."

Roger Backhouse has written three different histories of economic thought. Backhouse's *A History of Modern Economic Analysis* (1985) focuses on economic theory and on continuing the account to about 1980. Part I covers the background, political economy before 1870; part II, the "new systems" 1870–1890; part III, the neoclassical period, 1890–1939; and part IV, the modern period, 1939–1939. Part IV contains in ten of the thirty chapters and 140 of 415 pages the most comprehensive account of post-war developments found in any textbook. The chapter topics include scope and method; microeconomic theory; welfare economics; growth and capital theories; money, employment and inflation; international trade and development; alternatives to mainstream economics (oddly, the Chicago School is one of them); economics and policy in Britain; and comments on contemporary economics. And still it is selective and incomplete. But Backhouse self-consciously aims "to tell the story of how economic analysis has reached its present state" (1985: xi).

If his *History* is a story of theory, approximating an internalist (or absolutist) historiography, Backhouse's *Economists and the Economy* (1988) is externalist (or relativist); it combines economics and political economy with the history of economic ideas, with the former now dominant. It does not have the earlier book's concentration on the post-war period.

Backhouse's *The Ordinary Business of Life* (2002) is a combination of economic history and history of economic theory and ideas, a combination either more equal than the 1988 work or with more emphasis on theory and ideas. But it, like his first and unlike his second work, carries the story "to the present." Four chapters of 14, and some 90 of 330 pages, cover periods with varying beginning dates to the present: econometrics and mathematical economics, from 1930; welfare economics and socialism, from 1870; economists and policy, from 1939; and expanding the discipline, from 1960— all to the present.

Much of the foregoing is summarized in Table 2.1.

Non-textbook coverage largely stopping short of contemporary period

Many history-of-economic-thought writings deal with pre-war topics and subjects, for example, mercantilism, the Physiocrats, the classical economists, Marx, and so on. Here the question of recency of coverage does not arise. One group, some of which may slightly include the post-war period, is the Routledge series with volumes on Australia, Canada, France, and Sweden (Groenewegen and McFarlane 1990; Neill 1991; Faccarello 1998; and Sandelin 1991; see also Goodwin 1961; 1966) and more or less comparable books on the Netherlands and Spain (van Daal and Heertje 1992; Grice-Hutchinson 1993). Everett J. Burtt, Jr.'s *Social Perspectives in the History of Economic Theory* (1972), a study of controversy and its resolution, a very different type of work, commences with Petty to Quesnay and concludes with Walras to Pareto. Anthony Endres and Grant Fleming's (2002) study of economists' ideas in several international organizations covers the period 1919–1950 and thus complies, as it were, with Dorfman's rule, even extending it to a half-century, although one discussion relates to the literature of the 1970s to 1990s.

Non-textbook coverage of recent materials

Numerous non-textbook works and collections of pieces on recent individuals or schools or topics each amount to a structured history of economic thought for the topic and the period covered. Most, we suppose, have a termination date well before their date of publication (for example, D.K. Fieldhouse's *Economics and Empire, 1830–1914*, part I, "Explanations of Imperialism" (1973), John Creedy's *Development of the Theory of Exchange* (1988), which stops at the end of the nineteenth century, and June Flanders's *International Monetary Economics, 1870–1960* (1989); Philip L. Williams's *The Emergence of the Theory of the Firm* (1978), whose termination is, according to the subtitle, with Marshall, but which covers material published much later). But numerous such works and collections have been assembled for the post-war period; these include works which survey and interpret, and thereby provide proto-histories of economic thought for the periods and topics covered.

Essays on contemporary individual economists may not be, strictly speaking, history of economic thought. But such essays tend to identify and interpret the domain(s) in which the individual works so that identification and interpretation of both individual and domain(s) may constitute and certainly contributes to our understanding of the relevant history of the period.

Table 2.1   Coverage of recent topics in textbooks, alphabetical and by date of publication

Authors of textbook	Problem of recency explicitly discussed	Design change to acc. recent material	No/negligible coverage of recent materials	Some coverage of recent materials	Extensive coverage of recent materials
Asso 2001			X		
Backhouse 1985					X
1988				X	
2002					X
Barcer 1967			X		
Bell 1953	X			X	
1967	X			X	
Blaug 1962	X		X		
1968	X			X	
1978	X			X	
1986	X			X (less)	
1997	X			X (less)	
Boucke 1921			X		
Bowden 1981					X
Breit and Ransom 1971	X				X
1982	X				X

Table 2.1 continued

Authors of textbook	Problem of recency explicitly discussed 1	Design change to acc. recent material	No/negligible coverage of recent materials	Some coverage of recent materials	Extensive coverage of recent materials
Cannan					
1893			X		
Canterbery					
1976					X
1980					X
1987					X
1995				X	
Catlin					
1962			X		
Cossa					
1880					X
1893					X
Dasgupta					
1985				X	
Deane					
1978				X	
Dome					
1994				X	
Ekelund and					
Hébert					
1975				X	
1983				X	
1990					X
1997					X (no new)

Authors of textbook	Problem of recency explicitly discussed	Design change to acc. recent material	No/negligible coverage of recent materials	Some coverage of recent materials	Extensive coverage of recent materials
Ely					
2002 [1931]					X
Ferguson					
1938			X		
Finkelstein and Thimm					
1973			X		
Fusfeld					
1965					X
1972					X
1977					X
1982					X
1985					X
1990					X
1994					X
1999					X
2002					X
Gide and Rist					
1915				X	
1948				X	
Gill					
1967				X	

Table 2.1 continued

Authors of textbook	Problem of recency explicitly discussed	Design change to acc. recent material	No/negligible coverage of recent materials	Some coverage of recent materials	Extensive coverage of recent materials
Grey 1931			X		
Grey and Thompson 1980		X			X
Haney 1911			X		
1920			X		
1936		X		X	
1949		X		X	
Heilbroner 1953			X		
1961			X		
1967			X		
1976			X		
Heilbroner 1960	X				
Heimann 1945					X
Homan 1928					X
Hoover 1950				X	

Authors of textbook	Problem of recency explicitly discussed	Design change to acc. recent material	No/negligible coverage of recent materials	Some coverage of recent materials	Extensive coverage of recent materials
Hunt					
1979					X
1992					X
2002				X	
Hutchison					
1953			X		
Ingram					
1888				X	
Kastelein					
et al.					
1976					X
Kuhn					
1963	X		X		
1970	X			X	
Landreth					
1976			X		
Landreth					
and					
Colander					
1989				X	
1994		X		X	
2002		X		X	
Lekachman					
1959				X	

Table 2.1 continued

Authors of textbook	Problem of recency explicitly discussed1	Design change to acc. recent material	No/negligible coverage of recent materials	Some coverage of recent materials	Extensive coverage of recent materials
McConnell 1943			X		
Mitchell 1934-35[1949]					X
Napoleoni 1963					X
Neff 1946			X		
1950			X		
Negishi 1989	X		X		
Newman 1952				X	
Niehans 1990				X	
Oser 1963			X		
1970			X		
with Blanchfield 1975			X		
with Bruc 1988		X			X
1994		X			X

Authors of textbook	Problem of recency explicitly discussed	Design change to acc. recent material	No/negligible coverage of recent materials	Some coverage of recent materials	Extensive coverage of recent materials
by Brue 2000					X
Perelman and McCann 1998			X		
Pribram 1983			X		
Rima					
1967	X		X		
1972	X	X		X	
1978	X	X			X
1991	X	X			X
Roll					
1940	X				X
1942					X
1956					X
1974					X
Rogin 1956					X
Routh					
1975			X		
1989			X		

Table 2.1 continued

Authors of textbook	Problem of recency explicitly discussed	Design change to acc. recent material	No/negligible coverage of recent materials	Some coverage of recent materials	Extensive coverage of recent materials
Sandelin, Trautwein and Wundrak 2002				X	
Schumpeter 1912 [1967] 1954					X X X
Scott 1933			X		
Screpanti and Zamagni 1993					X
B. Seligman 1962	X				X
Sievers 1962					X
Skousen 2001					X

Authors of textbook	Problem of recency explicitly discussed	Design change to acc. recent material	No/negligible coverage of recent materials	Some coverage of recent materials	Extensive coverage of recent materials
Spiegel					
1971				X	
1983				X	
1991				X	
Staley					
1989				X	
Stark					
1943			X		
G. Stigler					
1948			X		
1965			X		
S. Stigler					
1986			X		
Suranyi-Unger					
1932					X
Taylor					
1960				X	
Walsh and Gram					
1980				X	
Weintraub					
1977					X
1985				X	

Table 2.1 continued

Authors of textbook	Problem of recency explicitly discussed	Design change to acc. recent material	No/negligible coverage of recent materials	Some coverage of recent materials	Extensive coverage of recent materials
Whittaker					
1940				X	
1960	X			X	
1980				X	
Zweig					
1950			X		

Note
[1] This column merely indicates whether the author(s) discussed the problem of recent economic thought. It does not mean that the author(s) who did so were in any agreement as to the nature of the problem or proposed solutions to dealing with the problem.

Emil Kauder's *A History of Marginal Utility Theory* (1965) carried the story into the 1960s.

John Presley's two co-edited volumes, *Pioneers of Modern Economics in Britain* (vol. 1, 1981, with D.P. O'Brien; vol. 2, 1989, with David Greenaway), include essays on economists active during and into the late post-war period.

Mark Blaug's *Great Economists Since Keynes* (1985b) presents material on contemporary economists, as do the three editions of his *Who's Who in Economics* (third edition, 1999); the latter's coverage is more comprehensive.

J.E. King's essays on *Economic Exiles* (1988) includes at least three (of eight) economists who were active in the post-war period.

W.W. Rostow's history of economic growth theorists (1990) not only advances to the present but gives "a perspective on the next century."

J.R. Shackleton's *New Thinking in Economics* (1990) surveys and interprets ten topics or areas; the coverage is very contemporary in relation to publication date. All but one of Shackleton and Gareth Locksley's subjects in *Twelve Contemporary Economists* (1981) (Kalecki) were producing contemporary work.

Edmund Phelps's (1990) *Seven Schools of Macroeconomic Thought* amounts to a broad history of post-war macroeconomics.

Douglas Mair and Anne Miller's *A Modern Guide to Economic Thought* (1991), close to being a textbook, surveys eight schools of modern economic thought.

The collections by Warren Samuels (1992b, and *inter alia* 1996b) and by Henry Spiegel and Samuels (1984) are entirely devoted to contemporary economists, as are Arnold Heertje's series, *The Makers of Modern Economics* (1993, 1995, 1997, 1999), Leonard Silk's *The Economists* (1976), and David Warsh's *Economic Principals* (1993), the latter two by leading economic journalists as is Sylvia Nasar's celebrated study of John Nash (1998).

Michel Beaud and Gilles Dostaler's *Economic Thought Since Keynes* (1995) is largely post-war in coverage and presents material by major topics and by individual.

John Davis's collection on recent developments in economics (1997) covers topics and themes not typically recognized as having taken place.

Ferdinando Meacci's collection, *Italian Economists of the 20th Century* (1998) has essays on twelve economists, five of whom have been active in the post-war period.

Steven Pressman's *Fifty Major Economists* (1999) starts with Thomas Mun but almost half the biographical entries worked in the post-war period and over half of them remain active.

David Reisman has authored no less than five intellectual biographies of important post-war economists (1977; 1980; 1990a; 1990b; 1997), thereby helping extend the period of recency to the present and contributing to the history of economic thought of the period.

The autobiographical essays in Michael Szenberg's *Eminent Economists* (1992) and *Passion and Craft* (1998)—together with biographical essays published elsewhere, such as in *American Economist* and *Banca Nazionale del Lavoro Quarterly*

Review—make often unique and insightful contributions to the understanding of post-war economics. The same applies to William Breit and Roger Spencer's collections of autobiographical essays by Nobel laureates in economics (1986; 1995).

All of these volumes constitute, in whole or in part, exercises in post-war history of economic thought.

Intentional interpretation of recent period

The authors of some books specifically attempt in some sense and/or within some scope to construct a particular interpretation of recent economic thought.

Richard Holt and Steven Pressman's *New Guide to Post Keynesian Economics* (2001) is a survey and interpretation that, like Alfred Eichner's earlier *Guide* (1978), somewhat doubles as a (selective) history of post-Keynesian economics. J.E. King's *A History of Post Keynesian Economics Since 1936* (2002) is an intentional and inevitably interpretive history carried to the end of the twentieth century.

Philip Mirowski's *Machine Dreams* (2002) is an interpretive account of certain sources of high theory in the post-war US and their role in the social construction of economics. Like his earlier *More Heat than Light* (1989) it is history of economics on a massively ambitious scale. He argues that economics has become a cyborg science (a concept he explores in depth), that neoclassical economics contributed to the other cyborg sciences at the same time that the other cyborg sciences influenced the development of economics. Central to this dual process was strategic decision-making, hence military finance of research, including game theory, the computer, and key elements of post-war economic theory. Mirowski's is a theory of the entire post-war period. So is E. Roy Weintraub's *How Economics Became a Mathematical Science* (2002), which also extends further back in history, as does his *Stabilizing Dynamics* (1991). Weintraub's *Toward a History of Game Theory* (1992) carries the story to well within Dorfman's quarter of a century. Whereas Mirowski's *More Heat than Light* traces the origin of modern economics to status emulation, i.e., economists emulating and copying both physics and the nineteenth-century mathematics of energy physics, Bruna Ingrao and Giorgio Israel's *The Invisible Hand* (1990) related developments in economics since the 1930s to parallel developments in mathematics. They too produced a status-emulation explanation of formalism, arguing that mathematization is not a secondary feature of general equilibrium theory but rather a basic reason for its creation and development.

Given, however, the long time frames of Mirowski's, Ingrao and Israel's, and Weintraub's books, the relevant notion of recency gives support to Dorfman's view that it will take some time before such systemic interpretations are possible. But only some support, and also support for the opposite view, assuming that interpretation of the post-war period to the present contradicts Dorfman's proscription.

Deirdre McCloskey's *The Vices of Economists, the Virtues of the Bourgeoisie* (1996) is in some respects an even wider interpretation that also contradicts Dorfman's rule (see also Brenner 1979).

Two different views of the origins of modern neoclassical microeconomics from that of Mirowski are provided by Endres (1997) and Ekelund and Hébert (1999).

An address and later book chapter on "The Evolution of Modern Economic Theory" by Lionel Robbins was given in 1960 and published in 1970. In it, Robbins has no hesitation in surveying, interpreting and evaluating work since Keynes into the 1950s.

Two essays recount, interpret and assess the development of economics during the middle half of the twentieth century, one (Spengler 1974) covering 1922–1972 and the other (Coats 1992) 1920–1970, well within Dorfman's period of recency.

Robert Hsu's study, *Economic Theories in China, 1979–1988* (1991) is as current history-of-economic-thought work as can be imagined.

Krishan Kumar's study of utopian and anti-utopian thought (1987) carries the history to its present day; so, too, do McNulty's history of labor economics (1980) and Noel Thompson's interpretive critique of British Democratic Socialist thought since 1979 (2002).

Part IV of Robert Nelson's *Economics as Religion* (2001) presents an interpretation of new institutional economics and its impact on American economics during the last three decades of the twentieth century.

Ben Fine's *Social Capital versus Social Theory* (2001) is both interpretation and critique of several concepts and trends.

A review essay by Melvin Reder (2003) considers both the decline of interest in issues of distribution and the change in the interpretation of the meaning and role of economic scientist by mainstream economists during the second half or last third of the twentieth century.

Theodore Rosenof's *Economics in the Long Run* (1997) is a study of principal New Deal theorists and their legacies for economic policy. The date of publication might seem to comport with Dorfman's rule but it is not clear how one would determine the starting date. A different treatment is McCarty (2001), a study of the shaping influence of Nobel laureates on various topics of post-war economic thought. Here the date of publication does not comport with Dorfman's rule.

The following sub-categories could easily be combined with elements of the foregoing.

Critiques of earlier work using recent work

Writings other than texts sometimes use recent materials in evaluating, critiquing, interpreting, rationally reconstructing and/or revising the work of earlier economists. Studies or collections of studies on earlier individual figures often use recent work, in part functioning to place the latter within and thereby reinforce a certain recent view of the history of economic thought. This is not recent history-of-economic-thought work *per se* but is close to it insofar as it points to recent work as important and may contribute to the understanding and/or social construction of the history of economic thought. Indeed, the uses of a theory, etc. may define its (original) meaning as much as if not more than the particular ideas of the economist whose name is associated with it. (If idea X could develop along paths X1, X2 or X3, and if it does develop (or is treated only as if it developed) as X3, X will take on the meaning and nuances of X3 rather than of X1 or X2, which, as noted above, will be forgotten.)

For example, many recent books have re-examined Adam Smith, critiquing and using other recent work on Smith, thereby changing, or rendering more complex if not more contradictory, both the nature and significance of Smith's work and the history of economic thought. These include works by Vivianne Brown (1994), Athol Fitzgibbons (1995), Charles Griswold (1999), Peter Minowitz (1993), Jerry Muller (1993), Spencer Pack (1991), Michael Shapiro (1993), Patricia Werhane (1991), Edwin West (1990), and Young (1997).

Other examples include Takashi Negishi (1994) on a variety of topics in the history of economic theory; Giovanni Caravale's collection on Ricardian economics (1985), Mark Blaug (1986a) on a variety of subjects, H.W. Arndt on the idea of economic development (1987), Horst Hanusch's collection on Schumpeterian economics (1988), Diana Hunt on competing paradigms in economic theories of development (1989), and Charles Oman and Ganeshan Wignaraja (1991) on varieties of development thinking.

Brian Loasby's *The Mind and Method of the Economist: A Critical Appraisal of Major Economists in the 20th Century* (1989) presents critiques of the work of economists from Alfred Marshall down to Frank Hahn, Herbert Simon and others, i.e., well into Dorfman's period. Neil de Marchi and Christopher Gilbert's collection, *History and Methodology of Econometrics* (1989) does likewise.

Sergio Nisticò and Domenico Tosato's *Competing Economic Theories* (2002) is a collection of studies of historical figures using recent work, functioning to place the latter in a certain view(s) of the history of economic thought.

It is easy to take for granted a work's definition of the history of economic thought in its area, if one takes it as obvious, but not if faced with rival identifications. Several different books on Vilfredo Pareto, for example, present more or less significantly different accounts of his work and thereby of his place in the history of economic thought and of his relation to present-day economics (see Bruni 2002; Cirillo 1979; McLure 2001; Samuels 1974a).

Critiques of Sraffian, radical, and Marx's economics by contemporary historians of economic thought and methodologists are presented in Fred Moseley's collection, *Heterodox Economic Theories: True or False?* (1995). Devotees or scholars of Sraffa and/or Marx have produced numerous volumes and articles critiquing their work.

Pierre Garrouste and Stavros Ioannides's *Evolution and Path Dependence in Economic Ideas* (2001) critiques and applies recent historiographical and other insights to the interpretation of earlier ideas. Their principal point is that all ideas have a history; they have meant different things at different times and to different people. One corollary is that the history is path dependent. Another emphasizes locked-in, if temporary, outcomes.

Critiques of recent work

Critiques of recent work sometimes provide contributions to the history of economic thought. Inasmuch as many new journal articles involve criticism or extension of other recent work, the positioning of each article relative to the preceding literature often constitutes a history of (relevant) economic thought. The same is true of book-length histories that also provide critiques.

Almost any issue of a journal will have at least several such articles. Numerous contributions to Fase *et al.* 1999 are good illustrations as are some in Caravale 1985; also Malinvaud 1977; Arndt 1987; McNulty 1980.

Readers in the history of economic thought

Attention should be given to readers in the history of economic thought. As with the textbooks in the field, while there is considerable variation at the level of particulars, i.e. individual excerpts, considerable structural homogeneity reigns at the level of the discipline as a whole—given date of publication, the sequence of major topics is fairly common. As to recency, however, Dorfman's rule is seemingly followed by some but not by all editors.

Starting with S. Howard Patterson's *Readings in the History of Economic Thought* (1932), the sequence defining the history of economic thought is pretty much the same as that edited by James A. Gherity, *Economic Thought: A Historical Anthology* (1965), given their respective dates of publication. The principal differences are: first, that Patterson starts with "Adam Smith and His Group" and Gherity with medieval economic thought; and, second, that Patterson concludes with "Miscellaneous American Writers," namely, Henry George, Francis A. Walker, and Simon Nelson Patten, and Gherity with the Stockholm School (Knut Wicksell). In other words, the two readers have in common an avoidance of recent economic thought, given their respective dates of publication. Patterson's coverage of economic theory ends with John Elliott Cairnes, William Stanley Jevons and Eugen Böhm-Bawerk; Carl Menger, Vilfredo Pareto, Leon Walras, Friedrich von Wieser and Alfred Marshall are absent. Patterson in effect follows Dorfman's rule, publishing in the early 1930s a collection that concludes near the end of the nineteenth century. Gherity, publishing in 1965, includes most of the aforementioned omitted by Patterson as well as Frank A. Fetter, John R. Commons, Thorstein Veblen, and Wicksell; in effect terminating in the early 1930s—also following Dorfman's rule.

The editor of *Masterworks of Economics: Digests of 10 Great Classics* (1946), Leonard Dalton Abbott, took no chances with Dorfman's rule. His latest-dated work is Veblen's *The Theory of the Leisure Class*, published in 1899. If Masterworks means "Great Classics," then a half-century version of the Dorfman rule would seem apposite.

Turning to *Source Readings in Economic Thought* (1954), edited by Philip C. Newman, Arthur D. Gayer, and Milton H. Spencer, the collection starts with Greek economic thought and concludes with a group on "Economic Stability and

Employment," namely, Wicksell, Bertil Ohlin, Keynes and Schumpeter. Further evidence that these editors do not follow Dorfman's rule is found in their relatively extensive coverage of work from the 1930s and 1940s, including Commons, the writers on imperfect competition, and Oskar Morgenstern and game theory.

The first edition of K. William Kapp and Lore L. Kapp's *Readings in Economics* (1949) commenced with excerpts from St. Thomas Aquinas and Martin Luther. The latest published items included in the collection are materials from Schumpeter, Abba Lerner, and Soviet and British planning (no Keynes). The second edition (1963) added or substituted materials from Keynes, Wassily Leontief, Arthur Spiethoff, John Kenneth Galbraith and Gunnar Myrdal. Dorfman's rule is not followed.

Howard L. Balsley's two volumes, *Economic Doctrines* (1961) seemingly followed Dorfman's proscription in one volume but not in the other. Volume 1, *Theory and Practice*, includes nothing later than excerpts from Lionel Robbins, Keynes, and Joan Robinson from the early and mid-1930s. Volume 2, *The Economy and Its Problems*, includes material from Alvin Hansen published in 1941, Roy Harrod in 1951, Roy Blough in 1952, Sumner Slichter in 1948, Edwin Witte in 1944, Theodore W. Schultz in 1945, Kenneth Boulding in 1945, Harold Moulton in 1949, Barbara Wooton in 1945, and Friedrich von Hayek in 1944. Recent materials are omitted from Volume 1 but are included in Volume 2. The explanation may be that Volume 1 deals with theoretical topics and Volume 2 deals more so, but by no means solely, with policy issues.

Personal citations

An analysis was made of the number of references included for certain names in the indexes of the history-of-economic-thought textbooks. The names, indicated below in the tables, are an arbitrarily chosen selection of eleven prominent post-war economists; no similar analysis was made of pre-war economists. The number of references for each person is a function of the idiosyncrasies and detail of indexing, the story being told and how it is told, the differential efficiency or verbosity of the author, and, *inter alia*, the author's emphasis on theory versus policy, etc. Not all citations are equal: one page should count for less than fourteen pages, and some citations are to text and others to notes, but no adjustments have been made (for a discussion of the issues involved in this type of approach, see Biddle 1996; see also Stigler and Friedland 1975). In some cases, perhaps especially that of George Stigler, some citations pertain to the subject's contributions as a practitioner and others as a historian of economic thought; no distinction is deemed either necessary or desirable for present purposes, as both types are indexed contributions. Apropos of the seeming idiosyncrasies in the citation identified below, we expect a different list of subjects would exhibit similar ones; it is the fact of oddities, not necessarily their particular substance that is important; and, we repeat, some references are to multiple pages (for example, the one reference to Samuelson in Routh 1989 is "316–37 *passim*").

In Table 2.2 the books are listed, ascending, by year of publication, so an overall sense of progression can be had. In Table 2.3, we list the sequence of editions by author of multiple editions, so a sense of their progression can be gained. (Roger Backhouses's three textbooks are not, strictly speaking, a series of editions.)

The tables suggest something of the variability of fortunes of these eleven individuals: (1) among authors; (2) between editions; and (3) over time overall. All eleven economists worked principally if not entirely in the post-war period. Of course, some of Samuelson's early works are now some fifty years old and, by Dorfman's rule, do not fall within the period of recency. The same applies to most of the others.

An enormous variety of citations and patterns for particular individuals is observed. This is due in part to different author interests, e.g., whether the text is oriented toward theory or to ideas and doctrines, whether the author largely accepts or rejects the development of economic thought as it came about, emphasis on particular topics, and the same themes being illustrated with different names. These are highly individualized accounts but within the relatively common overall structure.

The total number of index references for each individual is as follows:

Samuelson	383
Friedman	314
Hicks	255
Stigler	144
Galbraith	140
Arrow	89
Solow	77
Lerner	70
Becker	68
Debreu	46
Lucas	44

Clearly observable are the long periods, commencing with the publication of their first major work, that eventually important individuals are not recognized and included in the textbooks.

We cannot help but remark that it is likely that—with the principal exception of Backhouse's *A History of Modern Economic Analysis* (1985)—the bulk of student readers will not learn from the textbooks of the enormous paradigmatic and substantive importance of Paul A. Samuelson during the post-war period—like it or not. As Schumpeter foresaw, this has been the Age of Samuelson but the limited coverage of recent/contemporary work obscures him as a, if not the, principal source of the modern paradigm and high theory. This is not the only such example—Gerard Debreu and John R. Hicks are others—but it is a substantial one. That such judgments are subjective does not negate the perceived widespread failure. Two moderating considerations are, first, that in Table 2.2 Samuelson does receive the highest number of references; and, second, that various themes with regard to development can be illustrated with different names. Two persons who come off perhaps better than might be expected are George J. Stigler and Abba Lerner.

Table 2.6 presents dates of birth and of final earned degree plus age in degree year. Ages at final degree vary from twenty-one to forty; the average is twenty-nine (for many, because of World War II).

Tables 2.2 and 2.3 indicate that citations first increase and, after a while, notably in books with multiple editions, then decline. One could infer that greater emphasis on recency leads first to more citations and thereafter, with the passing of the recency of these individuals, to fewer citations. But individuals must wait to first be included.

Index references to Arrow are slow in coming. Some recognition is found in his second decade of post-PhD professional activity; it is increased in his third decade and the increase is continued in his fourth decade. The references are not concentrated in the theory textbooks but he is relatively popular in those books (see also Table 2.4). The maximum number of references to Arrow is fourteen, in Weintraub 1977; he received thirteen in Niehans 1990 and Screpanti and Zamagni 1993.

Becker receives some slight recognition in his second decade; this increases in his third and fourth decades. References tend to be concentrated in the theory texts (see Table 2.4). Becker's maximum number of references is fifteen in Ekelund and Hébert 1997, and twelve in their 1990 edition.

Debreu receives negligible and uneven recognition, even in the theory texts; recognition increases in his fourth decade. His largest number of references is seven, in Weintraub 1977; he receives six in Niehans 1990 and five in Backhouse 2002.

Friedman receives some recognition in his first and second decades; thereafter, wide and numerous, albeit uneven, recognition. His largest number of references is 119, in Skousen 2001, incidentally the most self-consciously and conspicuously ideology-driven, pro-mainstream textbook. The next highest number is forty-nine, in Breit and Ransom 1971; then twenty-two in Weintraub 1977, twenty in Blaug 1997, and between fourteen and nineteen in five books.

Galbraith receives some recognition in his third decade; thereafter, wide but uneven recognition. His largest number is sixty-four, in Breit and Ransom 1967. The next highest number is twenty-nine in Canterbery 1980, and between eighteen and twenty-four in five books—and fourteen in Skousen 2001.

Hicks is recognized in his second decade and widely, though unevenly, recognized thereafter. His largest number of references is forty-one, in Blaug 1978. The next highest number is thirty-seven in Blaug 1985a, and between eighteen and thirty-one in seven books.

Lerner received sporadic but significant references in his first and second decades, and widespread but relatively low numbers thereafter. His maximum is thirty-seven, in Breit and Ransom 1967; Blaug 1968 has twelve and Blaug 1978, eleven.

Lucas is given widespread recognition beginning in his second decade but with relatively low numbers. His largest number is five in Mair and Miller 1991; four textbooks have four references.

Samuelson is recognized early, in his first decade, by Haney 1949 (six references) and Schumpeter 1954 (sixteen references). His largest number is 100, in Skousen 2001, followed by 74 in Breit and Ransom 1967, 41 in Niehans 1990, 33 in Weintraub 1977, 31 in Backhouse 1985, 30 in Blaug 1985a and between 12 and 29 in thirteen other works.

Solow is referenced in his second decade and widespread thereafter, though unevenly in both periods. His largest number of references is seventeen, in Niehans 1990, followed by fourteen in Weintraub 1977 and seven or eight in six other works.

Stigler is given some early recognition in his first decade (two references in Haney 1949 and fourteen in Schumpeter 1954); recognition increases in his second and, especially, his third decade; altogether recognition is widespread but uneven. Ekelund and Hébert, who give him his maximum number of references, thirty-one, in 1990, increase their numbers in successive editions, decreasing in 1997 to twenty-seven. A similar pattern is found in Blaug, with a maximum of twenty-four in 1985a, decreasing to thirteen in 1996. Altogether, twelve textbooks have between twelve and thirty-one references to him.

One pertinent result of the foregoing is that most of these authors are first referenced in history-of-economic-thought textbooks in their second decade; some in their first. This conflicts with Dorfman's rule yet their inclusion would be hard to criticize.

Turning specifically to Table 2.3, multi-edition textbooks, one tendency is for the total numbers for all eleven individuals to increase and then decrease over time. This is true also for particular individuals but overall the individual patterns vary. For example, Blaug's totals for successive editions are 72, 113, 141, 144, and 119; Ekelund and Hébert's, 81, 95, 138, and 92; and Landreth and Colander, 35, 45, 56, and 30; in comparison, Rima's successive totals are 46, 43, 29, 39, 40, and 44. Through Blaug's five editions, for example, Arrow's, Hicks's and Stigler's references increase and then decrease; Friedman's increase; and Samuelson's increases and reaches something of a plateau. Roll's numbers increase dramatically: 1, 3, 3, 10 and 38.

The per-decade number of references increase:

1940s:	5
1950s:	11
1960s:	35 (23)
1970s:	37
1980s:	50
1990s:	62
2000s:	89 (30)

(The numbers in parentheses represent the omission of Breit and Ransom's 234 citations in 1967 and Skousen's 264 in 2001.) Given the cyclical pattern identified above, the total should be more stable; these numbers may be idiosyncratic.

The authorial totals in Table 2.4 indicate that the eleven economists, who are primarily theorists of various sorts, are highly referenced in the theory-oriented textbooks compared with the textbooks not oriented toward theory (included in Table 2.2). Table 2.5 indicates that these economists also figure prominently in the textbooks critical of the development of economics.

John R. Hicks is the clearly predominant figure of the group of eleven for the period of the 1940s and early 1950s; then come George Stigler, Abba Lerner and Paul Samuelson. Of course, several of the others had not commenced their careers; Gary Becker was born in 1930 and Lucas in 1937.

The number of books each with numbers of references between zero and, say, six into the 1970s is not insubstantial and is largely explained by design strategies excluding or having no need for current work.

For all of Joseph Schumpeter's (1954) breadth, his death precluded inclusion of work from the early 1950s but his total count represents a 52 percent increase over the previous totals leader, Haney (1949). But Schumpeter's total is surpassed by Blaug's 76 percent increase in 1962. Both claim to be focused on theory. Strikingly, the next book to exceed forty in total references is one that is highly critical of the development of economic theory, Seligman 1962, whereas Schumpeter and Blaug are largely laudatory.

The journal literature

Textbooks on the history of economic thought are limited in their breadth and depth of coverage of topics by their mission as textbooks. One might expect that, given the opportunity to choose their own topics, some historians of economic thought would elect to examine recent theory, people, or policy. However, we find both that recent economic theory garners only limited attention in history-of-economic-thought journals and that the extent and treatment of the problem of recency in the journal literature differs little from its treatment in textbooks. Four history of economic thought journals—*History of Political Economy, Journal of the History of Economic Thought, European Journal of the History of Economic Thought,* and *History of Economic Ideas*—were surveyed to determine and document the extent to which recent topics were covered, recent defined by Dorfman's twenty-five-year rule.[8] All articles, notes and comments were examined, though book reviews were not considered.

In *History of Political Economy,* through volume 33 (1969–2001), slightly less than 10 percent of articles dealt with recent economic theory or the recent history of economics as a discipline.[9] The vast majority of these articles dealt with either the present state of the economics discipline or with methodological issues, with a few articles on field-specific topics, the development of certain fields, and the development and use of mathematical economics and econometrics.

In the *Journal of the History of Economic Thought* approximately 15 percent of articles (1990 to 2001) can be considered to address recent issues in economic thought, with most of the articles examining the present state of economics.

Table 2.2 References to prominent post-war economists in all textbooks, by date of publication

Name	KJA	GSB	GD	MF	JKG	JRH	APL	REL	PAS	RMS	GJS	Total
1880 Cossa												
1888 Ingram												
1911 Haney												
1912 Schumpeter												
1915 Gide and Rist												
1920 Haney												
1921 Boucke												
1928 Homan												
1931 [2002] Ely												
1933 Scott												
1936 Haney												
1938 Ferguson												
1940 Roll	0	0	0	0	0	1	0	0	0	0	0	1
1942 Roll	0	0	0	0	0	3	0	0	0	0	0	3
1945 McConnell	0	0	0	0	0	0	0	0	0	0	0	0
1945 Heimann	0	0	0	0	0	0	0	0	0	0	0	0
1946 Neff	0	0	0	0	0	0	0	0	0	0	0	0

Table 2.2 Continued

Name	KJA	GSB	GD	MF	JKG	JRH	APL	REL	PAS	RMS	GJS	Total
1946 Roll	0	0	0	0	0	3	0	0	0	0	0	3
1949 Haney	0	0	0	0	0	12	7	0	6	0	2	27
1950 Neff	0	0	0	0	0	0	0	0	0	0	0	0
1952 Newman	0	0	0	0	0	6	0	0	0	0	0	6
1953 Bell	0	0	0	0	0	5	0	0	1	0	9	15
1953 Heilbroner	0	0	0	0	3	0	0	0	0	0	0	3
1954 Schumpeter	0	0	0	1	0	2	8	0	16	0	14	41
1956 Rogin	0	0	0	0	0	3	1	0	0	0	0	4
1956 Roll	0	0	0	1	0	4	0	0	5	0	0	10
1959 Lekachman	1	0	0	0	0	4	1	0	1	0	0	7
1960 Taylor	0	0	0	0	0	0	0	0	0	0	0	0
1960 Whittaker	1	0	0	0	1	7	0	0	0	0	1	10
1961 Heilbroner	0	0	0	0	3	0	0	0	0	0	0	3
1962 Blaug	2	1	1	8	1	27	6	0	13	0	13	72
1962 Catlin	0	0	0	0	1	7	0	0	1	0	2	11
1962 Seligman	4	0	0	5	4	9	4	0	12	1	9	48
1962 Sievers	0	0	0	0	12	0	0	0	0	0	1	13

Name	KJA	GSB	GD	MF	JKG	JRH	APL	REL	PAS	RMS	GJS	Total
1963 Kuhn	0	0	0	0	0	2	0	0	2	0	0	4
1963 Oser	0	0	0	0	0	0	0	0	0	0	0	0
1966 Fusfeld	0	0	0	0	3	0	0	0	1	0	0	4
1967 Barber	0	0	0	0	2	0	0	0	0	0	0	2
1967 Bell	0	0	0	2	0	6	0	0	8	3	11	30
1967 Breit and Ransom	0	0	0	49	64	6	31	0	74	6	4	234
1967 Gill	0	0	0	2	3	1	0	0	1	1	1	9
1967 Heilbroner	0	0	0	0	2	0	0	0	0	0	0	2
1967 Rima	1	0	0	2	0	18	6	0	6	4	9	46
1968 Blaug	4	3	3	13	2	31	12	0	19	5	21	113
1970 Kuhn	0	0	0	5	0	3	3	0	5	0	0	16
1970 Oser	0	0	0	0	2	1	0	0	1	0	1	5
1971 Spiegel	2	0	0	6	5	7	1	0	7	0	3	31
1972 Fusfeld	0	0	0	3	4	1	0	0	3	0	0	11
1972 Rima	5	0	0	3	3	13	3	0	7	4	5	43
1973 Finkelstein and Thimm	0	0	0	1	6	0	0	0	3	0	0	10
1974 Roll	3	0	0	7	4	8	1	0	13	2	0	38

Table 2.2 Continued

Name	KJA	GSB	GD	MF	JKG	JRH	APL	REL	PAS	RMS	GJS	Total
1975 Ekelund and Hébert	2	1	1	16	24	11	1	0	7	0	18	81
1975 Oser and Blanchfield	1	0	0	2	1	1	0	0	2	0	1	8
1975 Routh	0	0	0	0	7	3	1	0	1	0	0	12
1976 Canterbery	1	0	0	13	19	2	0	1	6	0	0	42
1972 Heilbroner	0	0	0	1	3	0	0	0	1	0	1	6
1976 Kastelein												
1976 Landreth	3	0	1	3	3	8	2	0	13	1	1	35
1977 Fusfeld	1	0	0	3	6	1	0	0	2	0	0	13
1977 Weintraub	14	4	7	22	6	33	8	1	33	14	9	151
1978 Blaug	6	2	4	16	2	41	11	0	26	8	25	141
1978 Deane	0	0	0	5	0	9	0	0	4	1	6	25
1978 Rima	1	3	0	6	2	9	1	0	2	1	4	29
1979 Hunt	0	0	0	3	0	0	0	0	3	0	0	6
1980 Canterbery	2	1	0	10	29	5	5	2	9	1	0	64
1980 Gray and Thompson	0	0	0	4	14	7	0	0	0	0	0	25
1981 Bowden	0	0	0	8	3	0	0	1	2	0	0	14
1982 Fusfeld	1	0	0	3	6	1	0	0	1	0	0	12

Name	KJA	GSB	GD	MF	JKG	JRH	APL	REL	PAS	RMS	GJS	Total
1983 Ekelund and Hébert	7	6	0	17	18	11	3	1	9	0	23	95
1983 Spiegel	3	2	0	8	5	11	1	0	10	0	4	44
1985 Backhouse	8	2	4	8	1	27	5	4	31	7	2	99
1985 Blaug	5	2	3	18	2	37	14	2	30	7	24	144
1985 Dasgupta	0	0	0	0	0	9	0	0	3	0	0	12
1986 Fusfeld	0	0	0	4	5	1	0	0	1	0	0	11
1986 Rima	0	3	0	9	4	15	3	0	4	0	1	39
1987 Canterbery	1	0	0	13	14	1	3	1	9	1	0	43
1988 Backhouse	2	1	1	5	0	0	0	2	2	1	0	14
1988 Oser and Brue												
1989 Landreth and Colander	4	1	2	1	3	6	6	1	11	8	2	45
1989 Negishi	6	1	2	3	1	11	0	0	16	1	2	43
1989 Routh	0	0	0	0	7	6	1	0	1	0	0	15
1989 Staley	2	2	1	7	1	12	0	2	20	3	12	62
1990 Ekelund and Hébert	8	12	4	19	21	20	4	1	16	2	31	138
1990 Fusfeld	0	0	0	8	6	0	1	0	2	0	0	17
1990 Niehans	13	1	6	14	1	28	8	3	41	17	11	143

Table 2.2 Continued

Name	KJA	GSB	GD	MF	JKG	JRH	APL	REL	PAS	RMS	GJS	Total
1991 Mair and Miller	1	0	0	14	3	6	2	5	2	0	0	33
1991 Rima	0	3	0	8	6	15	3	0	4	0	1	40
1991 Spiegel	3	2	0	8	5	11	1	0	10	0	4	44
1992 Hunt	0	0	0	4	0	0	0	0	6	0	0	10
1993 Screpanti and Zamagni	13	0	9	5	4	15	4	3	15	7	2	77
1994 Oser and Brue	3	8	1	8	6	7	7	2	17	3	9	71
1994 Dome	1	1	2	5	0	13	1	0	9	4	2	38
1994 Fusfeld	2	0	1	2	4	0	0	0	2	0	0	11
1994 Landreth and Colander	5	3	3	6	6	7	3	4	11	5	3	56
1995 Canterbery	0	0	0	7	24	4	2	4	12	3	1	57
1995 Rothbard	0	0	0	1	1	0	0	0	1	0	0	3
1996 Blaug	4	2	3	20	2	30	7	4	29	5	13	119
1996 Rima	4	3	1	7	6	11	5	0	5	1	1	44
1997 Ekelund and Hébert	8	15	3	10	3	10	4	3	8	1	27	92
1998 Perlman and McCann	2	1	2	5	1	1	1	0	2	0	12	27
1999 Fusfeld	3	0	1	3	4	0	0	1	4	1	0	17
2000 (Oser) and Brue												

Name	KJA	GSB	GD	MF	JKG	JRH	APL	REL	PAS	RMS	GJS	Total
2001 Skousen	3	6	0	119	14	7	2	0	100	5	8	264
2002 Backhouse	5	2	5	4	1	6	1	4	12	3	1	44
2002 Landreth and Colander	1	1	1	4	5	2	2	2	6	5	1	30
2002 Salanti *et al.*	0	0	0	3	1	2	0	3	5	2	0	16
2002 Hunt	0	0	0	5	0	0	0	0	6	0	0	11
2002 Fusfeld	4	0	2	3	4	0	0	1	4	1	0	19
Totals	176	95	74	608	439	663	207	58	793	145	368	3626

Note:
KJA Arrow   APL Lerner
GSB Becker   REL Lucas
GD   Debreu   PAS Samuelson
MF   Friedman   RMS Solow
JKG Galbraith   GJS Stigler
JRH Hicks

Table 2.3 References to prominent post-war economists in multi-edition textbooks

Name	KJA	GSB	GD	MF	JKG	JRH	APL	REL	PAS	RMS	GJS	Total
1985 Backhouse	8	2	4	8	1	27	5	4	31	7	2	99
1988 Backhouse	2	1	1	5	0	0	0	2	2	1	0	14
2002 Backhouse	5	2	5	4	1	6	1	4	12	3	1	44
1953 Bell	0	0	0	0	0	5	0	0	1	0	9	15
1967 Bell	0	0	0	2	0	6	0	0	8	3	11	30
1962 Blaug	2	1	1	8	1	27	6	0	13	0	13	72
1968 Blaug	4	3	3	13	2	31	12	0	19	5	21	113
1978 Blaug	6	2	4	16	2	41	11	0	26	8	25	141
1985 Blaug	5	2	3	18	2	37	14	2	30	7	24	144
1996 Blaug	4	2	3	20	2	30	7	4	29	5	13	119
1976 Canterbery	1	0	0	13	19	2	0	1	6	0	0	42
1980 Canterbery	2	1	0	10	29	5	5	2	9	1	0	64
1987 Canterbery	1	0	0	13	14	1	3	1	9	1	0	43
1995 Canterbery	0	0	0	7	24	4	2	4	12	3	1	57

Name	KJA	GSB	GD	MF	JKG	JRH	APL	REL	PAS	RMS	GJS	Total
1975 Ekelund and Hébert	2	1	1	16	24	11	1	0	7	0	18	81
1983 Ekelund and Hébert	7	6	0	17	18	11	3	1	9	0	23	95
1990 Ekelund and Hébert	8	12	4	19	21	20	4	1	16	2	31	138
1997 Ekelund and Hébert	8	15	3	10	3	10	4	3	8	1	27	92
1966 Fusfeld	0	0	0	0	3	0	0	0	1	0	0	4
1972 Fusfeld	0	0	0	3	4	1	0	0	3	0	0	11
1977 Fusfeld	1	0	0	3	6	1	0	0	2	0	0	13
1982 Fusfeld	1	0	0	3	6	1	0	0	1	0	0	12
1986 Fusfeld	0	0	0	4	5	1	0	0	1	0	0	11
1990 Fusfeld	0	0	0	8	6	0	1	0	2	0	0	17
1994 Fusfeld	2	0	1	2	4	0	0	0	2	0	0	11
1999 Fusfeld	3	0	1	3	4	0	0	1	4	1	0	17
2002 Fusfeld	4	0	2	3	4	0	0	1	4	1	0	19
1911 Haney												
1920 Haney												

Table 2.3 Continued

Name	KJA	GSB	GD	MF	JKG	JRH	APL	REL	PAS	RMS	GJS	Total
1936 Haney												
1949 Haney	0	0	0	0	0	12	7	0	6	0	2	27
1953 Heilbroner	0	0	0	0	3	0	0	0	0	0	0	3
1961 Heilbroner	0	0	0	0	3	0	0	0	0	0	0	3
1967 Heilbroner	0	0	0	0	2	0	0	0	0	0	0	2
1976 Heilbroner	0	0	0	1	3	0	0	0	1	0	1	6
1979 Hunt	0	0	0	3	0	0	0	0	3	0	0	6
1992 Hunt	0	0	0	4	0	0	0	0	6	0	0	10
2002 Hunt	0	0	0	5	0	0	0	0	6	0	0	11
1963 Kuhn	0	0	0	0	0	2	0	0	2	0	0	4
1970 Kuhn	0	0	0	5	0	3	3	0	5	0	0	16
1976 Landreth	3	0	1	3	3	8	2	0	13	1	1	35
1989 Landreth and Colander	4	1	2	1	3	6	6	1	11	8	2	45
1994 Landreth and Colander	5	3	3	6	6	7	3	4	11	5	3	56

Name	KJA	GSB	GD	MF	JKG	JRH	APL	REL	PAS	RMS	GJS	Total
2002 Landreth and Colander	1	1	1	4	5	2	2	2	6	5	1	30
1946 Neff	0	0	0	0	0	0	0	0	0	0	0	0
1950 Neff	0	0	0	0	0	0	0	0	0	0	0	0
1963 Oser	0	0	0	0	0	0	0	0	0	0	0	0
1970 Oser	0	0	0	0	2	1	0	0	1	0	1	5
1975 Oser and Blanchfield	1	0	0	2	1	1	0	0	2	0	1	8
1938 Oser and Brue												
1994 Oser and Brue	3	8	1	8	6	7	7	2	17	3	9	71
2000 (Oser) and Brue												
1967 Rima	1	0	0	2	0	18	6	0	6	4	9	46
1972 Rima	5	0	0	3	3	13	3	0	7	4	5	43
1978 Rima	1	3	0	6	2	9	1	0	2	1	4	29
1986 Rima	0	3	0	9	4	15	3	0	4	0	1	39
1991 Rima	0	3	0	8	6	15	3	0	4	0	1	40
1996 Rima	4	3	1	7	6	11	5	0	5	1	1	44

Table 2.3 Continued

Name	KJA	GSB	GD	MF	JKG	JRH	APL	REL	PAS	RMS	GJS	Total
1940 Roll	0	0	0	0	0	1	0	0	0	0	0	1
1942 Roll	0	0	0	0	0	3	0	0	0	0	0	3
1946 Roll	0	0	0	0	0	3	0	0	0	0	0	3
1956 Roll	0	0	0	1	0	4	0	0	5	0	0	10
1974 Roll	3	0	0	7	4	8	1	0	13	2	0	38
1975 Routh	0	0	0	0	7	3	1	0	1	0	0	12
1989 Routh	0	0	0	0	7	6	1	0	1	0	0	15
1971 Spiegel	2	0	0	6	5	7	1	0	7	0	3	31
1983 Spiegel	3	2	0	8	5	11	1	0	10	0	4	44
1991 Spiegel	3	2	0	8	5	11	1	0	10	0	4	44

Note:
KJA	Arrow	APL	Lerner
GSB	Becker	REL	Lucas
GD	Debreu	PAS	Samuelson
MF	Friedman	RMS	Solow
JKG	Galbraith	GJS	Stigler
JRH	Hicks		

Table 2.4 References to prominent post-war economists in theory-oriented textbooks

Name	KJA	GSB	GD	MF	JKG	JRH	APL	REL	PAS	RMS	GJS	Total
1985 Backhouse	8	2	4	8	1	27	5	4	31	7	2	99
1962 Blaug	2	1	1	8	1	27	6	0	13	0	13	72
1968 Blaug	4	3	3	13	2	31	12	0	19	5	21	113
1978 Blaug	6	2	4	16	2	41	11	0	26	8	25	141
1985 Blaug	5	2	3	18	2	37	14	2	30	7	24	144
1996 Blaug	4	2	3	20	2	30	7	4	29	5	13	119
1985 Dasgupta	0	0	0	0	0	9	0	0	3	0	0	12
1994 Dome	1	1	2	5	0	13	1	0	9	4	2	38
1975 Ekelund and Hébert	2	1	1	16	24	11	1	0	7	0	18	81
1983 Ekelund and Hébert	7	6	0	17	18	11	3	1	9	0	23	95
1990 Ekelund and Hébert	8	12	4	19	21	20	4	1	16	2	31	138

Table 2.4 Continued

Name	KJA	GSB	GD	MF	JKG	JRH	APL	REL	PAS	RMS	GJS	Total
1997 Ekelund and Hébert	8	15	3	10	3	10	4	3	8	1	27	92
1976 Landreth	3	0	1	3	3	8	2	0	13	1	1	35
1989 Landreth and Colander	4	1	2	1	3	6	6	1	11	8	2	45
1994 Landreth and Colander	5	3	3	6	6	7	3	4	11	5	3	56
2002 Landreth and Colander	1	1	1	4	5	2	2	2	6	5	1	30
1989 Negishi	6	1	2	3	1	11	0	0	16	1	2	43
1990 Niehans	13	1	6	14	1	28	8	3	41	17	11	143
1967 Rima	1	0	0	2	0	18	6	0	6	4	9	46
1972 Rima	5	0	0	3	3	13	3	0	7	4	5	43
1978 Rima	1	3	0	6	2	9	1	0	2	1	4	29
1986 Rima	0	3	0	9	4	15	3	0	4	0	1	39
1991 Rima	0	3	0	8	6	15	3	0	4	0	1	40
1996 Rima	4	3	1	7	6	11	5	0	5	1	1	44

Name	KJA	GSB	GD	MF	JKG	JRH	APL	REL	PAS	RMS	GJS	Total
1991 Rima	0	3	0	8	6	15	3	0	4	0	1	40
1996 Rima	4	3	1	7	6	11	5	0	5	1	1	44
1954 Schumpeter	0	0	0	1	0	2	8	0	16	0	14	41

Note:
KJA   Arrow
GSB   Becker
GD   Debreu
MF   Friedman
JKG   Galbraith
JRH   Hicks
APL   Lerner
REL   Lucas
PAS   Samuelson
RMS   Solow
GJS   Stigler

Table 2.5 References to prominent post-war economists in textbooks emphasizing criticism of development of economics

Name	KJA	GSB	GD	MF	JKG	JRH	APL	REL	PAS	RMS	GJS	Total
1956 Rogin	0	0	0	0	0	3	1	0	0	0	0	4
1959 Lekachman	1	0	0	0	0	4	1	0	1	0	0	7
1962 Seligman	4	0	0	5	4	9	4	0	12	1	9	48
1966 Fusfeld	0	0	0	0	3	0	0	0	1	0	0	4
1972 Fusfeld	0	0	0	3	4	1	0	0	3	0	0	11
1975 Routh	0	0	0	0	7	3	1	0	1	0	0	12
1976 Canterbery	1	0	0	13	19	2	0	1	6	0	0	42
1977 Fusfeld	1	0	0	3	6	1	0	0	2	0	0	13
1980 Canterbery	2	1	0	10	29	5	5	2	9	1	0	64
1982 Fusfeld	1	0	0	3	6	1	0	0	1	0	0	12
1986 Fusfeld	0	0	0	4	5	1	0	0	1	0	0	11
1989 Routh	0	0	0	0	7	6	1	0	1	0	0	15
1990 Fusfeld	0	0	0	8	6	0	1	0	2	0	0	17
1992 Hunt	0	0	0	4	0	0	0	0	6	0	0	10
1994 Fusfeld	2	0	1	0	4	0	0	0	2	0	0	11

Name	KJA	GSB	GD	MF	JKG	JRH	APL	REL	PAS	RMS	GJS	Total
1994 Fustfeld	2	0	1	2	4	0	0	0	2	0	0	11
1995 Canterbery	0	0	0	7	24	4	2	4	12	3	1	57
1999 Fustfeld	3	0	1	3	4	0	0	1	4	1	0	17
2002 Fustfeld	4	0	2	3	4	0	0	1	4	1	0	19
2002 Hunt	0	0	0	5	0	0	0	0	6	0	0	11

Note:
KJA Arrow   APL Lerner
GSB Becker   REL Lucas
GD   Debreu   PAS Samuelson
MF   Friedman   RMS Solow
JKG Galbraith   GJS Stigler
JRH Hicks

Table 2.6 Dates of final earned degree and of birth

Name	Date of final earned degree	Date of birth	Age in degree
Arrow	1951	1921	30
Becker	1955	1930	25
Debreu	1956	1921	35
Friedman	1946	1912	34
Galbraith	1934	1908	26
Hicks	1925	1904	21
Lerner	1943	1903	40
Lucas	1964	1937	27
Samuelson	1941	1915	26
Solow	1951	1924	27
Stigler	1938	1911	27

Note: (All PhD except Hicks (BA))

In the *European Journal of the History of Economic Thought*, 6 percent of articles dealt with recent economic topics in the journal's first seven volumes (1993–2000).

In the first nine volumes of *History of Economic Ideas* (1993–2001) approximately 10 percent of articles addressed recent topics, though fewer were focused on the current state of economics and methodological issues than *HOPE* or *JHET*, and more examined recent economic theory.

In all four journals, the number of articles devoted to recent economics and recent economic theory is consistent over time. Only two articles, Heilbroner (1979) and Porta (1994) directly addressed the problem of recency.

Materials not specifically history of economic thought

It is one of the principal findings of this study that Dorfman's proscription is inevitably negated by conventional and necessary practices by non-historian-of-economic-thought practitioners that contribute willy nilly to the history of economic thought. This point is no surprise but it makes more concrete and relevant Porta's point, attributed to Schumpeter (Porta 1994: 166; Schumpeter 1954: 4–6) that history helps satisfy a need for orientation and sense, and that any economist is "to some extent, a historian in a genuine sense" (Porta 1994: 169).

(1) should go without saying that the designed structure of a course in any field serves to define that field in the minds of students. Course materials can substantiate and/or amplify such definition. All this is inevitably recent economic thought insofar as the course covers contemporary materials. A

course in microeconomics in the late 1930s or early 1950s, to have recency, would have had to include the work on noncompetitive conditions by E.H. Chamberlin and Joan Robinson from the early 1930s. A course in medieval history or on medieval economic thought in the 1970s would have had to include post-war interpretive advances (such as Dempsey 1958). But whatever the degree of recency, a course helps define its field and possibly its history.

(2) Many journal articles and some books include literature reviews in order to define the field into which the author seeks to position his or her work. These often, even typically, constitute or at least contribute to a history of economic thought of a field or topic. The recency proscription seemingly never applies.

(3) Survey articles, such as have been published in the *Journal of Economic Literature, Economic Journal,* and other journals, tend to define their

respective fields, provide histories of the relevant work, and concentrate on the post-war period to the time they are written (see Ellis 1948; American Economic Association 1967). The Ellis volume, published for the AEA, contains interpretations and critiques of then-very recent developments of key topics. An influential recent survey is Mankiw (1990) on macroeconomic theory and policy. He shows how the varying characteristics of different approaches (different definitions of reality through varying readings of the history of economic thought and of the economy) impact the direction of research agendas, including identifying those approaches which have fallen out of favor with theorists.

(4) Readers in a particular field serve to define the field in terms of the literature deemed relevant and also tend to constitute or at least contribute to a history of economic thought of the field. The recency proscription seemingly rarely if ever applies (but see later in this chapter). Different readers define, even name, the field differently. Changes in focus by current writers are reflected in the contents of new editions. While these readers, each in their own way, help to define their field and its history, the element of change, if not faddism, calls Dorfman's injunction into play. Only in time will the field and its history, settling on the chief surviving literature, be defined. But that may well be precisely the problem. Such history is only a history of the surviving literature, perhaps only of the canonical literature, not a history of what went on at the time, which is more inclusive, survival (as of publication date) being only one aspect of the history.

Some if not most of the foregoing points apply to conventional textbooks in any field, such as money and banking, and public finance, as well as any more purely theoretical field, such as microeconomics. These textbooks must reflect new developments in institutions, policy, and/or theory, or face being out of date. Insofar as each edition serves to define the field and its history, Dorfman's injunction applies but only problematically. In retrospect particular editions will include, if not highlight, the impermanent; but that is part of the history of the field. There is no other way to present up-to-date material to students and other readers.

Examples include: (1) Mehmet Ugur's (2002) reader on open economy macroeconomics, which may be compared with Michael Rukstad's (1986) but also with M.G. Mueller's (1966) and, perhaps especially, Preston Miller's (1994) and Gregory Mankiw and David Romer's (1991) readers; (2) the respective sequences of editions of non-reader textbooks in monetary economics by Lester Chandler (first edition, 1953) and George Halm (first edition, 1942); (3) the readers in monetary economics by the AEA (1951), Richard Thorn (1966), Alan Entine (1968) and Robert Clower (1969); and (4) the readers in microeconomics by David Kamerschen (1967) and Edwin Mansfield (1971). The specific contents and structure of individual books define their field and its present state in the path of its history; comparisons reflect different conceptions of field and history and changes in domains of interest. And they all aim at currency—recency of coverage. Miller's subtitle reads "Readings from the Front Line," Clower's collection appeared in a series entitled "Penguin Modern Economics Readings" and Thorn's carries the subtitle "Major Contributions to Contemporary Thought."

To be specific, compare the overall structure of the three cited readers in monetary economics. The AEA committee's collection in 1951 had four parts: I. Integration of the theory of money and the theory of price; II. The demand for and the supply of money—the value of money; III. Money, the rate of interest and employment; and IV. Monetary policy. Thorn's 1966 collection had, after an introduction, five parts: II. The demand for money, comprised of A. Quantity theory and B. Asset preference theory; III. The integration of monetary and value theory; IV. The supply of money; V. The rate of interest; VI. Monetary policy. Entine's 1968 collection had seven parts: I. Commercial banking—problems of competition and control; II. Financial intermediaries and commercial banks; III. Monetary instruments; IV. Monetary indicators; V. Monetary theory and policy in a closed economy; VI. Monetary theory and policy in an open economy; and VII. Monetary policy—evaluation and alternatives.

Full appreciation of the differences/changes in content requires knowledge of the specific items included in each reader. Short of that, we see, first, differences in definition of the field, due to varying perceptions and/or changes in the field; second, differences in implication for the history of the field (supporting both of Dorfman's points, but only problematically); third, the deep problem of writing a history of the field that reflected all of the twists and turns of professional interest (in the 1960s the interests of monetary economists changed every half year or so) and not just the state of the field—what survived as timely topics—when the history was undertaken; and, fourth and most important for present purposes, the emphasis on recent/contemporary/modern, meaning up-to-date.

One can only wait with interest a contemporary alternative to the relatively unique collection in Geoffrey Hodgson's (2002) reader on institutional and evolutionary economics.

What is said above applies to hosts of similar, substitute books and to an almost infinite library of economics textbooks.

(5) A considerable literature surveys, critiques, uses, evaluates, and/or revises recent work on a subject that in one way or another provides a more or less partial history of economic thought of a field or topic. It is often difficult to separate survey or

critique and history of economic thought; the latter is produced in the course of undertaking either of the former. The recency proscription seemingly never applies to topics whose study extends toward and into the present. When different authors produce different summaries or critiques, the differences in the respective resulting histories of economic thought constitute evidence for the fact and significance of multiplicity in the social construction of the history of the discipline.

Compare Kaushik Basu's (2001) interpretive summary of law and economics with those in the Chicago and Virginia tradition, in part contained in Allan Schmid's list, mentioned earlier in this chapter, with respect to which see also Thrainn Eggertsson (1990), Eirik Furubotn and Rudolf Richter (2000), and C. Mantzavinos (2001); all are concerned with a largely post-war literature. A.I. Ogus (1995) is concerned not only with the past of law and economics but its future; albeit its domain is limited to the United Kingdom.

Further examples include Jack Birner *et al.*'s (2002) critique of Friedrich A. von Hayek as a political economist, and Allen Oakley's (1999) critique of Austrian subjectivism. Geoffrey Hodgson's 1995 essay reviews six books in evolutionary economics published between 1992 and 1994 and points to several dozen other post-war books. Hansjörg Klausinger (2002) summarizes and interprets the history of Walras's law and the IS-LM model in the post-war period. D. Wade Hands (2001) does likewise with the entire range of modernist and post-modernist methodology and philosophy of science. That Hands accepts the revisionism of the late twentieth century suggests how different an account, an interpretation and a history would emanate from someone who did not.

At least two of George Stigler's *Five Lectures on Economic Problems* (1949)— those on "Monopolistic Competition in Retrospect" and "The Mathematical Method in Economics"—define, evaluate and prescribe for their respective topics, in the course thereof presenting accounts of recent history of economic thought.

Several dozen late-twentieth-century books are devoted to interpreting the legacy of Austrian Economics, a comparable number to the legacy of Friedrich von Hayek, perhaps even more to the evaluation and reinterpretation of Keynes, and fewer to John R. Hicks. These books more or less vary in the pictures their authors paint. They attempt to simultaneously summarize and place in perspective their respective subjects, thereby contributing to the construction of the history of economic thought, and promoting one or another program for the future, thereby attempting to contribute to the future history of economic thought. The term "legacy" necessarily combines selective views of the past and of the future.

Philip Arestis and Malcolm C. Sawyer's *A Biographical Dictionary of Dissenting Economists* (2000 [1992]) paints a picture of contemporary economic heterodoxy and thereby helps create a story of the history of economic thought into the present.

A collection of conference papers celebrating the jubilee of the Conference on Research in Income and Wealth presents interpretations of findings and the related history of economic thought (Berndt and Triplett 1990), surely an exercise, however self-congratulatory (which it is not entirely), in recent history of economic thought.

(6) That survey and interpretation need not be only backward looking but can

use contemporary history-of-economic-thought materials to examine up-to-date developments and to suggest and probe future developments, is illustrated by Kenneth Arrow and Seppo Honkapohja's collection, *Frontiers of Economics* (1985), Klaus F. Zimmermann's *Frontiers in Economics* (2002), and John Foster and J. Stanley Metcalfe's *Frontiers of Evolutionary Economics* (2001). See also Alexander J. Field, *The Future of Economic History* (1987; new edition, 1995).

David Rich's *Contemporary Economics: A Unifying Approach* (1986) combines his view of post-war managerial capitalism and of economic theory in an effort to generate a new, unifying approach. Both implicit and explicit in his effort is the construction of a post-war history of economic thought.

(7) Much history-of-economic-thought material is found in specialized encyclope dias, companions and bibliographies. In the field of law and economics, for example, are Backhaus (1999), Bouckaert and De Geest (1992; 2000), and Newman (1998)—much of all three pertaining to the entire post-war period. Other examples include volumes on econometrics (Darnell 1994), theoretical econometrics (Baltagi 2001), methodology (Davis *et al.* 1998), 'economics' (Boettke 1994), institutional and evolutionary economics (Samuels *et al.* 1994), public choice (Shughart and Razzolini 2001), the modern politics of Southeast Asia (Leifer 2001), political economy (O'Hara 2000), international political economy (Jones 2001), radical political economy (Arestis and Sawyer 1994), environmental economics (Bromley 1995), Keynesian economics (Cate 1997), economics as a whole (Greenwald 1965; 1973; 1983; 1994) and contemporary economic thought as such (Greenaway *et al.* 1991). On a grand scale are the *Dictionary of Political Economy* (Palgrave 1894–1899), the *Encyclopaedia of the Social Sciences* (Seligman 1937), the *International Encyclopedia of the Social Sciences* (Sills 1968), and *The New Palgrave* (Eatwell *et al.* 1987). The contributors to these volumes include both historians of economic thought and practitioners in the covered fields.

(8) Policy history combined with relevant economic thought contributes to a history of economic thought for the topic(s) of policy during the period covered.

Ivo Maes's (2002) *Economic Thought and the Making of European Monetary Union* combines policy history with accounts of relevant interactions between politicians, bureaucrats and academic economists resulting in a partial history of economic thought, covering the entire post-war period to the present. An earlier book by Clarke (1988) covering comparable interactions over the ideas and policies of fiscalism and monetarism also carried the discussion to the then-present.

Several historians of economic thought have published books of this genre, with various beginning and ending dates. These include William Barber (1975; 1985; 1996), A.W. Coats (1981; 1986), Frank W. Fetter (1980), Mary O. Furner and Barry Supple (1990), Crauford Goodwin (1961; 1966; 1975; Goodwin and Nacht 1995), Barry Gordon (1977), Peter Hall (1989), Susan Howson and Donald Winch (1977), Richard Nathan (2000), and George Perry and James Tobin (2000). See also Anthony Endres and Grant Fleming (2002), McCarty (2001) and Rosenof (1997), already noted.

A substantial literature exists on the policies and influence of the major grant-dispensing foundations and think-tanks in the US. Apropos of Great Britain, see Cockett (1994).

(9) The international transmission of economic ideas has always operated with a lag but due to changes in the mode of distribution of materials, the rise of English as the dominant language of the profession, and, *inter alia*, the internet, for many countries the lag is now negligible. The imposition of a Dorfman-like rule, if such were possible, would help reintroduce long lags. Because of all the reasons identified above as to the inevitability of the treatment of recent, contemporary or modern work, in one form or another, enforcement is largely impossible. The mind boggles at the thought of proscribing European consideration of developments in US economic thought, or vice versa, until sufficient time has passed to better appreciate those developments—just as it does the idea of proscribing MIT economists from considering the work of Harvard economists. This is akin to the stipulation on a working paper, "Do Not Quote or Cite Without Permission" (Samuels 1999a). That which the rule or injunction would exclude is a critical part of the growth of knowledge. For general aspects of international transfer and reception, see Coats 2000; 1997; Colander and Coats 1989; Dorfman 1955; Goodwin 1973; Hutchison 1955; Llombart 1995; Mohr 1999; Spengler 1970. Much, though by no means all, of the material covered in these volumes qualified as "recent."

(10) An example of a small but important literature on theory choice in economics, which also deals with recent developments, is Christopher Mackie's *Canonizing Economic Theory* (1998); see also Forget and Peart (2001).

Conclusions

(1) The treatment in textbooks of recent developments is mixed. Some textbooks, for whatever reason, make little or no effort to bring the student to a point near the date of publication. Some make an extended effort, some a moderate effort. All efforts seem to be inevitably selective. More effort is made by some recent texts than earlier ones, though there are conspicuous exceptions. More effort is made by texts aimed at graduate courses than undergraduate courses. Overall, the treatment of post-war contemporary economic thought is limited, selective, incomplete and poor to the point of being abysmal.

(2) Most of the treatment of contemporary developments, however, is not to be found in the history-of-economic-thought textbooks. It is located in survey articles, literature reviews, integrative treatises, and critical writings. Most of these materials are not authored by historians of economic thought but by specialists in their respective fields. What these authors may lack in terms of training in historiography they perhaps more than compensate for in specialized knowledge of the development of their respective fields. It is a striking conclusion that most recent history-of-economic-thought work is undertaken by economists (and others) who are not historians of economic thought.

A difference among authors—both practitioners and historians of economic thought—should be noted. Some uncritically accept the disciplinary status quo as normal science. Some—the relatively orthodox who are more objective if not internally critical but still supportive or the heterodox who reject the mainstream—inquire into the origins of mainstream's normal science, and therefore into the conditions of its social construction and problematicity.

The selective, even idiosyncratic nature of efforts by the authors of history-of-economic-thought textbooks to cover contemporary developments reflects the authors' personal interests and expertise, their judgments as to what is centrally continuous to the overall story they tell in previous chapters (though in some cases no connections seem present), and their respective publisher's sense of what will differentiate their product for marketing purposes. It undoubtedly also reflects the impossibility of covering all that comprises modern economics and the limits of authorial expertise.

The history of economic thought, as a field, includes more than the work of technical historians of economic thought. The field must be seen to be broader than it is now seen to be and historians of economic thought should make greater use of specialized work by scholars who are not technical historians of economic thought.

(3)The textbooks manifest a great deal of the historical diversity within economics since, say, 1700. They do not, however, do so for the post-war period. This is because of limitations on and selectivity of coverage.

(4) Relatively little of the specialized research work of historians of economic thought finds its way into the textbooks. Blaug's *Economic Theory in Retrospect* is particularly attentive to the exegetical and interpretive literature, and some is found in most textbooks, but overall the use is sparse and selective, perhaps inevitably so. Making use of such work would enrich the stories we tell, in part thereby documenting many of the social-constructionist and other postmodernist themes widely found in contemporary technical work, and also familiarize the student with the work of historians of economic thought. Doing so would enhance their education and perhaps attract them to the field.

(5) The possibility exists to have textbooks specializing in the period since c.1945. That would solve the problem posed in (1), take advantage of the materials noted in (2), and solve the problems identified in (3) and (4). Perhaps only Backhouse's 1985 book comes close. Still, no history of the post-war period can approach completeness. The volume of publications in economics increased enormously during this period, in both general economics and the specialized fields. An exception might be a multi-volume collaborative effort by a team of historians of economic thought and specialists—though even here no coverage can fully relate what transpired, nor should it.

David Colander argues that the study of recent work is a worthwhile field in itself, that past work enters that field insofar as it sheds useful light on current work, and that modern economics is changing from within and is substantially different than perceived by many orthodox and many heterodox economists (email from Colander to Samuels, 19 August 2002). This is a matter of selective perception but the case can readily be made. The interesting point is that Colander in effect turns Dorfman on his head. Instead of seeking when the present is ready to help understand the past, for Colander the past is useful to help understand the present.

Another period seeking specialized treatment, oddly enough, is that between 1900 and 1940. Looking at the textbooks, one would never know how economists—say, other than Fisher—did economics during that period—no Taussig, no Fetter, no Davenport, no Stewart, no Adams, no Ely, no Fairchild, no Seligman, no Carver, no Gay, no Young, no Hollander, no Ripley ... to mention only US economists—unless, that is, one read Dorfman! The preceding sentence is admittedly hyperbolic but not by much.

(6) With the exception of monetary theory and economic development, perhaps international trade, and some idiosyncratic inclusions, the history of specialized fields (other than micro and macro theory) is significantly neglected in the history-of-economic-thought textbooks. Indeed, relatively few histories of specialized fields are undertaken, presumably because very few historians of economic thought have comparable specializations in other fields and most practitioners of specialized fields have no interest in, or no perceived payoff from, undertaking the history of their respective fields. Alas, much local knowledge is lost.

(7) Pressures exist for textbooks and other writings to cover contemporary work. Overall, attention to recent economic thought is inevitable, for the reasons given above. Given, however, Hume's injunction that an "ought" cannot be derived from an "is" alone, the fact that many history-of-economic-thought textbooks and other works attend to recent developments is insufficient ground on which to conclude that such ought to be done. Yet, if the positive analysis presented here is substantially correct, an affirmation of Dorfman's normative position is effectively negated by the inevitable.

(8)Another fundamental problem with the Dorfman position is its assumption that there is only one correct history of a period, one that adequate description and the correct perspective coming with the passage of time will provide; and, indeed, because of that, history writes itself. The problem is that this is not true. Every generation writes its own history. Each individual selectively identifies the past and selectively identifies with the past; each generation contributes to the process of rewriting, in part through the continuous discovery of simplicities. The tension is inescapable between a past never seen on its own terms and a past seen through some present terms. The history of economic thought is a process of continuous social construction as each individual and each generation emphasizes what it needs for its own purposes; each individual and each generation is a co-author of past texts and of "the past." Even if we all agree that there was something "the past" was all about, we disagree as to what it was.

(9) We have identified multiplicity, incompleteness and selectivity as critical findings in our study of authorial treatment of recency of publication. Multiplicity is truly fundamental when one looks not at individual textbooks (and other writings) but at all of the publications included in our study, some

by design, others at random. When one looks across publications one sees that many things are capable of being given, and are in fact given, different readings. For example, Keynesian and post-Keynesian economics, institutional economics, and neoclassical economics are interpreted and specified differently by different authors. There is an obvious common core to each of these schools of thought; but there are highly individualized accounts within the relatively common overall structure—idiosyncratic is not too strong a term. The version of neoclassicism, for example, learned by students will still be neoclassicism but each version will have its own twist, its own center of gravity, its own message. Given the relative paucity of attention given therein to the fullness of post-war developments, the textbooks in particular are contributing to selective myopia and avoiding the opportunity to enrich student education along these and other lines.

(10)In May 2002, Warren Samuels asked Roger Backhouse for his thoughts on the problem of recency by sending him a first draft of this material. Backhouse responded as follows:

> My initial reaction is that it is a non-problem. To say that we cannot write recent history presumes that there is a correct way to write it. Obviously there will be differences between the way we cover recent periods and longer ago, but so what? There are many types of history and I refuse to say that one is right and the rest wrong, as I suspect you do. There will be advantages and disadvantages to distance and which outweighs the other will depend on our purposes and why we are doing it. There is no problem, as I see it, with the same historian writing different types of history at different times.
>
> But I can't talk to you about pluralism!! Anyway, the interesting issue that I suspect you are really raising is "what are the implications of recency for the way we write history?" not "can we write recent history?" or "is it proper to write recent history?"
>
> Of course, when someone covers a long period (and my book that just came out is probably one of the worst ever for this) there is the issue of whether the treatment of the beginning is consistent with that of the end. I think mine is, though it would not surprise me if you or someone else were to point to inconsistencies, undermining the view that it is a seamless whole. But that is academic debate and will, hopefully, enable me to do even better should I do another edition.
>
> My reaction is that for nineteenth-century historians and for the early part of the 20th century, it was probably normal to take the story right up to recent events. I wonder whether it is correct to say that we have got more worried about it recently? I don't know the answer to that, but it would be a historical way of looking at it.
>
> But this is based on a rushed skim through, and I have not read it properly yet, as you probably realise. You probably answer all my doubts in the paper.
>
> (Backhouse to Samuels, 30 May 2002; spelling corrected)

This chapter does not take up all of the questions that Backhouse thought pertained to the problem of recency. We are interested in the issues raised by the problem and how the problem is handled in the literature. This interest includes the question, "what are the implications of recency for the way we write history?"—albeit only partly. We have shown an affirmative answer to the question, "can we write recent history?" We have not elaborately or seriously considered the normative question, "is it proper to write recent history?"—though we have cast doubt on the possibility of not doing so. We have suggested that, properly or not, intellectual, pedagogical and marketing forces promote the doing of recent history. Our principal conclusion is that, as with Samuels's argument concerning "The Problem of 'Do Not Quote or Cite Without Permission'" (Samuels 1999a), the injunction against recency is impossible, doing recent history is inevitable.

It is not the case that nineteenth- and early twentieth-century historians of economic thought took the story right up to then-recent developments. Some did and some did not (we do not examine this period here).

In any event, it appears that authors of history-of-economic-thought textbooks have an uneven but overall increased, perhaps renewed, commitment, however inescapably limited the results, to include recent, even the most recent, work. Such a conclusion is, however, problematic: Diversity of practice still reigns; any such conclusion must be, in part, the result of some weighting by market share of the various textbooks (and some assumption of professorial intentions); possible increasing reliance on practitioner-written literature reviews, and so on.

Other questions arise. Are historians of thought moving to more recent material because of the perceived gaps in the literature and because they feel that they have something to contribute? Or, are historians of thought moving to more recent material because of the perceived gaps in employment for historians of thought and because they had better have something to contribute? It would be necessary to pose these questions to current contributors to this area of research, keeping in mind agency problems when we hear their answers.

So far from being a "non-problem," we have an issue that apparently looks simple but is shown to be, in fact, extremely complex.

(11) The larger (largest?) frame of reference to which the problem of recency belongs has several tiers, each involving overdetermination, or interaction, between the objects of description and explanation *and* our concepts thereof (on which see Hacking 2002). First, the mutual influence of economic theory/thought and the story of its history. Second, the mutual influence of ideas and practice, e.g., the "Max Weber Problem" of the relation of the practices of capitalism and the ethic of capitalism. Third, the mutual influence of ideas and policy. Fourth, the mutual influence of policy and organized practice, i.e., recognizing the domain of policy—both influenced by and influencing ideas and interests—as a mode of social reconstruction, and the organization and control of the economic system. Without consideration of recent work in historical perspective—were that to be possible, which we deny—lags between

the several elements would develop. Some persons would applaud some lags but not all of them; some persons would condemn some lags but not all of them. All this is among what Backhouse calls "the implications of recency for the way we write history" to which we add "for the way in which history, however we write it, is made."

(12) Recency is one of a group of historiographical topics. They include internalism versus externalism, presentism, progress, discovery and innovation, social constructivism, hermeneutics and deconstruction, realism, selective perception, linguistics, and so on. Several of them have inevitably arisen in the foregoing discussion. None of them has been amply treated, nor has it been our intention to do so. Recency itself has not been the subject of any prior study; it has arisen principally in regard to the question of presentism and has been understood largely in that context (see, e.g., Heilbroner 1979; Porta 1994). Opportunities for further analysis surely exist.

(13) A.W. Coats has written, citing Dorfman's argument, that "It may never be easy to provide a brief and balanced assessment of the [recent] development of economics" and that "the task is especially difficult" at certain times (Coats 1992: 407). We have observed the truth of this position. We have also shown the impossibility of a universal proscription against doing recent economic thought—like it or not.

Notes

The authors are indebted to Roger Backhouse, John Davis, Luca Fiorito, Glenn Heuckel and Mark Perlman for comments on earlier drafts of this article. The authors apologize for any mischaracterization of a text, especially having emphasized that such readings are subject to selective perception.

1   In late 1973, for example, Warren Samuels sent Dorfman, out of courtesy, an advance typescript of his review of Dorfman's collection of Veblen essays, reviews and reports. In the last sentences of the review Samuels wrote, "We are again indebted to Joseph Dorfman. This reviewer, for one, looks forward to the additional indebtedness for a sixth volume of his *Economic Mind in American Civilization*" (Samuels 1974b: 963). In an accompanying letter Samuels indicated his wish "for the consummation of the object of the final sentence of the review!" (Samuels to Dorfman, 15 October 1973). Dorfman replied as follows: "I deeply appreciate the compliment in the statement about the next volume of *The Economic Mind*. While I am adhering to my resolution of 1959, I will, of course—as I have done in recent years—be discussing developments subsequent to those considered in Volume 5, in much of my writings" (Dorfman to Samuels, 31 October 1973). Thus even Dorfman finessed his own rule.

   Candor and full disclosure require that the following be said. Warren Samuels joined with Henry W. Spiegel to produce a two-volume sequel (Spiegel and Samuels 1984) to Spiegel's earlier collection of essays by economists on economists (Spiegel 1952). Spiegel's collection stopped with work done by the onset of World War II (hereafter "post-war" refers to post-World War II). The sequel was self-consciously devoted to the post-war period. The collection was necessarily selective. It also inevitably defined and structured the field of economics and its history during a nearly forty-year period. The collection had three parts. Part I covered "varieties of mainstream economics," divided into five sections: generalists; specialists; Keynesians, fiscalists, and post-Keynesians; anti-Keynesians and monetarists; and econometrics and quantitative techniques. Part II covered "eddies in the mainstream," nine economists who were orthodox but did unusual work. Part III covered "varieties of heterodox economics," and included Marxism and the Cambridge controversy, and the further development of institutional economics. The history of economics was thus defined in terms of various individual styles of doing economics. Much was omitted. Samuels also co-edited with Steven G. Medema collections on modes of contemporary economic research (1996) and on contemporary historians of economic thought (Medema and Samuels 2001), Samuels having already co-edited a similar collection which included the early post-war period (Spiegel and Samuels 1983). Samuels also edited volumes on contemporary economists (1992b; 1996b), on topics much of whose literature was published during the post-war period (1988; 1979; Samuels and Tool 1989a), and on the largely post-war Chicago School of Economics (1976). He also edited companion volumes much of whose content was post-war (1994; 2003).

The Recent Economic Thought Series published by Kluwer Academic Publishers, was initially edited by Warren Samuels, then co-edited with William Darity, Jr., who now co-edits it with James K. Galbraith. Each volume is a comprehensive and systematic attempt to identify and critique the current state of the field or topic covered in each book. Over seventy books have been published.

Samuels, while an enormous admirer of Dorfman and his work, is clearly no practitioner of the Dorfman position on this issue.

2 Fiorito also suggests two other, related cases of path dependency, cases driven by what may be called ceremonial adequacy. First, many accounts of the creation of the multiplier tend to neglect Clark's contribution. Perhaps an admission that the multiplier has institutionalist origins would disturb orthodox and Keynesian self-images. Second, it is conventional to stress that Veblenian and other institutionalists employed instinct theory, ignoring the situation that instinct theory was then the dominant approach to psychology and that many non-institutionalist economists—such as Frank A. Fetter and Frank William Taussig—used the theory.

3 Contemporary history is, of course, made difficult by selective memory, as well as through the monopoly and control of pertinent information. Individual economists control access to themselves, their thoughts, and their materials. Such is perfectly legitimate, but does limit historical research into their theories of economics. The contemporary historian of economic thought faces many of the same problems confronted by biographers of contemporary (living) figures that are different from the problems faced by historians working on much older material.

One eminent historian writes:

> Now the vanity of historians is to suppose that we understand better than the people who were there what the shouting was all about. ... 20–20 hindsight can be carried too far. There is always the risk of ... 20–20 hindmyopia. Too often we suggest that those poor chaps in the past may have thought they were acting for one set of reasons; but we, so much wiser, know that they were acting for quite other reasons. ... The assertion that people in the past did not really know why they were doing what they did leads to the conclusion that we do not really know why we are doing what we do today.
>
> (Schlesinger 2000: 365–366)

Another point of view is that in retrospect they did not know what they were doing, in the sense that the actual developmental path of ideas was not part of their intention or expectation, i e , the principle of unintended and unforeseen consequences.

4   The purpose of Samuels 1998 and 2002b was to rescue and restore to historical memory—and thus help achieve "adequate description"—the work of hitherto neglected continental economists.

5   One problem is access to materials, including, but not limited to data, letters, notes and drafts. This is an obvious problem associated with working with government documents, where access is often classified over long periods of time or where foreign governments might deny any access at all. But the problem is similar with access to archival materials for contemporary economic thought. Questions arise as to whether a living individual will provide information, whether the information is accurate, and whether the information is edited. Individuals attempt to shape views and history, both of themselves and of their work. Take, for example, James Buchanan's story that he "accidentally discovered" Knut Wicksell's *Finanztheoretische Untersuchungen* (1896) while browsing the stacks of the library at the University of Chicago. He claimed that this discovery shaped his entire view of economics and led to public choice analysis. While this story is part of the public choice mythology, its accuracy cannot be verified apart from Buchanan's claim. Milton Friedman is similarly interested in defining his own legacy, as evidenced by his and his wife's memoir (Friedman and Friedman 1998). Adam Smith instructed that his letters and drafts be burned on his death as an attempt to shape his legacy and the history written about him. In addition, contemporary history is made difficult by selective memory, as well as the monopoly and control of pertinent information—that Friedman controls access to himself, his thoughts and his materials, which is perfectly all right, but does limit historical research into his theories of economics. Thus, the contemporary historian of economic thought faces many of the same problems that biographers of contemporary (living) figures face that those working on much older material do not. If Adam Smith were alive today, we could ask him what he really meant by his use of the term "invisible hand" and other ideas. However, how do we know if he tells the truth? Is he allowed to change his mind over time? Can others interpret his phrase differently? What are the implications if they do? A modern example would be Ronald Coase and the interpretations of the Coase Theorem (Medema and Samuels 1997).

6   The distinction between normative, or value-laden, and positive, or value-free, statements is controversial. At least some of those who reject the distinction in practice feel that the distinction in theory is sound but that most putative statements of fact contain normative elements.

7   For the period 1880–1975 Howey lists roughly fifty-three textbooks published in English in the US, Canada and UK, counting each series as one. The group included from that period in this study is thirty-six. For the period 1976–2002 we estimate a higher proportion used in the study.

8   Certainly, more coverage and analysis of recent economic thought occurs in the primary economics journals, and especially in field journals, which contain surveys and critiques of recent economic thought.

9   At the same time, roughly 5 percent of *all* articles published in *HOPE* during this period dealt directly with Adam Smith. In *EJHET*, more articles were devoted to Smith than to all issues/topics/theories that would qualify as recent under the Dorfman rule.

3 What the authors of history-of-economic-thought textbooks say about the history of economic thought

Warren J. Samuels, Kirk D. Johnson and Marianne Johnson

Any book of limited scope will necessarily leave many questions unanswered. What role, if any, does the environment play in the development of economic theory? Do great empirical concerns (food shortages, income distribution, or the magnitude of unemployment and inflation) temper the nature and direction of analytical inquiry? If economic abstractions really do have a life of their own, has insularity led theorists to shut out potential areas of interest and benefit to economics? How do ideas filiate within countries and internationally? How are ideas related to the times in which they develop? How does philosophy relate to economic theory? We do not have conclusive answers to these questions, but we hope that this book will at least deepen appreciation and understanding of the issues.

(Ekelund and Hébert 1990: 8)

There is no *objective* measuring stick for *any*thing in economics.

There is *no established* economic usage for anything in economics.

Frank H. Knight (Ostrander 2005a)

Introduction: historiographical issues in the textbooks[1]

This chapter is concerned with what the authors of history-of-economic-thought textbooks say about historiographic topics in the various beginning and concluding sections of their books. These topics are multiple, complex, subtle and highly nuanced—thus much more difficult to deal with in a linear textual progression than the subjects of the first two chapters.

Each textbook of the history of economic thought tells a story about that history. There is an inherent problem with telling that story. It gets more difficult to tell as the literature of economics becomes vastly enlarged, diverse, increasingly technical and mathematical, and the authors of textbooks become more historiographically sophisticated (see, for example, Rima 1967: ix). One result is that the material presented to students is increasingly both an author-selected sample of the larger literature and a discussion about, rather than a presentation of, the objects of inquiry. But, however selective the sample, the author tells his or her story. For the most part, the elements of the story—the people, their writings, the principal topics and issues—are a given, though significant variations are inevitable. The stories vary in what the authors say in four ways: in what they include and exclude, the substance of the story they tell, the mode of presentation, and what they say about the history of thought as a whole as the work of historians of economic thought, i.e., historiographic issues. This essay examines the fourth of these four insofar as they are expressed in the prefatory, introductory and/or concluding sections of the textbooks.

The prefaces, introductions and concluding chapters of textbooks in the history of economic thought typically address historiographic questions and other topics that place the main account in some context. They can tell the reader why, and in what way, the author wrote what he or she did. They discuss such questions as: Where does all this history of economic thought lead? What are the issues and the several positions on each? What is the point or meaning of it all? The textbook authors can identify their purposes in writing the book either in general (none say to make money or establish reputation) or in the particular way they wrote it (some point, guardedly, to marketing considerations), explain why the history of economic thought should be studied, identify complications other than those of a purely epistemological type (though these too may be included), state conclusions as to the origins of economic theory and/or ideas and as to the nature of economic thought, and state explicitly where the study leaves us. More generally, these sections of a book explicitly introduce the reader to some of the dimensions and topics with which the author intends to stretch the mind and imagination of the reader. These may also say something about what the history of economic thought is all about, perhaps also how economic thought should be studied by going beyond the parade of names of people and theories and/or ideas. Insofar as the purposes of studying the history of economic thought are, *inter alia*, to provide perspective and to reveal how theoretical minds work, these historiographic discussions are a very important complement to the specifically historical chapters comprising the principal subject matter of the book. Indeed, textbooks can be compared as to how much historiographic insight they provide and how well they do so. By no means do all authors present all issues. Nor should one expect them to, as each author is entitled to discuss what interests them and/or what they want to make evident to their readers. No history of economic thought can do everything; scarcity is at work.

Generally, the narrowest purpose of prefaces and introductions is, in general, to provide a rationale for, and an introduction to, what follows. The common purpose of concluding chapters and epilogues is to reach some generalizing conclusions, or make other comments, with which to further educate the reader. Prefaces to multiple editions lay out changes in presentation and/or design strategy. Expected differences are based on (1) authorial attitudes toward mainstream, orthodox economics, though this does not always arise; (2) whether the intended or expected student reader is an undergraduate or graduate student; (3) whether the designed coverage stresses theory or, more broadly, ideas, or, in many cases, both; (4) the period covered in the book and a justification of the period chosen to be covered; (5) the period in which the text is written, e.g., whether—and if so, how—it is influenced by modern historiography, philosophy of science, discourse analysis, sociology of economics, and postmodernism generally; and (6) whether these sections are indeed intended to additionally educate, to provide a starting point or to put *finis* to the story, or even to provide a coda to the main body of the work.

We are interested in the topics chosen by the authors on which to comment and the substance of their comments. Among the principal substantive topics identified, in one way or another are: the nature and meaning or significance of (1) multiple theories, multiple methodologies, and/or multiple schools, i.e., multiplicity in one or more of its manifestations; (2) the pattern of sequential development of economic thought; (3) the phenomena of economic interconnections and interdependence; (4) the larger domain in which the history of economic thought has meaning; (5) problems of interpretation; and (6) the status of economics as described in the main text. Apropos of (4), one common topic is the set of issues that center on the larger issue of the purpose of knowledge: knowledge for knowledge's sake and/or control, making the world better, the status of the status quo, and so on.

We are operating within a three-tiered system of interpretation. The first level is comprised of the interpretations of the economy made by the people whose ideas are presented in the history-of-thought textbooks. The second level is comprised of the interpretations given those interpretations by the authors of the textbooks. The third is comprised of the interpretations principally of the latter but indirectly of the former given here. The work of historians of economic thought has primarily to do with the history itself, with how the history is done, and with the historians *qua* historians, and secondarily, but importantly, with how economics is done.

As historians of economic thought, we are sensitive, therefore, to the fact that we are engaged in an interpretive and selective exercise. By way of extension, this introduction is comparable to those of the textbook authors—both inevitably and by design. These comments constitute historiographic discussion of the textbook authors' historiographic comments.

One problem in identifying what the authors have to say about the history of economic thought is that their principal mode of doing so is their text itself, not solely their prefaces, introductions and epilogues. Some material pertinent to our interests resides in the texts' substantive chapters, for example, in passing comments (*obiter dicta*) and in the way substantive points and comparisons are presented. Schumpeter, for example, provides much editorial commentary in his extensive footnotes. Intensive attention to this material would have required numerous, time-consuming and lengthy discussions of possible nuances. We felt confident that most of what we wanted would be found in prefaces, introductory chapters, and epilogues, in which authors either intentionally or inadvertently provide more or less clear answers and positions. We have also generally omitted detailed analysis or interpretation of the more or less subtle historiographic differences between the several editions of a particular textbook. This is done with consideration of the space available and its best use for our purposes. Also because the topics rarely receive elaborate treatment in these sections.

In going through these materials on different occasions with different things in mind, we found relatively little tendency toward more or less different insights. *Inter alia*, this illustrates that what one brings to a book influences what one gets out of it, and that reading a book is indeed a joint venture with its author, and suggests that, in regard to these books, the differences in readings are not great.

It would seem efficient if we had a numbered list of topics and points and, alongside an entry for each book, were able to present the numbers for those presented therein. But incomplete treatments and subtle nuances distinguish one use from another and one totality of topics, points and their uses from another.

We have tried to avoid duplication of details presented in chapter 2 of this book on the problem of recency. We have also omitted providing exhaustive citations on every point, in order to avoid burden to the reader.

What if only, say, five (of over sixty) authors discuss a topic or make a point in the materials included in the study? Authorial silence on a matter may have several different explanations. One is a conscious decision not to discuss it. Another is a subconscious or non-cognitive failure to consider its discussion. Among the elaborations thereof can be an assumption that certain points or positions need not be discussed. Another is ignorance. The sensible result is to not infer anything from silence.

The content of this chapter is much more complex than that of chapter 2. Chapter 2 has only one topic, whereas this chapter and chapter 4 have multiple topics. In all four chapters we have the dual tasks of indicating conclusions and providing evidence. This presents little difficulty in chapters 1 and 2 because of their singular topics. Here, with multiple concerns, we face two problems. First, many authorial statements are pertinent to and evidence of a theme and while we are not happy with having so much quoted material, we feel that the evidence (actually only some of it) needs to be provided. The alternative (as in chapter 4) is to present only conclusions. Second, many statements are evidence on more than one topic; hence, the need for some repetition. As an example of the latter problem, consider the following quotation:

> rather than everyone contributing to an ever-progressing edifice, economics can and has proceeded in contentious, even zig-zag fashion, with later systemic fallacy sometimes elbowing aside earlier but sounder paradigms, thereby redirecting economic thought down a total erroneous or even tragic path. The overall path of economics may be up, or it may be down, over any give[n] time period.
>
> (Rothbard 1995a: x)

The statement provides evidence relevant to two themes, the dynamics of theoretical change and attitudes toward progress versus retrogression of economic theory.

The historiographic points made by each of the textbooks cannot be combined to form a composite whole. Each book stands independent of the others, each is a discrete unit of materials; together they form only—but informatively—an array of positions on various, and varying, issues.

For purposes of clarification, the term "thought"—unless it pertains specifically to the title of a particular book (or books) under discussion—is our generic, or default, term. The terms "theory" (or "analysis") and "ideas" (or "doctrines") are used in relation to the two major competing foci of textbooks. But that is not the practice of our textbook authors; Blaug, for example, uses "theory" in his title but both "thought" and "theory" in his text. Also, the term "authors" not otherwise specified refers to the authors of the history-of-economic-thought textbooks.

We again apologize for any mischaracterization of a text, especially having emphasized that such readings are subject to selective perception. Readers—and authors of textbooks—need to appreciate that we are interested in the positions the authors have taken on various issues. We are more interested, however, in the topics to which the issues relate and which the authors have chosen to bring up and on which to take a position. As indicated above, we are interested, but not very much so here, in the more or less highly nuanced statements of position in individual editions and in subtle changes of positions or in wording from edition to edition of multi-edition texts. Above all—except for apology for misrepresentation—we emphasize that authorial intent (or recollection of intent) is only one view of the meaning of a passage. The totality of authorial and reader interpretations of text forms a matrix of meanings, another level of interpretation.

The struggles of Mark Blaug, over his five editions, for example, to come to grips with relativism versus absolutism—what they mean, how they apply to the history of economic thought, and so on—are as important as they are legendary. For present purposes, however, they are important in two respects: that relativism versus absolutism *is* an important topic and that it is a difficult topic with which to deal adequately—no simple statement will suffice. And that is only one example. Another example relates to the tri-level interpretive problem noted above. Blaug (for example) maintains that economics is the economics of a market economy ("The history of economic thought, therefore, is nothing but the history of our efforts to understand the workings of an economy based on market transactions" (Blaug 1968: 6)). The problem of ideology versus rules of scientific procedure (on which Schumpeter and Blaug, for example, place so much reliance) arises on all three levels: that of the original authors, that of the textbook authors telling of the work of the original authors, and that of the present authors telling that the issue is or is not part of the textbook authors' historiographic comments (and if it is, what they have to say). Ideology and scholarly procedure can enter at each level.

Few authors undertake—at best they mention, hint at, or touch upon—a demonstration of the critique of their own practice; in other words, apply the rules, etc. of scientific procedure; in candor, neither do we. We illustrate this with a paragraph from Blaug (1968: 8). At first reading, it is a sensible paragraph, taking a sensible overall position and making sensible points. Nonetheless, it leaves many important questions unanswered, questions that Blaug further pursued in subsequent editions. We pursue the task of identifying those questions believing that Blaug's has been the best theory-oriented textbook available to graduate students. We hope to demonstrate strictness in both the use of language and of procedure. The paragraph—with inserted numbers referring to subsequent discussion—is as follows:

> And so, has there been progress [1] in economic theory? Clearly, the answer is yes: analytical tools have been continuously improved and augmented [2]; empirical data have been increasingly marshaled [3] to verify [4] economic hypotheses; metaeconomic biases have been repeatedly exposed and separated from the core of testable propositions which they enmesh [5]; and the workings of the economic system are better understood than ever before. [6] And yet the relativists do have a point. The development of economic thought has not taken the form of a linear progression towards present truths. [7] It has progressed, but many have been the detours imposed by exigencies of time and place. [8] Therefore, whether we adopt a relativist or absolutist interpretation of the subject depends entirely on the questions that we wish to raise. [9] If a commentator is interested in explaining why certain people held certain ideas at certain times, he must look outside the sphere of intellectual debate for a complete answer. But if he wants to know why some economists in the past held a labor theory of value while others believed that value is determined by utility, and this not only at the same time and in the same country but also in different countries generations apart, he is forced to concentrate on the internal logic of theory.

(1) No independent set of criteria of "progress" is given. The four illustrations in the next sentence become the tests of "progress" and do so without escaping the problem of the hermeneutic circle. Moreover, each has its own problems, a common one being that there is no independent conclusive test (either offered by Blaug or in practice) of either of the propositions.
(2) What is the test or criterion of continuous "improvement" and perhaps also "augmentation," and when has it been applied in an objective manner?
(3) The provision of empirical data has not been the province of economists; they generally rely on others—with some irony, on government and business, both of whom economists tend to distrust, albeit for different reasons.
(4) What does "verify" mean here—especially given Blaug's recognition that empirical testing can conclusively neither reject nor accept a hypothesis and his noted criticism and lament that neoclassicists engage in precious little testing?

(5) Ideological preconceptions—"metaeconomic biases"—are exposed but their extirpation is often strongly resisted. Blaug himself cites "competition" theory as both a positive and normative theory and notes the inevitable "element of judgment" (1968: 7).

(6) What is the test or criterion of "the workings of the economic system are better understood than ever before"—especially in a discipline whose principal modes of high theory are widely recognized, even by practitioners, *not* to apply to the actual economic system and whose practitioners disagree on important issues?

(7) The relativists do make the point. But it is not their principal point, which is the relativism indicated in points (1) through (6). To the extent that absolutists are philosophical or scientific realists, the absence of conclusive (or universally accepted) tests or criteria means that choice must be made. The point is not whether choice should or should not be made but that choice will be made willy nilly.

(8) How do we know a "detour" when we see one? When, and with respect to what, is a detour a detour? Is it the Truth about the real world—or a preferred rival theory, or the theory that becomes hegemonic or dominant (and how and why did it so become)? William Stanley Jevons was not the only economist who believed that a predecessor—in his case, David Ricardo—had shunted the train of political economy onto the wrong track, yet whether this is the case is a matter of judgment.

(9) "Entirely"? Are there absolutist questions and relativist questions, or questions to which one may apply absolutist and/or relativist approaches? Are absolutism and relativism definitions of reality, manifestations of certain sentiments of mindsets, or tools of analysis? Are they mutually exclusive?

Interestingly, the basis for most of the comments just made will be found in Blaug's chapter 16, "A Methodological Postscript."

The existence of multiple editions of a text can, but need not, offer the opportunity to see an author struggle over time with key questions and issues to which he is endeavoring to tease out meaningful and acceptable answers and positions. Blaug on absolutism versus relativism is a leading case in point.

Blaug writes,

> every new development in almost every branch of modern economics is liable to make us think again about some old familiar text in the history of economics or to revise the standard version of what the great thinkers of the past really meant to say.
>
> (Blaug 1997: xvii)

When Blaug writes that, he goes beyond those who would discuss only that part of the past that relates to the present and do so only on the basis of its putative contribution to the present. Through rational reconstruction he would identify the past based on the present. The former selectively adopts the past because of the present; the latter adapts the past because of the present. Given the present, only that which seems to have led up to it is included in the former approach; in the latter approach, the past is known only as its reformulation is based on the present.

As for rational reconstruction, he continues:

> The first edition of this book started with a statement of two diametrically opposed points of view to the study of the history of economic thought— relativism and absolutism—and held out programmatically for the latter view over the former. In due course I have had second thoughts about both the choice between these two viewpoints and the terms in which I posed that choice. In consequence, "relativism" and "absolutism" become "historical reconstruction" and "rational reconstruction" and I now see merits in both standpoints.
>
> (Blaug 1997: xvii)

But are rational reconstruction and historical reconstruction substitutes for absolutism and relativism (or internalism and externalism)? Is rational reconstruction actually the *history* of anything?

Our most important point, however, is this: of all our textbook authors it seems that *only* Blaug raises the rational reconstruction–historical reconstruction problem so effectively in the sections under consideration here. And his is the most extensive consideration of absolutism versus relativism as a historiographic problem. A third respect, therefore, in which Blaug's struggles are relevant should be obvious: he gives us an opportunity to illustrate the critique of historiographic practice.

The treatment of historiographic issues in selected textbook sections

Aspects of design strategy

The author(s) of any textbook must adopt a complex design strategy. Gide and Rist (1948 [1913]: xiv) is one of few that discuss the *problem* of design strategy as such, though most do identify the book's design strategy. In the case of history-of-economic-thought textbooks, the elements of authorial design include: intended audience, marketing considerations, orientation with regard to history of theory *vis-à-vis* history of ideas, the period covered, structure, and criteria of selectivity of coverage. As mundane as these topics may appear at first glance, several, perhaps all, have historiographic significance. The totality of positions taken on those elements constitutes a major part of the design of their textbook. There are, however, other elements entering into design, some of which motivate the positions taken on the foregoing elements. These other elements may be driven in turn by antecedent normative or subjective preferences or by deliberately chosen agendas. These may constitute either major themes—the primary motivation for writing—or subtexts—also a motivation for writing. These include: interpretation of economic thought as definition of reality, system of belief, set of tools; laudatory, critical or neutral attitudes toward the history of economic thought as it has developed; judgments as to the status of modern economics and the question of progress; how and why the study of the history of economics; the mode of doing history of economic thought; and so on. In this way, textbooks differ from non-textbook histories of economic thought, such as Meek (1977) and Stigler (1963), which deal with more abbreviated time frames, cover fewer topics, and comment less on historiographic issues.

A principal conclusion of this study derives from the multitude of design strategies used by authors of textbooks on the history of economic thought. The material not only accords them the opportunity but requires them to selectively design their work and of course they do so. These design strategies are constructed by the historian of economic thought; they are not conclusively presented to him or her by the history itself. While the *dramatis personae* (those whom Joseph Schumpeter called "the troops") are much the same, though not identical, from book to book, the story being told varies considerably. Even authors with similar design strategies will differ in the story told, because of the way in which each design strategy is nested in supplementary, supportive propositions.

What William Barber says of the work of the economists on whom historians of economic thought report through their story construction, can be rephrased to apply to the historians themselves: historians of economic thought have produced a variety of stories. In part, the differences between stories relate to the diversity of institutional conditions to which their original formulators addressed themselves, but also the differing purposes that each of the stories was constructed to serve, different perceptions of essential qualities and processes, and the differing themes around which they were originally organized and which, in turn, molded the categories used to fill out the analytical structure—by both the economist being discussed and the author undertaking the discussion. Different "ends in view" and "different set[s] of questions" as well as different images of what the history of economic thought is all about are all important. Historians of economic thought deploy intellectual and technical toolkits, with the tools shaped by the uses to which they are put.

The design strategies of textbooks in the history of economic thought vary enormously and reflect a substantial diversity of interests and orientations. Notwithstanding this diversity, a textbook in the history of economic thought is a textbook in that subject; the core material, given certain points shortly to be made, has been, at least since the mid-eighteenth century, roughly the same. All history is necessarily selective, and selectivity on certain matters leads to differences in the story being told. The substantive stories told by authors differ in terms of substantive fact—who and what is discussed—and in interpretation— e.g., Ricardo's theory of value and his and its place in the history of the discipline. The "reality" that is the history of economic thought is not singularly determinate in any conclusive sense.

Apropos of the implicit relativism of design strategy, one corollary of our general conclusion of the multiplicity of design strategies is that there is no one history of economic thought. The history of economic thought truly does not write itself. That history is constructed, constructed differently by different people—for reasons given throughout this chapter. We accept self-reflexivity, or self-referentiality: the four essays comprising this book could be written differently by different authors.

At the fundamental basis of each textbook are the specifics of design strategy. These specifics differ along the following lines, with considerable variation within each group.

Intended audience

Textbooks in the history of economic thought usually are expected to be read by students; some authors, however, seek wider readership. Some textbooks are written for undergraduate or beginning graduate (MA) students and others for advanced graduate (PhD) students. The market for the former is much greater than that for the latter; both are eclipsed by the potential market of general, non-academic readers. Very few find success in the non-academic market, Heilbroner's *Worldly Philosophers* (1953, 1961, 1967, 1972, 1976) is likely the biggest seller of all. Varieties of intended target and of related tone are indicated by the following. Soule's *Ideas of the Great Economists* (1952) attempts to convince the layman about how the ideas of great economists have shaped our daily lives.

Backhouse's *Economists and the Economy* (1988) is intended to have a wider audience than only those interested in pure theory, hence attention is given to economic history and how economists responded to practical problems (1988: 6, 3).

Bell's *History of Economic Thought* (1953: v) was designed primarily as a textbook for college courses; it is used principally at the graduate level.

Spiegel (1991: vi) targets advanced undergraduate and graduate courses.

Similarly, Haney's textbook (1949: vii) was designed to serve "the growing number of advanced students who study the history of Economics."

Ekelund and Hébert (1975: xi) target advanced undergraduate students.

Breit and Ransom's (1971: vii) expected/desired audience is "economics students and intelligent laymen." Finkelstein and Thimm (1973: ix) write for undergraduates and intelligent laymen. McConnell (1943: xi) writes "for the general reader with an interest in economics." Rima (1967: x) states that her book "is intended primarily for students whose background in economic theory does not go far beyond that presented in a one-year introductory course." Gray's textbook (1931: 5) is similarly intended for the beginner. Screpanti and Zamagni (1993: vi) write, "This book is not directed to a specialist public, nor solely to a student audience. We also hope to reach the educated person, or, rather, the person who wishes to educate herself or himself." And though "specialist training is not, therefore, necessary to understand this book; a basic knowledge of economics, however, especially the main themes of micro- and macroeconomics, would be of help" (1993: vi).

Taylor (1960: xiv–xv) has the objective of contributing to both education for enlightened citizenship and the technical training of professional economists.

> This is a book that should interest a rather wide variety of readers: economists, political scientists, philosophers, historians, university students (undergraduate and graduate) in all those fields, and mature, educated, and thoughtful citizens in all walks of life, beyond as well as within academic walls.
>
> (Taylor 1960: viii)

Canterbery (1976: iv) says that his only prerequisite is an inquiring mind.

Fusfeld's (1977: v) intention is to be useful to interested laymen and students in principles of economics courses.

Not surprisingly, by and large, the theory- or analysis-oriented textbooks are targeted at professional training of undergraduate and of graduate students rather than the general reader and general undergraduate. Educational specialization thus to some extent parallels historiographic emphasis on theory versus ideas. (In a discussion of the uses and dangers of mathematization, Ekelund and Hébert (1983: 542) write, "the system now operative for the transmission of economic knowledge might be responsible for keeping the discipline myopic. That system gives great weight to mathematical technique, often at the expense of history.")

One matter is beyond our capacities to consider without resorting to supposition. As Carpenter (2002: xxiv) has recently written of the impact of French (and other) translations of the *Wealth of Nations*, "a learned text can at various times be directed at different publics, who read it differently." We can only wonder at the different readings of each of these textbooks.

Marketing considerations

Design strategy is a function of many different variables. These include: authorial interest and orientation, and marketing strategy in the quest for market niche and share. No author seems to be very blunt about it, but the latter can be intuited from general statements on design strategy and changes therein, statements and practice in regard to recency in particular, and the Backhouse trilogy of textbooks, each oriented to a different market. One nonetheless expects that authorial considerations of intellectual interest and disciplinary history and historiography, as these are filtered through personal factors, are the primary sources. But textbooks are economic goods and one would expect authors of sequential editions to be at least somewhat responsive to the demands of professors contemplating course adoption and of their publishers' editors. Considerations of marketing strategy seem to help explain serial editions, change in "recent" or "contemporary" content, change in design strategy, and multiple books, such as those of Backhouse and Hunt.

Designing a textbook may well require the author to be professionally courageous and dedicated (a point that applies to more than the present topic). Do marketing considerations trump all others? Authors design and write textbooks for pedagogical reasons—including the desire to give their own account and/or the belief that they can do a better job than present authors—and sometimes these reasons are spelled out. The author is fortunate who finds a supportive publisher—and sympathetic manuscript referees. Outliers tend not to do well in professionalized disciplines, whose members are interested in status and safety; outliers tend to become outsiders. One cannot expect, for example, very many Murray Rothbards or E.K. Hunts. As Gray suggests:

> custom and convention very properly require that an author—at least of anything that looks like a textbook—should make suitable apologies for his action in accentuating the horrid and outrageous disproportion between supply and demand in the world of books, and that he should at the same time, for the benefit of reviewers and others, indicate what particular long-felt gap he imagines he is filling.
>
> (Gray 1931: 5)

Newman (1952: vii) similarly claims that "it is customary for an author to offer his apologia for writing another history of economic theory."

But, not all authors are silent on marketing topics.

The 1975 edition of Jacob Oser's textbook, authored by Stanley Brue, addresses marketing characteristics, including "Product Differentiation" (Oser 1975: v–viii). Other textbooks, which change content and structure in efforts to improve market position, are not so candid.

Ekelund and Hébert (1983: vii) note the mixed reactions to the allocation of space in their 1975 edition; their 1997 edition speaks of market acceptance and of revision responsive to market demand (1997: xvi). Rima (1972: ix) says that the reception of her 1967 edition was that it was "either too technical or not technical enough." The former undoubtedly relates to undergraduate use and the latter to graduate use. The situation led to revision favoring the former, larger market. Bell's *History of Economic Thought* (1953: vi) states its author's desire to avoid "overloading" the reader with "unimportant details." Similar thoughts pervade one-half of Landreth and Colander's preface to their third edition (1994: xx–xxi).

Blaug (1985a: xv) indicates both that the final chapter on methodology has been "drastically cut" since it duplicates the discussion in his *Methodology of Economics* (1980) and that "There is an entirely new chapter on the history of location theory, a subject almost totally neglected in rival histories of economic thought" (1985a: xv).

Why study the history of economic thought

Some authors present reasons for, sometimes identified as benefits from, the study of the history of economic thought. Presumably their purpose is to educate and/or motivate the student. An alternative explanation in some cases—considering the insecure position of the field in the curriculum—is to provide a defense against the decline of the field. A cursory survey of theory and field textbooks suggests that their authors do not feel the need to justify the endeavor, as the work is taken for granted as being important. Interestingly, Spiegel (1983) does not state why the study of the history of economic thought should be undertaken.

A variety of reasons for studying the history of economic thought is given. Few authors say that the field is useful in providing legitimacy and status for persons, ideas and theories, a historical cachet or imprimatur, as it were. Yet such is one of the uses of the field, as historians seek selectively to dramatize and glorify the past, in part to cast luster on the present. Roll (1946: 2), for example, says that interest in the history of economic thought is "[o]ften [due to] a desire for respectability and legitimacy which leads to the search for a pedigree."

Some, perhaps many, authors treat the possibilities and problems of historical work in a way similar to the teaching of mathematical and philosophical logic, namely, training the mind to think and reason correctly. Consideration of presentism; theory choice; absolutism versus relativism; the role of criticism; the relevance of structuralism, hermeneutics, discourse analysis (rhetoric of economics), sociology, epistemology, postmodernism, and so on, amount to training in sensitivity, for example, to subtle differences in meaning or nuance and their significance. The recognition, practice, and discussions of rational reconstruction and historical reconstruction, whatever their respective relations to absolutism and relativism, have raised historiographic discourse in the literature to a new level of sophistication, though explicitly only negligibly in the textbooks.

The following list provides insight into the reasons adduced by authors for studying the history of economic thought.

Backhouse (1985: 1–2):
Teach us about the ways of the human mind
Place contemporary economics in perspective
Enable study of methodological issues and status

Backhouse (1988: 3–4):
Acquire a historical perspective

Bell (1953: v):
Grasp recurring, complex problems of economics
Gain a fresh perspective for appraising current ideas and policies

Bell (1967: v):
Afford some pride in science of economics
Strengthen understanding of the use of prevailing doctrines

Blaug (1968: 681–682):
Become aware of the tendency to mistake chaff for wheat and to claim possession of the truth when all that is possessed are intricate series of definitions or
value judgments disguised as scientific rules
"One justification for the study of the history of economics ... is that it
provides a more extensive 'laboratory' in which to acquire methodological
humility about the actual accomplishments of economics."

Canterbery (1995: 2):
Satisfy intellectual curiosity
See ideas unfold
Broaden our vision, be more reflective, more thoughtful

Ekelund and Hébert (1975: 11, 484):
Rethink foundations of theoretical ideas
Insight into how ability to analyze problems changes
Ascertain the origin and determinants of new ideas; better understanding of
the creative process
Perspective on how the discipline developed theoretically and methodologi-
cally
Learn how men think, as economists
Acquire feel for ideas that have "staying power"
Better understanding of contemporary theory

Ekelund and Hébert (1983: 4–5):
Perspective on how the discipline developed theoretically and methodologi-
cally
Learn how humans think

Ekelund and Hébert (1990: 5–7):
Better understanding of the creative process
Fundamental insights into the sociology of scientific knowledge
Appreciation of the ways of the mind—perspective
Feel for the kind of ideas having "staying power"
Better understanding of contemporary theory
Understanding the thought processes followed by the great minds in
economics

Fusfeld (1966: v):
Understanding working of minds of the great economists, the grand themes
they produced, and the emergence of a discipline

Haney (1926: 6):
Emphasizes a certain unity in economic thought
Understanding the origin and position of a science

Acquire a broad basis for comparison—judgment broadened, and "a well-balanced and reasonable conservatism, or a wise progressivism"

Haney (1949: vi):
Understand the rapid changes brought by World War II and the use of new and revolutionary ideas in that context

Heimann (1945: 21):
"The beginning of intellectual integrity is veracity and modesty, and these are what a critical study of the history of economics teaches us."

Landreth and Colander (1989: 1, 19):
Better understanding of current economic thinking
Become a better economist by strengthening theoretical and logical skills
Learn humility
Foster new ideas

Oser (1963: 377):
Gives perspective and understanding of our past, of changing ideas and problems, of our direction of movement

Oser and Brue (1994: 11):
Enhances understanding of contemporary economic thought
Provides closer check on irresponsible generalizations
Provides perspective and understanding of our past, of changing ideas and problems, and of our direction of movement
Helps us appreciate that no group has a monopoly on the truth, and that many groups and individuals have contributed to the richness and diversity of our intellectual, cultural and material inheritance

Rima (1972: x):
Helps to end unfortunate schism between history of economic theory and contemporary theory

Roll (1938: 14):
Helps to challenge pre-existing ideas amidst interplay of conflicts of ideas
Corrective for neglect of essentially practical nature of the discipline, due to intricacies of modern theoretical refinements
Learn of contribution of economics to general human thought

Barber (1967: 13):
Provides a frame of reference, an organizing framework
Provides fuller appreciation of the ideas that have contributed to the shaping of the modern world

Learn views on the nature of the economic system and its potentialities and limitations that are shaped by less self-conscious and more implicit processes

Catlin (1962: 17):
Provides best safeguard against either fixity of ideas and overconfidence in existing institutions or an undue eagerness for change

Negishi (1989: 1–5):
Enables retention for possible future use of presently excluded programs, to maintain commensurability among programs, and to enable profitable competition among paradigms and programs

Niehans (1990: ix):
Enables present research to be more productive

Perlman and McCann (1998: 579):
Learn the critical significance of epistemic perceptions
Learn what type of economist one wants to be—a technocrat or an architect

Schumpeter (1954: 4–6):
Provides direction and meaning to current work
Provides material for new inspiration; explains what ideas succeed, why and how
Teaches us the ways of the human mind
Teaches that economics subject matter deals with different sets of fact and problems over time

Staley (1989: 1–2):
Learn how knowledge grows, both in factual content and in the theories used to organize and understand the facts, learning both the content of the theories and the process by which they changed, neither in a straight line nor a painless process
Gain perspective

Taylor (1960: xiv–xv):
Education for enlightened citizenship and technical training of professional economists

Initial selectivity

Considerations of intended audience and marketing aside, a prospective author has a number of further choices to make in working out a design strategy. These include: the starting point and ending point in time; theory versus ideas as orientation; selection between individuals, schools, concepts and theories; structure; the ontologies of definition of reality, system of belief, and tools; the reasons why the history of economic thought is important and should be studied; the mode of doing history of economic thought and the relative coverage of biography and historical events; and so on. Most authors do not address all these considerations

Table 3.1 The starting point in time

Starting Point	Theory	Ideas	Total
Ancient	5	18	23
Medieval	1	5	6
Merc.—17th century	5	7	12
18th century	6	11	17
19th century	1	1	2
Post-World War II	2	1	3
Total	20	43	63

explicitly; an outlier is Schumpeter (1954) who devotes the first four chapters of his textbook to such considerations.

The starting point in time

Authors must determine when they will commence telling their story, a determination that is tied into some other design issues, especially that between theory and ideas, considered independently below. That is a convenient topic with which to begin the present discussion of selectivity.

The list of textbooks used in this study, counting each series as one, comprises sixty-three. Of them, twenty are or are predominantly theory or analysis-oriented (a subjective matter as is also the identification of books that in one or two chapters survey economic thought up to their starting point for intensive discussion, e.g., the seventeenth or eighteenth century) and forty-three are idea-oriented. The starting points for the two groups are shown in Table 3.1.

Eleven of twenty theory-oriented books start before the eighteenth century; thirty of forty-three ideas-oriented books start before the eighteenth century. While this is a significant difference, not all theory-oriented books omit serious consideration of economic thought before the eighteenth century (which is widely but not universally identified as the beginning of modern economics). (Of books manifestly critical of the development of economics, the corresponding numbers are: ancient, 2; medieval, 1; mercantilism–seventeenth century, 4; eighteenth century, 3; nineteenth century, 1; i.e., seven of eleven commence prior to the eighteenth century.)

(Books starting in the sixteenth century are included in the medieval category. Starting points in the eighteenth century include but are not limited to the Physiocrats and Smith.)

Different authors, therefore, adopt different starting dates; all are aware of Backhouse's (2002: 5) question "When should the history of economics begin?" and give varying reasons for their choice.

Blaug (1968: xii) has the beginnings in the seventeenth century and elaborates thus:

> Economics, as a separate discipline of inquiry, did not emerge until the seventeenth century, perhaps because in preceding centuries economic transactions were not integrated on a national or even a regional basis, perhaps because economic institutions were severely circumscribed by military and political considerations, perhaps because economic motives were prevented from affecting more than limited aspects of social behaviour. It is not obvious why all economic reasoning before the seventeenth century was *ad hoc*, unsystematic and devoid of the recognition of an autonomous sphere of economic activity, but that it was so is hardly ever contraverted. And since this is a book about economics rather than economists, we will ignore what might be described as "the paleontology of the subject."

Per contra, Kuhn (1963: 1), for example, maintains that "the emancipation of economic from other social thought occurred during the second half of the eighteenth century" and Oser (1963: 3) commences with the mercantilists, out of concern that starting earlier "would make this book too long"—a decision presumably driven by (one view of) marketing considerations. Others decide coverage of the Greeks is worthwhile—such as Schumpeter (1954)—and Spiegel (1983) devotes chapters to biblical and pre-Greek times. In contrast, Screpanti and Zamagni (1993), for example, opt for a later starting point in order to devote more coverage to recent topics.

Individuals, schools or ideas

Ideas are often associated with individuals and individuals with schools, so focus on any one of the three typically includes consideration of the other two. Thus, Rima (1967: ix) maintains that the evolution of analytical tools and concepts can be divorced from neither the environment within which they were developed, nor the specific problems that inspired them, nor the individuals and schools whose "attitudes and preconceptions" they reflect.

Some authors nonetheless indicate their emphasis on one of the three. Haney (1949: vi) urged that:

> Particularly dangerous is the specious argument in favor of dealing with theories rather than with theorists. In no field of knowledge is thought so molded by the thinker and his environment as is the case with economics; and it is therefore always desirable to know something about circumstances.

Oser (1963: 4–7) and Oser and Brue (1994: 9–10) state their "major questions" in terms of schools—though Brue's edition concludes that individual economists have "mattered" (1994: 538).

A large number of authors explicitly identify the neoclassical mainstream as the focus of their book (see also the discussion of presentism, below). Some, like Backhouse (1985: xii), indicate the attention given in their text to alternative approaches.

As indicated in chapter 2 of this volume, several authors indicate that their texts focus on the past insofar as it has led to one school, the neoclassical mainstream. These authors "have read history through the lens of subsequent developments in economic theory and not as it actually unraveled" (Cariappa 1996: 10). Two points are relevant. First, if this plan were in fact to be carried out, a large proportion of the history of economic theory (and thought) would be omitted. The work would be a history of the present hegemonic school and its origins, more or less widely contemplated; it would be a history of neither economic theory nor economic thought. Or second, the plan is not carried out. The past covered in the textbooks is richer and more diverse than if it were. Surely books are written with the idea in mind, but, for whatever reason, some versions of heterodox, etc. economics are covered.

Bell (1953: v) says that his approach includes only those thinkers whose ideas, insights, and teachings have had substantial influence on the mainstream of economic thought. But also, "particular attention is paid to constructive criticisms of outstanding figures and doctrines by their contemporaries and successors." A somewhat different view is expressed in his 1967 edition: "brings together the most significant scholars and schools whose influence has left permanent imprint on the body of economic doctrines ... [but also] less well-known names and their contributions" (Bell 1967: v).

Ekelund and Hébert (1975: xi) say that their book covers the major figures plus "'supporting players' ... selected, in part, by using our own personal judgment as to which past writers the profession finds especially useful in interpreting contemporary economic problems or systems of thought."

Blaug (1962: ix) writes that his is "a study of the logical coherence and explanatory value of ... orthodox economic theory ... [whose] purpose is to teach contemporary economic theory ... as a legacy handed down from the past." He also says, "If, in the chapters that follow, there is little about Zeitgeist, social milieu, economic institutions, and philosophical movements, it is not because these things are unimportant but because they fall outside the scope of our inquiry" (1962: 7). There is, indeed, little, say, in comparison with Spiegel or Taylor's textbooks, but little is not none and there may be more than readily meets the eyes of the reader.

Ekelund and Hébert (1990: xiv) say that they pay more attention to mainstream economics and less to the institutional approach. This is to reflect both the authors' own methodological preference and their "informed judgment of what is more likely to be of immediate service to university students seeking historical perspective on the nature and the promise of contemporary economics."

Gray (1931) calls his an introduction, enabling current and accepted doctrine to be made more palatable by a "backward glance at the development of thought and opinion" (1931: 5) and selectively omitting developments and figures that seem "less important to-day," such as the old controversy over "method" (1931: 7).

Rima (1986: x) says that her fourth edition gives fuller treatment to institutionalism.

Whittaker's 1940 book is one of several which, as a history of ideas (its title), are structured ideationally, not chronologically. His view then was for "more emphasis on the evolution of leading ideas, and less on particular schools and individuals, than is provided by most of the textbooks available in the field" (1940: vii). Of course, he later wrote a more conventional, chronological text (Whittaker 1960).

Selectivity as to individuals and beyond

Whatever an author's attitude concerning individuals and schools, it is typically the work of particular individuals that is presented. But which individuals? Numerous authors inform the reader of the necessity of selectivity; many simply mention the point, others indicate something about how they have handled it. Almost all of the texts include the work of the canonical authors, such as Smith, Ricardo, Malthus, J.S. Mill, Marshall, and so on. Some unusual positions on inclusion are the following.

The scope of Breit and Ransom is "largely restricted to the ideas of American economists" (1971: ix). This approach is the exception, however. Still, even they must choose which American economists to cover. Also an exception— more possible then than now, i.e., relatively fewer omissions—is Haney's declared aim:

> to present a critical account of the whole development of economic thought in the leading nations of the Occidental world; and, while keeping the purely economic viewpoint, to indicate some of the most important relations of economic thought with philosophy and environmental conditions.
>
> (1926: v)

Gray (1931: 6–7) emphasizes the necessity for limits, and his own struggles with whom to cover and to what extent. Gray opts to cover "no writer unless I could find space for something like an intelligible account of what he stood for" (1931: 6).

Newman complains of all the textbooks and doctoral dissertations that:

> have dug deeper and deeper into the past, finding economic nuggets in the minds of every great thinker from Plato to Christ, and hopefully searching for a "neglected economist." This aversion to neglect can swing the pendulum too far in the other direction, to finding merit where merit there is none.
>
> (1952: 1)

Roll (1946: 4) points out that a history of ideas is necessarily selective and interpretive. His selection of individual economists has been guided by their having "significance in relation to present-day theory and controversy" and having exemplified "most clearly different trends of thought (1946: 7)." He also warns of the danger of neglecting non-academic theorizing.

Taylor (1960: ix) also says that the history of economic thought is necessarily highly selective, as does Weintraub (1977: xi) and Vaggi and Groenewegen (2003: xii, xv; as to both topics and authors).

Dasgupta (1985: 4–10) examines in detail the problem of defining each epoch and choosing representative figures.

Gill (1967: 2) views the development of a "certain mainstream ... not as a matter of taste but simply because it is better economics—more consistent, general, and realistic." He also says, "But economics is not a pure science; it is impure, uncertain, and *controversial.*"

Selectivity applies not solely to the mainstream. Ingram (1888) omits the Ricardian socialists, Karl Marx and other socialists.

Lekachman's (1959: xiii) selectivity applies to the choice of people and problems rather than concepts and doctrines. For Niehans (1990: 3), it applies to persons and subjects, especially subjects.

Rothbard is particularly critical of what

> in the 1940s, ... was an overwhelmingly dominant paradigm in the approach to the history of economic thought. ... Essentially, this paradigm features a few Great Men as the essence of the history of economic thought, with Adam Smith as the almost superhuman founder ... the creator of both economic analysis and of the free trade, free market tradition in political economy.
>
> (1995a: vii)

His overt selectivity centers on the choice of interpretive base: "an overall history of economic thought from a frankly 'Austrian' standpoint," one "grounded in what is currently the least fashionable though not the least numerous variant of the Austrian School: the 'Misesian' or 'praxeologic.'"

Staley (1989: 1) reports that his survey deals with the major figures who have contributed to the existing body of knowledge.

A further dimension of the foregoing concerns structure. Authors must adopt a design strategy and accordingly structure their story in terms of individuals, schools, epochs, modes of thought, and so on, including elements of variation within each type.

A further dimension concerns the internalist versus externalist approaches to the source of economic theory and ideas. This will be taken up below.

The volume of work undertaken and published by economists has become vastly more enlarged and its content more diverse and increasingly technical and mathematical. It has always been difficult to approach anything like a full coverage of economic thought (see the next paragraph). The difficulty has been increasing exponentially, underscoring the fact of selectivity. It has been increasingly difficult to fully portray contemporary economics, whether in terms of individuals, schools, ideas and theories, sub-fields, or what not.

Two points are relevant at this juncture. First, the inclusion of a particular name in the story of that history contributes to the perpetuation of that person and his or her work for posterity. Historians of economic thought, and others (see chapter 2), help make reputations. Omission from these textbooks means exclusion from disciplinary memory. Second, the inclusion of a particular name helps define both who is an economist and, thereby, the field or discipline of economics. It appears that authors do not articulate these points in the types of sections covered in this study; either they choose to ignore them—and their own roles in the defining of their subject matter—or they are unaware of them.

No textbook is or can be complete. Each is selective in its choice of representative or important figures, theories, and so on. Indeed, every single historian of economic thought has selective knowledge. Nonetheless, textbooks can be differentiated on the basis of how encyclopedic they are. Examples of the clearly encyclopedic variety are Spiegel (1971) and Schumpeter (1954). Spiegel's is intended to be a textbook, whereas Schumpeter's is a treatise.

Pervading several, perhaps all, of these statements is the notion of "importance." Hunt (1979: xv) rebuts the premise that historical importance conclusively derives from a hegemonic neoclassicism, saying, "But 'importance' is not a scientific category ... custom and tradition are the principal criteria." He says that

> My criteria [of selection] are based upon three general beliefs. ... First, I believe that social theories and social-historical processes are reciprocally interconnected. ... [S]ocial theories are the products of the social and economic circumstances in which they are conceived. But it is equally true that human beings act, create, shape, and change their social and economic circumstances on the basis of ideas they hold about these circumstances. Therefore, there is a sense in which ... social and economic circumstances are the products of ideas and social theories. ... Second, ... while today's capitalism is, in numerous respects, substantially different from capitalism of the late 18th century, nevertheless there are important and institutional foundations that have continually underlain capitalism.
>
> (Hunt 1979: xv)

> Third, ... all economists are, and always have been, vitally concerned with practical, social, political, and moral issues. Consequently, their writings have both a cognitive, scientific element and an emotive, moral or ideological element. Moreover, I do not believe these two elements are entirely separable. ... A thinker's moral feelings and ideological views give the direction to the cognitive, scientific inquiry and set the limits as to what will constitute "legitimate" range of solutions for that thinker. Moreover, moral feelings and ideological views are based on, and are always defended

by means of, the thinker's cognitive or scientific theories of how society actually functions.

(1979: xvi)

In my view, all theorists, all historians, and all human beings ... have values that significantly interpenetrate all cognitive endeavors.

(1979: xvi)

One of the frequently recurring themes in the history of economic thought—a theme that is central to this book—is the issue of whether capitalism is a social system that conduces toward harmony or toward conflict.

(1979: xvi–xvii)

Other themes include "the debate over the inherent stability or instability of capitalism" and

the question of the relationship between the pricing of consumer goods and the pricing of "the factors of production" or income distribution. The classical economists and Marx held that income distribution was an important determinant of the prices of commodities, whereas the neoclassical economists generally reversed the direction of causality. Most authors of history of economic thought books have accepted the neoclassical version without question and have treated the classical-Marx version as a historically antiquated curiosum.

(Hunt 1979: xvii)

Importance obviously depends in part on authorial attitudes toward the economic system and positions on different canonical authors or schools.

Haney (1949: vii) gives serious thought in his Preface to what constitutes "important," and suggests the application of a twofold test: (1) "what has been the writer's effect upon the stream of economics thought?"; and (2) "what important point in theory has he originated or developed?" He does not, however, offer any additional criteria to determine important points in theory.

Further selectivity: doing history of economic thought

Some historical perspective, no matter how implicit, is both inevitable and necessary for a coherent account of the history of economic thought. Certainly any account should and likely will reflect the heterogeneity and complexity of the subject. Critical to any account is the historian's attitude toward both the history of economic thought itself and how to do history-of-economic-thought work (see Samuels and Medema 1996).

We have already identified as design strategies certain modes of doing history of economic thought. The following identifies other, different sets of alternative modes of doing history of economic thought, and thus additional alternative elements of design strategies. All are selectively applied and pursue and give effect, each in their own way, to "understanding the thought procedures followed by the great minds in economics" (Ekelund and Hébert 1990: 7).

Theory versus ideas

As indicated previously, twenty books in our relatively comprehensive sample are oriented to economic theory or analysis and forty-three to economic ideas or thought. A vivid illustrative comparison is between Blaug, on the one hand, and Taylor or Spiegel on the other. Both types of design strategy cover the main persons, concepts, theories, and so on. The difference is that the former concentrates both more intensively and more exclusively on pure theory and/or theory alone and on tools than does the latter. The gap is substantial but less than one might surmise from the sections covered here, in part through attention to matters of biography, economic history, and philosophy. The remarkable—and well-known—case is that of Schumpeter's *History of Economic Analysis* which is extremely detailed and wide ranging in its coverage, notwithstanding its title. Rima's volumes were initially said to be devoted to tools and concepts. But they were broader than that, even in early editions, and became more like history-of-economic-thought texts in later editions.

Perhaps the major difference among texts is between those that *focus* on ideas and those that focus on theory (the second is criticism versus defense of economic theory). Theory- or analysis-oriented texts concentrate on the logical treatment of abstract conceptions and treat economic thought in and as due to an atmosphere of purism or formalism and as an effort to define and explain the economy, and to do so through the construction of deductive theory. These texts obviously are not devoid of ideas but the focus on theory is more substantive than that on ideas.

Ideas-oriented texts, usually with "thought" in the title, treat economic thought as a part of intellectual and cultural history and focus on ideas, including theory *qua* ideas. Most "ideas" books stress the flow from intellectual and/or cultural environment; very few stress the influence of economics on intellectual and cultural environment. These texts examine the theories and, perhaps especially, the ideational meaning of the theories. Perhaps in recognition of this issue, Deane (1978) calls her text, *The Evolution of Economic Ideas*.

Theory-oriented textbooks putatively derive the ontological and epistemological status of theory from the object of study—though "attribute" is more apposite than "derive." Ideas-oriented textbooks' status is derived from human intellect in all its subjective variety and complexity.

Textbooks on the history of theory deal with increasingly technical coverage, including correction and refinement. But they are not solely and totally focused on the tools and concepts of pure theory and the process of their development. Even with increasing emphasis on pure theory and technical tools, they, too, pay attention to aspects of political economy and economic thought, as well as topics of economic policy and methodology. While promising emphasis on tools and concepts, they also, inevitably, present the development of theories of the economic system for the analysis of which tools and concepts were developed. Books on theory or analysis are markedly different from books on ideas, though the difference is not total.

In summary, five somewhat contradictory points may be made. First, there are clear differences between books devoted to theory, such as Blaug's, and those devoted to ideas, such as Spiegel's. Each stresses its intended forte. Second, even books explicitly devoted to theory or analysis cover ideas, though not as broadly or as deeply as books on ideas. Both necessarily deal with the developing corpus of theory—as to the economic system *qua* system and as to explanations and/or descriptions of particular phenomena as well as the ideas ensconced in the theories. Even the "mainstream" of theory tends to be broadly developed. Third, books explicitly devoted to ideas cover economic theory, in some detail, even if in less detail than books devoted to theory. The foregoing points are even more complex because of the necessity for selectivity of coverage and the different arrays of coverage. Fourth, as suggested by Backhouse's trilogy, no *necessary* hiatus exists between theory- and ideas-oriented books. Indeed, the theory versus ideas conflict is, on the one hand, a matter of what is deemed important for the task at hand, and, on the other, a matter of design strategy. To author books in each genre requires only a well-informed, talented, open-minded, and precocious intellect. Fifth, theory-oriented textbooks appear to treat their subject in an internalist manner, whereas ideas-oriented textbooks seem to follow an externalist perspective. Each perspective amounts to a design strategy, although authors likely would say that their approach is congruent with the reality of how economic theory, even ideas, are formed.

An example of the fifth point is provided by Ekelund and Hébert. They say that their major focus is on the development of economic abstractions which "do indeed seem to have a life of their own" (1975: 10)—language usually employed in discussing internalism. They also note that questions about the role of environment lack conclusive answers; still, "Much of our treatment of theory will touch upon economic *thought*, i.e., upon environmental, philosophical, and social affiliations with abstractions" (1975: 11). In their 1983 edition the language changes from abstractions plus thought to abstractions and methodology. Their major focus now is

> the development of economic abstractions per se, although social and methodological issues are frequently considered as integral parts of the intellectual landscape. We believe that economic theories do indeed have a life of their own that … is both interesting and fruitful.
>
> (Ekelund and Hébert 1983: 6)

Haney (1926: 653; repeated in 1936: 780) presciently writes, "In fact, … one can realize some tendency toward general, 'pure' economics." Interestingly,

Haney (1949: 948) states, "And Institutionalism plays the useful part of criticizing abstract generalizations."

Landreth and Colander (1989: xvi) say that their textbook's emphasis is on modern theory but it also covers heterodox ideas and the workings of given theoretical structures, as well as the policy implications of theories and their impact on subsequent developments in theory and policy. Their 1994 edition suggests both how nondescriptive/uninformative or misleading a title may be and the putative influence of marketing strategy. What hitherto had been the title, *History of Economic Theory*, was now *History of Economic Thought*. Of this they wrote that they changed title to escape any suggestion of "a narrowly focused book dealing with how past ideas have contributed to the content of mainstream orthodox economic theory." Previous editions, they note, had given attention to both heterodox and orthodox ideas. "Thus, our change in title to 'thought' rather than 'theory' does not represent a change in content but a change in terminology to conform to nuances of current usage" (1994: xx). They also cite the greater attention given to economic thought as a basis for economic policy (1994: xxi).

We turn to a distinction not always drawn explicitly, though all texts must deal with it willy nilly, whether economic theory is pure theory or theory of actual economies. Pure theory deals with pure abstract a-institutional categories, such as firms, markets, commodities, and so on. It is seen either to have no or no direct application to actual economies or to have application. The late twentieth-century view was increasingly that it—in the form, for example, of general equilibrium theory—had/has no direct application. Theory pertaining to actual institutionalized economies was largely devoted to policy issues. (As Blaug (1962: 6) puts it, "Economic theory, even in its purest form, has implications for policy and in that sense makes political propaganda of one kind or another. This element of propaganda is inherent in the subject.") Newman (1952) includes a chapter attempting to identify the effects of Keynesian theory economic policy.

Ontologically, "economic reality" could be defined in terms of one type of theory or the other; economic reality could consist of general purely conceptual ideas or of certain existential phenomena. Each type of theory exhibits the problem of choice: Different bodies of pure theory exist and different "realistic" accounts of actual economies exist. Neither of the two different approaches to "reality" could provide necessarily conclusive descriptions and/or explanations. The closest the textbooks come to the problem at this level is when they discuss either the multiplicity of theories and the conflicts among them or the conflict between orthodox and heterodox schools—facts too patent to ignore but not emphasized by all authors.

All that being said, there is no conclusive need to discuss in detail the textbook authors' choices in design strategy as between those that fall in the two categories, theory and ideas. They are aware, at least for the most part, of what they are doing and of the compromises they are making. Still, some matters are worth citing.

Backhouse (1985: xi) writes that in this history of modern economic analysis the coverage is narrower than "thought" and broader than "theory."

Schumpeter (1954) says, first, that his subjects are "the history of the intellectual efforts … made … to understand economic phenomena or … the history of the analytical or scientific aspects of economic thought" and, second, "the Sociology of Science—… the theory of science considered as a social phenomenon" (1954: 3). In a discussion of "The Techniques of Economic Analysis," he further says that economic analysis is comprised of history, statistics, theory and economic sociology. Theory as an explanatory hypothesis is rejected in favor of theory as "mere instruments or tools framed for the purpose of establishing interesting results. … And it is the sum total of such gadgets— inclusive of strategically useful assumptions—which constitutes economic theory. In Mrs. Robinson's unsurpassably felicitous phrase, economic theory is a box of tools" (1954: 15). In a discussion of "The Sociology of Economics" Schumpeter further says that in addition to the Science of Science (logic and epistemology) we have the Sociology of Science analyzing

> the social factors and processes that produce the specifically scientific type of activity, condition its rate of development, determine its direction towards certain subjects rather than other equally possible ones, foster some methods of procedure in preference to others, set up the social mechanisms that account for success or failure of lines of research or individual performances, raise or depress the status and influence of scientists (in our senses) and their work, and so on.
>
> (1954: 33)

Especially relevant to the history of economic analysis are ideology, the "motive forces of scientific endeavor and the mechanisms of scientific development" and the personnel of economic science (1954: 33). Implicit in Schumpeter's approach are the many forms that theory can take.

Rima consistently says that she intends to present the development of "the analytical tools and concepts which comprise the body of economic theory" (1967: ix; 1972: ix). In her 1978 (p. x) and 1986 (p. ix) editions, she still writes of their being a history of theory, tools and concepts, but now uses the language of a "history of economics." The 1991 (pp. vii–viii) edition emphasized less the development of theory/analysis and became more of a conventional history of economic thought text encompassing both theory and ideas. The 2001 (pp. ix, xi) edition may have moved incrementally back toward the theory end of the spectrum.

All three of Spiegel's editions are said by him to have the "aim to strengthen the link between economics and the humanities and to relate the history of economic thought to the intellectual tendencies of the various periods." He says that he takes a cultural rather than a technical approach. Still, the central organizing question is said to be, "How did a writer or his school propose to cope with the fundamental economic problem of scarcity?"

(1991: v). If theory-oriented books are internalist, thought-oriented ones are externalist.

Hutchison (1953: v–viii) indicates an unusually broad agenda. He claims to focus on both pure theory and its application to problems of policy. The initial focus is on the internal logical development of each branch of economic theory, without presuming any simple regular development, and attention is given to "external" problems of economic change, dynamics and instability (1953: viii). He is interested in both the working of great minds and the external influences of ideas and problems (1953: viii). Static analysis, pursued for heuristical or propaedeutical reasons, has been characterized by both ambiguity and realism (1953: viii). Analysis has increasingly become less realistic and less relevant. The adequacy of a theory is to be judged in relation to the conditions it was devised to explain (1953: ix). Doctrines carry implicit and explicit assumptions and their applicability depends on the economic world to which they are applied (1953: ix–x). Early theory is said to be unrealistic today because of vast changes in actual economies (1953: x).

Rogin (1956: 6) addresses both "ideal theoretical models" and "ideal institutional premises." If, as he argues, the meaning of a theory resides in its use in policy making, then some specifics are driven by idealized antecedent normative premises.

Criticism and defense of economic theory

CRITICISM

Some critics of mainstream economics object to the body of theory and doctrine on substantive and methodological grounds. Others are primarily critics of the modern Western economic system; their criticism of the economic system drives their criticism of economics, in part presenting mainstream economic theory as the economic system's ideology. All tend to criticize *a priori* economic theory both as narrow and unscientific and as connected with *laissez-faire* policy. Some adopt a radical alternative (Hunt) and others an evolutionary and humanist position (Ingram 1888). Newman (1952: 3) attempts a middle of the road approach considering those "who were satisfied with neither Marxian nor with neo-classical theory." Peck (1935), however, offers an explicitly institutional reading of the history of economic thought

DEFENSE

Some authors explicitly seek to defend mainstream economic theory and analysis (Backhouse 1985) and some to defend and otherwise cast luster on the Western economic system (Skousen 2001). The key historiographic point is that some textbook authors accept their accounts as either truth or a story, and other authors do not.

Definition of reality, system of belief, or set of tools

Beyond the dualism of theory and ideas lies a still deeper issue: whether economic theory or thought constitute efforts to define reality, establish a belief system or create a set of tools with which to examine the economy. The temptation is to understand the phrase "examine the economy" as if the economy had an independently generated existence. But the economy is, for economists, formed in part by the tools used to define it. The discussion becomes particularly complicated because definitions of reality and systems of belief, as well as the definitions of the words used in their articulation, are, or can be seen as, so many tools. Circularity is insinuated partially by the use of definitions that embody theories. The underlying issue is the ontological (and epistemological) nature of the theories and ideas constituting the history of economic thought. No one, to our knowledge, denies the existence of "an economy" to study. The question is whether the economy as economists know it corresponds to a given, transcendent economy or is a matter of human interpretation, of human social construction (in two senses: creation and interpretation). The textbooks are largely silent on the matter but nonetheless provide implicit suggestions. One discussion that comes near to this matter is methodology, especially the authors' treatment of economics as a science; another is philosophical realism. Two considerations pertaining to science are of present relevance. One is the difference between economics *being* a science and economics *being seen* as a science. The other is the problematic, probabilistic nature of science, to wit, the difficulty of ascertaining justified truth.

In any event, our task at this point is to establish the distinctions between the three alternatives. Some textbooks project the history of economic theory/thought as a history of tool-making and using. Other textbooks tell the story of the history of economic thought as one of ideas, ideas whose progenitors and users may contemplate them as efforts to know economic reality but which, for practical and analytical purposes, constitute a system of belief. Other authors present the case or assume that the task of economists is to define reality; tools and ideas are not ends in themselves but means to the definition of reality, i.e., economics is more than a system of mere belief (except insofar as it is problematic and tentative). Since this is a matter on which the textbooks typically are silent, we must seek the ways in which they nonetheless provide, in their own ways, implicit suggestions.

Textbooks that teach the history of economic theory strongly tend to adopt the economics-as-tools approach but may go further toward the definition-of-reality approach. The classic case is Schumpeter's *History of Economic Analysis* (1954). Schumpeter writes that his subject is "the history of the efforts to describe and explain economic facts and to provide the tools for doing so" (1954: vii). (Invocation of "economic facts" can constitute philosophical realism and that may be the case for Schumpeter. The idea of theory-laden facts is not central to his point of view. Still, he may have a soft rather than hard conception of "facts.") He favors, as we have seen, theory understood as mere instruments or tools framed for the purpose of establishing interesting results. ... And it is the sum total of such gadgets—inclusive of strategically useful assumptions—which constitutes economic theory. In Mrs. Robinson's unsurpassably felicitous phrase, economic theory is a box of tools.

(1954: 15)

However, tools are used in telling stories. For Schumpeter the scientific process—vision and its results subjected to rules of scientific procedure (1954: 41–47)—is another set of tools. They are tools for working out the definition of reality. Here he has high hopes but, ever realistic, knows the results are likely to be problematic.

Blaug (1962: 4) affirms that unequivocal progress has been made in the matter of tools and analytical constructs and that "the history of economics is not so much the chronicle of a continuous accumulation of theoretical achievements as the story of exaggerated intellectual revolutions, in which truths already known are neglected in favor of new revelations"—in other words, both progress by some standard and through misapprehensions. Others, such as Deane (1978) and Hutchinson (1978), debate what constitutes revolutions or major turning points in history, attempting to determine whether one can identify progress in economics, as well as how progress comes about.

Other authors have adopted the tools approach, more likely in combination with the realist rather than the belief approach but with a sense of the problematic. Rima (1967: ix), after indicating her goal as tracing the "development of the analytical tools and concepts that comprise the body of economic theory," says that "efforts to explain economic phenomena [have] resulted in the forging of analytical tools and concepts ... refined, and sometimes rediscovered or discarded, by later writers."

Barber (1967: 14) follows Robinson in viewing economics as a toolkit, with the tools shaped by the uses to which they are put.

Dome (1994: xv) writes that the development and improvement of analytical tools enables us "to know economic phenomena more finely than before," though "new ideas and methods ... are sometimes partly a refashioning of past doctrines" and "we have to judge what is mere refashioning and what is real progress."

Niehans (1990: 1) writes that "Economic theory may be regarded as a perpetual inventory of analytical tools," with deletions and additions. The inventory at a given time

may be called the mainstream economics of that period. Opinions about the content of mainstream economics will inevitably differ. There is no dogmatic authority watching over the purity of the faith and unity of doctrine. The basic test of mainstream economics is whether a particular piece of analysis is found useful in practical application or promising for further research.

(1990: 1)

In other words, he emphasizes the usefulness of tools rather than correspondence with reality, and free thinking rather than doctrinaire representations of a supposed reality.

Perlman and McCann (1998: 570), notwithstanding their modes-of-thought design/interpretation, say that the patristic legacies shape our perceptions, have an ability to remain dormant for long periods, and are tools or frameworks both "useful in making sense of, and even giving structure to, an amorphous mass of sometimes contradictory conclusions" and serving "to shape perceptions further."

More than tools are involved for Heilbroner, though the reader is uncertain whether the definition or reality or system of belief is involved. In his 1953 edition, he writes,

> When the economists were done, what had been a humdrum and chaotic world became a living society with a life history and a meaning of its own.
>
> It is this search for the meaning of the world which lies at the heart of economics.
>
> (Heilbroner 1953: 7)

In the 1961, 1967 and 1972 editions, the first statement is unchanged (1961: 3) and the second is replaced with "It is this search for the order and meaning of social history which lies at the heart of economics" (1961: 4). The task, even the social function, of the economist is to provide meaning, not necessarily knowledge, i.e., a sense of order, to set minds at rest (very much in the tradition of Adam Smith and George Shackle).

Routh (1989), rejecting the tenacious realist claims of orthodox mainstream economics, denies

> the cluster of beliefs that constitutes the [mainstream] economist's perception of the economic world—the hard core, paradigm or vision. … They do not see the world in terms of a paradigm, they aver, but simply note, examine and explain what is there.
>
> (1989: 340–341)

Theirs is a creed, "impervious to argument" (1989: 342).

A similar skeptical position was voiced by Boucke (1921: 319), who wrote, apropos of the use of certain terms, "Not mere metaphors these, but analogies held to be real!"

A. Bosman (Kastelein *et al.* 1976: 129) seemingly takes a realist position when he says that teleological rationality enables the concept of a procedural system (1976: 131), whose central question is the validity of the representation of a problem (1976: 132).

Landreth and Colander (1989: 5–6) point to related problems of presenting diversity. Their 2002 edition, distinguishing "modern economics from neoclassical economics," says that modern economics is "characterized more by its method—an eclectic, formal model-building and model-testing approach—than by specific beliefs" (2002: xx).

Apropos of diversity, Mair and Miller (1991: 19) claim that diversity among schools is a sign of maturity and a cause of some optimism. "No individual, no school of thought has a monopoly of the truth in economics." It is not made clear whether they intend a lower- or higher-case meaning of "truth."

Rothbard (1995a) writes that his is "an overall history of economic thought from a frankly 'Austrian' standpoint," one "grounded in what is currently the least fashionable though not the least numerous variant of the Austrian School: the 'Misesian' or 'praxeologic'" (1995a: vii). Thus he adopts as his design strategy one variant of the Austrian economics paradigm. Austrian economics is the test of what is to be praised or denigrated, although he is not specific as to the presently relevant reasons why

> rather than everyone contributing to an ever-progressing edifice, economics can and has proceeded in contentious, even zig-zag fashion, with later systemic fallacy sometimes elbowing aside earlier but sounder paradigms, thereby redirecting economic thought down a total erroneous or even tragic path. The overall path of economics may be up, or it may be down, over any give[n] time period.
>
> (1995a: x)

But the late Rothbard, it would seem, was no postmodernist. The social constructivist implication was not his. He emphasized neither interpretation *per se* nor the role of choice, and neither economic theory as system or belief nor as toolkit. For Rothbard, and for many others, the matter is not interpretation as a key activity, it is a matter of the correct versus the wrong definition of reality, given the essential—shall we say, following Mises, apodictic—nature of things. On the one hand, he can be read as a constructivist who says, let's get it right normatively; on the other, as a realist who says, let's get it right positively and objectively. Either way, Smith, according to Rothbard, got it wrong.

The tone of some textbooks seems to reflect a belief that the economy is "out there," that it is the economists' object of study, and that economic study, particularly economic theory, is ever more drawn toward a correct description and explanation of it derived from the object of study itself. The text of some other textbooks seems to reflect a belief that whatever it is that economists study, the stories they tell are socially constructed and reflect authorial preconceptions, ideologies, personal ambitions, academic pressures and problems, and so on. Realists disagree about substance, rendering their claims as to Truth putative and inconclusive and their realism a mode of approbation and legitimation. Whatever one's personal view of philosophical realism, it seems clear, as many authors acknowledge, that writing the history of either economic theory or economic thought is an *interpretive* exercise. Both positions reduce, therefore, to *interpretation*.

But not all textbooks on the history of economic thought consider multiplicity *per se* and the reasons for it (Barber 1967: 14 and passim; see also p. 259). The neoclassical hegemony of late twentieth-century economics is their lodestar and most if not all prior and competing schools of thought are seen as stepping stones to recent neoclassicism, even those leading to dead ends or comprising error, i.e., an essentially unilinear path. Some textbooks identify the array of competing schools at important points in time. For the most part, however, it is left to the reader to recognize the existence of the array; it is negligibly discussed as a topic suitable and important for the author to cover. Some textbooks identify late twentieth-century economics in terms of competing schools or paradigms (e.g., Rima 1986: x and part VI; 1996: ch. 25; 2001: 4–5). Negishi (1989: 385) makes a point of insisting, "Throughout this book, we have emphasized the coexistence of many different paradigms in economics." Gray (1931: 370, 369), discussing what he identifies as an age of transition—in which "there are so many streams of thought that the result is an obvious whirlpool"—argues, "When there is no dominant school, when theory is in solution and truth may be anywhere, ideas of all kind, mutually contradictory, jostle against each other in the pot in which public opinion is cooked"—but ceases his story with the Austrian School.

Ekelund and Hébert (1983: 4), in the face of a hegemonic school (itself, ironically, diverse), say—in effect echoing Knight's statement quoted in the epigraph—that "The plain truth is that economics is anything but a settled body of thought. Even among mainstream economists, gnawing questions persist ... not all economists approach the subject in the same way."

The writing of any history is a matter of construction, a function of selective perception. The result is an array of interpretations, each more or less different than the others. Each written history, therefore, is inevitably an interpretation. Theory-oriented texts tend to emphasize tools, and ideas-oriented ones, system of belief and/or tools. Both groups understand that tools and system of belief function to define reality.

Modes of doing history of economic thought

MODERNISM VERSUS POSTMODERNISM

It is fair to say that all of our authors accept and most if not all stress that economic theory is neither perfect nor complete, and is subject to revision. This is true of authors who more or less accept the modernist view that a discipline like economics—and its history—is a quest for truth, even Truth, especially those who view economics in a positivist, scientific manner. Among this latter group, seemingly significant differences occur in how "positivism" and "science" are understood and presented. Something of a standard mix of objectivity, empiricism combined with deductive theory, and the like is, however, common. Important for present purposes, methodological views are often not developed in the sections chosen for this study.

But it is true in a different way or context for those who adopt a postmodernist view. To them, economics remains a quest for truth but (1) Truth is unlikely or impossible and/or (2) economics is and should be considered to be a matter of socially constructed stories. The modernist tends strongly to adopt or exhibit strands of philosophical and/or scientific realism, and to emphasize that economic theory is both driven and tested by recourse to economic reality. The postmodernist tends to emphasize that economic reality is socially constructed in two senses and not so easily if at all driven and tested by reality. In one sense, *economic reality* is a product of human action, even if not by overt human design; there is nothing, or very little, given and transcendent. In the other sense, the operative *picture* painted of the economy is socially constructed, whatever the ontological status of the economy/economic reality. Postmodernism says that, like it or not, pretty much "anything goes," hence the necessity of choice. Even if everyone were a modernist realist, they would differ as to content and therefore would manifest "anything goes" and the necessity of choice, and amount to social constructionism. But the typical modernist realist does not see matters this way and resists doing so.

Social-constructionist ideas tend to be anathema to those with conservative attitudes who identify Reality as an absolute in terms comfortable to them. Ironically, conservatives who want to substitute their design for that of liberals rarely explicitly adopt a social-constructionist position but nonetheless exhibit that position.

The authors of both some very old and some very recent textbooks qualify, as it were, as postmodern in their attitudes toward problematicity and the social construction of economics (science as a social phenomenon), the history of economic thought, science and Truth.

A problem posed by some more recent authors involves the hermeneutic or discourse nature of economic thought, the idea of economics as rhetoric. This involves the study of ideas *qua* ideas more than of pure theory. This is hardly a new element of design strategy, but it now includes the study of economic ideas, including theory, as modes of language and systems of belief.

Very few authors, at least until the rise of the study of economics as rhetoric, have pointed out the importance of implicit definitions and identifications that act as settled definitions of reality but are problematic hypotheses. Thus for Backhouse (2002) classical situations involve fundamental changes in the definitions of central concepts and in how economists understood what they are doing. For example, formalization meant a definitional change such that "Competition ceased to be a process and had become an end-state" in which firms had no incentive to compete (2002: 327). Also, "What constitutes a 'detour' is crucially dependent on what one takes to be the true story" (2002: 328).

Another problem posed by some more recent authors, also found in Schumpeter (1954), is the difference between the history of economics and the history of economic thought, though in some cases the latter encompasses the former. The history of economic thought is the history of ideas, theories and/or doctrines. The history of economics is the history of the sociology of the discipline of economics and the history of the motivations and behavior of individual economists.

Gray was idiosyncratic: he concludes his preface with the hope that his book "may serve as a useful stepping stone to the more comprehensive works of Haney and of Gide and Rist," having noted a few lines earlier, "I flatter myself that in no other book professing to be a history of economic doctrine are so many names entirely unmentioned" (Gray 1931: 7). He was candid: At the beginning of his first chapter, in a prelude to the doctrines of Greece and Rome, he finds economic meaning in institutions: "all customs, institutions and laws must contain implicitly a certain measure of economic theory, even if it be never expressly propounded" (1931: 11). And he was a precursor of postmodernism—political meaning in economic doctrine is a function of society: "economic doctrine ... reflects the condition of the society to which it relates" (1931: 12; see also Boucke 1921: 6; meaning flows from economic production to speculations on property and government). And economic theory is explanation not of some transcendent reality but of the implicitly transient status quo:

> Political economy throughout has been in large measure an attempt to explain, within the existing framework and assumptions of society, how and on what theory contemporary society is operating. ... [A]ny body of economic doctrine can have only limited validity.
>
> (Gray 1931: 12)

The foregoing elements of postmodernism combine to render more problematic, probabilistic and putative the definition of reality ensconced within and reinforced by mainstream, neoclassical economic theory. For some historians of economic thought, postmodernism is another mode of attacking neoclassicism; for others, however, postmodernism, subject to self-referentiality, *is itself a definition of reality*. More generally, truth, even Truth, remains part of the consciousness of both theorists and historians—each tends to think that *their* view is the correct one, even though the postmodernist part of their consciousness tweaks their hubris by reminding them that, in the larger scheme of things, theirs is but a story too (on this, see Deane 1978: xi–xiii).

MODES OF THOUGHT

As seen in chapter 2, some authors interpret the history of economic thought in terms of deep interpretive structures, preconceptions, or modes of thought (e.g., Barber 1967; Boucke 1921; Perlman and McCann 1998; Pribram 1983). A less abstract and less remote approach is that of Dasgupta (1985) and Dome (1994), who write of three systems or epochs of economic theory, namely, classical, marginalist and Keynesian.

SOCIOLOGY OF ECONOMICS

Some texts analyze the discipline of economics in terms of small-group sociology, including professionalization, hierarchy, socialization through the training of new economists, incentive and reward system, the role of status emulation, and so on (Schumpeter 1954; Deane 1978; Landreth and Colander 1989: 1–16). They treat the development of hegemonic ideas as due, at least in part, to factors and forces of disciplinary structure.

ORIGIN OR LATER USE OF THEORIES AND IDEAS

Ekelund and Hébert (1983), after questioning whether contemporary work is "new" or "merely an extension of the self-interest paradigm" (1983: 540), answer: "[P]recious few contemporary ideas may be thought of as original in that they created new and seminal ways of interpreting and analyzing economic and social happenings in the real world. ... The problem, as always, is a matter of degree" (1983: 541). In their 1990 edition they explore the conditions of originality:

> geniuses responsible for the major mutations in the history of thought seem to have had certain features in common. ... [They] held a skeptical, almost iconoclastic, attitude toward traditional ideas. ... [T]hey maintained (at least initially) an open-mindedness verging on naive credulity toward new concepts. Out of this combination sometimes comes the crucial capacity to see a familiar situation or problem in a new light. ... Another precondition ... is the "ripeness" of the age.
>
> (Ekelund and Hébert 1990: 5)

Dome (1994: xv) distinguishes two approaches to studying history of economic doctrines. One focuses on an author's personality and historical context, "the process by which his ideas and work were produced." The other involves the re-interpretation, re-evaluation and re-use by later economists "in different manners for different purposes"; hence "we are confronted with several versions of the doctrine wearing different clothes" (1994: xv). His book follows the second approach. (See also Routh 1975.)

Landreth and Colander (1989: 17) indicate that their emphasis is on those who most influenced, rather than those who originated, economic ideas.

Roll (1946: 3) focuses on the "interplay between objective conditions ["economic practice," "circumstances and exigencies of time and place"] and the theorizing of man" as the basis for understanding "the conflicts of ideas."

By this he means that "The ideas of the past had their roots in institutional arrangements, in the relations between social classes and groups, in their conflicting interests" (1946: 3).

As for the manner in which conditions and ideas can be connected, Barber (1967: 13) writes, for example, "Many widely held views on the nature of the economic system and its potentialities and limitations are shaped by less self-conscious and more implicit processes."

ECLECTIC OR SINGLE PRINCIPLE

Heimann (1945: 13–14) distinguishes the following models for writing the history of economic thought:

1   Eclectic, "without any dominant, unifying principle of presentation."
2   "Describe the evolution of economic theory as the progress in analytic thinking—the technical growth of theory ... toward the ideal of a completely adequate science of economics." Pursuit of the latter too often seeks to fit theories into a "procrustean pattern supposedly exhibited in history," whereas there are "the rich diversity of points of view, ... and ... the mutual inconsistency and irreducibility of conflicting theories."
3   "[R]educe the variety of conflicting theories to the class interests of those who advance or defend them. Each doctrine is then interpreted as a ratio-nalization of the interests of the economic class which it is supposed to serve, and the conflict of doctrines is taken to reflect the conflict of classes. ... In this way, a theory may come to be used as a weapon. ... But this is only part of the truth, and to present it as the whole truth is misleading."

(Heimann 1945: 13–14)

The first is eclectic and the second and third are examples of singular principles. All three compose a point of selectivity in design strategy.

MICROECONOMICS, MACROECONOMICS AND STATISTICS:—
AND BEYOND

Hutchison (1953: 424–429) traces three lines in the advance of economic theory, each worked on further from different points of view, lines that can be followed by historians of economic thought. One is the microeconomic analysis of normal value, price, production and distribution, upon the assumption of a self-adjusting mechanism. The second is the study of crises and cycles and other fluctuations in economic aggregates. (Many pioneer contributors of the latter, he argues, were skeptical or ignorant of or little interested in the former.) The third is the growth of economic statistics, affecting economists' work and public opinion on economic problems.

Bell (1953: 658–659) writes of two "well-defined generic groups": those who study the money–price analysis of the economy, and those who study the operation of and changes in institutional arrangements within the present socio-economic order (1953: 658–659). This picture was revised in Bell's 1967 edition, in which the latter group is treated as having "little or no staying powers" (1967: 706). The next year, Blaug wrote:

> But in the final analysis, institutionalist economics did not fulfill its promise to supply a viable alternative to neoclassical economics and for that reason, despite the cogency of much of the criticisms of institutionalists, it gradually faded away. The moral of the story is simply this: it takes a new theory, and not just the destructive exposure of assumptions or the collection of new facts, to beat an old theory.
>
> (Blaug 1968: 681)

Per contra, the authors of books critical of mainstream development point to the sociology of the discipline and related exclusionary practices for at least part of the story of the decline of heterodoxy in general and institutionalism in particular.

Bell (1967: 706) also says that the "brief" life of institutionalism was due in part to "the absence of theory. Economists were a lonely group without a *raison d'être* —economic theory." Again, authors of critical books would raise two points: First, that theory *per se* should not be the *raison d'être* of a school; and, second and more important, that it is not true that institutionalists were either anti-theory or had no theory—they had their own versions of theory (see chapter 4 of this volume).

Bowden (1981: 217), like Bell, identifies groups, his being the theorist-explainers and the activist-changers, with a few individuals managing to play both roles.

Here, therefore, is another set of structural choices for authorial design strategy.

ANTIQUARIANISM, ERROR AND SERIOUS STUDY

Ingram (1888: 2) first rejects as obsolete J.B. Say's dismissal of the history of economic thought as the history of "absurd and justly exploded opinions." The Say point of view (though Ingram does not say so) is correlative to limiting the study of the history of economic theory/thought to the origins of contemporarily accepted theory, leaving "error" to the dusty and useless history books. Ingram then distinguishes between antiquarianism and the serious study of history, i.e., between pedantry and modes of thought that have prevailed and "largely and seriously influenced practice in the past, or in which we can discover the roots of the present and of the future."

MAJOR OR MINOR FIGURES

Most history-of-economic-thought texts present the work of a more or less standard, or canonical, group of great economists. These are typically supplemented by attention to some number of not-so-great, lesser, or minor figures, who, together, have made important contributions—including the decision to follow one or another great figure or to go their own way. (The question of who is a "great" economist can be seen as tautological. Inclusion in the text-book(s) means *ipso facto* that they are great; otherwise they would be excluded.) Some textbook authors elect to cover a relative handful of "greats" in order to concentrate attention and to avoid confusion. Some others have become almost encyclopedic in their coverage. Advocates of non-hegemonic, perhaps even unorthodox, if not heretical, points of view may invoke selected "minor" figures in order to give their perspective a suitable, legitimizing pedigree (see Rothbard 1995a: viii). Newman (1952: 2–3), in defense of the non-economist, points to the engineers, mathematicians, and philosophers who influenced the development of economic thought, as well as noting that "the government economist has become a fixture."

CONSERVATIVE AND LIBERAL ECONOMISTS

Sievers (1962) and Skousen (2001) are examples of several books that construct disciplinary history in terms of a contest between conservative and liberal economic theories/ideas. Books critical of the development of mainstream economics present their own favored body of ideas in juxtaposition to and criticism of mainstream economic theory. What constitutes "conservative" and "liberal" changes and is elusive.

CLASSICAL AND MODERN THEORY

A further distinction "focuses on developing the story of how economics evolved by means of a dual division between classical political economy ... and modern developments." Classical economics deals with the "requirements for reproduction, the generation of surplus product and the accumulation of capital" as well as the "explanation of value and price, of production theory, of accumulation, and of a theory of distribution" (Vaggi and Groenewegen 2003: xi). Modern economics has "greater emphasis on the market, on exchange, on supply and demand" with marginalism as the unifying principle (2003: xiii).

Attitudes toward the substantive history of economic thought

Different attitudes are shown toward the substantive history of economics and its present status. The long, complex history of defense and criticism of economic ideas, theories, and modes of analysis is reflected in the positions taken in the history-of-economic-thought textbooks. Some are critical of the history and present state of economics, even hostile; others present criticisms without hostility; and others defend the history and especially the present state of economics. Those who not only accept—both as fact and normatively—but laud the neoclassicist mainstream can either denigrate, disregard, acknowledge or accept heterodox alternatives.

The widespread postmodernism of historians of economic thought coupled with their more or less limited desire to serve as either cheerleader or high priest to the discipline leads some practitioners of economics to perceive the sub-discipline as hostile to the practice and content of mainstream economics. The arguments of both those who are overtly hostile to neoclassical hegemony and those who include important criticisms along with their overall affirmation also contribute to the same perception. The perception is reinforced by the widespread questioning by historians of economic thought of the possibility of unequivocal progress in economics (see the next section).

Spiegel is one of a small genre of authors who, while inevitably presenting their respective interpretive accounts, decline to adopt a strikingly distinctive further agenda as critic or defender. Spiegel chooses to write a history of ideas that *inter alia* are a part of larger cultures, instead of either an account of the progressive development of high theory and analytical technique or a dismissive critique of the development of economic thought and/or theory. He does not affirm his design strategy to be *the* correct one. It is only the one that suits his announced purpose; his is a neutralist relativism of design strategy. He neither criticizes nor makes a case for an analysis-laden design. Similarly he neither condemns nor lauds the modern economic system and its relation to economics. He has his own selectively perceived story of the history of economic thought. This includes criticism and praise for individuals, their ideas and theories. Unlike those who go further and either defend or condemn that history, he has no driving supplementary objective; he has no further design strategy.

Per contra, Spiegel's attention to ideas and the larger culture enables him to take up topics and themes typically excluded when the focus is pure theory and advanced analytical technique. The topics include the pursuit of power, ideology, and so on (one can imagine a history-of-economic-thought textbook written by Douglass North). Accordingly, for Spiegel these topics become part of the history of economics and, therefore, of economics as such; they are part of his design strategy. Some writers, like Spiegel, are unusually sensitive to important and/or intriguing subtleties, and seek to convey a sense thereof to their readers. Some of these writers, unlike Spiegel, concentrate on high theory and technique, and seek to educate along the lines of different subtleties. The names of the authors covered in Spiegel's book's concluding paragraph are indicative of the mind-stretching Spiegel sought to accomplish. The names include Fernand Braudel, Michel Foucault and Jacques Attali.

It is fair to say that all authors accept and that most, asymptotic to all, stress that economic theory is neither perfect nor complete, and is subject to revision. This is especially true of authors who more or less accept the modernist view that a discipline such as economics is a quest for truth, even Truth, especially those who view economics in a positivist, scientific manner.

Perhaps explicable by the impact of the Cold War on sensitivities, is Whittaker's (1960: viii) statement, "The controversial nature of some of the theories which are discussed makes it desirable to state an author's disclaimer of personal responsibility for the ideas examined. The historian does not make history."

Both Haney (1949) and Roll (1956) point to the economic, social, and political changes engendered by World War II and its aftermath as reasons to reevaluate the history of economic thought.

Among the authors who affirm and defend the neoclassicist mainstream are Backhouse, Blaug, and Ekelund and Hébert. Among those who would dethrone neoclassicism are Canterbery, Hunt, Routh, and Seligman. Some illustrations follow.

Boucke (1921: 12) told his readers that the "elusive character of so much that is important" in economics accounts for the naturalness of a "skeptical attitude." "Economics has been over-confident, not to say over-pretentious and officious."

Backhouse affirms the progressive (in the sense of Lakatos) nature of the neoclassical research program (1985: 409–412). He defends abstract theoretical work and finds no need "to replace mainstream economics with something radically different" (1985: 412–413). He affirms, albeit with criticism, its economic analysis and its methodological status. But that "does not imply a complete rejection of the arguments put forward by the proponents of alternatives to mainstream economics" (1985: 414). He himself indicates unease, because as many awkward questions have been pushed aside as have been answered (1985: 2). Mathematization, for example, has enhanced the study of some topics, but others have been neglected (1985: 3)—a view reflecting the dissidents' argument that method has driven attention to substance.

Negishi (1989) presents a different but related argument pertaining to the rational reconstruction of past economic theories in rigorous mathematical models, with the hope that they can provide clues to questions of present interest and/or techniques to apply to modern problems, or enable the solution of old problems using modern techniques. The mathematical method, he suggests, can reveal the implicit assumptions on which the propositions of a theory are based (1989: xi), but inevitably with the loss of something of the original content because of mathematical translation (1989: xii).

Backhouse's earlier affirmation-with-qualifications view is also found in his *Economists and the Economy* (1988), in which he defends economic theory and its criteria of theory choice in both theory and practice while recognizing the discipline as having strengths and weaknesses (1988: 184–194). He laments that too much is claimed for economic theory. Economic theory is a part of economics, not economics proper. It is a powerful, though limited, engine for the discovery of concrete truth. Economic theory has been greatly refined and is increasingly powerful, but it and its application are still dependent on prevailing, though ever-changing, circumstances and the fact that the use of theory can change the way the world works. Improvement has been in quantity and quality of available information, statistical techniques, and economic theory itself, though it is still subject to severe limitations (1988: 194–196). This view also pervades but is not spelled out in *The Ordinary Business of Life* (Backhouse 2002; see pp. 7–9).

Blaug is a critic of what he sees as the methodological faults and limitations of neoclassical economics but he views it "as a legacy handed down from the past" (Blaug 1962: ix) and defends its overall position of orthodoxy. What is negative by one criterion is positive by another:

> It may well be that the neoclassical distinction between economic and noneconomic factors is itself a hindrance in the study of long-run development ... the weight of tradition is such that economics has resisted and may well continue to resist the blurring of a distinction that has long given economics a status as a separate field of study.
>
> (Blaug 1962: 612)

When Blaug writes

> Alas, the history of economics reveals that economists are as prone as anyone else to mistake chaff for wheat and to claim possession of the truth when all they possess are intricate series of definitions or value judgments disguised as scientific rules. ... To be sure, modern economics provides an abundance of empty theories parading as scientific predictions or policy recommendations carrying concealed value premises
>
> (Blaug 1968: 681–682)

he parallels Canterbery: "economists have tended to formulate economic laws as if they were immutable laws of nature. ... We question this" (Canterbery 1976: iv). But a world of difference exists between the positions taken in their respective series of editions.

Ekelund and Hébert acknowledge disciplinary myopia (Ekelund and Hébert 1983: 542), but find that "mainstream economics represents the consensus of what economics is all about" and argue that their textbook "is a lesson ... on how men think, as economists" (Ekelund and Hébert 1975: 484).

In his 1956 edition, Roll writes that even though modern theory has not reached perfection (Roll 1956: 522), "the state of affairs is fairly reassuring" (1956: 523). In 1974 he cites recent criticisms of the "whole theoretical scheme" in economics (Roll 1974: 603) but finds that economics is prospering in both theoretical and applied areas and is decidedly not in a critical state (1974: 604). "Many economists," he finds, "naturally avoid" confrontational issues "and take refuge in more and more refined theoretical work"—comforted by the sense that the "weaknesses and failures" of the free enterprise economic system "lie outside the field of the mechanics of exchange under the theoretical conditions of perfect competition"—albeit in a reality in which consumption desires are "the product of social influence" and "productive capacities ... are derived from an uncertain mixture of conscientious effort, inheritance, pure luck and outright force and fraud" (1974: 608, quoting Frank H. Knight) and in which "the possession of power ineluctably corrupts the pure power of reason" (1974: 610, quoting Immanuel Kant).

Routh catalogs varieties of criticism but claims that "orthodox theory has survived and flourished" (1975: 25). The "paradigm that provides the inner framework for economic thought has not changed since the seventeenth century." Marginalism and Keynesianism were not "revolutions in the Kuhnian sense. On the contrary, they were the means by which the survival of the existing paradigm was ensured" (1975: 27). But, "The magnificent edifice, with all its disparate parts, is built of air, a mirage that misleads the seeker from his goal … paralyzing attempts to reach real understanding"; "the overall effect is soporific" (1975: 294). "It has been used not to explain, but to explain away" (1975: 295). Routh's 1989 edition likewise deals with orthodoxy's tenacity and existence as a creed, "impervious to argument" (1989: 342).

In 1913, Gide and Rist wrote that, "Nothing could be more harmful than the dogmatism which the science has only recently escaped" (Gide and Rist 1948: 647). Deane (1978: x–xii) writes of the decline of dogmatism over "progress" (see below).

Seligman (1962: xii) presents a critique of "technique for its own sake." Technical competence is "a requirement for effective economic reasoning. … But … the profession has bogged itself down in technical refinement" (1962: xii). And "When rebuffed, the economist consoles himself with the fiction that his theory indeed possesses validity because all he, the theorist, need do is to suppose that businessmen behave in marginalist ways" (1962: 789). (Rogin made the point differently, saying that "The pure theories … acquiesced in the shift, first effected by Ricardo, of conceiving the competitive equilibrium model as descriptive of the prevailing economy" (Rogin 1956: 11).)

Attitudes toward progress in economics

Some historians of economic thought proclaim progress in economics. Some deny all affirmations of progress except, perhaps, those of a superficial, even technical, nature. Many historians of economic thought question the objectivity of any such judgment. When one speaks of "technique for its own sake" (Seligman, quoted in the immediately preceding paragraph) the operative meaning—aside from inculcated training and habit—is status emulation. Functional, too, are claims of "progress" with regard to status-seeking both internal and external to economics. As can be inferred from the preceding section, a substantial variety of positions has been presented in the history-of-economic-thought textbooks. Some illustrations follow.

Backhouse illustrates the historian who favors mainstream neoclassicism without losing perspective. Examining "the past in order to understand the present need *not* mean telling the story as one of progress" (Backhouse 2002: 7). Lines of inquiry change, some die out, others depart from dominant interests, and different generations ask different, sometimes un-understandable, questions; the result is that the "notion of progress becomes problematic" (2002: 8).

Blaug commenced as an absolutist (see below) and gradually moved toward relativism; the absolutism included a univocal claim that progress had been made in the matter of tools and analytical constructs (Blaug 1962: 4). But in his 1968, 1978, 1985a and 1997 editions, substantially repeating the 1962 edition, one reads,

And so, has there been progress in economic theory? Clearly, the answer is yes: analytical tools have been continuously improved and augmented; empirical data have been increasingly marshaled to verify economic hypotheses; metaeconomic biases have been repeatedly exposed and separated from the core of testable propositions which they enmesh; and the workings of the economic system are better understood than ever before. And yet the relativists do have a point. The development of economic thought has not taken the form of a linear progression towards present truths. It has progressed, but many have been the detours imposed by exigencies of time and place. Therefore, whether we adopt a relativist or absolutist interpretation of the subject depends entirely on the questions that we wish to raise.

(Blaug 1968: 8)

The issue is not linear progression; the issue is whether the tools have improved and whether our knowledge of the economic system has improved—perhaps also whether our abilities to predict and to control the economic system have improved—all of which goes to indicate some of the complexity of the question of "progress." At any rate, for Blaug, it seemed, not every practice of economics constitutes or contributes to the progress of the discipline.

Blaug's position echoed that view of Schumpeter in which he relied on the application of the rules of scientific procedure to vision, to ideology derived from class identification, and so on. But Schumpeter also stipulated that "there is no objective meaning to the term progress in matters of economic or any other policy because there is no valid standard for interpersonal comparisons" (1954: 40). In other words, it is grandiose, wishful thinking for an economist to claim that he or she knows *the* criterion of progress and/or how that criterion works out in its application.

Canterbery dislikes such criteria as success in toying "with trivial normal science puzzles" (Canterbery 1976: 266). In *The Literate Economist* (1995: 2) he writes, "Historical perspective puts the lie to any claim that economics is a progressive science—operating like nuclear physics, outside time and in pursuit of eternal verities."

Ekelund and Hébert argue that once theory is extricated from motives, it is a neutral concept "which may be used in alternative and very different situations" (Ekelund and Hébert 1975: 9). Still, they also maintain, "men's ability to analyze problems changes, not always progressively, over time" (Ekelund and Hébert 1975: 11). One reads in Ekelund and Hébert (1983: 542) that economic myopia results from giving "great weight to mathematical technique, often at the expense of history"—a position not obviously different from that of Seligman, who, of course, has other criticisms to levy as well. Ekelund and Hébert (1983: 7) also state that because "*every* idea is a more or less faithful expression of the time period in which it emerged," it is impossible to evaluate progress in the history of ideas.

Fusfeld (1966: ii; repeated in subsequent editions, with minor changes) wrote early on that, with the exception of Marxism, "There are many disputes among economists, ... but not about the fundamental principles of the science." "[E]conomics is the only social science with a generally accepted body of theory whose validity almost every practitioner would accept." But he later added, "Whether our theories are 'better' or more advanced is debatable" (1982: 5; 1986: xiii; 1990: xiii; 1999: 5).

Dasgupta (1985) informs his readers that unlike the world of physical sciences, the worlds of both economics and the other social sciences change, and not equally everywhere (1985: 2). Thus, it is misleading to see the development of economic theory as continuous and cumulative, as satisfying the universality criterion, and progressive (1985: 1). Changing context will mean changing relevance (validity) (1985: 3). Systems of economic theory evolve in response to new questions elicited by changing circumstances or attitudes. Some particular theories do progress, but others do not; epochal systems are independent and merely different (1985: 4), provoked by changes and problems. The development of economics through successive epochs has not been smooth, but breaks have not constituted revolutions (1985: 5). Every system of economic theory, each answering different sorts of questions at different points of time, is incomplete, a partial theory, dealing only with aspects of an economy (1985: 7–8).

After noting the two main lines of advance—in the study of microeconomics and of crises and cycles—Hutchison (1953: 431) nonetheless cautions the reader about the sense in which that is to be understood, saying that by the 1930s, "the common naïve attitude to scientific progress had been considerably shaken up."

Niehans (1990) is more accepting of the idea of progress. He says that his book is "about the progressive evolution of modern economic theory" (1990: ix). Given modern mainstream economics as the standard, he argues that history is necessarily a tale of cumulative progress, based on neither belief in progress nor optimism about the blessings of science; modern mainstream is the best economics known (1990: 2–3).

Heimann (1964: 15) accepts the idea of, at minimum, technical progress, though he is more circumspect as to whether one can declare progress in analytic thinking. While he finds some truth in this form of presentation, he is concerned that "the rich variety of theories is disregarded or their inner integrity is violated in order to make them fit into the procrustean pattern supposedly exhibited in history" (1964: 13).

Rothbard rejects the idea of progress *per se*, stating:

Thomas Kuhn demolished the "continual progress, onward-and-upward approach" ... the "Whig theory of the history of science". ... The Whig historian ... really maintains that ... "whatever was, was right", or at least better than "whatever was earlier". The inevitable result is a complacent and infuriating Panglossian optimism. ... Kuhn ... demonstrated that this is not the way that science has developed. ... One need not adopt Kuhn's nihilistic philosophic outlook, his implication that no one paradigm is or can be better than any other, to realize that his less than starry-eyed view of science rings true both as history and as sociology. ... [R]ather than everyone contributing to an ever-progressing edifice, economics can and has proceeded in contentious, even zig-zag fashion, with later systemic fallacy sometimes elbowing aside earlier but sounder paradigms, thereby redirecting economic thought down a total erroneous or even tragic path. The overall path of economics may be up, or it may be down, over any give[n] time period.

(Rothbard 1995a: ix–x)

It is not only over the idea of progress, but over the form of progress that historians of economic thought disagree. Scott (1933: v) offers the analogy that economic thought, like economic society, progresses through stages of development, though he does not comment on whether this "progress" necessarily is an improvement. Newman (1952: 2) claims that chronology is not always the best method of presentation for the history of economic thought, or the presentation of a particular historical school. Roll (1956: 15) also argues against a strictly chronological approach, since the use and development of economic theory differs so significantly across countries. Both suggest progress is not linear.

Screpanti and Zamagni (1993: 6) spend much effort considering the idea of progress in economics, and present two different theories by which progress can occur: the incrementalist approach, which they themselves adopt, and the catastrophic approach. The incrementalist approach suggests that there is a "slow and continual growth in knowledge" (1993: 4) and they categorize the work of Knight, Stigler and Blaug as incrementalist. Others, they argue, believe that "economic thought proceeds in jumps and advances by revolutions"—the catastrophic approach (1993: 4). Ultimately, Screpanti and Zamagni argue

We do not share the idea that economics is a "Darwinian" discipline, an idea which claims that the last link in the evolutionary chain contains all the preceding developments, and that these can all be dismissed as irrelevant or superseded. Certainly we do not deny the existence of some form of evolution in the process of historical change of economic ideas. However, we deny that it is a unidirectional, homogeneous, and unique development; above all, we deny that the key to understanding this process must necessarily be provided by the theories which are in fashion today.

(1993: 8)

Aspects of the development of economic thought

What characterizes the development of economic thought? What constitutes the dynamics of theoretical change? What generalizing themes are important enough about—what are the lessons of—the substantive history to lead authors to point them out in prefaces, introductions, epilogues and concluding chapters?

Several authors raise these questions more or less directly. Others make their points in passing. Some deal with aspects of the history of economic thought and others with the dynamics of theoretical change.

Aspects of the history of economic thought

Whittaker (1940: 745) remarks that "it is apparent that few beliefs have been widely held without some reason for them, either in the circumstances in which they appeared or the objectives that were sought by the men and women who held them" (1940: 745). He also says:

> Another lesson is the antiquity of many ideas that seem novel to the present generation. … As society progresses, men seem to have few important ideas or experiences that are really new, but they have many repetitions and developments of old thoughts and old experiences.
>
> (1940: 745)

Bell articulates what is evident throughout the literature: "The role of government appears in practically every page of the development of economic thought" (Bell 1953: 661).

Not unrelated, Gide and Rist (1948: xi) write that " 'schools' only began with the appearance of those two typical doctrines, individualism and socialism, in the earlier half of the nineteenth century." They also call attention to the "segmentation of economic science into a number of distinct sciences, each of which tends to become more or less autonomous. Such separation does not necessarily imply a conflict of opinion, but is simply the outcome of division of labour" (1948: 645).

Blaug makes points concerning the work of historians of economic thought that also apply to the development of economic thought itself:

> What has been revived … is not quite the good old history of economic thought that we knew fifteen or twenty years ago. Some have argued in recent years that we have long misrepresented the historical evolution of modern economics. …
>
> These sorts of arguments open up questions in the history of economic thought that many had long considered closed. Suffice it to say that the history of economic thought now seems to be becoming the arena in which some of these controversial questions will be fought out.
>
> (Blaug 1978: xii–xiii)

The points include the possible past misrepresentation of "the historical evolution of modern economics," the presence of perennial controversial questions, and the sub-field of the history of economic thought sharing both these controversial questions with economics as a whole and participation in the process of working out ongoing solutions.

The cultural importance of economic ideas, including economic theory, in Western society is given in Fusfeld (1966: i; repeated in editions of 1972, 1977 and 1986 with minor changes):

> The writings of economists have defined the major social philosophies of the past two hundred years.
>
> Economists have become the high priests of a world of money, wealth, and aspirations for material goods. Like the Schoolmen of the Middle Ages, they define for a secular world the relationships between man and man, man and nature, man and society.

Fusfeld further identifies four themes:

> One of the great themes in the advance of economics, then, has been the interaction of ideology and science.
>> (Fusfeld 1966: iii; 1990: xi and thereafter, "ideology and theory")

> A second grand theme is the relationship between economic theories and practical problems. ... With control comes choice, and choice begets policy.
>> (1966: iii)

> A third theme in the development of economics is its close relationship to the climate of opinion.
>> (1966: iv)

> A fourth and overriding theme is the development of economics as a science.
>> (1966: v)

In his 1982 edition, he states what other authors have either stated or implied: "Indeed, one conclusion that emerges from this survey ... is that there are no clear answers to the more fundamental questions the discipline has struggled with over the years. It is a sobering thought" (1986: 189; 1990: 176 has "most" replacing "more" in the penultimate sentence).

In a chapter on the origin and tardy development of economic thought, Haney (1926: 24–28) presents lists of subjective and objective reasons for the relatively insignificant development of economics in the ancient world that are cultural in origin, which makes the explanation of the origin of modern economic thought also cultural in nature.

Screpanti and Zamagni (1993: v) claim that you cannot separate history from economics, and "knowledge of the 'environment' in which a theory is formed is just as important as knowledge of its logical structure."

Hunt (1979: xvii), in distinguishing between different versions of income-distribution theory, says,

The classical economists and Marx held that income distribution was an important determinant of the prices of commodities, whereas the neoclassical economists generally reversed the direction of causality. Most authors of history of economic thought books have accepted the neoclassical version without question and have treated the classical-Marx version as a historically antiquated curiosum.

Landreth and Colander's 2002 edition presents Colander's argument that neoclassicism is no longer the hegemonic school, saying that their aim is to "more clearly separate modern economics from neoclassical economics," starting around 1950 onward. Modern economics is "characterized more by its method—an eclectic, formal model-building and model-testing approach—than by specific beliefs" (Landreth and Colander 2002: xx).

Both Roll (1974: 608) and Routh (1975: 27) direct attention to the field of the mechanics of exchange as the paradigm constituting the inner framework for economic thought since the seventeenth century—a useful period in plotting the origins of the modern, post-late-feudal economic system. The publisher's preface to Pribram's *History of Economic Reasoning* (1983: xiv) thus quotes the author, that the work is "intended to show that economic reasoning has developed as an integral part of Western thinking."

Heimann (1945) writes that a free economy is not chaotic but constitutes an order; economics has as its task "to discover and analyze the hidden law of co-ordination and integration in a free economy" (Heimann 1945: 9). "[E]conomic theory is the doctrine of the system of free enterprise, and originally of nothing else" (1945: 10). "[W]hat economics must explain is the functioning of an order" (1945: 10). "[T]he term 'order,' as we use it to describe a free economy, has no apologetic connotation; it merely denotes the highly specific arrangement which makes possible any kind of life, organic or social, and which must be fully understood and appreciated before it can be reconstituted" (1945: 11).

Boucke (1921: 3) writes, "The historical viewpoint is now only a species within the genus Genetics."

Bowden (1981: 217) argues that the flow of history is driven in part by two groups, the theorist-explainers and the activist-changers, with a few individual economists managing to play both roles.

Dynamics of theoretical change

Roll (1946), in a lengthy comment on the genesis of economic ideas writes that in comparatively settled periods, "[e]conomic relations and political and legal institutions are taken for granted, and theoretical refinements are developed. But in the more revolutionary epochs … the connection between economic relations and ideas is clearly revealed" (Roll 1946: 5–6). "Ideas which have arisen in a past social order … [help] shape contemporaneous social change; and … it is not always easy to say which is the proximate and which the remote influence" (1946: 6). In a later edition, writing about "The abandonment of providential harmony in order to introduce the scientifically more defensible concept of equilibrium," he says, "It is one of the ironies of the history of ideas that changes introduced in order to buttress a particular position temporarily should, in the end, help to undermine it still further" (Roll 1956: 547; *per contra*, Barber (1967: 259) notes that his four modes of economic reasoning began in criticism of established institutions or patterns of thought; however, some of their doctrines later were appropriated to justify the status quo; such complacency, however, is alien to innovators; economics is actually a dangerous science).

In a still later edition, Roll calls attention to his "greater emphasis on the interrelationships among the different schools of thought and on the continuity of economic thought between older ideas and current thinking" (Roll 1970: vii). (Oser and Brue (1994: 538), conclude that new ideas seldom lead to the total abandonment of the existing heritage. Dasgupta (1985: 142–143) says that we cannot afford to ignore old economic theories just because they are old: since systems of economic theory have grown in response to specific situations, each system has relevance in appropriate contexts; an older theory may be more appropriate to an economy with conditions similar to those that had evoked it.)

Dasgupta (1985) suggests that systems of economic theory evolve in response to new questions elicited by either changing circumstances or changing attitudes. Some particular theories do progress, but others do not; epochal systems are independent and merely different (1985: 4), provoked by changes and problems. The development of economics through successive epochs has not been smooth, but breaks have not constituted revolutions (1985: 5).

Numerous writers present the history of economic thought explicitly against the background of major changes in society. Several, in effect following Adam Smith, identify the different periods or stages in terms of the institutional structure of society, especially law and politics (and not Karl Marx's foundational mode of production). As to the flow of causation, Gray (1931: 12) writes, "In a sense therefore, a study of comparative politics, meaning thereby an analysis of the changing structure of society, is a presupposition of a correct understanding of the development of economic doctrine." Others, like Boucke (1921: 6) have it the other way: "To understand the speculations on property and government of any one epoch relate them to the mode of living of its people, to their social organization as dictated by principles of production." As with most other topics, the identification of the topic or problem and its relevance to the history of economic thought is more important for present purposes than the individual author's particular position.

One implication of both the immediately foregoing and earlier discussions follows from the development of economic thought being so complex, so multi-faceted, and so much constituted of recursive relationships. The implication is that some or many authors of textbooks believe that it is impossible to make any simple generalization about the history of economic thought. That implication is in addition to the more controversial, widespread, though by no means universal, rejection of the belief in the unequivocal progress of economics and the non-controversial belief in the necessity of selectivity. A correlative implication is that no one substantive position can be held about a serious historiographical issue in the history of economic thought that cannot be contradicted by a different if not opposite reasonable position. These implications are further elaborated by the state of findings in the textbooks as to the problems of presentism, relativism, the sources of economic ideas and theories, and methodology—the issues to which we now turn.

The problem of presentism

One of the historiographic topics most widely discussed in the textbooks concerns how historians of economic thought, writing in the present, are, on the one hand, to treat the past in terms of the present and, on the other, to treat the present in terms of the past. The principal issue is not about writing a history of the antecedents of contemporary theory as such but writing an accurate history of economic thought/theory (the meaning of "accurate" is another, subsidiary issue). The textbooks on the history of economic thought, in the sections under consideration here, take four different positions.

The first, perhaps the most obvious one, is articulated by a few authors, though it may be implicit in the statements by others. As expressed by Backhouse (2002: 7), one cannot avoid viewing the past from the perspective of the present: "anyone who writes a history of economic thought *necessarily* views the past, to some extent, from the perspective of the present. However much we try to do so, we can never completely escape from our preconceptions attached to the questions we are trying to answer. It is better to state these preconceptions as completely as possible than to pretend that they do not exist."

He goes on to say that to approach the past from the perspective of the present can make for very unconvincing history, and that "Critics of such work are right when they argue that this approach misses the important historical questions and frequently results in a caricature of what actually happened."

Boucke (1921: 4–5) made the same point six decades earlier. He wrote that it is "practically impossible to speak of the past without putting into it something of the present. … The fact itself is little or nothing, the interpretation much or everything. The *value* put upon events of the past is the core of historiography."

Landreth and Colander (1989: 16) make the general point by saying that emphasis should be on current economics in relation to the past and not vice versa.

Blaug (1962: 1) calls attention to the dangers of both arrogance toward past writers and ancestor worship—the sins of judging older writers by modern theory and of not recognizing equivalent content in older writers because they do not use modern terms and symbols.

Screpanti and Zamagni (1993: v) make the same point:

we have tried to resist the double temptation of rereading the past only in the light of the present and explaining the present only by the past, or, to be more precise, to avoid searching in the traditional theories for the seeds of the modern theories and explaining the latter as simple accumulations of knowledge.

Barber (1967: 12) presents a variant of the position. He argues that carica-turization does injustice to "the analytical subtlety of the pioneers" and may venerate modern theory as universal truth superior for all purposes, thereby contributing to a mood of self-congratulation.

Blaug (1968: 8), however, in a later edition, partly narrows and possibly greatly strengthens (though perhaps not) his warning in the succeeding edition:

> We opened the chapter with the declaration: "Criticism implies standards of judgment, and my standards are those of modern economic theory." ... [E]ven this innocent sentence is subject to a variety of interpretations, and ... it is not at all obvious what it means to apply the standards of modern economics.

In his 1997 edition, Blaug says that "every new development in almost every branch of modern economics is liable to make us think again about some old familiar text in the history of economics or to revise the standard version of what the great thinkers of the past really meant to say" (Blaug 1997: xvii). The first is innocuous but the second gives effect to or constitutes presentism (see the section on Landreth and Colander 1994: 4–5 later in this chapter; rational reconstruction—Blaug's next topic and second point here—is included in the section on sources of economic ideas and theories).

Screpanti and Zamagni (1993) present yet another variant, writing that, "We have endeavoured to present traditional theories as living matter, as well as presenting modern theories as part of a historical process and not as established truths" (1993: v). Thus they say that "our endeavour [is] to treat the present as history" (1993: vi). The same point was implicitly made by Ekelund and Hébert (1975: 3) in saying that they do "regard economics as a finished inquiry or a closed set of issues."

Staley (1989: 2) makes two points frankly. First, "Much of this book is Whig history"—judging "the past as to whether it led to the present"—studying "the past from the standpoint of the present state of economic science." Second, however, "parts of the past of economics do not lend themselves to the Whig approach ... because it is not a good idea to believe that wisdom is exclusively concentrated in the present."

Several writers, particularly those who say that they select from the past that which contributed to the present mainstream, in effect posit that we cannot elude either the interpretive perspective of the present or the differential valua-tions put on past thought because of what is important today (e.g., Bell 1953:

v; Gray 1931: 7; Newman 1952: vii; Niehans 1990: 2–3). (Roll (1946: 3) argues that our interest in particular past ideas depends on the circumstances and exigencies of our time and place.) Roll (1956: 16) thus decides that "only those have been included whose contributions to economic thought appear to have significance in relation to present-day theory and controversy." Heimann (1964: 13) states that while treating "different periods in the history of economics … from different points of view as the occasion seems to suggest" is an interesting approach that allows for "highly erudite treatment", it "can only add to the bewilderment" of students. Therefore, it makes more sense to treat past theories in light of the present state of economic theory.

Second, and arguably the most widely treated point, concerns making our view of the past depend on the present. As Backhouse (2002: 5) puts it, does viewing the past through the lens of the present distort the past, and if so, how? As indicated above, the danger is Whig history, one version of which is to consider the historical antecedents to present-day hegemonic or popular theory (thus he writes, "Given that my main aim is to explain how the discipline reached its present state, developments within its theoretical 'core' are clearly prominent. However, they are not the whole story" (Backhouse 2002: 9)).

The problem and its critique are found in Schumpeter (1954: 34) where we read that attempts to interpret human attitudes, especially attitudes of people far removed from us in time or culture risk our "crudely substitut[ing] our own attitudes for theirs." This is aggravated by the fact that the "analyzing observer himself is the product of a given social environment—and of his particular location in this environment—that conditions him to see certain things rather than others, and to see them in a certain light," even endowing "the observer with a subconscious craving to see things in a certain light."

Schumpeter sees this not only as the problem of presentism but as that of ideology:

> This brings us up to the problem of ideological bias in economic analysis … [and the] habit of our minds that we call rationalization. This habit consists in comforting ourselves and impressing others by drawing a picture of ourselves, our motives, our friends, our enemies, our church, our country, which may have more to do with what we like them to be than with what they are.
>
> (1954: 35)

We shall again encounter the phenomenon—absolutist legitimization—in the next section.

The lesson that Schumpeter draws from his discussion goes beyond constricting the history of economic thought to economic theory itself: "The historical or 'evolutionary' nature of the economic process unquestionably limits the scope of general concepts and of general relations between them ('economic laws') that economists may be able to formulate" (1954: 34).

Anticipating another point to arise in the next section, we note that

Whittaker (1940: ix) avers that "In studying the originals [original works], the reader should bear in mind the conditions of the times in which they appeared."

Opposition to Whig history of economic thought is found in Landreth and Colander (1994: 4–5). However, in their 2002 edition they explicitly follow the lead of interpreting at least part of the past on the basis of the (changed) present, saying

> In previous editions, our discussions of classical economics were written from a neoclassical perspective, emphasizing those parts of classical economics that highlighted issues in neoclassical economics. Since modern economics deals with issues different from those of neoclassical economics, our coverage of classical economics, being written from a modern perspective, has changed ... more interest in growth and dynamics.
>
> (Landreth and Colander 2002: xxi)

Not all the textbook writers condemn using the present to construct selectively the history of the past (e.g., Newman 1952: vii). Catlin (1962: 1) writes, "The true historian ... is still primarily interested in progress; and in this realm of ideas what he comes to hold significant and valuable in the past is largely determined by what remains true and applicable in the present." This is not a defense of writing a history of the origins of presently hegemonic theory; it is a defense of equating that with writing a history of (all) economic theory. In other words, mercantilism, Quesnay, Smith, Ricardo, Marx, and so on would be presented not as they thought in their entirety but only as they are rationally reconstructed in light of present-day theory. Catlin, however, does not rigidly enforce his rule. (It would be interesting to compare the texts of authors who did strictly enforce the rule, to see wherein they agreed and differed. Is the classicist's labor theory of value an antecedent to modern price theory? To what today is Say's Law antecedent?)

A comparable view is offered by Niehans (1990). He argues that

> modern mainstream economics is the standard of reference; it includes what has survived. The implications of that position include the following: (1) There is no need for criticism; survival indicates that the essential criticism has been performed by the history of economics itself. (2) Each generation writes its own history, because it has its own mainstream. (3) Even failures can shed light on the dynamics of science. (4) Given modern mainstream economics as the standard, history is necessarily a tale of cumulative progress, based on neither belief in progress nor optimism about blessings of science.
>
> (1990: 1–3)

Aside from the defense of presentism itself, the most striking is the first implication, which engenders the query whether new theory cannot challenge the old. The second implication tends to be true willy nilly; but in light of the textbooks that are critical of the past development of economics, there are exceptions.

Third, if presentism, however, ineluctable, is a problem of the past being interpreted on the basis of the present, what of the present as a function of the past? Several positions on this question are found in the textbook sections.

One is that the past has led to, engendered, the present. Blaug (1962: ix) has put it, "the logical coherence and explanatory value of ... orthodox economic theory ... [is] a legacy handed down from the past." In his 1968 edition, Blaug is a bit more tentative but makes the same point: "The history of economic thought is a proving ground for answering such questions ... the practice of past generations still shapes what economics now is" (Blaug 1968: 7). Boucke (1921: v) said he would show, "how far economics even today rests on concepts worked out during the eighteenth century."

Another is comprised of the "interpretations of recent theory grounded in the knowledge of past literature" (Landreth and Colander 2002: xix), a position also held by Rima (1972: x): "much about contemporary theory will never be understood except in retrospect." Apropos of the familiar theme that the meaning and truth-status of a theory are independent of their provenance, a theme usually applied to biography, one wonders if it applies to earlier versions of the theory and their context.

As an example of another position, namely, changing practices by economists, we have already seen Backhouse's points that different generations ask different, sometimes un-understandable questions (Backhouse 2002: 8) and that fundamental changes occur in the definitions or meanings of central concepts (2002: 327). To different questions and changes in definitions other authors "add," as it were, interests or changing interests (Whittaker 1960: vii) and economic and social environments and other circumstances (Kapp and Kapp 1963: v; Gide and Rist 1948: xiii); and the same theory may serve different groups of people (Oser 1963: 4–7). All impact the influence, even if oblique or negative, of the past on the present. A contrary position, perhaps only an additional critical line of reasoning, is that the past and the present are non-comparable—though no textbook author seems to bring it up. The reasons for this are numerous and varied but can be summed up in the proposition that the past and present are a function of different, i.e., changed, circumstances.

Fourth, if (what we take to be) the past is a function (selectively) of the present, and if the present is a function, in one way or another, of the past, the possibility arises that present and past mutually interact in a recursive process of cumulative causation or over-determination. Blaug has stated this position succinctly: "There is a mutual interaction between past and present economic thinking for ... the history of economic thought is being rewritten every generation" (Blaug 1962: ix).

The problem of relativism

The problem of relativism is another topic to which reference is made in the selected textbook materials, either directly or by clear implication. The problem, insofar as it applies to economic theory and its status (separate from moral rules), is due to multiple principles, different conditions, complex topics, and so on, each situation necessitating the making of choice. Whenever multiple principles co-exist and compete, for example, scarcity exists in the form that choice must be made between the principles. Two considerations militate against this type of situation in the minds of many people. One is a desire for certainty (or certitude) and closure, correlative with a disdain for ambiguity and open-endedness. Every problem should have one, and only one, solution and it should be knowable. The other is the practice of absolutist legitimization, in which particular solutions are supported by reasons deemed absolute—e.g., what nature, reason, common sense, human nature, the US constitution, and so on, unequivocally mandate. Every problem should have one, and only one, solution and it should not only be knowable but absolutely required. Whether these considerations are, in any given instance, a matter of belief or a matter of manipulating political psychology (latent versus manifest function) is beyond the scope of this study and, most likely, beyond the ability of the relevant materials to cast light. The problem of relativism arises in several circumstances.

First, as indicated earlier, some people appear sensitive to anything resembling relativism—or, worse, nihilism.[2]

Backhouse (1985) writes that a particular theory (set of equations) can be interpreted in different ways but that to stress this is not relativism

> for it is not being claimed that a particular philosophy or particular circumstances in any way "justify" defective economic theories. It is rather that examining economists' systems as wholes, distinguishing philosophical attitudes from what we might think of as pure economic logic, is valuable in helping to distinguish those claims which depend for their validity on certain philosophic presuppositions, from those which depend on economic logic alone.
>
> (1985: 9)

This statement can be read as either descriptive or sensitive; we leave it to the reader to decide.

The twin interpretive possibilities are similarly found in Oser:

> There are certain dangers in the doctrine of cultural relativism, or "situational ethics," or "the new morality." Accepting the customs and mores of any society without critical judgment leads to a conformity that tends to stifle necessary or desirable changes. ... Does cultural relativism abjure all value judgments? Obviously it cannot.
>
> Cultural relativism can help us understand other cultures.
>
> (Oser 1970: 443; repeated in Oser and Blanchfield 1975)

Material from Blaug (1968: 6–8) has been quoted earlier. The lines presently relevant are these, particularly the first and third:

> Are we then driven into the arms of relativism? Surely, there are universal standards that can be applied to all theories?
>
> (1968: 6–7)

> And yet the relativists do have a point.
>
> (1968: 8)

> There are no simple rules for distinguishing between valid and invalid, relevant and irrelevant theories in economics. … In short, a good deal of received doctrine is metaphysics.
>
> (1968: 681)

This account is clearly mixed.

Unequivocal is Gray's closely related statement that economics professors today "suffer from economic agnosticism, if indeed the agnosticism does not amount to an active lack of faith in all dogma" (Gray 1931: 366). Such indecision and agnosticism is due to an impasse in and weariness with controversy and having entered an age of transition (1931: 366–367).

Apropos of nihilism is Rothbard's mixed statement: "One need not adopt Kuhn's nihilistic philosophic outlook, his implication that no one paradigm is or can be better than any other, to realize that his less than starry-eyed view of science rings true both as history and as sociology" (Rothbard 1995a: ix).

Second, what amounts to a case for relativism, although apparently rarely articulated as such, pervades the textbooks. It is a case all the more strong for seemingly arising inadvertently to the authors but derived from their materials.

Conspicuous by its absence with one exception (see later in this chapter), at least in the sections included in this study, is any mention of price theory as being relativist. For a long time in the history of economic thought, people sought the explanation of "value," meaning the absolute and invariable basis of price. With the ascendance of price theory, especially general equilibrium theory, no such absolute and invariable basis of price was posited. Instead, price was seen as a function of relative supply and demand functions and of the factors and forces forming and operating through them. Absolutist value was discarded; relativist price remained.

On the other hand, hints of absolutism, few as they may be, are found in these materials. Bell (1953: 663) writes, "the few doctrines which have survived to this day are universal economic truths." But this is only a hint, and perhaps misleading. Earlier in this edition, Bell writes:

> What was true under given circumstances of time and place may not be true at some later time. Because of this fact alone, the student of economic thought must be tolerant of economic doctrines and dogmas which are no

longer accepted and try to view them objectively by placing them in their proper setting.

(1953: 4)

And in his 1967 edition we read, "While it is true that some elements of history never change, it is possible for new interpretations to be placed on events as a result of further research" (Bell 1967: v).

Taylor (1960: xi) writes of a belief in a universe of all knowledge that "has a unity whereby its different parts illuminate each other."

An explicit affirmation of relativism is also to be found. Haney presents a case only slightly limited:

> The concept of relativity, the point of view according to which ideas are not judged with dogmatic absolutism, but are critically examined in the light of the times and places in which they were formed, becomes very real.
>
> (Haney 1926: 6–7)

But, "in emphasizing the relativity of economic doctrine, men have often been too prone to overlook the element of direct continuity" (1926: 645). Still, "Economists are realizing the interrelation of things; more and more the quest for absolute laws of causation is modified by a knowledge that things move in circles and mutually determine one another" (1926: 659).

In a later edition, Haney also says that he finds "some truth in all" schools and "complete truth in none" (Haney 1936: vi; repeated in 1949: vi–vii). Haney is echoed in

> Oser and Brue (1994: 11): "no group has a monopoly on the truth."
> Mair and Miller (1991: 19): "No individual, no school of thought has a monopoly of the truth in economics."

> Boucke (1921): makes the explicit case arguing that all ideas are subject to revision and destruction and that "the whole history of thought testifies to the relativity of our understanding" (1921: 2). "The historical viewpoint is now only a species within the genus Genetics" (1921: 3).

> Sandelin *et al.* (2002: 101): "different schools have co-existed, often with one school dominating. ... [H]ow difficult it is to regard one school as the 'correct' one. Different schools emphasize different aspects and may be 'right' or [']wrong' in different respects." The status of ideas may change over time. "... [A] combination of respect for, and criticism of, different opinions is an advisable attitude for a serious economist."

> Dasgupta (1985): Unlike the world of physical sciences, the world of economics and the other social sciences changes (1985: 2). Thus, it is

misleading to see the development of economic theory as continuous and cumulative, as satisfying a universality criterion, and progressive (1985: 1). Changing context means changing relevance (validity) (1985: 3). Systems of economic theory evolve in response to new questions elicited by changing circumstances or by changing attitudes. Some particular theories do progress, but others do not; epochal systems are independent and merely different (1985: 4), provoked by changes and problems. Each system of economic theory, each answering different sorts of questions at different points of time, is incomplete, a partial theory, dealing only with aspects of an economy. Synthesis, the construction of a unified system of economic theory, is unlikely, due to the changing character of economic reality (1985: 7–8).

Ingram (1888) presents a wide-ranging case for relativism and in such a way as to suggest that internalist explanations of the development of economic thought have an absolutist character and externalist explanations have a relativist one (which is in part why the terms are substitutes):

> The rise and the form of economic doctrines have been largely conditioned by the practical situation, needs, and tendencies of the corresponding epochs. ... [T]he theories prevailing in each period have owed much of their influence to the fact that they seemed to offer solutions of the urgent problems of the age. Again, every thinker ... is yet a child of his time.
>
> (1888: 3)

But the "connection of theory with practice" can "be expected to produce exaggerations in doctrine, to lend undue prominence to particular sides of the truth, and to make transitory situations or temporary expedients be regarded as universally normal conditions" (1888: 3). He also stresses the connections of economic doctrine to the development of other branches of inquiry—"by the prevalent mode of thinking and even the habitual tone of sentiment." Accordingly, Ingram affirms the formation of "less absolute and therefore juster" views of "successive phases of opinion" and economic theory (1888: 4). Earlier views often had a relative justification, resting on a different social order. Present theoretic positions are not definitive, for they, too, will change with the practical system of life. Internal factors are secondary and subordinate in influence, affecting the spirit or form of doctrines: the thinkers' particular situations, relation to special predecessors, native temperament, early training, religious prepossessions and political views. Common social factors dominate the individualist ones.

Not surprisingly, in E.J. James's preface to Ingram's *History of Political Economy*, James says that one lesson of the book is "the essential relativity of economic theories" (Ingram 1888: vii). Screpanti and Zamagni (1993: 8–9) also affirm the relativity of economic theories, influenced by cultural climate.

"Society as a whole decrees the importance of the problems to be studied, establishes the directions in which solutions should be sought, and, ultimately, decides which theories are correct" (Screpanti and Zamagni 1993: 9).

Third, relativity with respect to what? What generates relativity? The textbook material is rich and varied in respect to these questions. Relativity arises with respect to and/or because of (giving a few examples):

> Dependence of economic ideas on circumstances: historical, ever-changing (Backhouse 1988: ix, 194–196; Roll 1956: 14); evolutionary nature of the economic process (Schumpeter 1954: 34; see also p. ix: "the conditions of the time" in which original works appeared); changes in institutional structure and emergence of new practical problems (Blaug 1962: 5); "the condition of society" (Gray 1931: 12); specific situations and context (Dasgupta 1985: 142–143); circumstances a theory was designed to explain (Hutchison 1953: ix); theories as part of historical process, not established truths (Screpanti and Zamagni 1993: v); economics as a response to political theory and political practice (Roll 1956: 15).

> Changes in meaning and/or definition: Backhouse (2002: 327), including the meaning of "detour" (2002: 328).

> Class structure "and the group minds or attitudes that form in it" (Schumpeter 1954: 38).

> Differences in the questions asked: Blaug (1962: 7); Fusfeld (1982: 176); new sets of questions in new epochs (Dasgupta 1985: vii, 7–8).

> Assumptions made: Blaug (1962: 610, 611).

> Absence of a single view of the development of economics: Ekelund and Hébert (1983: 6).

> Whether contemporary work is new or an extension of the old: Ekelund and Hébert (1983: 540).

> A variety of approaches to economics: Ekelund and Hébert (1990: 4).

> Epochs of capitalism: Dasgupta (1985).

> Progress as a matter of judgment: Dome (1994: xv).

> Conflicting theories: Gide and Rist (1948: 644).

> Forms and methods of understanding: Heimann (1945: 17).

> No theory is able to do everything: Mair and Miller (1991: 5).

> Economics is but one way of looking at the total complex of social behavior (Seligman 1962: 786).

A suggestive example with regard to the relativism latent if not manifest in macroeconomics is Blaug's statement,

> The persistent debate on "what Keynes really meant" … has aggravated rather than alleviated the problem of making sense of Keynes' arguments. … [M]y chapter on Keynes … is now a history of interpretations of Keynes over a period of almost 50 years.
>
> (Blaug 1985a: xv)

A view expressing the operational approach to knowledge, in which knowledge is a function of the tools used in its production, is Heimann's: "the choice of a method largely determines the results to which it will lead. … No science merely 'mirrors' reality as it is" (Heimann 1945: 17).

All of the foregoing examples have *multiplicity*, including multiplicity due to change, and the *necessity of choice*, in common. There are many phenomena to explain, many approaches and many theories to take toward them, many different applications of each theory, and so on. Multiplicity is the father of the necessity of choice and of relativism—or so we interpret the textbook sections to be saying.

Fourth, our final relativist theme is recursiveness, or cumulative causation or over-determination. Recursiveness signifies that an object under study is both cause and consequence in its relations to another(s), such that, for example, any generalization about either object must include the other and something of their relations and of the changes in each wrought by the other. This theme is also found in the materials.

Whittaker is explicit about this, saying "It cannot be over-emphasized that ideas and environment react upon each other. What men think is explained by what they do, and vice versa" (Whittaker 1940: ix).

We have already quoted Haney in regard to relativism. His place in the sub-discipline was so important for so long and his statement apropos of recursiveness is so dramatic that we reproduce it again: "The concept of relativity, the point of view according to which ideas are not judged with dogmatic absolutism, but are critically examined in the light of the times and places in which they were formed, becomes very real" (Haney 1926: 6–7). But, "in emphasizing the relativity of economic doctrine, men have often been too prone to overlook the element of direct continuity" (1926: 645). Still, "Economists are realizing the interrelation of things; *more and more the quest for absolute laws of causation is modified by a knowledge that things move in circles and mutually determine one another*" (Haney 1926: 659; italics added). The point is repeated and restated in later editions, notably in part in regard to price, thus:

> Economists are realizing the interrelation of things; more and more the quest for absolute laws of causation is modified by a knowledge that, while

some things are primary and others secondary, changing economic phenomena react upon one another, as do supply, demand, and price.

(Haney 1936: 659; 1949: 948)

Backhouse (1988: 194–196) argues that economic theory has been greatly refined and is more powerful, but is still dependent on ever-changing prevailing circumstances and the fact that the use of theory can change the way the world works. The belief that the ideas of the great economists both have enormous influence on societies and are molded by the cultural milieu that nurtured them, is expressed by Canterbery (1995: 1); and by Hunt (1979: xv):

> social theories and social-historical processes are reciprocally intercon-nected. … social theories are the products of the social and economic circumstances in which they are conceived. But it is equally true that human beings act, create, shape, and change their social and economic circumstances on the basis of ideas they hold about these circumstances.

The sources of economic ideas: internalism and externalism

Our penultimate historiographic topic found in the textbook material has to do with the genesis of economic ideas and theories. The textbooks raise the topic principally in two ways, in general and in terms of the issue called either inter-nalism versus externalism or absolutism versus relativism (a different but not unrelated use of the terms). The former attributes the development of theory to the minds and interests of theorists; the latter, to the influence of external factors.

But the matter of source is not simple. Several points: first, logically, consid-eration of source should have two components: the origination of ideas and/or theories, and the selection or adoption of them. Origination has to do with conjecture; adoption, with acceptance. The materials of this study do not make this distinction. Second, the same external conditions may and very likely will yield different theories and ideas. That being the case, the connections between external conditions require examination, e.g., the heterogeneity of external conditions and of economists' mentalities. The materials of this study pursue as such neither the multiplicity of theories and ideas nor the connections. Factors such as social structure are mentioned in this or another connection (ideology), but individuals within the same socioeconomic class can have different ideas, signifying that some other factor(s) is also operative.

Several positions on internalism versus externalism in the history of economic thought are found in the textbook literature. These include: (1) a long period of dominant externalism followed by a long period of dominant internalism; (2) the perennial, continued dominance of externalism; (3) the perennial co-existence of both; and (4) the dichotomy as a tool and design strategy. Some authors, such as Screpanti and Zamagni (1993: v) simply declare the debate void: "we have attempted to distance outselves from the implicit banality of the great historiographical alternatives, such as 'internal' and 'external.'"

Several characteristics of the interpretation given in the materials of this study can be identified. (1) Except as part of perennial co-existence, or as a result of a declared decision to exclude external factors from discussion, little emphasis is placed on or attention given to internalism. (2) The gradual emergence to positions of dominance of perennial co-existence and of externalism.

EXTERNALISM

Those authors for whom externalism explains or helps explain *pro tanto* the development of economic theory and ideas, identify the external factors and forces in various ways. These include:

Culture: Backhouse (1988: 2).

Circumstances: Backhouse (1988: 194–196); Haney (1926: v); Boucke (1921: 327); Niehans (1990: 516ff).

Economic background: Backhouse (1988: 4–6); Kapp and Kapp (1963: v); Gide and Rist (1948: ix–x, 646); Scott (1933: vi).

Ideology: (see below).

Philosophical climate of opinion or intellectual culture: Blaug (1962: 5); Spiegel (1991: v); Scott (1933: vi).

Controversies over economic policies and social reforms: Kapp and Kapp (1963: v); Rogin (1956: xiv, 3–4).

Society's needs and problems: Oser (1963: 377); Deane (1978: ix); Ingram (1888: 3).

Specific historical and socioeconomic situations: Dasgupta (1985: viii); Finkelstein and Thimm (1973: ix).

Problem situation: Deane (1978: xiv).

Among statements elaborating the externalist position are the following. Schumpeter posits the sociology of science or of economics analyzing

the social factors and processes that produce the specifically scientific type of activity, condition its rate of development, determine its direction towards certain subjects rather than other equally possible ones, foster some methods of procedure in preference to others, set up the social mechanisms that account for success or failure of lines of research or individual performances, raise or depress the status and influence of scientists (in our senses) and their work, and so on.

(Schumpeter 1954: 33)

Fusfeld interprets the history of the Keynesian-neoclassical synthesis in externalist terms:

The breakup of the post-Keynesian synthesis was not caused primarily by faults in its internal logic. It came because the world of which the theory was a part reached a crisis. As the institutions and modes of that world change and adapt, economics will change and adapt also.

(1977: 173; see also 1982: 158)

Dasgupta identifies the history of economic theory as one of successive epochs, each marked by "specific historical and socio-economic situations," especially "the metamorphosis of capitalism" (Dasgupta 1985: viii). Each epoch is a system of economic theory attempting to answer specific questions deemed important, i.e., new epochs give rise to new sets of questions and to new theories for answering them (1985: vii; indeed, epochs come close to being *defined* in those terms—new questions and new theories).

Ingram takes a predominantly externalist view of the development of theoretical ideas:

The rise and the form of economic doctrines have been largely conditioned by the practical situation, needs, and tendencies of the corresponding epochs. ... [T]he theories prevailing in each period have owed much of their influence to the fact that they seemed to offer solutions of the urgent problems of the age. Again, every thinker ... is yet a child of his time.

(Ingram 1888: 3)

Newman (1952: viii) cautions his reader that his book presents "a history of theories, but theorists and theories are products of their times."

Rogin identifies the uncriticized premise that theory can be tested by appeal to fact, freed from subordination to social ideals and social goals, and asserts that the externalist opposite is true: "significant new orientations in economic theory first emerge (and persist, often in a changed role) in the concealed or unconcealed guise of arguments in the realm of social reform" (Rogin 1956: xiv). He interprets Malthus versus Ricardo on the Corn Laws to mean that their "selective appeal to fact is subordinated to the theorist's sense of values," hence "the constitution of the science" depended "on the manner in which the Corn Laws issue was resolved" (1956: 3)—a function of different values, different class interests, and different positions on practical problems (1956: 3–4). All schools of thought are arguments for one kind of reform or another (1956: 5)—another version of externalism.

COMPLEMENTARINESS

The position of perennial co-existence—or co-determination or complementariness—is explicitly taken by many authors.

Backhouse (1988: 4–6) makes the case for the two approaches being complementary and intertwined, especially via the relationship between economic ideas and the economic background against which they were composed. He goes on to say that economic theory is a part of economics, not economics proper, and is a powerful, though limited, engine for the discovery of concrete truth. Economic theory has been greatly refined and is more powerful, but is still dependent on ever-changing prevailing circumstances and the fact that the use of theory can change the way the world works (1988: 194–196). "Economists' preconceptions and ways of thinking are inevitably formed by the culture in which they are writing" (1988: 2; the point made above means that a particular culture can give rise to different perceptions and ways of thinking).

Blaug (1962: 2ff) says there are immoderate and moderate versions of absolutism and relativism as to the source of ideas. Relativism permits valuable fusion; neither alone, however, can furnish the key (1962: 3). He is doubtful that "dramatic shifts in the focus of attention can be explained solely in terms of intellectual forces." Some changes "must surely have been associated with changes in the institutional structure of society and with the emergence of new practical problems" (1962: 5). He notes that Schumpeter said that economic analysis has never been shaped by economists' philosophical opinions; but this "dogmatic 'positivism'" is negated by his devoting half of his text to narrative history, political theory, and philosophical climates of opinion. "It turns out that Schumpeter did not mean that economic analysis is logically independent of philosophy but rather that the philosophical beliefs of economists are not relevant to its validity" (Blaug 1962: 5). He subsequently goes on to say, "The task of the historian of economic thought is to show how definite preconceptions lead to definite kinds of analysis and then to ask whether the analysis stands up when it is freed from its ideological foundation" (1962: 6).

Later in that edition Blaug notes that economic-system performance evaluation has been "the great driving force behind the development of economic thought; ... the source of inspiration of almost every great economist" (Blaug 1962: 608). (Of course, this formulation posits the active evaluating mind of the theorist or policy analyst.)

Blaug, possibly alone, also has transformed internalism and externalism—absolutism and relativism are the terms he uses—into rational reconstruction and historical reconstruction. In his 1997 edition he relates that he has had "second thoughts about both the choice between these two viewpoints and the terms in which I posed that choice. In consequence, 'relativism' and 'absolutism' become 'historical reconstruction' and 'rational reconstruction' and I now see merits in both standpoints" (Blaug 1997: xvii).

Distinguishing between the two types of reconstruction, the historical attempts to state the ideas of past thinkers in terms they would have recognized and accepted, and the rational attempts to analyze their ideas in our terms, correcting their errors and making their ideas more coherent. "[H]istorical reconstructions are literally impossible, while rational reconstructions are invariably anachronistic" (1997: 7–8)—the former because we can view the past only from the present, the latter because it pretends to omniscience and is superfluous, omniscience because we presume present knowledge of absolute truth, and superfluous inasmuch as given such knowledge, one does not need the past (1997: 8). Both can be pursued, with adequate appreciation of their respective limitations. They must be

> kept distinctly apart. Unfortunately, what is separable in principle is almost impossible to keep separate in practice: every interpretive exercise in the history of economic thought starts out either as a historical or a rational reconstruction but, in the course of argument, these tend invariably to shade into another. What is explicitly claimed to be a reworking of, say, Ricardo in modern dress is soon claimed to be at the same time a statement of what Ricardo really would have meant to say if only he had been as analytically advanced as we now are, as if a historical reconstruction is an unexpected bonus of a rational reconstruction. Likewise, although less frequently, many an examination of what Ricardo actually said ends up being at the same time a rendition of what he should have said, thus capping a historical with a rational reconstruction.
>
> (Blaug 1997: 8)

Canterbery finds that economists have responded to social and economic conditions. The historian of economic thought must consider the "relationship between *what* an economist thinks and *why* he thinks it." "[M]ost economists reflect the values of their society and want to be accepted by their fellow citizens as responsible members of society. Their thinking, therefore, is a reflection of their social world, and vice versa" (Canterbery 1980: 1). (The following sentence in the 1976 edition was omitted in the 1980 and 1987 editions, otherwise largely unchanged: "Yet many of today's economists seem inured to such crises" (hunger, depression, war, social discontent, etc.) (1976: 2).)

In *The Literate Economist* (1995), which has less discussion of methodology, Canterbery indicates his dislike of absolutist history, rational reconstruction, and Whig history of thought: they ignore lives and times, and are pretentious, with excessive relentless optimism (1995: 1). He affirms that the ideas of the great economists both have enormous influence on societies and are molded by the cultural milieu that nurtured them (1995: 1). Rational reconstruction is rejected for historical reconstruction (1995: 2).

Heimann argues that the proposed correlation is not between economic interests and economic theories but "between changing forms of man's understanding of himself in his changing existence … and changing methods employed in economic thinking" (Heimann 1945: 17).

Ekelund and Hébert tell the reader that their major focus is on the development of economic abstractions *per se*; these "do indeed seem to have a life of their own" (1975: 10). They feel that questions about the role of environment lack conclusive answers; still

> Much of our treatment of theory will touch upon economic *thought*, i.e., upon environmental, philosophical, and social affiliations with abstractions. In sum, the best approach to economic thought and theory does not appear to be at either absolutist or relativist poles. Perhaps the distinctions are themselves overdrawn and somewhat old-fashioned. The determinants of new ideas (or theories) are likely so complex as to defy such simple classification.
>
> (1975: 11)

The argument is repeated in their 1983 edition. They are concerned "more with the question of *what* constitutes our economic heritage (and the implications that flow from it) than with the questions of why or how this heritage came about" (1983: 5). Their book's major focus is "the development of economic abstractions *per se*, although social and methodological issues are frequently considered as integral parts of the intellectual landscape. We believe that economic theories do indeed have a life of their own that ... is both interesting and fruitful." They have no conclusive answers to important questions and do not attempt "to confirm any single view of the development of economic analysis" (1975: 6). Their view is, like Blaug, perhaps more sympathetic to absolutism (= internalism), but the end result is a model of complementarity.

Ekelund and Hébert also examine some of the internalist sources of theoretical change:

> geniuses responsible for the major mutations in the history of thought seem to have had certain features in common. ... [They] held a skeptical, almost iconoclastic, attitude toward traditional ideas. ... [T]hey maintained (at least initially) an open-mindedness verging on naive credulity toward new concepts. Out of this combination sometimes comes the crucial capacity to see a familiar situation or problem in a new light. ... Another precondition ... is the "ripeness" of the age.
>
> (Ekelund and Hébert 1990: 5)

Haney combines both internalism and externalism in a manner unusally both outspoken and subtle:

> Particularly dangerous is the specious argument in favor of dealing with theories rather than with theorists. In no field of knowledge is thought so molded by the thinker and his environment as is the case with economics; and it is therefore always desirable to know something about circumstances.
>
> (1949: vi)

Kuhn (1963: v) distinguishes between the individual's contribution and "the external circumstances which propelled the contributors on their chosen paths."

Oser (1963: 4) expresses complementarity as follows: "In economics, social relationships and institutions probably are as important as individual efforts and accomplishments."

Pervading many pertinent statements is an identification problem: how to know an individual's position when it is influenced by environmental factors; and how to know the meaning of external factors when they are given effect by individuals—and neither is homogeneous.

Rima (1967: ix) holds that the "development of the analytical tools and concepts which comprise the body of economic theory," their forging and their refinement, cannot be divorced from the environment within which they were developed, the specific problems that inspired them, nor from the individuals and schools whose "attitudes and preconceptions" they reflect.

Roll early took a position that at first reading seems externalist but upon reflection is more accurately designated complementary. He argued that his book is

> based on the principle that the appearance of certain ideas is not fortuitous, but dependent upon causes which can be discovered ... [and] on the conviction that the economic structure of any given epoch and the changes which it undergoes are the *ultimate* determinants of economic thinking ... [a] conviction ... shared by most writers ..., though ... seldom admitted ... [because] the general principle ... is often stated in a way which appears to make the economic system the *sole* determinant.
>
> (Roll 1946: 4)

"[T]he economic factor is the determinant only in the final analysis and ... it is generally difficult to make this final analysis." Other factors include the already existing body of economic theory, political theory and political practice—"many a theory bears the mark of the political struggle in which it was conceived" (Roll 1946: 5).

In comparatively settled periods, "[e]conomic relations and political and legal institutions are taken for granted, and theoretical refinements are developed. But in the more revolutionary epochs ... the connection between economic relations and ideas is clearly revealed" (Roll 1946: 5–6). "Ideas which have arisen in a past social order ... [help] shape contemporaneous social change; and ... it is not always easy to say which is the proximate and which the remote influence" (Roll 1946: 6).

Roll later indicated his belief that neither the view "that the appearance of ideas is wholly fortuitous" nor the view "that it is ultimately dependent on some permanently operating factors, in particular, the material ... can be relied upon by itself to provide consistently an adequate explanation" (Roll 1974: 7).

Catlin (1962) approaches the problem of the source of economic ideas and theories in an unusual manner, and one that also at first resembles externalism but is more aptly seen to be close to complementarity. He summarizes Francis A. Walker's presidential address of 1888 as to those influences which, in the previous half-century or less, had made ... progress [in economics] a matter of intelligent research rather than the blind acceptance of tradition or of chance. As he stated them, they included: (*a*) the separation of political economy from natural theology, with its implications of an overruling providence and the assertion that "all is right with the world"; (*b*) the abandonment of the doctrine of *laissez-faire* as an infallible and universal principle; (*c*) a new conception of human nature, proceeding from the doctrine of evolution, as opposed to that of an "economic marionette," postulated by the older economists; (*d*) the rise of democracy, and the "coming of age" of Labor; and (*e*) the spirit of scientific inquiry, "including a more careful observation of phenomena, and assisting to a sounder interpretation of facts and statistics."

(Catlin 1962: 32)

Barber relates "the differences between economists' analytical systems to the diversity of institutional conditions to which their formulators addressed themselves," but also "the differing purposes each of the major systems was constructed to serve," different perceptions of essential qualities and processes, and "the differing themes around which they were originally organized and which, in turn, molded the categories used to fill out the analytical structure" (Barber 1967: 14). Different "ends in view" and "different set[s] of questions" as well as different images of what the economy is all about are all important. It is in this context that he argues that economics is a toolkit, with the tools shaped by the uses to which they are put (1967: 14).

Niehans (1990: 516–523) includes among the sources of scientific progress such driving forces as external conditions, resources, logical flaws, and creative minds—a position of complementarity.

Screpanti and Zamagni (1993: v), we again note, inform their reader that they want "to distance [them]selves from the implicit banality of the great historiographical alternatives, such as 'internal' and 'external' history or 'continuism' and 'catastrophism.'" They want

> to avoid the dichotomy ... which seems to us to cause misleading simplifications, between the "pure" historians of thought, who dedicate themselves exclusively to studying "facts", and the "pure" theorists, who are only interested in the evolution of the logical structure of theories. We believe that knowledge of the "environment" in which a theory is formed is just as important as knowledge of its logical structure, and we do not accept the view that an analysis of the emergence of a theory must be considered as an alternative to the study of its internal structure.
>
> (Screpanti and Zamagni 1993: v)

Taylor tells of his concern with both the history of economic theory and the relations of its main developments with their wider intellectual background, "the broad, general patterns of philosophical and over-all social, moral, and political thought" (1960: vii)—notably "the late-Victorian conservative liberalism as the ruling climate of political thought" in relation to neoclassical economic theory (Taylor 1960: viii; see also pp. ix, xii).

Blaug candidly indicates his awareness of the importance of authorial design strategy in explicating the source of economic theory and ideas: "whether we adopt a relativist or absolutist interpretation … depends entirely on the questions that we wish to raise" (Blaug 1978: 8; 1985a: 7). "If, in the chapters that follow, there is little about Zeitgeist, social milieu, economic institutions, and philosophical movements, it is not because these things are unimportant but because they fall outside the scope of our inquiry" (1978: 8; 1985a: 7). In view of frequent misunderstanding, he restates his aim:

> Presented with the ultra-Marxist thesis that the economic theory of a given period is nothing but a reflection of the prevailing historical and political circumstances, I have wondered whether the diametrically opposite thesis— economic theory for economic theory's sake—is not less misleading. … Of course it would be limited and inadequate, but that is true of all monocausal interpretations of intellectual history. It is perfectly obvious that much of what we think of as economics had its origin in intellectual responses to major unsettled policy questions. … But equally obviously, it must be insisted, great chunks of the history of economic thought are about mistakes in logic and gaps in analysis, having no connection with contemporary events. And so, without pretending that this is the whole story, or even the best part of the story, but merely that it is a part rarely told, I have tried to write a history of economic analysis which pictures it as evolving out of previous analysis, propelled forward by the desire to refine, to improve, to perfect, a desire which economists share with all other scientists.
>
> (Blaug 1968: xi)

In this light, internalism versus externalism becomes a tool of analysis and not a settled definition of the reality of the genesis of theoretical or ideational change. As a tool it provides a framework for analysis, and does not itself constitute the analysis. As such it becomes a design strategy for telling a story.

Deane (1978) also is explicit in revealing her design strategy as such. She identifies two approaches to the study of the development of ideas in a discipline, each raising different sets of questions. One concentrates on the dialectical sequence of change of the substance of the discipline, and is primarily concerned with the rational justification and critique of theory in successive epochs. The other traces the historical process of change in how generations of scientists have adapted their explanatory techniques to the solution of problems regarded as important and soluble, and is concerned with explaining the historical process of innovation and adaptation in their theoretical framework. The two are not mutually exclusive; both are used. This book pursues the second approach, for pedagogical reasons (Deane 1978: ix).

Shortly thereafter she discusses her externalist approach, paying attention to matters of acceptance, longevity and content. She calls attention, *pace* Thomas Kuhn, to connections between the sociology of a discipline and its development of theory (Deane 1978: xii–xiii). Also, she says, the "philosophical and ideological premises of an economic theory … play an important role both in its initial acceptance and in its tenacity" (1978: xiii). But the empirical content, analytical boundaries, theories and concepts, and problem priorities of a discipline are changeable, due in part to changes in institutions and economic reality. Doctrinal changes may derive more from autonomous changes in the problem situation than from efforts to test the logical or empirical validity of existing theory (1978: xiii). Deane postulates, first, that "shifts in economists' views about what problems they ought to be solving, as well as how they ought to be solving them, are the key to understanding the historical changes … in the ruling paradigm for economics"; and, second, that "leading theorists have adapted their theories and concepts—and with them the research orientation of the discipline—to major changes in the problem-situation confronting them" (1978: xiv).

Design strategy also seems central to Boucke's (1921) statement, apropos of the "*economic* interpretation of history"—which he considers to be "the only accurate one" (1921: 6) though "Intellectual history stands on its own ground" (1921: 8). "In the end," he says, "the crux of the question lies in the definition of 'economic' and of 'cause.' … We know only by definition, that is by hypothesis. … We accept distinctions because they serve to emphasize aspects or to focus our attention upon particular purposes" (1921: 9).

Methodological considerations

Methodology is not, strictly speaking, a matter of historiography. But methodology has implications for historiography. Moreover, historians of economic thought and economic methodologists form a sociological professional group, and many individuals work in both fields, such as Backhouse, Blaug and Hutchison. Of course, there are others such as Taylor (1960: x), who declares such methodological issues "impossible to resolve" and therefore states his own position without much defense.

Several preliminary points should be made.

(1) Methodology (inclusive of epistemology and philosophy of science) deals with the criteria by which statements acquire credentials as one form of knowledge or another.
(2) Very few authors of history-of-economic-thought textbooks present extensive coverage of methodological topics. Heimann (1964: 15) explicitly claims his textbook is a study of methods of solving problems, and therefore emphasizes technical progress and the methodologies employed by different economic theorists. Screpanti and Zamagni (1993: vi) also claim to give attention specifically to methodology in economics.
(3) In the period since c.1960, attention increasingly was given to the approaches of Karl Popper, Thomas S. Kuhn and Imre Lakatos. For present purposes,

Popper was interested in establishing falsification as a test of positivism, or science, as well as the sociology of science; Kuhn was interested in the processes of theoretical or scientific change and the sociology of science (giving rise to a variety of approaches to the empirical study of science, etc.); and Lakatos was interested in the sociology of scientific conflict and theory choice. Such work both greatly enriched the possibilities of doing history of economic thought and greatly complicated historiography—both increasingly reflected in the textbooks.

(4) The work of Popper, Kuhn and Lakatos combined with the work of people in such fields as hermeneutics, deconstruction, discourse analysis, literary criticism, socio-linguistics, rhetoric, sociology of knowledge, structuralism, and so on, to help form and fill out the content of what came to be called postmodernism. Briefly, postmodernism uprooted or reoriented such topics as Truth, correspondence with reality, predictive power, induction versus deduction and so on, in favor of social construction of reality, belief systems, science as language, and so on. Such work also both greatly enriched the possibilities of doing history of economic thought and greatly complicated historiography—both also increasingly reflected in the textbooks (e.g. Deane 1978; Screpanti and Zamagni 1993).

(5) A number of postmodernist points were advanced by pre-1960s authors. It is not widely appreciated, for example, how much Joseph Schumpeter in his *History of Economic Analysis* (1954) adopted ideas that eventually became postmodernism. However much they conflict with his positivism, they make his positivism both more limited and more realistic. The authors of both some very old and some very recent textbooks qualify, as it were, as postmodern in their attitudes toward problematicity, the political nature of theories and ideas, and the social construction of economics (science as a social phenomenon) and the history of economic thought, science and Truth. The same applies in respect to modernism.

(6) The result of the foregoing is reflected in revisions made to successive editions of at least one series. The addition of Colander to make Landreth and Colander significantly introduced postmodernist themes while remaining within the textual mainstream. Blaug's restructuring of his chapter 16, "A Methodological Postscript," which in his 1962 edition substantially covered topics of theory development and choice, resulted in the 1968 edition focusing on verifiability, falsifiability, the limitations of the falsifiability criterion in economics, hypotheses as heuristic statements, the presence and role of value judgments, and so on. The 1978 edition provided for revised treatment of the limitations of the falsifiability criterion in economics and a new section on paradigms versus research programs and another on scientific revolutions in economics—generally emphasizing Lakatos and internalism. The chapter on methodology in subsequent editions was "drastically cut" (Blaug 1985a: xv) to avoid duplication with *The Methodology of Economics* (Blaug 1980). Blaug's overall position on internalism versus externalism became more ecumenical.

Notwithstanding the foregoing, the proportion devoted to methodological topics in most textbooks is relatively small. As with the discussions on historiography, those on methodology are wide ranging, if often cursory; they are typically more of the nature of comments and positions taken on issues than extended discussions. Among the topics or points are the following, and a few examples.

Economists' desire for economics to be and to be seen as a science:
Backhouse (1985: 127); (Rima 2001: ix): status emulation following physics and other natural sciences.

Whether economics is, or can be, a science:
Schumpeter (1967 [1912]: ch. I), on the development of economics as a science. Kuhn (1963: v), showing "economics as a body of scientifically developed propositions." Ingram (1888: 240 and passim) criticizes the non-scientific nature of much economic work, its theological–metaphysical encumbrances and deformities. Seligman (1962: 789): "As matters now stand, economics is not a science when it is economics and not economics when it is a science." Taylor (1960: xi) claims that economics is often presented as "in some degree at least a science and the history of economic theory is a history of progressive, scientific-theoretical investigations and discoveries." However, economics also involves the study of political theory and philosophy, which are "local and transitory" and are "purely speculative, void of demonstrable or verifiable truth or validity, as largely emotional as intellectual" and therefore not science (Taylor 1960: xi–xii). Taylor (1960: xii) thus concludes that economic inquiry is "*in some degree* a science" and while sharing with science "phases of progress," economics cannot be "absolutely scientific—objective, unbiased, neutral." Spann (1972: 10) does not share Taylor's conflict, declares economics a science in so much as biology is a science, since biology, like economics, studies "the living (which lacks unimpeachable objective characteristics)."

Conflicting ideas of the nature of "science"
Schumpeter (1954: 6, 9 and passim). Neff (1950: 2) hedges with the phrase the "science of economics."

That the objective, scientific character of a proposition is independent of the biography, motive, etc. of its propounder:
Schumpeter (1954: 10): that "the scientific character of a given piece of analysis is independent of the motive for the sake of which it is undertaken." Blaug (1962: 5): "Schumpeter did not mean that economic analysis is logically independent of philosophy but rather that the philosophical beliefs of economists are not relevant to its validity."

The ideological-subjectivist limits of science in particular and methodology in general:

Neff (1946: 6–7; see also Haney 1926: 21): Comte's stages—theological, metaphysical, and positive. Heimann (1945: 15): "Method reflects the prevailing philosophy of the age." From conception of world, its history "as subject to supernatural control or intervention" (1945: 15), to "emphasis on fact and on cause and effect" (1945: 15). Emphasis on nature implies that forms of society are relatively stable; emphasis on history, to possibility of fundamental change in social organization (1945: 16).

Economics comprised of positive and normative economics:
Oser and Brue (1994: 539).

Revolutions in economics:
Numerous authors note Thomas Kuhn's work on scientific revolutions (and also that of Karl Popper and Imre Lakatos) and some pronounce a judgment on whether economics has had revolutions. For example, Rima (1986: x) writes of how intellectual revolutions in economics differ from those of the natural sciences. Dasgupta's (1985: 5) judgment is that the development of economics through successive epochs has not been smooth, but breaks have not constituted revolutions. Niehans (1990: ch. 37) devotes an entire chapter to the dynamics of scientific progress, part of which presents a revolutionary model. (See also Mair and Miller 1991: 4ff, 9ff; Negishi 1989: 1–5.) Blaug (1962: 4) says, "the history of economics is not so much the chronicle of a continuous accumulation of theoretical achievements as the story of exaggerated intellectual revolutions, in which truths already known are neglected in favor of new revelations." Blaug (1978: ch. 16) emphasizes the approach of Lakatos and internalism (absolutism).

The importance of criticism:
Backhouse (1988: 4): "The distinguishing feature of science is not that its theories are known to be true, but that it possesses a mechanism by which theories are tested and inadequate theories discarded." Landreth and Colander (2002: xx): "This emphasizes that every mainstream school has had its critics and that the economic thought of a period is best understood by considering both the mainstream thought and the criticisms of that thought within the period."

Backhouse's point is instructive. A number of authors—by no means only those critical of mainstream economics—stress the importance of criticism, in part for the correction of error but in larger part, we surmise, for the identification of and insistence upon the conceptual and technical limits of theories and ideas. Backhouse's statement amounts to an authorial caution that a sensible student will be necessarily no more taken with a criticism of a theory, because it is criticism or for some other appeal, than with the praise of a theory, because it is praise or for some other reason. Professors are figures of authority to many students but their position does not necessarily mean that their statements or positions are true. Such a view antedates the type of critique known as post-modernism.

Nonetheless, Bell (1967: 10) can point to a certain invulnerability of economics: "The anvil has a peculiar way of wearing out the hammers; so also have economic truths weathered the storm of criticism." In his 1953 edition, Bell says of his book that

> particular attention is paid to constructive criticisms of outstanding figures and doctrines by their contemporaries and successors.
>
> (Bell 1953: v)

> The role of criticism in the development of economic thought must not be overlooked. … Indeed, criticism appears to have been a favorite diversion of most writers in political economy.
>
> (Bell 1953: 656; 1967: 705)

Historians of economic thought and methodologists, even those who identify with mainstream neoclassical economics, have been, in comparison with other economists, much more prone to be sensitive to and to emphasize the sociological, epistemological, ontological, political and other ideological characteristics of the development of economics in general and theory in particular. Given their expertise, derived from the intra-disciplinary division of labor, such attention is only to be expected. The position of the historian of economic thought moved increasingly in these directions after the 1960s. Earlier historians of thought could be critical and even those not critical as such could candidly present sufficient sociological and epistemological data as to inadvertently support many of the same positions.

The design strategy of entire textbooks, indeed their *raison d'être*, is criticism, giving vent to a belief in and the practice of criticism: the texts by Canterbery, Hunt, Ingham, Routh, and Seligman, for example, but also and Rogin and Rothbard.

Ideological, subjective and normative considerations

Our final historiographic topic is one on which unanimity seems to reign in the materials relevant to this study: the relevance of ideology, subjectivity and normative judgments to the development of economic thought and theory. Some authors, like Schumpeter (1954), examine the tension between ideology and scientific procedure and have an important place for ideology. Among the variety of authorial positions pertinent to this topic are the following.

Backhouse (1988: 194) holds that disagreements among economists are due only slightly to differences over economic theory and more to differences over value judgments and the interpretation of empirical evidence; political and ideological issues are especially mixed up with economic ones.

For Schumpeter (1954) ideology—manifest in part through an economist's "vision"—is an important force in the history of economic thought and the sociology of economics, and is a matter of social location, or class structure. To Schumpeter, the "analyzing observer himself is the product of a given social environment—and of his particular location in this environment—that conditions him to see certain things rather than others, and to see them in a certain light," even endowing "the observer with a subconscious craving to see things in a certain light" (1954: 34). "This brings us up to the problem of ideological bias in economic analysis" and the

> habit of our minds that we call rationalization. This habit consists in comforting ourselves and impressing others by drawing a picture of ourselves, our motives, our friends, our enemies, our church, our country, which may have more to do with what we like them to be than with what they are.
>
> (1954: 35)

One danger threatening economic analysis, says Schumpeter, "proceeds from the inveterate habit of economists to pass value judgments upon the processes they observe. An economist's value judgments often *reveal* his ideology but they *are not* his ideology" (1954: 37). It is ideology that is important. Economic thought is not homogeneous but divided on the basis of "the class structure of the corresponding society and the group minds or attitudes that form in it" (1954: 38). The history of economic thought traces out "the historical change of attitudes, mentioning analytic performances in passing." He also says that "Our own plan is exactly the opposite one" (1954: 39), apropos of which it is clear that he does not follow the plan, inasmuch as the plan is internalist but the execution in the book is one of complementarity.

Blaug (1968: 6–7) echoes Schumpeter's model in which ideological vision and rules of scientific procedure are in perpetual conflict: "Propaganda and ideology are always there, but so is the discipline exerted by rules of scientific procedure built into economics by generations of practitioners: economics is forever catching up with the biases of yesterday."

Breit and Ransom, and also Roll, are among numerous authors who identify the ideology principally affecting mainstream economics as that of classical liberalism and *laissez-faire*:

> neoclassical economics—the body of thought with largely laissez-faire implications.
>
> (Breit and Ransom 1971: 2)

> economists seem to have given up any implicit, unquestioning belief in the virtues of *laisser faire*, and, to some extent, even in the capitalist system. Yet there seems still to be lurking in their minds an inherited regard, if not for

the Smithian "hidden hand," at least for the so-called economic case for *laisser faire*.

(Roll 1942: 544)

the general belief in the beneficence of *laisser faire* and of the existing economic system remained.

(Roll 1942: 546)

It is this ideology that forms for Fusfeld (1966: i; repeated in editions of 1972, 1977 and 1986 with minor changes) the content of economics as religion:

The writings of economists have defined the major social philosophies of the past two hundred years.

Economists have become the high priests of a world of money, wealth, and aspirations for material goods. Like the Schoolmen of the Middle Ages, they define for a secular world the relationships between man and man, man and nature, man and society.

What is true of ideology is also true of the subjective and normative in economics. Writing about the belief system of capitalism and economists' role in the ideological defense of capitalism since the late eighteenth century, Hunt says in part, that the writings of economists

have both a cognitive, scientific element and an emotive, moral or ideological element. Moreover, I do not believe these two elements are entirely separable. ... A thinker's moral feelings and ideological views give the direction to the cognitive, scientific inquiry and set the limits as to what will constitute "legitimate" range of solutions for that thinker. Moreover, moral feelings and ideological views are based on, and are always defended by means of, the thinker's cognitive or scientific theories of how society actually functions.

(Hunt 1979: xvi)

In my view, all theorists, all historians, and all human beings ... have values that significantly interpenetrate all cognitive endeavors.

(Hunt 1979: xvi)

For Roll (1942: 547) this defense included "The abandonment of providential harmony in order to introduce the scientifically more defensible concept of equilibrium."

Spiegel goes so far as to say that ideology enables well-meaning people to "attribute effects to unreal causes that make them feel more comfortable or convey other benefits to them" (Spiegel 1991: xix). "[T]he dividing line between science and ideology is not always easily drawn," and is subject to both selective perception (1991: xix) and the "historical and social determinants of thought" (1991: xx).

In Taylor's judgment, economics "is in some degree at least a science" (Taylor 1960: xi) but it is also an expression of subjective individual moods and movements,

> purely speculative, void of demonstrable or verifiable truth or validity, as largely emotional as intellectual in content or substance, and intent not purely on discovering truth or understanding actualities but largely on inspiring and directing political action toward particular goals and along particular paths. And they are always biased, partisan, fervent, and dogmatic—in short, they are in every way antithetical in spirit and nature to all science.
>
> (Taylor 1960: xi-xii)

> Economics ... is, and long has been, *in some degree* a science, though I emphasize the qualifying phrase.
>
> (Taylor 1960: xii)

> I do not think that economic science, or theoretical work in it, is or has been or can be so perfectly or absolutely scientific—objective, unbiased, neutral ...—as to make it possible to say ... that the great contributions ... have been wholly uninfluenced by ... political philosophies ... [and by] the social philosophies.
>
> (Taylor 1960: xii)

Conclusion

One conclusion of this study is the multiplicity of understandings given effect by a multiplicity of authorial design strategies in what is essentially a selective, interpretive process. The history of economic thought does not write itself.

A huge number of original and derivative articles and books comprise the bulk of the literature of economics. Another part of that literature is articles and books, especially textbooks, that interpret the history of the former. Both are conducted with dedication and passion, driven by love of subject, an agenda of reform, and/or desire for status by those who would be the next Jacob Viner, Joseph Schumpeter or Joseph Spengler. From their work arises our understandings of the economy and of the history of economic thought; not understanding, but understandings, plural.

The authors of textbooks on the history of economic thought employ a multitude of design strategies. These design strategies are constructed by the historian of economic thought; they are not conclusively presented to him or her by the history itself. The material not only accords them the opportunity but requires them to selectively design their work, and they do so. Authors with similar design strategies will differ in the story they tell, because of the way in which each design strategy is nested in supplementary, supportive propositions.

From textbook to textbook the *dramatis personae* (Schumpeter's "troops"), given by history, are much the same, though by no means identical, and the story being told varies considerably. The stories derive from design decisions on the starting point from which the story will begin and the combination of individuals, schools and ideas covered in the story.

The domain of decisions entering into design strategy includes an array of deep and subtle historiographic topics and issues. These topics and issues include the most recent, late twentieth-century developments called postmodernism. These topics have, gradually but increasingly, become central to the consciousness of professional historians of economic thought. The aforementioned opportunity for multiple understandings and multiple design strategies is due, to no small degree, to the richness of these historiographic topics and issues.

Textbook authors have decided to introduce historiographic topics and issues to their readers and to take positions or state conclusions on them. The resulting multiplicity of interpretations is anathema to those who identify their favorite economic theory with the natural order of things or who require unique determinacy and closure. This chapter has reported on our study of the treatment of these topics and issues, and the positions and conclusions, expressed by authors of history-of-economic-thought textbooks in prefaces, introductions, conclusions and epilogues. Our work injects a third level of interpretation, one closer to that of the historian of economic thought him/herself than to that of the practitioner of economic theory or history.

These historiographic topics and issues are not purely esoteric academic matters. Numerous authors make it clear that the history of economic thought since the seventeenth century is an important part of Western society and civilization. Of what other social science has this been true so widely and deeply? Only political science qualifies, which should surprise no one, since much of the histories of economic and of political thought have to do with the relations between government and economy. While economists are prone to stress the automatically self-regulating market, such can occur only with a propitious political and legal system—and what constitutes such a system is often the point at issue. Problems of the history of economic thought are also problems of epistemology, ontology, language and historiography, as well as the history of political, social and economic change. Historiography does not exist in a vacuum. All of the foregoing complicates the analysis and understanding of historiographic topics and issues, perhaps most especially when existential experience is believed to relate automatically to something postulated to be given and transcendent, i.e., a matter of absolutist legitimation.

Two authors who believe that there is one true story of the history of economic thought nonetheless likely will tell two different stories, each a matter of interpretation. No one believes that "anything goes" but in practice, "anything does go." All are caught up in the hermeneutic circle, with each different interpreter giving effect to particular different preconceptions. Each of those who do not believe that there is one true story to tell nonetheless proposes their favored story. Each author is driven by training (intellectual capital accumulation), parochial or other loyalty, intellectual appeal, and/or other factors. Each seeks to satisfy their hunger of imagination, to set their and their auditors' and/or readers' minds at rest. Each, in other words, seems to be following the account of the work of the philosopher-scientist given by Adam Smith in his *History of Astronomy* and apparently practiced by him in articulating an etiology for the division of labor (see chapter 1 in this volume); an account incorporating social recognition, moral approval, and establishing connections.

The great majority of textbook authors accept, even insist upon, the argument that the writing of the history of economic thought is an exercise in interpretation. The domain of interpretation includes selectivity not only as to starting date and period and the individuals and schools covered but, most importantly, over focusing on theory versus ideas; attitude toward the history itself; treatment of such problems as presentism, relativism, and internalism versus externalism; and whether the history of economic theory, and of ideas, is a matter of belief system, definition of reality, or tools; and so on. If Smith, in his affirmation of setting minds at rest over Truth as the typical case, is an early postmodernist, then the authors of history-of-economic-thought textbooks are *pro tanto* postmodernist too. That conclusion applies to authors whose views on the mainstream and on economic policy/ideology vary significantly. In some cases, adjustment has to be made for strong, assertive personalities and deeply held views, but once the adjustment is made, it seems clear that subjectivist interpretation rules their work and that they affirm it. More broadly, historiographic topics and issues, and authorial positions on them, constitute the historian's set of tools.

Apropos of the implicit relativism of design strategy, one corollary of our general conclusion of the multiplicity of design strategies is that there is no one history of economic thought. The history of economic thought truly does not write itself. That history is constructed and constructed differently by different people—for reasons given throughout this chapter. We accept self-reflexivity, or self-referentiality: The four essays comprising this book likely would be written differently by different authors.

In partial summary, six somewhat contradictory points may be made. First, there are clear differences between books devoted to theory, such as Blaug's, and those devoted to ideas, such as Spiegel's. Each stresses its intended forte. Second, even books explicitly devoted to theory or analysis cover ideas, though not as broadly or as deeply as books on ideas. Both necessarily deal with the developing corpus of theory—as to the economic system *qua* system and as to explanations and/or description of particular phenomena as well as the ideas ensconced in the theories. Even the "mainstream" of theory tends to be broadly developed. Third, books explicitly devoted to ideas cover economic theory, in some detail, even if in less detail than books devoted to theory. Fourth, the foregoing points are even more complex because of the necessity for selectivity of coverage and the different arrays of coverage. Fifth, as suggested by Backhouse's trilogy, no *necessary* hiatus exists between theory- and ideas-oriented books. Indeed, the theory-versus-ideas conflict is, on the one hand, a matter of what is deemed important for the task at hand, and, on the other, a matter of design strategy. To author books in each genre requires only a well-informed, talented, open-minded and precocious intellect. Sixth, theory-oriented textbooks appear to treat their subject in an internalist manner, whereas ideas-oriented textbooks seem to follow an externalist perspective. Each perspective amounts to a design strategy, although authors likely would say that their approach is congruent with the reality of how economic theory, even ideas, are formed.

Just as no theory can do everything, so too no textbook can do everything. The principle of scarcity, and therefore the principle of opportunity cost, applies to textbook design strategy. But some statements of design strategy are either misleading, i.e., reflect authorial sentiments rather than execution, or use words with elastic, subjective definitions. We have in mind those textbooks whose authors claim to be dedicated to the history of theory or analysis but nonetheless include material on ideational history. Perhaps the point is that some ideational history is necessary to make sense of the history of theory; after all, theory is composed of ideas. Certainly books on the history of ideas must encompass the history of theory.

Beyond the dualism of theory and ideas lies an arguably still deeper issue: whether the pursuit of economic theory or thought constitutes efforts to define reality, establish a belief system or create a set of tools with which to examine the economy. The temptation is to understand the phrase "examine the economy" as if the economy had an independently-generated existence. But the economy is, for economists, formed in part by the tools used to define it. The same is true of the history of economic theory or thought.

A reader must be careful to attribute neither too much nor too little. One example is the historiographic conflict between interpreting the past on the basis of the present and interpreting the present on the basis of the past. More than likely, neither will always be right—and neither will always be wrong. A reason for taking care in all such cases is given by Keith Tribe: "We could say that a text is composed in a binary manner, out of explicit statements and implicit omissions" (Tribe 1999: 617). This is certainly the case with textbooks on the history of economic thought. We have tried, however, to concentrate on the explicit, the interpretation and summarization of which is difficult enough, without taking up the implicit. The task is both facilitated and exacerbated by our decision to concentrate on prefaces, introductions, conclusions and epilogues, thereby omitting the main texts.

If economic theory is contested ground, so also is the history of economic theory. The theoretical and ideational conflict spills over into its own history. Some history-of-economic-thought textbooks affirm and defend and others criticize and oppose the history they relate. Some critics of mainstream economics object to the body of theory and doctrine on substantive and methodological grounds. Others are primarily critics of the modern Western economic system;

their criticism of the economic system drives their criticism of economics, in part presenting mainstream economic theory as the economic system's ideology. All tend to criticize *a priori* economic theory both as narrow and unscientific and as connected with *laissez-faire* policy. Some adopt a radical alternative (Hunt) and others an evolutionary and humanist position (Ingram 1888). Some authors explicitly seek to defend mainstream economic theory and analysis (Backhouse 1985) and some to defend and otherwise cast luster on the Western economic system (Skousen 2001). The key historiographic point is that some textbook authors accept their accounts as either truth or story, and other authors do not.

As several authors, not all of them critical of the theoretical mainstream of economics, have pointed out, economics has often been on the conservative side, whatever the substance of the status quo. But economics has also been in the army, even in the front ranks, of those who practice economics and/or the history of economic thought as a means to liberalism. The problem is what constitutes liberalism and conservatism, notably with regard to a propitious political and legal system, especially in a world of subtle linguistic usage and contrivance. The history of economic thought is both cause and consequence of the spread of liberalism, however difficult and problematic it is to define the term. The worlds of economics and its history are vaster because of the spread of freedom of speech, including the right to publish, and vice versa. "[T]he production and diffusion of the printed word" has had important "connections with political and social change"; the impact of Gutenberg's invention was related to "long-term social and economic phenomena such as the organization of scriptoria, the price of rags and parchment, and the development of trade routes" (Darnton 2003: 45).

Postmodernism, in one form or another, is widespread among historians of economic thought. These historians exhibit a more or less limited desire to serve as cheerleader or high priest to the discipline. These two characteristics lead some practitioners of economics to perceive the sub-discipline as hostile to the practice and content of mainstream economics. The arguments of both those who are overtly hostile to neoclassical hegemony and those who include important criticisms along with their overall affirmation contribute to the same perception. The perception is reinforced by the widespread questioning by historians of economic thought of the possibility of unequivocal progress in economics. Consider internalism versus externalism (absolutism versus relativism): in the internalist story, the theoretician is, by postulate, the intellectual entrepreneur, the unequivocal hero. Insofar as historians of economic thought seem to settle upon either externalist explanations or explanations of complementariness (in which externalism looms large), they are denying finessing the theoretician's identity and status as intellectual hero.

Historians of economic thought and methodologists, in comparison with other economists, have been much more sensitive to and have emphasized the sociological, epistemological, ontological, political and other ideological characteristics of the development of economics in general and of theory in particular. Given their expertise, derived from the intra-disciplinary division of labor, such attention may be expected. Early historians of thought could be critical and even those not critical as such could candidly present sufficient sociological and epistemological data as to inadvertently support many of the same positions. It may boggle some minds that several postmodernist themes may be found in Schumpeter (1954).

Authors of textbooks on the history of economic thought do three things. They adopt their design strategy. They take positions on historiographic issues. They tell their story. In doing so, they vary in the design strategies they adopt, in the positions they take on the historiographic issues on which they comment, and in the stories they tell. Historiographic topics and issues are present and treated in various ways, though only occasionally in depth, more typically in a conclusionary manner. The complaint that sundry historiographic topics are only superficially treated requires caution. It is not the function of the sections of textbooks covered in this study to present extended analysis of such topics. It is enough and important that the authors educate their readers that such topics exist, that they pertain to the book in hand, and that they enter into the author's design strategy.

We sense the presence of some escapism. Roll (1974: 604) finds that economics is prospering in both theoretical and applied areas and is decidedly not in a critical state. "Many economists," he finds, "naturally avoid" confrontational issues "and take refuge in more and more refined theoretical work"—comforted by the sense that the "weaknesses and failures" of the free enterprise economic system "lie outside the field of the mechanics of exchange under the theoretical conditions of perfect competition"—albeit in a reality in which consumption desires are "the product of social influence" and "productive capacities ... are derived from an uncertain mixture of conscientious effort, inheritance, pure luck and outright force and fraud" (1974: 608, quoting Frank H. Knight) and in which "the possession of power ineluctably corrupts the pure power of reason" (1974: 610, quoting Immanuel Kant).

In the pure theory of science, that which is currently held to describe and/or explain reality is juxtaposed to the prospect and legitimacy of future correction, the latter showing that the former had been less a definition of reality and more a system of belief. If a serious conflict exists between historians of economic thought and practicing mainstream economists it may well turn in part on two points: First, heterodox economists having a home in the field. Second, on the greater sensitivity of historians of economic thought to the role of correction, hence to the problematicity of economic ideas and techniques, whereas practicing mainstream economists rely in part on the assumed correctness of their work for their personal gratification and professional status and esteem. It is characteristic of human nature for a person to resist relativist interpretation of what is important to them. Thus is the historiography of a discipline influenced by personal psychology.

An identification problem pervades historiography: how to know an individual's position when it is influenced by environmental factors; and how to know the meaning of external factors when they are given effect by individuals—and neither is homogeneous.

Most if not all textbooks spell out the conflicts of doctrines and of schools, commencing in the early nineteenth century, derivative of two complex sets of positions, designated left and right, liberalism and conservatism, individualism and collectivism, capitalism and socialism, and so on. Gide and Rist represent the few authors (other than the critics) who make a point of it. All authors must somehow deal with the predicaments of multiplicity and of tension and with the significance of conflict and how conflict is handled within the discipline. How authors handle this predicament says much about them and the state of the sub-discipline of the history of economic thought.

Notes

1   For surveys of historiographic topics, see Samuels *et al.* 2003: part II.
2   Candor requires that reader's attention be called to Samuels 1993a. The purpose of the present study is to report on the materials covered, not promote any particular argument. Still, it is an interpretive venture.

4 Thorstein Veblen as economic theorist

Warren J. Samuels

[Theory is] instruments or tools framed for the purpose of establishing interesting results. ... And it is the sum total of such gadgets—inclusive of strategically useful assumptions—which constitutes economic theory. In Mrs. Robinson's unsurpassably felicitous phrase, economic theory is a box of tools.

(Schumpeter 1954: 15)

Bad theory is still better than no theory at all. [Even if non-testable, it should draw] attention to a significant problem [and provide] a framework for its discussion from which a testable implication may some day emerge.

(Blaug 1962: 605, 606)

The "older" American Institutional Economics is often perceived and described ... particularly by those who neither know nor want to know much about it, as monolithically mostly anti-abstract theory, but such is a silly judgment, and has too often been made by people who ought to know better.

(Perlman 1996: 227)

Introduction

The claims have been made that institutional economists are anti-theoretical and that their work is devoid of economic theory. For example,

> The institutional attack in the 1920s had little or no staying powers; among the many reasons that contributed to making its life history rather brief was the absence of theory. Economists were a lonely group without a *raison d'être*—economic theory.
>
> (Bell 1967: 706)

> But in the final analysis, institutionalist economics did not fulfill its promise to supply a viable alternative to neoclassical economics and for that reason, despite the cogency of much of the criticisms of institutionalists, it gradually faded away. The moral of the story is simply this: it takes a new theory, and not just the destructive exposure of assumptions or the collection of new facts, to beat an old theory.
>
> (Blaug 1968: 681)

The objective of this chapter is to demonstrate the falsity of both claims, in part by considering the diverse nature of "theory" and in part by identifying institutionalist economic theories. The latter is a comparatively simple task; the former, more complicated, but showing the many forms that theory can take enables one to see the narrow and myopic basis on which the false claims rest.

It will be most appropriate to rebut the two claims by demonstrating their falsity as applied to Thorstein B. Veblen. This is so for several reasons, including his stature as the first major institutionalist, the breadth of his work, and his often being the principal target of the claims. Apropos of Veblen, Rick Tilman has remarked that "the elaboration of theories was one of Veblen's specialities. … Veblen had little in common with those institutionalists [of the 1930s] who were atheoretical" (Tilman 1987: 151). I am not sure who Tilman had in mind. The institutionalists active in the 1930s were not the equal of Veblen or Commons, having little if any of Veblen's flair or Commons's depth. But they, too, were not anti-theoretical, only opposed to a narrow and exclusivist neoclassical theory.

The procedure will be as follows. First, I consider the nature of theory. I next review neoclassical economics as theory. Finally I examine Veblen as a theorist. It should be clear that the issue is not whether one type of theory is to be preferred over another, nor whether one theory of theories is to be preferred over another, nor whether neoclassical theory is true, nor whether Veblen's theory is true, nor whether one body of theory is to be preferred to the other, nor whether the two are supplementary or mutually exclusive. The sole issues are whether Veblen was anti-theoretical and whether his work is theoretical.

By way of preface, concerning the substance of institutional economics in general, the author has argued (Samuels 2003) that the historic meaning of institutionalism resides in its roles as, first, a protest movement directed at both the capitalist dominated market economy and mainstream market economics seen as providing the former's legitimation; second, an approach to problem-solving; and third, a body of knowledge. As a body of knowledge, the difference between institutional and neoclassical economics is apparent in two ways: first, institutionalism's wider range of variables providing a different, deeper and/or broader answer to the same problems; and second, institutionalism's basic problem being the organization and control of the economy as a system, hence different from neoclassicism's emphasis on the price mechanism and the "efficient" allocation of resources. In contrast to neoclassicism's general modern focus on pure a-institutional conceptual abstract markets, institutionalists have studied markets as institutional complexes operating within, and in interaction with, other institutional complexes. Institutionalists have identified the problem of the institutional organization and control of the economy as the fourth basic economic problem (in addition to the allocation of income, the level of aggregate income, and the distribution of income). They emphasize several alternative issues: the mutual impact of the problem of organization and control upon others and of others upon it; that the resolution of the basic economic problems is a function of institutional arrangements (and vice versa) and not market forces alone; that institutions are regulatory systems; and that the organization-and-control problem is one of the distribution of power in society. They therefore also emphasize the importance of the structure of power and that the problem of organization and control is part of the larger problem of order. They also take a holistic or system-level, and evolutionary, view of the economic process, envision power structure as a phenomenon of collective action, and consider psychology and knowledge as correlative to power as the main facets of institutional economics. Finally, in further consideration of the problem of power, they examine the functioning of the working rules of law and morals, the interrelation of legal and economic processes, how relative rights govern the power structure (allocation of power), and how the working rules govern both relative rights and the transmutation of private into social interests and vice versa. In short, institutionalists focus on the determination of whose interests count and take seriously the theme that institutions matter. These are the subjects on which institutionalists, e.g., Veblen, have theorized. If one believes that these subjects are not part of economics, then the institutionalists are not economists. Not only, however, is that not the issue here but inasmuch (for example) as Nobel Prizes in Economics have been awarded in some of these subjects,[1] the issue is no longer seriously operative.[2]

The nature of theory

Theory

Theory has two lives: one is abstraction, the process of formulating the object of inquiry and limiting and structuring the proposed explanations thereof, in part giving effect to the need/desire to make the inquiry manageable; the other is deduction, the process of drawing conclusions from premises, or assumptions.[3] We deal with them together, with the understanding that, to paraphrase Mark Blaug in a different but related connection (Blaug 1992: 11), any comprehensive view encounters too much material to permit a single "rational reconstruction." That is not our only problem: Blaug quotes Peter Achinstein, "It is in fact difficult to define the notion of *theory* even when the term is employed in a narrow, technical sense" (Blaug 1992: 33 n. 25). Alexander Rosenberg says, on a matter that includes but goes beyond definition, that "Economic theory is a perplexing subject. ... I have never been confident that I or anyone else for that matter really understand its cognitive status" (Rosenberg 1992: 216).

What follows is true of theory in both neoclassical and institutional economics, including Veblen's institutional economics. Theory is ubiquitous, albeit taking different forms; and theory is always subject to limits. In what follows little or no attention is given to the conflicts of interpretation and/or meaning that exist in epistemology and philosophy of science on every point. One type of theory attempts to facilitate or provide our knowledge of our objects of inquiry, the physical and social worlds. Another type of theory attempts to facilitate or provide our knowledge of theory itself. Conflicts abound in both types. The following statements about theory—its domain and its types—abstract from the issues over which these conflicts take place.

To theorize is to reason deductively from premises to conclusions, given the system of logic. Theory requires the reduction of the number of variables to a manageable number. Theory also requires the specification of subject matter and thus of that which is to be explained.

Among the limits of a theory is the impact of the excluded variables. If X is that which is to be explained, and if actually X is a function of A, B, C, ... N variables, and if the theory is limited to X = f(A, D, F), then B, C, etc. have no place in the theory and the theory is constrained. But if Y is also present, and a candidate for explanation, but is not taken up by theorists, it too has no place in either the theory or the discipline.

Accordingly, because a theory is geared to a particular topic, because of the exclusion of certain variables, and because theorists structure the included variables in particular ways, the process and the result are matters of science fiction—intended to be understood non-pejoratively.

The products of this hypothetico-deductive procedure are valid conclusions. Given the premises, given the social space, or domain, to which the theory is applied, and given the proper use of the system of logic used, the conclusion follows logically and is a matter of validity. *Validity* conveys only that, the proper drawing of implications given premises, social space or domain, and system of logic.

Many economists write as if mathematics necessarily deals with reality, and thus with the category of truth. Fundamentally, mathematics is both a language and a matter of deduction. Mathematical exposition of an economic theory or model allows conclusions to be drawn from premises in a manageable manner. The conclusions (and the structures from which they are derived) may or may not pertain to actual economies—in which actual economic actors do not necessarily worry about the logical requirements of their actions, etc., and in which auctioneers have narrowly specified job descriptions not including systemic coordination.

Truth is a different matter. Whereas validity conveys proper deduction, *truth* involves accurate description or correct explanation.

That truth depends on specification of domain is illustrated by the comparison of Euclidian and non-Euclidian geometry on a certain fundamental point concerning the number of degrees in a triangle. Euclidian geometry assumes that through a point, parallel to a line, only one line can be drawn, and, through a series of proper logical steps, concludes that triangles have 180 degrees. Non-Euclidian geometry assumes that through a point, parallel to a line, more than one line can be drawn, and, through a series of proper logical steps, concludes that triangles can have a number of degrees equal to, less than, or more than 180 degrees. Here are two valid but contradictory conclusions. The dependence of truth on specification of domain results from noting that the Euclidian formulation applies to a plane and the non-Euclidian formulation applies to space, or curved objects. Euclidian geometry works on the Earth's surface so long as the distance being measured is small relative to the curvature of the Earth; but non-Euclidian geometry is required in the vast distances of space.

That truth varies from validity is illustrated by the following use of Aristotelian logic: if all men are immortal and if Adam is a man, then Adam is immortal. The conclusion follows logically from the premises but, because one premise is false, the conclusion is untrue. Validity differs from truth.

Theory narrowly defined is not the only meaning conventionally given to "theory" in the foregoing sense of deduction. A *model* is a set of included variables given a particular structure in explanation of a particular object of inquiry. It may or may not be accompanied by a particular specification of domain, or social space. The object of inquiry, the set of included variables, and their particular structure may be, indeed likely are, generated by a particular theory. Y = C + I + G ± X is a model of income as a function of spending.

A *theory* more technically defined comprises an object of inquiry, the list of included variables, a particular structuring of those variables, the social space or domain to which the theory applies, a particular hypothesis as to how the included variables accurately describe or correctly explain the object of inquiry, and a decision rule governing when (under what conditions) the hypothesis will be accepted.

Whereas validity depends only on the proper use of logic within the process of deduction, and if so, then the conclusion necessarily follows, the case of truth is different. A theory confirmed in accordance with the procedure outlined in the immediately preceding paragraph will be true with regard to its elements, e.g., its specific domain, specific hypothesis, and specific decision rule. It is not necessarily true in other cases (the argument of this chapter applies to Veblen and may or may not be true for others). Truth is problematic and conditional.

A model is more general than a theory, and a paradigm is more general than a model—and in part for that reason is more difficult to define in this context. A *paradigm* is a general system of belief, a general cognitive or symbolic system comprised, pointing to, signifying, and re-enforcing what is deemed true and important, and the elementary components thereof and their relations. It is our most basic definition of reality. It is a generically specific, generally structured, self-cognizant or unconscious intellectual system, and more or less consonant with, even derivative from, the dominant cosmology, ontology or ideology.

Both validity and truth comprise exercises in *abstraction*. This is because each specific example abstracts from what it excludes, for example, certain variables, other social space, other structuring of the variables, other specifications of the object of inquiry, other specifications of the hypothesis, and other decision rules. Because this is the case, no theory can answer all of our questions. The result is science fiction. Each and every particular theory has its limits.

To take a particularly simple example, assume some X is to be explained by some D. If D consists of unspecified psychological variables, not much is said. If

D becomes D_1, a particular psychological theory, then the foregoing limits apply to it; and similarly with some D_2. In these latter cases, it is rare that meaningful testing is undertaken through the comparison of particular theories.

It is also the case that important "facts" do not speak for themselves. Facts are derived from theory, either implicit or explicit theory; facts are theory-laden. Conversely, theories are laden with research–design strategy and selectively perceived "facts." A paradigm might be seen as what simultaneously gives meaning to a theory and to certain facts.

The predominant protocol of "science" calls for the empirical testing of conclusions reached through either deduction or induction (out of necessary considerations of essay length, a topic not considered here). Leading methodologists (e.g., Mark Blaug) and practitioners (David Hendry, Edward Leamer, Deirdre McCloskey) affirm, if not confirm, that not much testing is undertaken in economics and that much testing (such as is done) is not very meaningful. In particular, it is rare that meaningful testing is undertaken through the comparison of particular theories. It is also the case that some, though by no means all, methodologists have been critical of neoclassicism on other grounds.

In economics, theorizing comprises several levels of thought. Shackle identifies three such levels, or worlds:

> There is the world of what we take to be "real" objects, persons, institutions and events; on the axis of abstract–concrete this world is at the concrete pole. There is the logical or mathematical construct or machine, a piece of pure reasoning, almost of "pure mathematics", able to exist in its own right of internal coherence, as a system of mere relations amongst undefined thought-entities; this world lies at the abstract pole. And between these two worlds there lies the world of names, linking the real-world elements with the undefined entities of the abstract machine.
>
> (Shackle 1967: 294)

All three, it cannot be emphasized too much, are worlds of thought and theory.

Also noteworthy is the perennial conflict between two approaches to economic methodology. *Prescriptivism* would prescribe certain epistemological criteria by which conclusions should be judged. Whole groups of theories have been denigrated and dismissed on the grounds of some epistemological criterion. "Science" defined in terms of deduction, or mathematical formalism, or induction/empiricism, and so on, has been used to dismiss and ignore other specifications. *Credentialism* rejects the prescription of any single prescribed criterion in favor of simply identifying and attaching to a theory the criterion actually employed, and letting others make of it what they will (a position that may accurately describe practice; see Hands 2001).

Another conflict is between different specifications of particular but nonetheless general theories. The quantity theory of money, Keynesian macroeconomics, the theory of the firm, the Ayresian technology–ceremony dichotomy, the consumption function, the corporation, public expenditure and public-sector decision making, and so on, each may be given different readings and therefore different specifications for testing (such as there is). It is easy to dismiss a theory *qua* theory because one dislikes its subject, its implications, particular specifications of it, and so on.

Theory, therefore, is a generic term used throughout economics. If a model is a set of variables, structured in a particular way with regard to a specific problem (object of inquiry), a theory adds thereto a particular hypothesis (a specific formulation of the theory to be tested), a particular specification of the social space to which the hypothesis-theory applies, and a decision rule by which the hypothesis may be confirmed or refuted. Theories enter into models, theories *per se* (technically defined), and paradigms, and fill every nook and cranny in economics.

To theorize is thus not only to reason deductively from premises to conclusions, given the system of logic. Theorizing is also to organize experience as the basis, and for the purpose, of either description or experimentation or explanation (or the testing of other theories), and to do so by formulating types of dependence among phenomena and/or variables. A theory is a tool and repository of representation and explanation and their application to other materials, other premises and other explanations than those directly, if only generally, encompassed in the theory.

Ernest Nagel's four types of description and explanation thus include the deductive, the probabilistic, the functional or teleological, and the genetic (or historical or evolutionary) (Nagel 1961: 20–26; see also p. 117ff). There are other approaches to the variety of conceptions of explanation and modes of discovery (see, e.g., Briefs 1960; Diesing 1971). Theory need not be formal, using the language of mathematical or philosophical logic.

Both institutional and neoclassical economics encompass theory—as description and/or explanation—in all the foregoing manifestations.

Some further considerations

Lawyers, in writing briefs, have a technique open to them designated by the term "incorporate by reference." Needless to say, they seek to construct the array of possible precedential cases in such a way as to advance their cause. They also wish to bring to bear on the argument presented in their brief certain other materials whose inclusion in the brief is physically burdensome if not impossible. The author does likewise here.

The reader is invited to reflect on at least the last half-century of controversy in epistemology and philosophy of science. This includes the efforts to establish what is called the Received View, albeit in various forms; the variety of attacks on the Received View; the moves made to defend, resuscitate, and revise the Received View; the varieties of alternatives to the Received View; the criticism of each of these alternatives; the various attempts to formulate an acceptable resolution; and so on. To deal adequately with the foregoing, one would have to write one or more books, say, along the lines of those written or edited by

Roger Backhouse, Wade Hands, Daniel Hausman, D.N. McCloskey, Philip Mirowski, Alexander Rosenberg, Andrea Salanti, and Roy Weintraub, as well as by Mark Blaug, Lawrence Boland, and Bruce Caldwell. Caldwell's *Beyond Positivism: Economic Methodology in the Twentieth Century* (1982) and Hands's *Reflection without Rules: Economic Methodology and Contemporary Science Theory* (2001) are particularly useful as surveys and for their points of view. One would have to do more than touch base with some major integrative or survey works by non-economists, such as May Brodbeck's *Readings in the Philosophy of the Social Sciences* (1968), Gordon DiRenzo's *Concepts, Theory, and Explanation in the Behavioral Sciences* (1966), Ernest Nagel's *The Structure of Science* (1961), Maurice Natanson's *Philosophy of the Social Sciences* (1963), Frederick Suppe's *The Structure of Scientific Theories* (1977), and so on. In addition, the huge literature on such major domains of social theory as holism, evolution, and deep structures—separately and in combination and in conjunction with similar philosophical issues to those dealt with in the literature of economic methodology and philosophy—need to be brought to bear. Naturalism, realism, methodological and theoretical pluralism, relativism, and so on, are all relevant topics. Peter Berger, Pierre Bourdieu, Donald Davidson, Michel Foucault, Jurgen Habermas, Ian Hacking, Thomas S. Kuhn, Tony Lawson, Andrew Pickering, Hilary Putnam, Richard Rorty and others are all names additionally relevant to the foregoing and other topics and approaches.[4]

Reflection arguably will lead one to conclude that many more works have dealt with the methodological and substantive criticism, defense, and reconstruction of neoclassical economics than of institutional economics. The reasons for this are clear: the hegemonic position of neoclassicism attracts methodological attention; and the epistemological and philosophy-of-science nature of neoclassical economics is variegated and its status from different points of view is open to criticism. Neither of these reasons, especially the second, should be objectionable as matters of fact inasmuch as any body of analysis will rank high by some criteria and low by others. Indeed, the same is true of institutional economics. Just as no one theory can answer all our questions, no methodological position can satisfy all our methodological requirements or desires. Neoclassical theory is variegated and each variety, and each specific theory, is open to certain relevant criticisms. The same is true of institutional theory. And the same is true of what passes for empirical research in each school.

Reflection arguably will lead one to further conclude, therefore, that no reasonable grounds exist for denying that each school practices theory or for affirming that either school is anti-theoretical. Different theories advanced by members of each school will be subject to different mixes of general and specific criticisms. But they will be theories and those who develop them—and perhaps those who use them—are theorists and none of these people are anti-theoretical. To say that only price theory is theory makes no more sense than to say that only theories of the legal and other foundations of capitalism are theory or that only theories of the deep structures of economic knowledge are theories or that only theories of the planets, and not of non-solar system phenomena, are theories in astronomy.

Part of the problem, to reiterate, is the uneven development of theory and empiricism, the respective limits of each, and the different subjects of neoclassical and institutional economics. The subjects of the former tend to be more quantitative, in part through its use of what Alfred Marshall called the measuring rod of money; but there is considerable quantitative material in the domains of both schools. Not, however, that quantification must be accepted as a *sine qua non* of science.

Consider George Stigler's *The Theory of Price* (1952). Stigler's preface to his revised edition tells the student that he has sought "to emphasize the intimate relationship between theory and empirical evidence: how the theory is tested by evidence—not merely by logic—and how evidence instructs us on the forms of the relationships." Stigler says he hopes "this emphasis will make the theory more comprehensible," perhaps even to "incite the student to attempt to test parts of the theory for himself" (Stigler 1952: v). Nowhere does Stigler tell the student much if anything about "theory" and of the different types of theory presented together in the book, pretty much as the seamless web of "the theory of price." Nor is the façade of "testing"—how little really is done and the limits thereof—revealed to the student. Even the chapter on methodology has been deleted! But "theory" the book is, propounded by a splendid theorist—no more and no less than books by Thorstein Veblen, albeit different in content. To return to the illustrations at the end of the immediately preceding paragraph, even if I were to prefer a price theory different from Stigler's, a theory of the legal and other foundations of capitalism different from John R. Commons's, or a theory of the deep structures of economic knowledge different from, say, Foucault's, theirs would still be theories.

In the third edition of *The Theory of Price*, three points are relevant. In its preface, Stigler identifies the theory of value (= price) as "the traditional central core of economic theory" (Stigler 1966: v), thus coming close to equating price theory with economic theory. The price, or value, theory Stigler has in mind is, of course, neoclassical theory, not the classical or Marxian versions. In his introductory chapter, he has a section entitled "Science as Fiction," in which he bases the title on the inexorable generality of a useful theory to the neglect of details (1966: 5–7). Inevitable unrealism, therefore, renders economics *science fiction*. This is as true of institutional economics as it is of neoclassical price theory. And in his discussion of tastes, after arguing that the "defenses of the assumption of constant tastes are not wholly implausible," Stigler goes on "to retract. There is no strict boundary over which the economist dare not step, and many studies of tastes have been made" (1966: 39). This position shows how questions of the scope of economics can get mixed up with questions of theory and empiricism, with the possibility, for Stigler, of a supplemental or complementary relation between institutional and neoclassical economic theory (see note 2).

At least one irony pervades all discussions of epistemology and philosophy of science. Brief notice will be taken below of the market as metaphor. The irony can be presented in a question: "What if science is a metaphor?" The argument has been made (e.g., Olson 1971). So has the argument that it, the social sciences, is sorcery (Andreski 1972).

Different schools of thought use different terminology to label what is either the same point or a nearly identical one: general interconnectedness, general equilibrium, recursive relations, cumulative causation, and over-determination. Symbolically: A↔B. The latter two terms are probably the widest: A and B both influence each other with regard to impact and each changes in response to the operation of the other; i.e., one impact of each is the reshaping of the other. The usage of all five terms is both universal and often finessed in the search for unilinear unique determinate results. This means that the theory that contains A↔B will almost certainly not yield unique determinate results. Consequently, both prediction and refutation are substantially excluded. The alternative is termed pattern models, a methodology, as is now understood, adopted by Friedrich A. von Hayek (apropos of Veblen, see Wilber and Harrison 1978; Diesing 1971; and Ramstad 1986). These encompass multiple statements of tendency (or statements of multiple tendencies) rather than unique determinate results. What transpires will depend on the presence and relative strength of pertinent variables. Without knowing those, prediction and refutation is impossible.

Many of Veblen's theories and neoclassical theories at first read as providing unilinear unique determinate results but soon become obvious pattern models, although they are rarely called that by name. A neoclassical claim that a Veblen theory explains everything and therefore nothing is compromised by the pertinence of the same point to neoclassical theories. But a theory is not a non-theory because it involves a pattern model and cannot itself alone be used to predict or be refuted—and, indeed, it is very difficult, if not impossible, to (conclusively) refute any theory. A common neoclassical argument or line of reasoning is that some development is reflected in the capital market. This reasoning is *a priori* and non-empirical and non-refutable. It also fails to specifically encompass and indicate the effect of variables—such as information and power—that are asymmetric and others that are absent— such as organization.

An economics of tendencies or of pattern models avoids both the presumptuous quest for unique determinate solutions and sole reliance on equally question-begging, purely abstract entities. Such an economics recognizes that no one theory can either answer all of our questions or cope with the variety of institutions, evolutionary and other processes, and outcomes.

Indeed, neoclassical constrained-maximization models inexorably require specification of that which is to be maximized. Different specifications are possible. Litigation and lobbying are economic alternatives. Inasmuch as different interests may count, economic agents allocate resources to change the law (and the interpretation/application of moral rules) so that their interests will count (for more), i.e., others' interests will be economized. (For example, marginal-cost pricing requires choice from among multiple extant margins (Samuels 1980).)

No blanket prescription can be properly given. Theories and models are not given and transcendent; they are tools of analysis to be adopted for and adapted to the pragmatic/instrumental/utilitarian purposes of the analyst. For certain purposes, it may be useful to the analyst to posit a unique equilibrium and examine how the system converges to that equilibrium regardless of initial conditions and independent of structural and environmental conditions. For other purposes, it may be useful to drop the idea of a unique equilibrium, even the idea of equilibrium, and inquire into the process of adjustment to changes of all sorts, including structural and environmental conditions. The existence of different levels of abstraction in theory is legitimate, with greater or less attention to detail, to behaviors, and to processes, all of which can be variegated. Methodological pluralism is joined by theoretical pluralism.

All that notwithstanding, the neoclassical propensity to make propitious assumptions, in order to generate deductively the desired unique determinate optimal equilibrium result, is both worrisome and a source of humor directed at the discipline. Still, making the number and content of assumptions manageable is the nature of deduction. Moreover, institutionalist theory operates no differently; being less formal and less overtly deductive, the limited number, nature and role of assumptions may be less clear.

Even that notwithstanding, institutionalism seems more willing to accept and give effect to recursive relations, cumulative causation, and over-determination. Frank H. Knight was recorded at one point as saying in class, "The individual preference or choice scale becomes a social scale via the price system" (Ostrander 2004). At another point he said, "saving a result of social mores." So Knight was seemingly willing to recognize the two-way causal relationship— though not together and very unlike conventional neoclassical practice. Knight also said, "The psychology of saving is chiefly a matter of getting ahead in life— a question of power"—this from an economist who later tried to exclude power from both his economics and his social theory. Perhaps the problem is, in part, not what people know or do not know but what they are prepared to include in their theories and models, even in economics, as dependent or independent variable or as explicandum or explanandum.

Definitions often assume, embody, and give effect to theories, theories, for example, as hypotheses. Definitions not only define words, when the words are used they define the world for us and that definition may mislead or incompletely define the world.[5]

When a metaphor is used to define a metaphor, not much of substance has been said. If the "invisible hand" is a metaphor and if "market" is a metaphor, then identifying the invisible hand as the market—to answer the question, what is the invisible hand?—is not very informative. Doing so leads to a profound difference between pure abstract a-institutional conceptual markets *and* actual markets which are a function of the institutions/power structures that form and operate through them. Then one has to ask, what is an institution? The use of primitive, undefined terms can meaningfully go only so far.

The notion of a market as characterized by a single price for a given commodity can be considered a definition, an assumption, or a conclusion. If a conclusion, the question arises whether it is a matter of logical validity or an empirical fact. Here, too, the theory built upon it may be a tautology, such that finding more than one price does not negate the proposition but implies multiple markets.

Terms are often used in a generic sense. Terms such as "private," "public," "voluntary," "freedom," "coercion," "property," "morality," "liberty," and so on, are used as primitive terms with unspecified meaning. They are kaleidoscopic, subject to selective perception, and almost invariably given variable specification. Their use facilitates the entry into analysis or argument of selective implicit antecedent normative premises. This allows an author to escape questions of both substantive content and the mode of its determination, thereby usually begging an, if not the, important substantive question, leaving it to each reader to provide substantive content. Such terms are often identified with the status quo somehow selectively perceived—often the point at issue. They permit implicit, if variable, apologia, for example, by selective reification of some status quo.[6]

Economics discourse has numerous examples of primitive terms used in such a way as to lead each user to adduce selective, private meanings or a meaning that is wrong or misleading.

For example, the phrase "Government interference in free markets" is misleading if not wrong because markets are in part a function of government action, action promoting certain interests and not others, and actions changing the interests to which government gives its support.

Other examples include: phrases such as "properly designed institutions" and "properly designed institutional change"—with the meaning of "properly," as well as "institution," left unspecified. Statements such as, "If the most is to be made of the new technology, the proper infrastructure must be in place," or that a policy "left things worse, not better," or that a policy "worked," "failed," or "distorted" results, leave unspecified both the substantive meaning of the key terms—proper, worse, better, worked, failed, distorted—and how to determine what they mean. It is left to each reader to provide substantive content.

Yet another example: phrases such as "correct solutions," "minimal standards," "deficient versus excessive budgets," "distortion," "good versus bad policy," and that "the function of rules is to restrain harmful behavior"—leave unspecified the meaning of each critical term. Phrases such as "the optimal set of laws," "the optimal tax and expenditure system," "the optimal balance between private and public sectors," when something is "best served" by each sector, and so on—with the precise substantive meaning and/or conditions of "optimal," and "best," "private" and "public" left unspecified.

A further problem is that the so-called status quo is not a given; it is a matter of interpretation. The status quo is selectively perceived and identified. The status quo itself is the ultimate object of inquiry. By identifying it in particular, selective terms and identifying it with the pure conceptual model, economists selectively reify the existing system, rendering it more concrete than it really is. A further problem is that the primitive terms of the descriptive model itself—such as "competition"—can be given variable specification.

The foregoing and still other problems of language compromise the meaningfulness of certain theories. But the pertinence of these problems does not negate the status of the theories *qua* theories. Institutional economics has its share of these problems (as indicated in the second set of examples). In part because it works with a pure abstract a-institutional conceptual model of the economy (Shackle's second world), neoclassical economics is particularly susceptible to these problems.

The roles of theory

Some of the foregoing discussion has dealt more or less necessarily but also more or less in passing with the roles of theory.[7]

Theory is known not only by epistemological considerations but by the roles it performs—not that everything that performs these roles is theory nor does the performance by a theory of one role necessarily constitute performance of another. Also, the role of a theory is derived from the specific purpose for which it is created or used by the economist. Theories are shaped by their builders, who are guided consciously or unconsciously by a theory's potential role in society. Theory making and theory using are social phenomena. Politicians, including politically active economists, use, even manufacture, economic theory so as to create an aura of respectability and coherence for policies determined on ideological grounds. Among professional economists, the perceived performance of a particular function of theory may constitute a mode of theory choice. Especially important is that the creation and use of theory is part of the political-economic process; for those, like Frank Knight, who see economics as an emanation from a particular culture, whose simultaneous explanation and legitimation it pursues, economic theory takes on a different aura in comparison with those, like Veblen, who saw economics as a cultural emanation but rejected legitimation masquerading as explanation. Theories are both of and about this world; they are part of the world that some theories are used to explain.

The roles of theory are multiple. In an analysis of those roles (Samuels 1994) the present author has identified them as follows: explanation, description, prediction, hypothesis, confirmed hypothesis, definition of reality, providing a sense of economic order or disorder, understanding in the sense of understanding (*verstehen*), heuristic, and tool of analysis. Theory also performs several discursive or rhetorical roles, such as systematizing ideas, providing a framework of discussion, serving as an organizing principle, and a mode of concentrating attention. In addition, theory facilitates manageability, is an element in a logical/epistemological structure, is used for prescriptive purposes, is the basis of the social construction of reality (in either of both senses, artifact creation and interpretation), is used as the basis of legitimation and criticism, as a means of projecting perceptions, as social control, as psychic balm, to tell a story, to give economics the status of a science, and as a vehicle of ideology, wishful thinking, and paradigm. Finally and highly apposite for present purposes, theory is used to refer to neoclassical economics—seeking to give it an honorific status, a privileged hermeneutic and disciplinary position while treating invidiously all other forms or schools of economic thought.

Theories are indeed part of the world and one function of theory in economics is to legitimize (and in the case of heterodoxy, to criticize) mainstream, neoclassical economics itself. Given Veblen's critiques of neoclassical economics (he coined the term), it is not surprising that neoclassicists saw him as both anti-theoretical and un-theoretical: If one equates theory with neoclassical theory, to reject the latter is to reject the former. But that was not the case with Veblen, nor could it have been the case, for he too was a theorist in most if not all the aforementioned respects. There is more to economic theory than price theory. For Veblen as well as for Knight, for example, the subject matter of theory included the problem of organization and control; indeed, one can comprehend the neoclassical paradigm centering on, say, the competitive market price mechanism as itself an approach to the problem of organization and control. But this one theory cannot answer all of our questions about organization and control.

Neoclassical economics as theory

Neoclassical economic theory has several forms.

One form is the Marshallian. It seeks to develop theories about the "real" world, with actual firms and actual markets, however generalized through abstraction. It seeks to develop tools for the analysis of the "real" economic world. It seeks to develop an economics of statements of tendency and of pattern models. On a number of issues, e.g., "economic man" and "maximum satisfaction," it is relatively "soft." It comports with Shackle's first world, "the world of what we take to be 'real' objects, persons, institutions and events; on the axis of abstract–concrete this world is at the concrete pole."

Another form comports with Shackle's second world, "the logical or mathematical construct or machine, a piece of pure reasoning, almost of 'pure mathematics', able to exist in its own right of internal coherence, as a system of mere relations amongst undefined thought-entities; this world lies at the abstract pole." Whereas the Marshallian practitioner is comfortable—however reluctantly—with open-endedness and ambiguity, this second practitioner seeks closure and determinacy. This world's research protocol prescribes reaching unique determinate optimum equilibrium results or solutions. It works with pure abstract a-institutional conceptual markets. Neither its markets nor its analytical conclusions apply directly to actual firms or actual markets.

Both of the preceding two forms are largely deductive in character, the Marshallian within its ambit of generalized actual firms, and the other within its specific research protocol and its notion of pure conceptual markets. Each in its own way conducts abstraction to render the number of variables manageable.

Still another form is an array of empirical approaches. Some test theory. Some reach conclusions as to factual description. Some are used to help formulate and/or reconstruct theory. Some operate in the Marshallian mode; some in combination with the purely conceptual a-institutional mode.

Accordingly, neoclassicism is not alone laden with controversies as to which of all these and still other forms is "scientific" and "theoretical." The relations of theory and empiricism to each other and to "science" are also controversial, even though epistemologically in practice they are not mutually exclusive.

So neoclassical theory is not homogeneous. Ronald Coase, for whom "institutions matter," is a theoretician in the Marshallian mode. Gerard Debreu and Hal Varian are theoreticians of the second of Shackle's worlds of thought. John R. Hicks started in the Marshallian mode, helped generate its rival, and eventually shifted more or less substantially back to his original mode—distressing those who followed obediently his second set of footsteps. Theory in neoclassical economics thus takes different forms and is differently nested as between the first two of Shackle's three worlds. Alas, very little work has been done on the development of theories "linking the real-world elements with the undefined entities of the abstract machine."

Knight himself, in a discussion of Marshallian wage theory, anticipated and may even have gone beyond Coase's much later criticism of "blackboard economics." Notes from his lectures (Ostrander 2004) record, in part, "Knight doesn't put any stock in any of this—it is a mere logical exercise," "We don't know *anything* about all this," and "Try to get some idea of realistic psychology." This type of neoclassical theory was not for everyone, though Knight did not criticize it much in public.

Knight (Ostrander 2004) also was seemingly willing to recognize the two-way causal relationship—very unlike conventional neoclassical practice. We have already noted his reported statement, "The individual preference or choice scale becomes a social scale via the price system" coupled with "saving a result of social mores." At another point Knight has labor supply as a function in part of standard of living and standard of living as a function in part of labor supply.

Neoclassicism's self-perception of its central problem exhibits several dimensions, and these are often combined. One such combined explication is of the market and price mechanism. Another is the explication of resource allocation and income distribution. Another is working out the logic of choice. Another is the explication of the foregoing to the working out of the problem of organization and control of the economic system. And so on. All these involve, insofar as theory *per se* is involved, an enormous array of theories (each performing the aforementioned roles to one degree or another). Some of the theories are *a priori*. Some are grounded in other theories. Some are hypothetical or conjectural. Some are based on readings of empirical evidence. And so on. All are driven, in part, by status emulation.

Some theories are theories in accordance with certain conceptions of theory; others seem not to be theories because they conflict with other conceptions of theory. Each of the great controversies in the history of economics has tended to include such conflicts: the controversies over capital theory with and without measurement, rent theory, the theory of exploitation, marginalism, and so on.

As a deductive system, neoclassical theory is based on premises. Three presently relevant problems arise. One problem is that implicit antecedent normative premises can enter ostensibly positive analysis through the selective use of assumptions; these can be the premises that drive the conclusions. The second problem is that analysis that is supposed to be a-institutional can be, and often is, joined with a selective reading of the status quo in order to reach further deductive conclusions, conclusions made applicable to policy. Thus, neoclassical theory assumes the existence of *some* system of property but cannot properly adopt (some reading of) the existing property system as *the* basis of the price mechanism. Affirmation of the general integrity and security of some institutionalization of property is one thing; transforming that affirmation into a set of particular positions on legal change of property rights in the working out of the conflicts of freedom and control and of continuity and change is something else. Third, and related to both of the foregoing, is the conventional neoclassical solution to the problem of determining property rights. The solution is to adopt that definition and that assignment of rights that is most efficient, the optimal one. The analytical problem is that optimality is a function of rights, not the other way around. The neoclassical solution is reached by the introduction of implicit normative premises as to whose interest should count through legal protection, thereby foreclosing the process of policy determination. These problems are so serious and so widespread that, coupled with the problems of language (which overlap), the resulting body of theory is seriously flawed. The nature of the theory *qua* theory is not negated but the methodologically complacent use of that theory renders it flawed—almost, perhaps actually, that the theorist—having been told of the infirmities—does not care, surely something of an anti-theoretical position. The neoclassical response to all questions about premises is to point, following Milton Friedman, to predictive power and not realism of assumptions. Yet economics is notorious for the difficulties if not impossibility of prediction, for its reliance on internal consistency (logicality and validity) and coherence, and for its unlabelled reliance on pattern models. All this seems more a matter of rhetorical moves and less one of conjecture and refutation, etc. It is not clear that institutionalism performs better along these lines than neoclassicism.

Neoclassical economics encompasses theory—as description and/or explanation—in all the foregoing manifestations and more. It organizes experience as the basis of and for the purpose of either description or explanation (or the testing of other theories), and does so by formulations of types of dependence among phenomena and/or variables. Its theories are tools and repositories of representation and explanation; its theories are applied to other materials, other premises and other explanations than those directly, if only generally, encompassed in the theory. It encompasses Nagel's four types of description and explanation, and while neoclassical economics has increasingly used the formal language of mathematical or philosophical logic, it includes non-formal language as well.

On 24 December 2002 the present author posed to several economists the following question: "In what precise ways/senses … is neoclassical economics a 'theoretical' discipline? Please answer in whatever length is comfortable or necessary." Their replies are as follows.

Roger E. Backhouse, after pointing out that "any answer must be historically specific. An answer that makes sense today would not necessarily have been appropriate circa 1900," wrote:

> the answer hinges on our current understanding of economic theory and its relation to the rest of economics. Theory and empirical work have increasingly become separated—even when economists do both, possibly in the same article, they make a distinction—and we have chosen to define neoclassical economics as what lies on the theoretical side of this divide. In short, I would suggest that neoclassical economics is a theoretical discipline because we have constructed our understanding of what neoclassical economics is to make it so.

Backhouse, having focused attention on the problem of the construction of the idea of the "theoretical," then noted the same problem with "neoclassical" itself, saying, "there are also questions about what is neoclassical" (Backhouse to Samuels, 6 January 2002).

Mark Blaug wrote, "Economics is the discipline. Neoclassical economics is a phase in the history of the discipline" (Blaug to Samuels, 1 January 2003). For Blaug, the problem is not that of theory.

Bruce J. Caldwell wrote that he finds the question

> too big to try to answer. I think the short answer is that it is, definitely, a theoretical discipline. The key question is how well the theory helps us to understand real economic phenomena, and whether other frameworks are in some cases better. I think here that the story is mixed.
>
> But there is also a troubling self-reflexivity in my answer. I think I know what I mean by "real economic phenomena." But we (you and I) may differ on what we consider these to be. And the way I come up with "my" list depends on, well, my theory of the way the world works. So it would seem (and perhaps this is due to my having studied the Austrians) it is theory all the way down for me. It's just that, on different levels, different conceptions of theory are relevant.
>
> (Caldwell to Samuels, 14 January 2002)

John B. Davis suggested that:

> If for Marshall neoclassical economics is the study of people in the ordinary business of life, then it could be termed a practical discipline. If for Robbins (following JS Mill) neoclassical economics is the study of the implications of a specific abstraction, homo economicus, then it could be termed a theoretical discipline. A theoretical discipline proceeds essentially in a deductive

manner; a practical discipline proceeds essentially in an inductive manner. The former also emphasizes positive explanation; the latter makes a less sharp distinction between positive and value-laden discourse.

(Davis to Samuels, 6 January 2002)

Anthony M.C. Waterman responded that

Neoclassical economics is a "theoretical discipline" for exactly the same reason as all other branches ("schools", sub-disciplines etc) of economics are "theoretical disciplines". Indeed, for the same reason that ALL scientific inquiries whatsoever are "theoretical disciplines".

So far as we humans are able to observe ourselves in our intellectual activity, we think we can say that human minds seem to go about the business of constructing "knowledge" of their external environment by inventing concepts, by postulating relations between those concepts, by using these relations to construct models intended to capture—in some public or at any rate interpersonally recognisable way—what we all seem to think we are observing; and to prove the usefulness of these models by deriving from them hypothetical predictions about the things we think we are observing. If those predictions work well enough and often enough to be useful, we stay with the model(s). If not, we try to do better. "Doing better" means getting a better "theory" (i.e., assemblage of related models and the logical structure that connects them).

This statement is intended to cover everything from nuclear physics to musicology. All forms of economics come somewhere in the middle of such an imaginary continuum.

(Waterman to Samuels, 7 January 2002)

Considering all the foregoing replies to the author's query, the emphasis is on the social construction of what constitutes "theory" (Backhouse, Caldwell, Davis, Waterman); the distinction between the Marshallian and the abstract forms (Davis); theory as deductive (Davis, Waterman); present neoclassicism as theoretical (in the sense of deduction) (Backhouse, Caldwell; cf. Blaug); theory as conceptual, distinct from but not unrelated to the observational (Caldwell, Waterman); all forms of economics are (at least in part) theoretical (Waterman); and the relevance of different concepts of theory (Caldwell).

These replies provide an affirmation, at least an expectation, of plural types or forms of economic theory, presumably in all schools of thought. Devotees of particular types of theory often are unable to recognize other types as theory too.

Thus, the manifest results of selective perception are exhibited within neoclassical economics. As Tom Mayer notes, "theory" and "theorist" are honorific terms (Mayer 1995: 51). He quotes McCloskey: "The leading middle-aged economists laugh when Gary Becker is described as a theorist ... and the leading young economists do not even think it funny" (Mayer 1995: 51, quoting

McCloskey 1991: 14), and comments: "Yet Becker's work is surely theoretical, as that term is used in the natural sciences and in philosophy of science" (Mayer 1995: 51; for an elaborate treatment of the issues, see Hands 2001).

Thorstein Veblen as theorist

Veblen was not a neoclassical theorist, of any type or form. He knew neoclassicism (he gave it its name) as it then existed. He provided leading critiques of neoclassical doctrines. As Wesley Mitchell put it, "His fundamental criticism is that economists have asked the wrong questions. Their conception of science and its problems is antiquated, pre-Darwinian" (Mitchell 1936: xxiii; Mitchell also pointed out that Veblen had his own theory of human nature/psychology to accompany his criticism of the neoclassical theory). Not anti-theory, not without theory, but for the correct questions and the right and appropriate theories.

I wrote earlier, "Veblen was not a neoclassical theorist, of any type or form." This is not strictly true. Neoclassicism deals with price, market determination of price, price governing resource allocation, price as cost, price–cost differentials (profits, losses), and so on. Veblen dealt with the pecuniary economy inclusive of masses of those same phenomena. Wesley Mitchell's Veblenian project on the pecuniary economy became, at NBER, his empirical, pecuniary business cycle theory, laden with pecuniary and other theory.

Veblen was a theorist.[8] Pursuant with what has been said above, he theorized—and theorized in much the same way, including the *a priori*—about some of the same subjects as did neoclassicists. He did so with different perceptions, different premises, a wider range of variables, and with different theories—for example, on monetary and cyclical topics. He also theorized—in various ways—about different problems than did neoclassicists. Veblen was critical of neoclassical value and price theory but he was not anti-theoretical; he was, indeed, a theorist.

Veblen's economics encompassed theory—as description and/or explanation—in all the manifestations given above and more. His corpus of theory organized experience as the basis of and for the purpose of either description or explanation (or testing of other theories), and did so by formulating types of dependence among phenomena and/or variables. His theories were tools and repositories of representation and explanation and their application to other materials, other premises and other explanations than those directly, if only generally, encompassed in the theory. They encompassed Nagel's four types of description and explanation. Veblen, however, did not use the formal language of mathematical or philosophical logic.

One form in which Veblen theorized, in the mode of abstraction, was through his use of "type-forms" (Veblen 1998 [1917]: 10, 82). These approximate Max Weber's ideal types in that they are constructions that concentrate upon and intensify the traits of certain processes, structures or values through exaggerating their characteristics, using them like Weber to explicate and clarify by comparison and contrast. In Veblen's case the ideal types emphasize *becoming* rather than *being* and are akin to the *verstehen* concept (see Tilman 1973). A comparable example is Joseph Schumpeter's entrepreneur as a "constructed type" (Carlin 1999 [1956]).

Having referred to Hayek's and Wilber's emphasis on pattern modeling, let me elaborate briefly. Veblen argued that the economic world was much more vast and much more complex than mainstream economics allowed it to be. This meant to him that the search for unidirectional principles and unique determinate solutions (as I would put it) was misguided; the only feasible approach, especially if one added (non-teleological but path-dependent) evolution, was the identification of factors and forces, and of tendencies from among the many possibilities constituting both cumulative causation and the relevant pattern model. Veblen found both that certain problems interested him and that these problems were both important and largely ignored (to some extent given ideologically christened and safe formulations and analyses) by mainstream economists. His interest in these problems was engendered by his reading and led him to other works, so that his eventual analyses were predicated upon the assumptions in the form of those problems and of the putative facts he found in his reading and, presumably, observation, all inevitably with a heavy dose of interpretation. In this context he practiced neither pure deduction nor pure induction but various forms of their combination, or Peircian abduction. (Veblen's analyses of imperial Germany and Japan and of peace in the contest between two types of states, the predatory dynastic and pacific modern states, are splendid examples.) The result was what has been called the compositive method and pattern modeling and prediction and it all comes under the heading of theory. All this must be combined with Veblen's co-evolutionary model or theory. The implication for policy is of a kind: non-teleological natural selection and, in the absence of an independent test, the ubiquitous need to work out solutions to problems on a trial and error basis, the problems having to do with substantive issues within a given structure and with decision-making structure itself. The working out of policy paralleled abduction, pattern modeling, and the compositive method—and all involved theory of one type or another.

Veblen has been treated by institutional economists and by scholars from other disciplines around the world as not only a theorist but a great theorist, even while being criticized by them. Some neoclassical economists have made the charges here rebutted; they were presumably sensitive to his criticisms of them, feeling a sensitivity to competition, unwilling to consider his theories in terms of central problem and/or substance on disciplinary and/or ideological grounds, and, ironically, driven by considerations of status. Other scholars, some of whom are neoclassicists, either accept, tolerate, or prefer his topics, his theories, and/or his mode of theorizing, finding them deeper and broader, more holistic and evolutionary, less mechanical and formal, more ideational and intellectual, and less metaphysical and ideological. Be all that as it may, Veblen was not anti-theoretical; he was a theorist.

Perhaps the two most significant indicators that so far from being anti-theoretical, Veblen was a theorist, are, first, the seeming acceptance by most neoclassicists of the propriety of his theories being included in economics—for example, by neoclassicist historians of economic thought—and, second, the criticisms of Veblen's theories *qua* theories by a variety of critics. The former is too vast a topic to be dealt with here in detail. One example is the use of Veblen's theory of status emulation in macroeconomics in explaining the gradual rise of the consumption function over time (other examples are given below). The latter is also vast, but the basic work has been produced by Rick Tilman in his *Thorstein Veblen and His Critics, 1891–1963* (1992; see also Tilman 1999). That scholars in a variety of fields have found some or much in Veblen's writings to criticize, typically in the context or on the basis of their own theories, seems more reliable evidence, if not confirmation, of Veblen as theorist than his rejection by a few antagonistic and myopic neoclassicists unable to tolerate criticism or possessed of a narrow definition of the scope of economics and/or its methodology.

It is not only neoclassical historians of economic thought concentrating on theory (e.g., Ekelund and Hébert 1975 and later editions; Landreth 1976; Negishi 1989; Niehans 1990) who include Veblen. He has been included on reading lists in theory courses given by neoclassicists. For example, Veblen's *The Theory of Business Enterprise* was listed on the reading list for Melchior Palyi's course on Business Cycle Theory, Economics 333, at the University of Chicago during 1933–1934. Veblen was in good company; other authors included Albert Aftalion, R.G. Hawtrey, Friedrich Hayek, W.C. Mitchell, A.C. Pigou, Denis Robertson and Knut Wicksell. On Frank H. Knight's reading list for Economics 303, Current Tendencies, at Chicago during the same academic year, were Veblen's *The Instinct of Workmanship*, *Theory of the Leisure Class*, and *Place of Science in Modern Civilization* ("The Limitations of Marginal Utility," "Professor Clark's Economics," and "Gustav Schmoller's Economics"), in similar good company.

Henry Simons, in a course also that year, in a discussion of excise taxation, is recorded as saying of diamonds, "a product whose demand is *entirely* due to *invidious competition*" (Ostrander 2005d).

Frank Knight is a special source of insight into the status of both Veblen as theorist and his theories. For that purpose I use four sets of notes taken by a student in Knight's classes in 1933–1934. The student was F. Taylor Ostrander (see biographical sketch: Samuels 2004) and the courses were Economic Theory (Economics 301), History of Economic Thought (302), Current Tendencies (303), and Economics from Institutional Standpoint (305).

Knight was ambivalent about institutional economics in general and Veblen in particular. He affirmed the importance of institutions but not what institutionalists made of them. Knight is reported to have said of institutional economics, "*Institutional[ism]* (largely a revolt for sake of revolt)." His basic position on institutionalism was different and more thoughtful, if still negative: the institutionalists dealt with important questions, but not in the right way (or came up with the wrong answers), i.e., they needed to be less dismissive and less sarcastic. Nonetheless, his negative view shows when he says of "cumulated change" that it was "Veblen's phrase, didn't know what it meant" (Ostrander 2005a).

Knight's position on institutional economics is ironic. The Chicago School opposed much of institutionalist theory and policy, defending and rendering the market system as an absolute, whereas the institutionalists were critical of the capitalist-dominated form of the market system and tried to demystify it as well. The institutionalists saw regulation as a mode of changing property rights, whereas the Chicago School saw it as redistributive and inefficient, and so on. The Chicago Economics Department during the pre-World War I and interwar periods had a number of institutionalists, including Veblen. Knight and other Chicagoans paid attention in their own way to institutionalist topics. (See Rutherford 2002 and Tilman 2001.) For example, in Economics 301, the assignment sheet included "Veblen—Place of Science in Civilization," "The Limitations of Marginal Utility," "Prof. Clark's Econ." and Knight refers to John Maurice Clark's overhead cost.

In the history-of-economic-thought course, Economics 302, Knight says that given the "assumption that ... the meaning of goods and services is something outside themselves, as social prestige, it does no good to try to construct utility curves for goods and services." This is a remarkable statement, in part for the deep use made of Veblen's analysis. Knight accepts the Smith–Veblen theory of status emulation. The statement suggests why conventional microeconomic theory must finesse status emulation in order to produce determinate and ostensibly welfare-relevant results.

Knight's treatment of Veblen as theorist and his use of Veblen's theories explodes in Economics 303, Current Tendencies.

Knight again uses Veblen's theory of pecuniary emulation, conspicuous consumption, and the pecuniary standard of living: "Corporate heads are not paid for *services*, but so they can *live* the way it 'befits' a corporate head to live—their salaries are window-dressing." Given Knight's more or less respectful hostility toward Thorstein Veblen and his ideas ("Only real institutionalist in U.S. was Veblen. ... Knight can find no contribution."), it is striking to read him validating Veblen's portrayal of the mainstream conception of the economic actor. Knight's own view was: "Ordinary economic theory treats of *behavior* as *motivated*, but of the *motivation* as *mechanical*." Compare Veblen's famous language:

> The hedonistic conception of man is that of a lightning calculator of pleasures and pains who oscillates like a homogeneous globule of desire of happiness under the impulse of stimuli that shift him about the area, but leave him intact. He has neither antecedent nor consequent. He is an isolated definitive human datum, in stable equilibrium except for the buffets of the impinging forces that displace him in one direction or another. Self-imposed in elemental space, he spins symmetrically about his own spiritual axis until the parallelogram of forces bears down upon him, whereupon he

follows the line of the resultant. When the force of the impact is spent, he comes to rest, a self-contained globule of desire as before. Spiritually, the hedonistic man is not a prime mover. He is not the seat of a process of living, except in the sense that he is subject to a series of permutations enforced upon him by circumstances external and lien to him.

(Veblen 1997 [1898], vol. I: 19–20)

Knight anticipated the core argument of the characteristics theory of demand, that people demand not goods but certain of what they believe are the characteristics of goods. Knight: "What do people do when they buy commodities? What do they buy? *Commodities are not human wants.* A list of one and a list of the other would have no word on both lists." And as to what drives the demand for those characteristics, according to Knight, "We want mainly *distinction* and *conformity.*" Status emulation through conformity and distinction—a position in distinctive conformity to what Veblen, in his *Theory of the Leisure Class*, called status and pecuniary emulation under the aegis of the canons of invidious comparison, pecuniary standards of taste, and conspicuous consumption and leisure. Veblen, again.

In a discussion of cost theory and resource allocation, Knight once again borrows from Veblen, saying, "one knows that people value things according to their price. ... And sellers put up the price accordingly."

When his discussion turns to Veblen's use of Darwin's analysis, of particular interest is Knight's seeming implicit acceptance of a conflict between institutions that work to inhibit change and those that promote change. The notes read, "Preindustrial society has a definite aversion to *change.* ... Western, post-Renaissance history has changed to a belief in the improvement of life through change." The final use of Veblen is spectacular but, alas, undeveloped: "The whole *content* of economics *is* of institutional origin." The implications are that institutions matter and that economics—"the whole content of economics"—is derived from, an emanation of, the institutions of the market economy. Economics is, indeed, like markets, a function of the institutions that form and operate through it.

Not surprisingly, Veblen's work is a feature in the reading list for Knight's course, Economics from Institutional Standpoint, Economics 305, offered the same academic year (and other years). Without repeating what I say above and elsewhere, the course was not an exposition of the institutional economics of Veblen, Commons *et al.* It was a tribute to the importance of the questions they raised, plus a condemnatory dismissal of their analyses, especially those by Veblen—largely because Knight found them wrong or wanting. Missing, however, are the claims that Veblen had no theory and that he was anti-theoretical.

Consider the type of remark that Knight made about Veblen's approach to history, an important topic given Veblen's advocacy of an evolutionary economics. Knight recognizes Veblen's emphasis on non-teleological Darwinian evolution and on cumulative causation but considers, as noted above, that Veblen did not know what they meant—meaning that he did not have Knight's view of them. The notes record Knight saying

–What does Veblen believe Darwinism to be?

–Biological survival, <u>or social</u> selection.

–Do those <u>ideas</u> and <u>social habits</u> which tend to protect and increase the race tend to survive?

–Do social institutions lead to biological survival?

–This is what Darwinism [is].

and

Veblen has no <u>explanation</u> of change, nor Marx, nor Sombart.

–Does Veblen give a real answer to the problem of the effect on human nature of machine technology?

Does Knight intend to toss out all economic and/or all technological theories of history? What would count as a "real" answer, especially a *correct* "real" answer?

Consider Knight on Veblen's theory of status emulation, which is fundamentally, though not in development, that of Adam Smith:

–All drive for accumulation is based on desire to emulate.

–And in the end, <u>all</u> consumption is also based on desire for emulation—a "<u>theory</u>" of consumption. [This is the closest Knight comes to saying Veblen had no theory. It is followed by discussion every bit as satiric as he claims Veblen to be.]

–Would Veblen have placed himself on the productive or unproductive side of human activity?

–Conspicuous leisure—

–"Theory of leisure class" (1899)—a psychogenetic rationalization of Marxian theory of class struggle.

[Alongside the following three questions, in the margin: "F.T.O."]

1. Was not Veblen a <u>puritan</u>—dislike of <u>consumption</u> and <u>leisure</u>?
2. Is <u>his</u> kind of deduction just the same as that of classical and neo-classical economists, as Harris says?

3. Could he make his statement of the place of science as following invention for <u>modern</u> industry, which is largely chemical?
–What would be Veblen's <u>real values</u>?
–Knight says puritanism is only one possibility.
–And Knight says that Veblen is more closely allied to Carver's point of view—a biological or physical ideal—<u>physical life</u> is the ultimate end.—(Is not Carver also a Puritan?) [F.TO. question?]
–Veblen's work gave him a large degree of "invidious distinction"!
–Cf. Laski's review of Veblen in Economica, 1925; <u>Dorfman</u>, Political Science Review, 1932, "The Satire of the Theory of the Leisure Class"
–Veblen only understood in terms of satirizing Spencer.
–Knight objects: Classical economists did not view life as a struggle for existence.
–Puritanism is "activist asceticism."
–The Instinct of Workmanship, 1914 [by Veblen]
–(Knight) Did Veblen ever give any thought to the <u>difference</u> between work by/to savages and by/to moderns.
And as to the total array constituting Veblen's system:
Veblen thinks there is no validity in a <u>preference</u> for <u>future</u> value.—Knight agrees but individual future value can not extend beyond death.
–Capital accumulation does, it is never consumed.
–What does Veblen mean by any of his terms?—exploitation, servic-eability.
–Some ethical theory, plus some theory of imputation, are both necessary for a theory of the origin of wealth.–Veblen's system

<u>Instincts</u> = give the objective ends of action.

<u>Instinct of Workmanship</u> = is a means to achieve an end—

–Most of our "<u>propensities</u>" are in this class.

[Alongside preceding two lines, in margin: "Contradiction in terms here"]

<u>Intelligence</u>

<u>Institutions</u>

–How does Veblen work instincts, intelligence, and institutions into a comprehensive system that has inner consistency? He doesn't!

If we take this last question of Knight's, it is clear that Knight found Veblen's system defective. He disagreed with Veblen's theory of psychology, his theory of the role of intelligence (how many other economists even thought of "intelligence" as part of their theory?), and his theory of institutions. His jibe coming closest to the claim that Veblen had no theory concerns, ironically, Veblen's theory of consumption—that part of Veblen's total array of theories that people both in and outside of economics know best and which has been both denigrated and used by neoclassical economists. Not only that, as we have seen an inkling of earlier, Knight voiced important themes of Veblen's *in his own theory of consumption*. One can only suspect that Knight's rambunctious, even difficult, personality coupled with his general displeasure with Veblen's heterodox position in economics led Knight to the negative views he expressed in this course.

Further, powerful support for the present argument is available. Robert Dimand has reminded me of two and informed me of a third. The oldest is by Milton Friedman (1950), making the argument that being a theorist need not entail being a Cowles Commission-style Walrasian general equilibrium theorist. Next in time is Kenneth Arrow's (1975) examination of *The Theory of Business Enterprise* as a contribution to economic theory. The third is an article by Eaton and Eswaran (2003), arguing that evolutionarily stable preferences (preferences that evolve by natural selection in a competitive environment) include preferences over relative payoffs, as in Veblen's theory of invidious competition, and that this is consistent with anthropological evidence and would explain, Dimand emphasizes, some surprising results in experimental game theory.

It is neither possible nor necessary to elaborate in detail the substance or theoretical methodologies of Veblen's several theories and the variety of forms, or of conceptions, of theories taken by his theories.[9] An in-depth account of one or two theories—room for such is all that could be justified in one chapter—would apply only to those theories. All that is necessary to further and conclusively rebut the charge that he was anti-theoretical and had no theory is to identify those theories.

It was stated earlier that both institutional and neoclassical economics encompass theory—as description and/or explanation—in numerous manifestations. One reader of this chapter in draft form, Dan Hammond, understandably felt that the impression I created is that "anything and everything in economics is theory, and if so, then the whole issue is trivial. The discussion must then be on the level of good theory versus bad or not-so-good theory." Although I sympathize with this view I choose not to follow his suggestion that I demonstrate that a few of Veblen's theories were novel, useful in his time and useful today, i.e., that he developed theory, theory that was good theory.

I choose not to follow this route in part for the reason given in the preceding paragraph—it would do the job but be too narrow—and in part on methodological grounds already treated. There is no one methodology of theory. There is no one methodology, no one prescriptively sound and correct methodology. Wade Hands's *Reflection without Rules* (2001) makes both a positive and normative case for this; I rely only on the positive case centering on the practice of methodological (and theoretical) pluralism. In the past I have emphasized credentialism over prescriptivism and Paul Feyerabend's position (as I read him) that "anything goes" willy nilly whether one likes it or not, as both positive and normative positions, but especially the former.

Another reason for my decision concerns the issue of good versus bad theory. I think I know—within a limited range of expertise—the difference between good and bad statements/formulations of theory but good versus bad theory is a matter of what one finds interesting and useful—and that I have argued is a function of confirmation by consonance with one's paradigm.

Let me reiterate that neither abstraction *per se* nor degree of abstraction is at issue (though that is an important matter). Abstraction is both inevitable and legitimate (*vide* Shackle's two worlds). Much of Veblen's theorizing involves abstraction. Nor is formalism the issue. Much neoclassicism and most institutionalism is not formalist. But it is all theory.

The same is true of the theoretical work of John R. Commons and Robert Lee Hale, whose theories I use in my own law and economic work (Samuels 1992a). Take, for example, Commons's *Legal Foundations of Capitalism*. In my (Reader's Guide) (Samuels 1996a) I have identified the topics on which he theorized, spelled out the theories, and called the reader's attention to the evidence he presents in support of the theories—including what constituted formalism in law in his time. These are theories of description and explanation. These theories are closer to the theories found in the legal history of James Willard Hurst than to the theories found in the work of Ronald Coase and Harold Demsetz. But all these are theories, open to varying subjective judgments of good and bad, useful and not useful, and, of course, theory and non-theory. And the same is true of John Kenneth Galbraith's array of theories, to mention one late twentieth-century institutionalist whose work (and style) has been compared to Veblen's.

Veblen's theories—each of which is an attempt to describe and explain—include and may be classified (with some overlap) as follows:

General Theory of Society[10]
- Society as system of interacting sub-systems
- Increasing tension between technology, seen as progressive force, and institutions, seen as repositories of traditional social norms and beliefs and vested interests: a theory of institutional resistance, especially to technological change, as part of general analysis of technology and institutions (including organizations) changing at different rates
- Theory of economic evolution: the Darwinian genetic approach as unfolding sequence without teleology applied to evolution and selection of institutions and to institutional environment
- Theory of social control
- Theory of social change
- Theory of adaptation
- Relations between religion and capitalism
- Cumulative causation
- Theory of class
- Theory of economic conflict
- Theory of war and peace
- Savagery in modern industrial society

General Theory of Capitalism and Its Development
- Capitalism as a scheme of institutions
- Allocation of resources and distribution of income as a function of institutions
- Increasing tension between industrial and pecuniary activities and between technology and institutions
- Pecuniary culture and the pecuniary nature of capitalist economy
- The cultural incidence of the machine process
- The savage and predatory state of industry
- Theory of property and ownership
- Theory of capital
- Capitalism as plutocracy
- Theory of the entrepreneur
- Rationalization through vertical integration and replacement of markets by vertically integrated firm
- Role of absentee ownership
- Penalty of taking the lead
- Theory of technicians, the price system, and revolution
- Religion and economic development
- Religion and science
- Finance capitalism
- Theory of competition
- Theory of exploitation
- Theory of waste
- Theory and critique of socialism
- Theory of higher learning in a pecuniary culture
- The cultural meaning of America

Methodology
- Evolutionism
- Holism
- Instrumentalism

Theory of Belief System
- Theory of institutions as habits of thought
- Theory of patriotism
- Ownership and business principles
- Systemic origins of economic preconceptions
- Economics as metaphysics
- Theory of preconceptions:
  - Animistic or teleological vs. matter-of-fact
  - Theory of reality and of preconceptions

Theory of Behavior
- Theory of leisure class
- Theories of status and pecuniary emulation, of invidious comparison, and of pecuniary standards of taste

- Conspicuous consumption and leisure
- The pecuniary standard of living and the pecuniary canons of taste
- Instinct of workmanship
- Idle curiosity
- The cultural incidence and discipline of machine technology and the machine process
- Invidious and non-invidious behavior

Theory of the State
- Predatory dynastic and pacific modern states
- War and peace
- Theory of patriotism
- Legal–economic nexus
- Business control of government
- Economic roles of government

Theory of the Firm
- Rationalization through vertical integration and replacement of markets by vertically integrated firm
- Role of absentee ownership; separation of ownership and control
- Industrial sabotage
- The entrepreneur as captain of industry
- The role of the engineers
- The decay of the business enterprise
- The penalty of taking the lead

Theory of Economic Instability
- Theory of business cycle as a function of structural and monetary factors
- Theory of credit
- Theory of disequilibrium

If the foregoing are not theories of one form or another, then one does not know what they are. If they take different forms, they are no different from the theories of neoclassical economics.

Some of Veblen's most important theories are echoed in and supported by the following. In an article in the 27 November 2002 issue of *Business Week*, entitled "Biting the Invisible Hand," Martin Fridson, the chief high-yield strategist at Merrill Lynch, is quoted for making a critical distinction apropos of the Enron scandal (Farrell 2002). His first point was that the invisible hand, in his view a metaphor for harnessing individual self-interest to serve the general well-being, is a powerful principle. His second point was that it is a "very convenient cover story for people who are actually trying to stack the deck in their favor"—for people who preach the virtues of competitive capitalism but practice the crony variety. Here we have the failure of neoclassicism's arguably most fundamental principle and support for Veblen's theory of business control of government, of ideology as a system of preconceptions, of capitalism as predatory behavior, and so on. Predictive power is generally not very powerful in economics, but absent a desire to predict precisely who will act in a predatory manner and precisely how they will do so, Veblen's theories predict these types of behavior very clearly. The likelihood of business-oriented because business-dominated government being complicit in arguably numerous ways is another successful Veblenian prediction.

The neoclassicist record runs the gamut from sanctioning (in the affirmative sense) business decisions within the law—even if business is responsible in one way or another for making the law what it is—to predicting such behavior whenever and however money is to be made, to pious remonstrations that such should not be allowed, and so on. The problem is that in following, explicitly or implicitly, the market plus framework approach, neoclassicists generally side with the market against intervention. Perhaps all that reduces to a successful prediction of predatory behavior but one would not know it from, e.g., the Chicago School approach to antitrust, in which so-called predatory activity is largely aggressive pursuit of the bottom line.

Although predation and other strategic behavior are both relevant and important, a broader matter is involved, namely, the theory of the firm. Firms operate under conditions of uncertainty, especially radical uncertainty as to the future. They involve different cognitive and different moral communities. Firms must work out substantive definitions of goals (objective functions) and therefore their internal plan and array of productive competencies, all partly path dependent. All this constitutes a theory of the firm, one comprised of several subsidiary theories. And as Foss (1998) argues, these theories are to be found in Veblen's work as key themes.

One difference between the histories of institutional and of neoclassical economics is that neoclassicists have been much more prolific in developing, extending, and refining their corpus of theory than have the institutionalists. Much of the work of both schools has been rehearsal of earlier ideas—most conspicuously, however, the institutionalists' work, because of the relative paucity of developmental efforts. Relative paucity, but not non-existence. Modern institutionalists have enlarged and extended Veblen's (and, e.g., Commons's) work on technology, institutions, the legal foundations and operation of capitalism, and so on. Moreover, neither school has an edge on the conduct of theorizing *qua* theorizing, including testing, in the manners described earlier in this chapter—this, notwithstanding the impressive statistical and mathematical techniques of modern neoclassicism.

Finally, consider for a moment Veblen's work in the eyes of a small sample of other writers—no less important than those who deny Veblen is a theorist. Robert Heilbroner, among others, has pointed out that to many observers Veblen was an isolated, impenetrable and strange figure, walking "through life as if he had descended from another world," whose *Theory of the Leisure Class* "appeared to be nothing more than just … a satire on the ways of the aristocratic class, and a telling attack on the foibles of the rich" (Heilbroner 1953:

205, 216). For Heilbroner the core theory is that of status emulation and related ideas.

Geoff Hodgson, like Heilbroner, has pointed to a very different view of *The Theory of the Leisure Class*. He argues that the book had a "core theoretical project" and that it was a theory of "cultural and institutional evolution," both the concept of and a theory of "the evolution and selection of institutions," a theory of "institutions as the objects of selection in socio-economic evolution." "[T]he principles of Darwinian selection" were applied "to emergent social structures or institutions" (Hodgson 2003: 5–7) The result was, in Veblen's own formulation, "an evolutionary economics" that is "the theory of a process of cultural growth as determined by the economic interest, a theory of a cumulative sequence of economic institutions stated in terms of the process itself" (Hodgson 2003: 7, quoting Veblen 1898: 393, reprinted in Veblen 1990 [1919]: 77).

Consider the entry on Veblen in *The Routledge Dictionary of Twentieth-Century Political Thinkers*. Veblen is included not because he is a political thinker as such but because of what he, as an economist, has to say of importance for political theory. The entry at one point reads thus:

> Although his significance is still widely disputed, his ideas of conspicuous consumption, display and emulation have been shown to have significance in explaining not only ruling-class hegemony but also consumer predation, international politics, militarism, sport and fashion changes. Veblen is also credited with demonstrating the link between obstentatious [*sic*] display and the oppression of women.
>
> (Benewick and Green 1998: 226)

Here we have affirmation of Veblen's ideas, or theories, for the explanation of a wide range of phenomena. The entry also lists Veblen's ideas of trained incapacity and withdrawal of efficiency and his contributions to the theories of latent and manifest functions, of social stratification and the sociology of knowledge. Not only theory but prediction: in work published during World War I, Veblen predicted the later "resurgence of authoritarianism in Germany and Japan" (Benewick and Green 1998: 227). As for the relevance of Veblen for political theory, the entry reads: "Characteristically, Veblen did not distinguish between economics and politics. For him, business interests dominated both industry and politics" (Benewick and Green 1998: 227). Veblen's theories of the legal–economic nexus and of business control of government are among his most powerful; they parallel the comparable theories of Commons—and myself and many others.

The entry on Veblen in *The New Palgrave* does not equivocate on the subject of Veblen as theorist. Thomas Sowell, the author and critic of Veblen, writes that Veblen understood the nature of theory, that "Veblen's aim was theoretical work" and that "Veblen was a theorist, in the sense of producing many theories." But Sowell also notes that Veblen sought economic understanding "in a wider social context" which "blurred the line between economics and sociology or history." Such a view arguably presumes a narrow and insular concept of economics; compare Schumpeter (1954) who includes economic sociology along with economic theory, history and statistics in economics (compare also Benewick and Green 1998: 227, quoted earlier; what Sowell faults, they laud). Sowell also says that Veblen "was neither a systematic analyst nor a systematic tester of theories against empirical evidence" (Sowell 1987: 799–800). These views are odd; Veblen's use of language is unusual but the analysis in every one of his works is systematic and supported with evidence; and as for testing, very few economic theories are subject to serious testing (see above). These criticisms go beyond the questions of whether Veblen was anti-theoretical and a theorist; here is a critic who makes the same affirmation as is done here: Veblen was not anti-theoretical and he was a theorist. In comparison, Mark Blaug has written that Veblen's books are not about economic theory at all but rather about how to interpret the values and beliefs of those whom he ironically labeled as "captains of industry" (Blaug 1986b: 257). For Blaug, economic theory seems to be neoclassical economic theory, period.

Daniel H. Borus's entry on Veblen in *A Companion to American Thought* (1998) correctly identifies the importance of a central proposition of Veblen's institutional theory: it is institutions and not the pure conceptual price mechanism that govern the allocation of resources, for the price mechanism operates within markets that are the product of institutions which form and operate through them. As Borus puts it, "production and distribution were best understood [insisted Veblen] as the result of the action of evolving institutions" (Borus 1998: 702).

Veblen lives on—in Coase, notwithstanding his hostility.

Conclusion

One test of neoclassical economics's hegemonic position is provided by asking how much of the modern economist's and others' view of the world is provided by neoclassical definitions. Definitions including short run, income, cost, utility, supply and demand, growth, capital, investment, money, and so on. These definitions are the result of and embody theories or proxies for theories. None of them are given words or categories; they are socially constructed definitions. That many definitions have been and remain contested underscores the point. The definitions are neither right nor wrong except on the basis of some theory; that is what the teaching of economic principles is largely all about. The same is true of much of Veblen's economics, i.e., his terminology and the theories embodied in them. To the claim that Veblen, unlike neoclassical economists, produced ideas and not theories, the replies are, first, that Veblen produced theories along many of the same numerous modes as neoclassicism; and, second, that both Veblen and neoclassicism developed theories and terms that defined and gave force to ideas.[11]

To see the last point, one need only compare Veblen's theories of conspicuous consumption and status emulation with such theories as Alfred Marshall's representative firm and short run–long run, Joseph Schumpeter's creative destruction, John R. Hicks's fixed price, Milton Friedman's permanent income, John Maynard Keynes's liquidity preference, Ronald Coase's theories of the firm and social cost … and scores if not hundreds of terms in any dictionary of economics.

And then one can compare Veblen's theories of increasing tension between industrial and pecuniary activities and between technology and institutions, disequilibrium, capitalism as plutocracy, business control of government, institutions as habits of thought, property and ownership, status and pecuniary emulation, invidious comparison, and of pecuniary standards of taste, with Hicks's theory of general equilibrium, Herbert A. Simons's theory of decision making under uncertainty, Kenneth J. Arrow's theory of welfare economics, Frank H. Knight's theory of risk and uncertainty, George J. Stigler's theories of information and regulation, Robert Lucas's theory of rational expectations, Gary Becker's theory of human behavior, James Tobin's theories of investment behavior and their consequences, James M. Buchanan's theories of the contractual and constitutional bases of the theory of economic and political decision making, the theories of economic growth and/or development of Theodore W. Schultz, W. Arthur Lewis and Robert Solow, and Simon Kuznets, the theories of Robert W. Fogel and Douglass C. North on economic history, John Nash's theory of equilibrium, and the theories of asymmetrical information of George A. Akerlof, A. Michael Spence and Joseph Stiglitz.

Again, one may prefer one group of theories to another or one theory to its rival, but that—like relative success in conquering the discipline—is beside the point. There are epistemological differences within each of the two groups of theories *qua* theories. But there are no epistemological differences between the two groups of theories *qua* theories. And the reader will have noticed that most of the second group of neoclassical theories led to the awarding of the Nobel Prize in Economic Science. To cite but two juxtapositions: are either Buchanan's theory of the state or Nash's theory of equilibrium more of a theory, more scientific, and/or epistemologically different from Veblen's theory of the state or his theory of disequilibrium? I think not.

The mathematical formalism of neoclassicism is not a fundamental epistemological difference between it and Veblen. Nor is the greater availability of quantitative data and technique, especially when one remembers Veblen's quantitative work in the *Journal of Political Economy* (Veblen 1892; 1893; reprinted in Hamilton *et al.* 1962). Not each and every neoclassical theory performs all the roles of theory identified above; the same is true of Veblen's theories. The chasm between the two schools resides, rather, in neoclassicism's transformation of the market price mechanism into a paradigm for the economic system.

Veblen pointed out the preconceptions underlying neoclassical theory. When empirical facts were stressed, Veblen pointed out the theory-ladenness of facts; at other times, how theory gave effect to theory-laden facts.[12] The facts often, therefore, gave effect to the theory, the same theory used to organize and make sense of and, perhaps especially, to test the facts, the same facts used to organize and make sense of and, perhaps especially, to test the theory. The presence of the preconceptions was ubiquitous, in the domains of both fact and theory. In this regard, though Veblen surely believed in the descriptive accuracy and explanatory correctness of his own theories, the case can be made that he applied his critical analysis in principle to both neoclassicism and himself, i.e., that he was self-referential or self-reflexive (Samuels 1990b).

If economic theory means that the central object of theory is to explain the allocation of resources by the market price mechanism, all terms narrowly defined, then Thorstein Veblen was no theorist. If economic theory means the use of mathematical formalism, then Thorstein Veblen was no theorist. If either or both of the foregoing constitutes neoclassical economics, then Thorstein Veblen was no neoclassical theorist. And if such neoclassical economics is equated with being an economist, then Thorstein Veblen was no economist. But none of the premises of those statements are necessarily correct.

And none of them fully describe neoclassical economics (see note 2). If behavior is a function only of price, then Thorstein Veblen was no economist. Ronald Coase, for example, in holding that institutions matter, affirms that behavior is a function of price and institutions. Gary Becker, Coase's Chicago colleague, emphasizes economic change as a function of price change. But Becker, an apostle of economic imperialism, insists that prices can take non-monetary forms and that prices therefore pertain to areas of life and take forms hitherto not deemed "economics." Institutional change thus involves changes in the relative prices of opportunities—a theme resonant throughout Veblen's work. The language of the two sets of theories may be different but the theories are not mutually exclusive; more importantly, they are theories.

So far from being anti-theoretical and not a theorist, Thorstein Veblen practiced theory—"did" theory—and did so in various ways. That he was not a neoclassicist does not prevent such from being true. To envision Veblen as anti-theoretical and not a theorist, one has to have a myopic, narrow, and limited conception of theory in general and of economic theory in particular.

Notes

The author is indebted to Bob Dimand, Dan Hammond, Yngve Ramstad and Rick Tilman for helpful comments on earlier drafts and other help, and to Gerald F. Vaughn for assistance. In particular, Tilman reminded me of Veblen's use of "type-forms," and Bob Dimand (when the manuscript was in production) reminded me of two sources and told me of a third.

1 They include James M. Buchanan, Ronald Coase, Robert Fogel, Daniel Kahneman, Simon Kuznets, Douglass North, Amartya Sen, Herbert Simon, and Vernon L. Smith. Their interests tend to be on legal-economic and other institutions and other structural factors, psychology, and system dynamics and evolution.
2 David Colander, among others, argues that neoclassicism is broader, more open, and more variegated than it was. He makes two relevant points: first, that a variety of new mathematical techniques permits economists to deal with subjects of complexity, change and multiple equilibria that economists have hitherto shied away from; and second, that the foregoing developments coupled with developments in

psychology, experimental economics, and evolutionary game theory now allow "behavioral economists to explore and test other assumptions rather than simply accept the rather sterile rationality that characterized neoclassical economics" in the past. This is correct; moreover, neoclassicism has always been more variegated and complex than its usual caricature (deployed by both disciples and critics) allows. See Colander 1991.

3 "The question how two or more separately observed facts hang together, whether some may be causes or effects of others, is tentatively answered by a mental scheme of interrelationships which we call theory. ... According to the degree of abstraction we may distinguish general theories, special theories, applied theories, and implied theories" (Machlup 1978: 112, 113).

4 I cannot refrain from noting the two books on methodology I read a few years after their publication (within a year or so of my doctorate), two books which further opened my eyes to what is involved and which showed the myopia of what then, and for some time thereafter, posed as principles of economic methodology: Tjalling C. Koopmans's *Three Essays on the State of Economic Science* (1957) and Andreas G. Papandreou's *Economics as a Science* (1958).

5 This subsection is adopted from Samuels 2001a.

6 Adam Smith recognized and used language to "allay this tumult of the imagination" (Smith 1980: 45–46), the sequel to which is G.L.S. Shackle's (1967: 288–289) argument that the function of a theory is to set minds at rest.

7 Performance of the roles of theory is heavily dependent on the operative criteria of theory choice, a topic, however, of only oblique relevance to that of this chapter. Suffice it to say that the usual criteria—conventionalism, generality, realism, simplicity, usefulness, verisimilitude and predictive power (see, e.g., Boland 1989: 193 and pages there cited)—by no means exhaust the field. Other related topics include economic theory as applied mathematics (see, e.g., Rosenberg 1992: 223ff; Mayer 1995: 51) and as analytic versus synthetic statements (a version of which is presented below).

8 So was Mitchell, the view that he practiced "empiricism without theory" notwithstanding. Mitchell knew that theory was inevitable; the way in which he searched his statistical data presumed a pecuniary economy and accompanying relationships. Fact was theory laden; theory was influenced by perceptions of facts (see below). Mitchell objected, as did Veblen, to the then-practiced theories.

9 Among the most useful collections of Veblen's writings are by Ardzrooni (1934), Dorfman (1973), Lerner (1948), Mitchell (1936), Rutherford and Samuels (1997, two volumes), Tilman (1993), and Veblen (1919, 1990)

10 Akin to those of Adam Smith, Karl Marx, Max Weber and Vilfredo Pareto.

11 It is clear from Mitchell's essay on the place of Veblen in the history of ideas that to speak of Veblen's ideas is also to speak of his theories (Mitchell, in Horowitz 2002: 41–63).

12 "[M]ost of the supposed facts are in effect 'implied theory'" (Machlup 1978: 74, 1167). Machlup favorably quotes Veblen in rejecting the idea that history is prior to theory (1978: 106). Machlup also says that "Anything that looks substantially different to different observers or from different points of view, or that lends itself to different 'interpretations'[,] should not be called a fact" (1978: 112).

Bibliography

Aarsleff, H. (1982) *From Locke to Saussure: Essays on the Study of Language and Intellectual History*, Minneapolis: University of Minnesota Press.

Abbott, L.D. (1946) *Masterworks of Economics: Digests of 10 Great Classics*, Garden City, NY: Doubleday.

Ahiakpor, J.C.W. (1992) "Rashid on Adam Smith: In Need of Proof," *Journal of Libertarian Studies*, 10: 171–180.

——(1999) "Did Adam Smith Retard the Development of Economic Analysis? A Critique of Murray Rothbard's Interpretation," *Independent Review*, 3 (Winter): 353–383.

American Economic Association (1951) *Readings in Monetary Theory*, New York: Blakiston.

American Economic Association and Royal Economic Society (1967) *Surveys of Economic Theory*, 3 vols, New York: St. Martin's Press.

Andres, A.M. and Fleming, G.A. (2002) *International Organizations and the Analysis of Economic Policy, 1919–1950*, New York: Cambridge University Press.

Andreski, S. (1972) *Social Sciences as Sorcery*, New York: St. Martin's Press.

Aoki, M. (2001) *Towards a Comparative Institutional Analysis*, Cambridge, MA: MIT Press.

Ardzrooni, L. (ed.) (1934) *Essays in Our Changing Order*, New York: Viking.

Arestis, P. and Sawyer, M.C. (eds) (1994) *The Elgar Companion to Radical Political Economy*, Brookfield, VT: Edward Elgar.

——(eds) (2000 [1992]) *A Biographical Dictionary of Dissenting Economists*, 2nd edn, Brookfield, VT: Edward Elgar.

Arndt, H.W. (1987) *Economic Development: The History of an Idea*, Chicago, IL: University of Chicago Press.

Arrow, K.J. (1975) "Thorstein Veblen as an Economic Theorist," *The American Economist*, 19(1): 5–9.

Arrow, K.J. and Honkapohja, S. (eds) (1985) *Frontiers of Economics*, New York: Basil Blackwell.

Asso, P.F. (ed.) (2001) *From Economists to Economists: The International Spread of Italian Economic Thought: 1750–1950*, Firenze: Edizioni Polistampa.

Aune, J.A. (2001) *Selling the Free Market: The Rhetoric of Economic Correctness*, New York: Guilford Press.

Backhaus, J.G. (ed.) (1999) *The Elgar Companion to Law and Economics*, Northampton, MA: Edward Elgar.

Backhouse, R.E. (1985) *A History of Modern Economic Analysis*, New York: Basil Blackwell.

——(1988) *Economists and the Economy: The Evolution of Economic Ideas, 1600 to the Present Day*, New York: Basil Blackwell.

——(1994) *Economists and the Economy: The Evolution of Economic Ideas, 1600 to the Present Day*, 2nd edn, New Brunswick, NJ: Transaction.

——(2002) *The Ordinary Business of Life: A History of Economics from the Ancient World to the Twenty-First Century*, Princeton, NJ: Princeton University Press.

Balsley, H.L. (ed.) (1961) *Readings in Economic Doctrines*. Volume 1: *Theory and Practice*. Volume 2: *The Economy and Its Problems*, Paterson, NJ: Littlefield, Adams.

Baltagi, B.H. (ed.) (2001) *A Companion to Theoretical Econometrics*, Malden, MA: Blackwell.

Barber, W.J. (1967) *A History of Economic Thought*, Baltimore, MD: Penguin.

——(1975) *British Economic Thought and India, 1600–1858: A Study in the History of Development Economics*, Oxford: Clarendon Press.

——(1985) *From New Era to New Deal: Herbert Hoover, the Economists, and American Economic Policy, 1921–1933*, Cambridge: Cambridge University Press.

——(1996) *Designs within Disorder: Franklin D. Roosevelt, the Economists, and the Shaping of American Economic Policy, 1933–1945*, New York: Cambridge University Press.

Barnes, C.W. (1979) *Historiography, Historical Theory, and the Advance of Human Consciousness*, unpublished thesis, Michigan State University.

Basu, K. (2001) "The Role of Norms and Law in Economics: An Essay on Political Economy," in Scott, J.W. and Keates, D. (eds) *Schools of Thought: Twenty-Five Years of Interpretive Social Science*, Princeton, NJ: Princeton University Press.

Beaud, M. and Dostaler, G. (1995) *Economic Thought Since Keynes: A History and Dictionary of Major Economists*, Brookfield, VT: Edward Elgar.

Bell, J.F. (1953) *A History of Economic Thought*, New York: Ronald Press.

——(1967) *A History of Economic Thought*, 2nd edn, New York: Ronald Press.

Benewick, R. and Green, P. (eds) (1998) *The Routledge Dictionary of Twentieth-Century Political Thinkers*, New York: Routledge.

Berkowitz, P. (2000) "And Lofty Flows the Don," *The New Republic*, 13 November: 42–45.

Berndt, E.R. and Triplett, J.E. (eds) (1990) *Fifty Years of Economic Measurement: The Jubilee of the Conference on Research in Income and Wealth*, Chicago, IL: University of Chicago Press.

Biddle, J. (1996) "A Citation Analysis of the Sources and Extent of Wesley Mitchell's Reputation," *History of Political Economy*, 28: 137–169.

Biggart, N.W. (ed.) (2002) *Readings in Economic Sociology*, Malden, MA: Blackwell.

Bini, P. (2003) "Umberto Ricci: Profile of a Militant Economist," in Samuels, W.J. (ed.) *European Economists of the Early 20th Century*, vol. 2, Northampton, MA: Edward Elgar.

Birner, J., Garrouste, P. and Airmar, T. (eds) (2002) *F. A. Hayek as a Political Economist*, New York: Routledge.

Blaug, M. (1962) *Economic Theory in Retrospect*, Homewood, IL: Richard D. Irwin.

——(1968) *Economic Theory in Retrospect*, revised edn, Homewood, IL: Richard D. Irwin.

——(1978) *Economic Theory in Retrospect*, 3rd edn, Homewood, IL: Richard D. Irwin.

——(1980) *The Methodology of Economics*, New York: Cambridge University Press.

——(1985a) *Economic Theory in Retrospect*, 4th edn, Homewood, IL: Richard D. Irwin.

——(1985b) *Great Economists Since Keynes*, New York: Cambridge University Press.

——(1986a) *Economic History and the History of Economics*, New York: New York University Press.

(1986b) *Great Economists before Keynes*, Atlantic Highlands, NJ: Humanities Press International.

——(ed.) (1991) *The Historiography of Economics*, Brookfield, VT: Edward Elgar.

——(1992) *The Methodology of Economics*, 2nd edn, New York: Cambridge University Press.

——(1997) *Economic Theory in Retrospect*, 5th edn, New York: Cambridge University Press.

——(1999 [1983; 1986]) *Who's Who in Economics*, 3rd edn, Northampton, MA: Edward Elgar.

Boettke, P.J. (ed.) (1994) *The Elgar Companion to Austrian Economics*, Brookfield, VT: Edward Elgar.

Boland, L.A. (1989) *The Methodology of Economic Model Building*, New York: Routledge.

Borus, D.H. (1998) "Thorstein Veblen," in Fox, R.W. and Kloppenberg, J.T. (eds) *A Companion to American Thought*, Malden, MA: Blackwell.

Bouckaert, B. and De Geest, G. (eds) (1992) *Bibliography of Law and Economics*, Boston, MA: Kluwer.

——(eds) (2000) *Encyclopedia of Law and Economics*, 5 vols, vol. 1, *The History and Methodology of Law and Economics*, Northampton, MA: Edward Elgar.

Boucke, O.F. (1921) *The Development of Economics, 1750–1900*, New York: Macmillan.

Boulding, K.E. (1956) *The Image: Knowledge in Life and Society*, Ann Arbor, MI: University of Michigan Press.

Bowden, E.V. (1981) *Economic Evolution*, Cincinnati, OH: South-Western.

Boyer, R.A. (2001) *The Regulation Approach as a Theory of Capitalism* in Labrousse, A. and Weisz, J.D. (eds) *Institutional Economics in France and Germany*, Berlin: Springer.

Breisach, E. (1983) *Historiography: Ancient, Medieval, and Modern*, Chicago: University of Chicago Press.

Breit, W. and Ransom, R.L. (1971) *The Academic Scribblers*, New York: Holt, Rinehart and Winston.

——(1982) *The Academic Scribblers*, revised edn, New York: Dryden Press.

——(1998) *The Academic Scribblers*, 3rd edn, Princeton, NJ: Princeton University Press.

Breit, W. and Spencer, R.W. (1986) *Lives of the Laureates*, Cambridge, MA: MIT Press.

——(1995) *Lives of the Laureates*, 3rd edn, Cambridge, MA: MIT Press.

Brenner, Y.S. (1979) *Looking into the Seeds of Time*, Assen: Van Gorcum.

——(1998) *Looking into the Seeds of Time*, 2nd edn, New Brunswick, NJ: Transaction.

Briefs, H.W. (1960) *Three Views of Method in Economics*, Washington, DC: Georgetown University Press.

Brodbeck, M. (ed.) (1968) *Readings in the Philosophy of the Social Sciences*, New York: Macmillan.

Bromley, D.W. (1989) *Economic Interests and Institutions: The Conceptual Foundations of Public Policy*, New York: Basil Blackwell.

——(ed.) (1995) *Handbook of Environmental Economics*, Cambridge, MA: Blackwell.

Brown, V. (1993) "Decanonizing Discourses: Textual Analysis and the History of Economic Thought," in Henderson, W., Dudley-Evans, T. and Backhouse, R. (eds) *Economics and Language*, New York: Routledge.

——(1994) *Adam Smith's Discourse: Canonicity, Commerce and Conscience*, New York: Routledge.

——(2002) "On Some Problems with Weak Intentionalism for Intellectual History," *History and Theory*, 41: 198–208.

Brubaker, L. (2001) "Adam Smith's Prudence: A Skeptical Philosopher Contemplates Religion," manuscript.

Bruni, L. (2002) *Vilfredo Pareto and the Birth of Modern Microeconomics*, Northampton, MA: Edward Elgar.

Buckle, S. (1991) *Natural Law and the Theory of Property*, Oxford: Clarendon Press.

——(2001) *Hume's Enlightenment Tract*, Oxford: Oxford University Press.

Burtt, E.J., Jr. (1972) *Social Perspectives in the History of Economic Theory*, New York: St. Martin's Press.

Caldwell, B. (1982) *Beyond Positivism: Economic Methodology in the Twentieth Century*, London: George Allen & Unwin.

Cannan, E. (1917 [1893, 1903]) *History of the Theories of Production and Distribution in English Political Economy*, 3rd edition, London: P.S. King.

Canterbery, E.R. (1976) *The Making of Economics*, Belmont, CA: Wadsworth.

——(1980) *The Making of Economics*, 2nd edn, Belmont, CA: Wadsworth.

——(1987) *The Making of Economics*, 3rd edn, Belmont, CA: Wadsworth.

——(1995) *The Literate Economist: A Brief History of Economics*, New York: Harper-Collins.

Caravale, G.A. (ed.) (1985) *The Legacy of Ricardo*, New York: Basil Blackwell.

Cariappa, C.A. (1996) "The Political Origins of Neoclassical Economics," dissertation proposal, University of Texas. Online at: http://www.eco.utexas.edu/Homepages/faculty/Cleaver/chipprop.html

Carlin, E.A. (1999 [1956]) "Schumpeter's Constructed Type—The Entrepreneur," in Hanusch, H. (ed.) *The Legacy of Joseph A. Schumpeter*, Northampton, MA: Edward Elgar.

Carpenter, K.E. (2002) *The Dissemination of the Wealth of Nations in French and in France, 1776–1843*, published for The Bibliographical Society of America, New Castle, DE: Oak Knoll Press.

Carson, K.A. (2002) "The Iron Fist Behind the Invisible Hand," Online at: http://flag.blackened.net/daver/anarchism/iron_fist.html

Cate, T. (ed.) (1997) *An Encyclopedia of Keynesian Economics*, Lyme, NH: Edward Elgar.

Catlin, W.B. (1962) *The Progress of Economics: A History of Economic Thought*, New York: Bookman Associates.

Chandler, L.V. (1953) *The Economics of Money and Banking*, New York: Harper & Row; 5th edn and 6th edn with Goldfield, S.M.

——(1959) *The Economics of Money and Banking*, 2nd edn, New York: Harper & Row.

——(1969) *The Economics of Money and Banking*, 3rd edn, New York: Harper & Row.

——(1973) *The Economics of Money and Banking*, 4th edn, New York: Harper & Row.

Chandler, L.V. and Goldfeld, S.M. (1977) *The Economics of Money and Banking*, 5th edn, New York: Harper & Row.

——(1986) *The Economics of Money and Banking*, 6th edn, New York: Harper & Row.

Cirillo, R. (1979) *The Economics of Vilfredo Pareto*, Totowa, NJ: Frank Cass.

Clarke, S. (1988) *Keynesianism, Monetarism and the Crisis of the State*, Brookfield, VT: Edward Elgar.

Clower, R.W. (1969) *Monetary Economics: Selected Readings*, Baltimore, MD: Penguin.

Coase, R.H. (1960) "The Problem of Social Cost," *Journal of Law and Economics*, 3: 1–44.

——(1993) "Law and Economics at Chicago," *Journal of Law and Economics*, 36: 239–254.

——(1998) "The New Institutional Economics," *American Economic Review*, 88: 72–74.

Coats, A.W. (ed.) (1971) *The Classical Economists and Economic Policy*, London: Methuen.

——(ed.) (1981) *Economists in Government: An International Comparative Study*, Durham, NC: Duke University Press.

——(ed.) (1986) *Economists in International Agencies: An Exploratory Study*, New York: Praeger.

——(1992) "Economics in the United States, 1920–70," in *On the History of Economic Thought: British and American Economic Essays*, London and New York: Routledge.

——(ed.) (1997) *The Post-1945 Internationalisation of Economics*, Annual Supplement to *History of Political Economy*, 28, Durham and London: Duke University Press.

——(ed.) (2000) *The Development of Economics in Western Europe Since 1945*, London and New York: Routledge.

Cockett, R. (1994) *Thinking the Unthinkable: Think-Tanks and the Economic Counter-Revolution, 1931–1983*, London: HarperCollins.

Colander, D.C. (1991) *Why Aren't Economists as Important as Garbagemen?*, Armonk, NY: M.E. Sharpe.

Colander, D.C. and Coats, A.W. (1989) *The Spread of Economic Ideas*, Cambridge and New York: Cambridge University Press.

Comin, F. (2002) "The Scottish Tradition in Economics and the Role of Common Sense in Adam Smith's Thought," *Review of Political Economy*, 14(1): 91–114.

Oxford English Dictionary (1971) *Compact Edition of the Oxford English Dictionary*, 2 vols, New York: Oxford University Press.

Cooper, A.A., Lord Shaftesbury (1964) *Characteristics of Men, Manners, Opinions, Times …*, 2 vols, ed. Robertson, J.M., Indianapolis: Bobbs-Merrill.

Corballis, M.C. (2003) *From Hand to Mouth: The Origins of Language*, Princeton, NJ: Princeton University Press.

Cossa, L. (1880) *Guide to the Study of Political Economy*, London: Macmillan.

——(1893) *An Introduction to the Study of Political Economy*, London: Macmillan.

Coulthard, M. (1994) *Advances in Written Text Analysis*, London: Routledge.

Creedy, J. (1988) *Development of the Theory of Exchange*, Northampton, MA: Edward Elgar.

Curti, M. (1943) *The Growth of American Thought*, New York: Harper & Row.

——(1951) *The Growth of American Thought*, 2nd edn, New York: Harper & Row.

——(1964) *The Growth of American Thought*, 3rd edn, New York: Harper & Row.

Darnell, A.C. (ed.) (1994) *A Dictionary of Econometrics*, Brookfield, VT: Edward Elgar.

Darnton, R. (2003) "The Heresies of Bibliography," *The New York Review of Books*, 29 May: 43–45.

Dasgupta, A.K. (1985) *Epochs of Economic Theory*, New York: Basil Blackwell.

Davis, J.B. (ed.) (1997) *New Economics and Its History*, Durham, NC: Duke University Press.

Davis, J.B., Hands, D.W. and Mäki, U. (eds) (1998) *The Handbook of Economic Methodology*, Northampton, MA: Edward Elgar.

de Jouvenel, B. (1962) *On Power*, Boston, MA: Beacon Press.

de Marchi, N. and Gilbert, C. (eds) (1989) *History and Methodology of Econometrics*, New York: Oxford University Press.

Deane, P. (1978) *The Evolution of Economic Ideas*, New York: Cambridge University Press.

Dempsey, B.W. (1958) *The Functional Economy: The Basis of Economic Organization*, Englewood Cliffs, NJ: Prentice-Hall.

Denis, A. (2001) "Collective and Individual Rationality," manuscript, City University, London.

Denis, A. (forthcoming) "Epistemology, Observed Particulars and Providentialist Assumptions: The Fact in the History of Political Economy," *Studies in History and Philosophy of Science*.

Diesing, P. (1971) *Patterns of Discovery in the Social Sciences*, Chicago, IL: Aldine-Atherton.

DiRenzo, G.J. (ed.) (1966) *Concepts, Theory, and Explanation in the Behavioral Sciences*, New York: Random House.

Dome, T. (1994) *History of Economic Theory: A Critical Introduction*, Brookfield, VT: Edward Elgar.

Dooley, P.C. (2002) Review of Harry Landreth and David C. Colander, *History of Economic Thought*, 4th edn, Boston: Houghton Mifflin, 2002. *History of Economic Thought Newsletter*, 68 (summer): 3–6.

——(2003) "Francis Hutchison and the Division of Labour," manuscript.

Dopfer, K. (1998) "The Participant Observer in the Formation of Economic Thought," *Evolutionary Economics*, 8: 139–156.

Dorfman, J. (1934) *Thorstein Veblen and His America*, New York: Viking Press.

——(1955) "The Role of the German Historical School in American Economic Thought," *American Economic Review*, 45(2): 17–28.

——(1959) *The Economic Mind in American Civilization*, vol. 4, New York: Viking Press.

——(1973) *Thorstein Veblen: Essays, Reviews, and Reports, Previously Uncollected Writings*, New York: Augustus M. Kelley.

——(1997) *Economic Theory and Public Decisions*, Brookfield, VT: Edward Elgar.

Durkheim, E. (1933) *The Division of Labor in Society*, Glencoe, IL: Free Press.

Eaton, B.C. and Eswaran, M. (2003) "The Evolution of Preferences and Competition: A Rationalization of Veblen's Theory of Invidious Comparisons," *Canadian Journal of Economics*, 36(4): 832–859.

Eatwell, J., Milgate, M. and Newman, P. (eds) (1987) *The New Palgrave: A Dictionary of Economics*, 4 vols, New York: Stockton Press.

Edgell, S. (2001) *Veblen in Perspective: His Life and Thought*, Armonk, NY: M.E. Sharpe.

Eggertsson, T. (1990) *Economic Behavior and Institutions*, New York: Cambridge University Press.

Eichner, A.S. (1978) *A Guide to Post Keynesian Economics*, Armonk, NY: M.E. Sharpe.

Ekelund, R.B., Jr. and Hébert, R.F. (1975) *A History of Economic Theory and Method*, New York: McGraw-Hill.

——(1983) *A History of Economic Theory and Method*, 2nd edn, New York: McGraw-Hill.

——(1990) *A History of Economic Theory and Method*, 3rd edn, New York: McGraw-Hill.

——(1997) *A History of Economic Theory and Method*, 4th edn, New York: McGraw-Hill.

——(1999) *Secret Origins of Modern Microeconomics: Dupuit and the Engineers*, Chicago, IL: University of Chicago Press.

Ellis, H.S. (ed.) (1948) *A Survey of Contemporary Economics*, Philadelphia, PA: Blakiston.

Ely, R.T. (2002 [1931]) *The Story of Economics in the United States*, in Samuels, W.J. (ed.), *Research in the History of Economic Thought and Methodology*, 20(C).

Endres, A.M. (1997) *Neoclassical Microeconomic Theory: The Founding Austrian Version*, New York: Routledge.

Endres, A.M. and Fleming, G.A. (2002) *International Organizations and the Analysis of Economic Policy, 1919–1950*, New York: Cambridge University Press.

Entine, A.D. (ed.) (1968) *Monetary Economics: Readings*, Belmont, CA: Wadsworth.

Evensky, J. (1998) "Adam Smith," in Davis, J.B., Hands, D.W. and Mäki, U. (eds) *The Handbook of Economic Methodology*, Northampton, MA: Edward Elgar.

——(2001) *"An Inquiry into the Nature and Causes of the Wealth of Nations" and Its Relationship to Adam Smith's Full Moral Philosophical Vision: Books II and III*, manuscript.

——(2003) " 'An Inquiry into the Nature and Causes of the Wealth of Nations', Book 1: Its Relationship to Adam Smith's Full Moral Philosophical Vision," *Research in the History of Economic Thought and Methodology*, 21(A): 1–47.

Faccarello, G. (ed.) (1998) *Studies in the History of French Political Economy: From Bodin to Walras*, New York: Routledge.

Farrell, C. (2002) "Biting the Invisible Hand," *Business Week Online*, 27 November. Online at: http://www.businessweek.com/bwdaily/dnflash/nov2002/nf20021127_9554.htm

Fase, M.M.G., Kanning, W. and Walker, D.A. (eds) (1999) *Economics, Welfare Policy and the History of Economic Thought*, Northampton, MA: Edward Elgar.

Ferguson, A. (1966 [1767]) *An Essay on the History of Civil Society*, Edinburgh: Edinburgh University Press.

Ferguson, J.M. (1938) *Landmarks of Economic Thought*, New York: Longmans, Green.

Fetter, F.W. (1980) *The Economist in Parliament, 1780–1868*, Durham, NC: Duke University Press.

Field, A.J. (ed.) (1987) *The Future of Economic History*, Norwell, MA: Kluwer.

——(ed.) (1995) *The Future of Economics* (new edition of *The Future of Economic History*), New Brunswick, NJ: Transaction.

Fieldhouse, D.K. (1973) *Economics and Empire, 1830–1914*, Ithaca, NY: Cornell University Press.

Fine, B. (2001) *Social Capital versus Social Theory: Political Economy and Social Science at the Turn of the Millennium*, London: Routledge.

Finkelstein, J. and Thimm, A.L. (1973) *Economists and Society: The Development of Economic Thought from Aquinas to Keynes*, New York: Harper & Row.

Fiori, S. (2001) "Visible and Invisible Order: The Theoretical Duality of Smith's Political Economy," *European Journal of the History of Economic Thought*, 8(4): 429–448.

Fitzgibbons, A. (1995) *Adam Smith's System of Liberty, Wealth and Virtue: The Moral and Political Foundations of "The Wealth of Nations"*, Oxford: Clarendon Press.

Flanders, M.J. (1989) *International Monetary Economics, 1870–1960*, New York: Cambridge University Press.

Fligstein, N. (2001) *The Architecture of Markets: An Economic Sociology of Twenty-First-Century Capitalist Societies*, Princeton, NJ: Princeton University Press.

Forget, E.L. and Peart, S. (eds) (2001) *Reflections on the Classical Canon in Economics: Essays in Honor of Samuel Hollander*, New York: Routledge.

Foss, N.J. (1998) "The Competence-Based Approach: Veblenian Ideas in the Modern Theory of the Firm," *Cambridge Journal of Economics*, 22(4): 479–495.

Foster, J. and Metcalfe, J.S. (eds) (2001) *Frontiers of Evolutionary Economics: Competition, Self-Organization and Innovation Policy*, Northampton, MA: Edward Elgar.

Friedman, M. (1950) "Wesley C. Mitchell as an Economic Theorist," *Journal of Political Economy*, 58 (December): 465–493. Reprinted in Arthur F. Burns (ed.) (1952) *Wesley Clair Mitchell: The Economic Scientist*, New York: National Bureau of Economic Research.

Friedman, M. and Friedman, R.D. (1998) *Two Lucky People: Memoirs*, Chicago, IL: University of Chicago Press.

Furner, M.O. and Supple, B. (eds) (1990) *The State and Economic Knowledge: The American and British Experiences*, Cambridge: Cambridge University Press.

Furubotn, E.G. and Richter, R. (2000) *Institutions and Economic Theory: The Contribution of the New Institutional Economics*, Ann Arbor, MI: University of Michigan Press.

Fusfeld, D.R. (1966) *The Age of the Economist: The Development of Modern Economic Thought*, Glenview, IL: Scott, Foresman.

——(1972) *The Age of the Economist: The Development of Modern Economic Thought*, revised edn, Glenview, IL: Scott, Foresman.

——(1977) *The Age of the Economist: The Development of Modern Economic Thought*, 3rd edn, Glenview, IL: Scott, Foresman.

——(1982) *The Age of the Economist: The Development of Modern Economic Thought*, 4th edn, Glenview, IL: Scott, Foresman.

——(1986) *The Age of the Economist: The Development of Modern Economic Thought*, 5th edn, Glenview, IL: Scott, Foresman.

——(1990) *The Age of the Economist: The Development of Modern Economic Thought*, 6th edn, Glenview, IL: Scott, Foresman.

——(1994) *The Age of the Economist: The Development of Modern Economic Thought*, 7th edn, Glenview, IL: Scott, Foresman.

——(1999) *The Age of the Economist: The Development of Modern Economic Thought*, 8th edn, Glenview, IL: Scott, Foresman.

——(2002) *The Age of the Economist: The Development of Modern Economic Thought*, 9th edn, Glenview, IL: Scott, Foresman.

Gabriel, R.H. (1940) *The Course of American Democratic Thought*, New York: Ronald Press.

——(1956) *The Course of American Democratic Thought*, 2nd edn, New York: Ronald Press.

Gabriel, R.H. and Walker, R.H. (1986) *The Course of American Democratic Thought*, 3rd edn, New York: Ronald Press.

Gans, J.S. and Shepherd, G.B. (2000) "How are the Mighty Fallen: Rejected Classic Articles by Leading Economists," in Gans, J. (ed.) *Publishing Economics: Analyses of the Academic Journal Market in Economics*, Northampton, MA: Edward Elgar.

Garrouste, P. and Ioannides, S. (eds) (2001) *Evolution and Path Dependence in Economic Ideas*, Northampton, MA: Edward Elgar.

Gerrard, B. (1993) "The Significance of Interpretation in Economics," in Henderson, W., Dudley-Evans, T. and Backhouse, R. (eds) *Economics and Language*, New York: Routledge.

Gherity, J.A. (1965) *Economic Thought: A Historical Anthology*, New York: Random House.

Gide, C. and Rist, C. (1948 [1913]) *A History of Economic Doctrines: From the Time of the Physiocrats to the Present Day*, Boston, MA: D.C. Heath.

Gill, R.T. (1967) *Evolution of Modern Economics*, Englewood Cliffs, NJ: Prentice-Hall.

Goodwin, C. (1961) *Canadian Economic Thought: The Political Economy of Developing Nations, 1814–1914*, Durham, NC: Duke University Press.

——(1966) *Economic Enquiry in Australia*, Durham, NC: Duke University Press.

——(1973) "Marginalism Moves to the New World," in Black, R.D.C., Coats, A.W. and Goodwin, C.D.W. (eds) *The Marginal Revolution in Economics: Interpretation and Evaluation*, Durham, NC: Duke University Press.

——(ed.) (1975) *Exhortation and Controls: The Search for a Wage-Price Policy 1945–1971*, Washington: Brookings Institution.

Goodwin, C. and Nacht, M. (eds) (1995) *Beyond Government: Extending the Public Policy Debate in Emerging Democracies*, Boulder, CO: Westview Press.

Gordon, B. (1977) *Political Economy in Parliament, 1819–1823*, New York: Barnes & Noble.

Granovetter, M. (2002) "A Theoretical Agenda for Economic Sociology," in Guillen, M.F. *et al.* (eds) *The New Economic Sociology: Development in an Emerging Field*, New York: Russell Sage.

Gray, A. (1931) *The Development of Economic Doctrine: An Introductory Survey*, New York: Longmans, Green.

Gray, A. and Thompson, A. (1980) *The Development of Economic Doctrine: An Introductory Survey*, 2nd edn, New York: Longman.

Greenaway, D., Bleaney, M. and Stewart, I.M.T. (eds) (1991) *Companion to Contemporary Economic Thought*, New York: Routledge.

Greenwald, D. (ed.) (1965) *The McGraw-Hill Encyclopedia of Economics*, New York: McGraw-Hill.

——(ed.) (1973) *The McGraw-Hill Encyclopedia of Economics*, 2nd edn, New York: McGraw-Hill.

——(ed.) (1983) *The McGraw-Hill Encyclopedia of Economics*, 3rd edn, New York: McGraw-Hill.

——(ed.) (1994) *The McGraw-Hill Encyclopedia of Economics*, 4th edn, New York: McGraw-Hill.

Greif, A. (1998) "Historical and Comparative Institutional Analysis," *American Economic Review*, 88: 80–84.

Grice-Hutchinson, M. (1993) *Economic Thought in Spain*, Brookfield, VT: Edward Elgar.

Griswold, C.L., Jr. (1999) *Adam Smith and the Virtues of Enlightenment*, New York: Cambridge University Press.

Groenewegen, P. (1987) "Division of Labor," in Eatwell, J., Milgate, M. and Newman, P. (eds) (1987) *The New Palgrave: A Dictionary of Economics*, vol. 1, London: Macmillan.

Groenewegen, P. and McFarlane, B. (1990) *A History of Australian Economic Thought*, New York: Routledge.

Grotius, H. (1964 [1625]) *De Jure Belli ac Pacis Libri Tres*, trans. F.W. Kelsey, New York: Oceana Publications.

Guelzo, A.C. (2000) Review of Daniel Walker Howe, *Making the American Self: Jonathan Edwards to Abraham Lincoln*, Cambridge, MA: Harvard University Press, 1996. Online posting, available by e-mail (1 October 2000): conservativenet@listserv.uic.edu

Guidi, M.E.L. (1999) "Towards a History of Emulation: Hobbes, Smith and Bentham," 2nd edn, manuscript.

Hacking, I. (2002) *Historical Ontology*, Cambridge, MA: Harvard University Press.

Hall, P. (ed.) (1989) *The Political Power of Economic Ideas: Keynesianism across Nations*, Princeton: Princeton University Press.

Halm, G.N. (1942) *Monetary Theory*, Philadelphia, PA: Blakiston.

——(1946) *Monetary Theory*, 2nd edn, Philadelphia, PA: Blakiston.

Hamilton, E.J., Rees, A. and Johnson, H.G. (eds) (1962) *Landmarks in Political Economy*, Chicago, IL: University of Chicago Press.

Hands, D.W. (2001)*Reflection without Rules: Economic Methodology and Contemporary Science Theory*, Cambridge: Cambridge University Press.

Haney, L.H. (1911) *History of Economic Thought*, New York: Macmillan.

——(1920) *History of Economic Thought*, revised edn, New York: Macmillan.

——(1926) *History of Economic Thought*, revised edn, New York: Macmillan.

——(1936) *History of Economic Thought*, 3rd edn, New York: Macmillan.

——(1949) *History of Economic Thought*, 4th and enlarged edn, New York: Macmillan.

Hansen, G.E. (2002) *The Culture of Strangers: Globalization, Localization and the Phenomenon of Exchange*, Lanham, MD: University Press of America.

Hanusch, H. (ed.) (1988) *Evolutionary Economics: Applications of Schumpeter*, New York: Cambridge University Press.

Heertje, A. (ed.) (1993) *The Makers of Modern Economics*, vol. 1, London: Harvester Wheatsheaf.

——(ed.) (1995) *The Makers of Modern Economics*, vol. 2, London: Harvester Wheatsheaf.

——(ed.) (1997) *The Makers of Modern Economics*, vol. 3, London: Harvester Wheatsheaf.

——(ed.) (1999) *The Makers of Modern Economics*, vol. 4, Northampton, MA: Edward Elgar.

Heilbroner, R.L. (1953) *The Worldly Philosophers*. New York: Simon and Schuster.

——(1960) *The Future as History*, New York: Harper Brothers.

——(1961) *The Worldly Philosophers*, revised edn, New York: Simon and Schuster.

——(1967) *The Worldly Philosophers*, 3rd edn, New York: Simon and Schuster.

——(1972) *The Worldly Philosophers*, 4th edn, New York: Simon and Schuster.

——(1976) *The Worldly Philosophers*, newly revised 4th edn, New York: Simon and Schuster.

——(1979) "Modern Economics as a Chapter in the History of Economic Thought," *History of Political Economy*, 11(2): 192–198.

Heimann, E. (1945) *History of Economic Doctrines: An Introduction to Economic Theory*, New York: Oxford University Press.

——(1964) *History of Economic Doctrines: An Introduction to Economic Theory*, reprint edn, New York: Galaxy.

Henderson, W. (n.d.) "A Very Cautious, or a Very Polite, Dr. Smith?: Hedging in The Wealth of Nations," manuscript.

——(1995) *Economics as Literature*, New York: Routledge.

Henderson, W., Dudley-Evans, T. and Backhouse, R. (eds) (1993) *Economics and Language*, New York: Routledge.

Herman, A. (2001) *The Scottish Enlightenment: The Scots' Invention of the Modern World*, London: Fourth Estate.

Hill, L. (2001) "The Hidden Theology of Adam Smith," *European Journal of the History of Economic Thought*, 8(1): 1–29.

Hobsbawm, E. and Ranger, T. (eds) (1983) *The Invention of Tradition*, New York: Cambridge University Press.

Hodgson, G.M. (1993) *Economics and Evolution: Bringing Life Back Into Economics*, Cambridge: Polity Press.

——(1995) "The Evolution of Evolutionary Economics," *Scottish Journal of Political Economy*, 42(4): 469–488.

——(2002) *A Modern Reader in Institutional and Evolutionary Economics: Key Concepts*, Northampton, MA: Edward Elgar.

——(2003a) "The Ubiquity Exchange: Spiritualism or Fact?," *Research in the History of Economic Thought and Methodology*, 21(A): 351–366.

——(2003b) "Veblen in Chicago: The Winds of Creativity," manuscript.

Holt, R.P.F. and Pressman, S. (eds) (2001) *A New Guide to Post Keynesian Economics*, New York: Routledge.

Homan, P.T. (1928) *Contemporary Economic Thought*, New York: Harper & Brothers.

Hoover, G. (ed.) (1950) *Twentieth Century Economic Thought*, New York: Philosophical Library.

Horowitz, I.L. (ed.) (2002) *Veblen's Century*, New Brunswick, NJ: Transaction.

Howey, R.S. (1982) *A Bibliography of General Histories of Economics, 1692–1975*, Lawrence KS: Regents Press of Kansas.

Howson, S. and Winch, D. (1977) *The Economic Advisory Council, 1930–1939: A Study in Economic Advice during Depression and Recovery*, Cambridge: Cambridge University Press.

Hsu, R.C. (1991) *Economic Theories in China, 1979–1988*, Cambridge: Cambridge University Press.

Hume, D. (1965 [1739]) *Treatise of Human Understanding*, ed. Selby-Bigge, L.A., Oxford: Clarendon Press.

——(1975 [1777]) *Enquiries Concerning Human Understanding and Concerning the Principles of Morals*, ed. Selby-Bigge, L.A. with revisions by Nidditch, P.H., Oxford: Clarendon Press.

Hunt, D. (1989) *Economic Theories of Development: An Analysis of Competing Paradigms*, Savage, MD: Barncs & Noble.

Hunt, E.K. (1979) *History of Economic Thought: A Critical Perspective*, Belmont, CA: Wadsworth.

——(1992) *History of Economic Thought: A Critical Perspective*, 2nd edn, New York: HarperCollins.

——(2002) *History of Economic Thought: A Critical Perspective*, updated edn, Armonk, NY: M.E. Sharpe.

——(2003) *Property and Prophets: The Evolution of Economic Institutions and Ideologies*, updated 7th edn, Armonk, NY: M.E. Sharpe.

Hutchison, T.W. (1953) *A Review of Economic Doctrines, 1870–1929*, Oxford: Clarendon Press.

——(1955) "Insularity and Cosmopolitanism in Economic Ideas," *American Economic Review*, 45(2): 1–16.

Ingram, J.K. (1888) *A History of Political Economy*, New York: Macmillan.

Ingrao, B. and Israel, G. (1990) *The Invisible Hand: Economic Equilibrium in the History of Science*, Cambridge, MA: MIT Press.

Jasinski, J. (2001) *Sourcebook on Rhetoric: Key Concepts in Contemporary Rhetorical Studies*, London: Sage.

Jensen, H. (1971) Motivation and the Moral Sense in Francis Hutcheson's Ethical Theory, The Hague: Nijhoff.

Johnson, M. (2002) "Colonial Dissent: Thomas Pownall's Letter to Adam Smith", presented at the History of Economics Society, 6 July, UC Davis.

Jones, R.J.B. (ed.) (2001) *Routledge Encyclopedia of International Political Economy*, London: Routledge.

Jorgensen, E.W. and Jorgensen, H.I. (1999) *Thorstein Veblen: Victorian Firebrand*, Armonk, NY: M.E. Sharpe.

Kalyvas, A. and Katznelson, I. (2001) "The Rhetoric of the Market: Adam Smith on Recognition, Speech, and Exchange," *Review of Politics*, 63(3): 549–579.

Kamerschen, D.R. (ed.) (1967) *Readings in Microeconomics*, Cleveland, OH: World.

Kapp, K.W. and Kapp, L.L. (eds) (1949) *History of Economic Thought: A Book of Readings*, New York: Barnes & Noble.

——(eds) (1963) *History of Economic Thought: A Book of Readings*, 2nd edn, New York: Barnes & Noble.

Kastelein, T.J., Kuipers, S.K., Nijenhuis, W.A. and Wagenaar, G.R. (eds) (1976) *25 Years of Economic Theory: Retrospect and Prospect*, Leiden: Martinus Nijhoff.

Kauder, E. (1965) *A History of Marginal Utility Theory*, Princeton, NJ: Princeton University Press.

Kemp-Smith, N. (1964) *The Philosophy of David Hume*, London: Macmillan.

Khalil, E.L. (2000a) "Beyond Natural Selection and Divine Intervention: The Lamarckian Implication of Adam Smith's Invisible Hand," *Journal of Evolutionary Economics*, 10: 373–393.

——(2000b) "Making Sense of Adam Smith's Invisible Hand: Beyond Pareto Optimality and Unintended Consequences," *Journal of the History of Economic Thought*, 22(1): 49–63.

Kibritcioglu, A. (2002) "On the Smithian Origins of 'New' Trade and Growth Theories," University of Illinois-Urbana-Champaign Commerce and Business Administration Working Paper, No. 02–0100.

King, J.E. (1988) *Economic Exiles*, New York: St. Martin's Press.

——(2002) *A History of Post Keynesian Economics Since 1936*, Northampton, MA: Edward Elgar.

Kitch, E.W. (1983) "The Fire of Truth: A Remembrance of Law and Economics at Chicago, 1932–1970," *Journal of Law and Economics*, 26 (April): 163–233.

Klausinger, H. (2002) "Walras' Law and the IS-LM Model: A Tale of Progress and Regress," in Boehm, S., Gehrke, C., Kurz, H.D. and Sturn, R. (eds) *Is There Progress in Economics?*, Northampton, MA: Edward Elgar.

Koopmans, T.C. (1957) *Three Essays on the State of Economic Science*, New York: McGraw-Hill.

Kuhn, T.S. (1962) *The Structure of Scientific Revolutions*, Chicago, IL: University of Chicago Press.

Kuhn, W.E. (1963) *The Evolution of Economic Thought*, Cincinnati, OH: South-Western Publishing.

——(1970) *The Evolution of Economic Thought*, 2nd edn, Cincinnati, OH: South-Western Publishing.

Kumar, K. (1987) *Utopia and Anti-Utopia in Modern Times*, Cambridge, MA: Basil Blackwell.

Landreth, H. (1976) *History of Economic Theory*, Boston, MA: Houghton Mifflin.

Landreth, H. and Colander, D. (1989) *History of Economic Theory*, 2nd edn, Boston, MA: Houghton Mifflin.

——(1994) *History of Economic Thought*, 3rd edn (of *History of Economic Theory*), Boston, MA: Houghton Mifflin.

——(2002) *History of Economic Thought*, 4th edn (of *History of Economic Theory*), Boston, MA: Houghton Mifflin.

Lawson, T. (1997) *Economics and Reality*, London: Routledge.

Leff, M. (1997) "Hermeneutical Rhetoric," in Jost, W. and Hyde, M.J. (eds) *Rhetoric and Hermeneutics in Our Time*, New Haven: Yale University Press.

Leifer, M. (2001) Dictionary of the Modern Politics of South-East Asia, London: Routledge.

Lekachman, R. (1959) *A History of Economic Ideas*, New York: Harper.

Lerner, M. (ed.) (1948) *The Portable Veblen*, New York: Viking.

Levy, D.M. (1992a) "Adam Smith and the Texas & Rats," in Levy, D.M. *The Economic Ideas of Ordinary People: From Preferences to Trade*, New York: Routledge.

——(1992b) "Adam Smith's 'Natural Law' and Contractual Society," in Levy, D.M. *The Economic Ideas of Ordinary People: From Preferences to Trade*, New York: Routledge.

——(1997) "Adam Smith's Rational Choice Linguistics," *Economic Inquiry*, 34(3): 672–678 (reprinted in Levy, D.M. *How the Dismal Science Got Its Name: Classical Economics and the Ur-Text of Racial Politics*, Ann Arbor, MI: University of Michigan Press, 2001).

——(1999a) "Adam Smith's Katallactic Model of Gambling: Approbation from the Spectator," *Journal of the History of Economic Thought*, 21(1): 81–91.

——(1999b) "Katallactic Rationality: Exploring the Links between Co-operation and Language," *American Journal of Economics and Sociology*, 58: 729–747 (reprinted in Levy, D.M. *How the Dismal Science Got Its Name: Classical Economics and the Ur-Text of Racial Politics*, Ann Arbor, MI: University of Michigan Press, 2001).

——(2001) *How the Dismal Science Got Its Name: Classical Economics and the Ur-Text of Racial Politics*, Ann Arbor, MI: University of Michigan Press.

——(2002) "George Stigler as Dissertation Director," *American Journal of Economics and Sociology*, 61: 617–622.

Levy, D.M. and Diamond, A.M., Jr. (1994) "The Metrics of Style: Adam Smith Teaches Efficient Rhetoric," *Economic Inquiry*, 32(1): 138–144.

Lewis, T.J. (2000) "Persuasion, Domination and Exchange: Adam Smith on the Political Consequences of Markets," *Canadian Journal of Political Science*, 33(2): 273–289.

Leifer, M. (ed.) (2000) *Dictionary of the Modern Politics of Southeast Asia*, London: Routledge.

Llombart, V. (1995) "Market for Ideas and Reception of Physiocracy in Spain: Some Analytical and Historical Suggestions," *The European Journal of the History of Economic Thought*, 2(1): 29–51.

Loasby, B.J. (1989) *The Mind and Method of the Economist: A Critical Appraisal of Major Economists in the 20th Century*, Brookfield, VT: Edward Elgar.

McCarty, M.H. (2001) *The Nobel Laureates: How the World's Greatest Economic Minds Shaped Modern Thought*, New York: McGraw-Hill.

McCloskey, D. (1996) *The Vices of Economists, the Virtues of the Bourgeoisie*, Amsterdam: Amsterdam University Press.

——(1998) *The Rhetoric of Economics*, 2nd edn, Madison, WI: University of Wisconsin Press.

——(1991) "Economic Science: A Search Through the Hyperspace of Assumptions," *Methodus*, 3 (June): 6–16.

McConnell, J.W. (1943) *Basic Teachings of the Great Economists*, New York: Barnes & Noble.

McLure, M. (2001) *Pareto, Economics and Society: The Mechanical Analogy*, New York: Routledge.

McNulty, P.J. (1980) *The Origins and Development of Labor Economics*, Cambridge, MA: MIT Press.

Machlup, F. (1978) *Methodology of Economics and Other Social Sciences*, New York: Academic Press.

Mackie, C.D. (1998) *Canonizing Economic Theory: How Theories and Ideas are Selected in Economics*, Armonk, NY: M.E. Sharpe.

Maes, I. (2002) *Economic Thought and the Making of European Monetary Union*, Northampton, MA: Edward Elgar.

Magnusson, L. (2004) "Bertil Ohlin—A Centennial Celebration," *Research in the History of Economic Thought and Methodology*, 22(A).

Mair, D. and Miller, A.G. (eds) (1991) *A Modern Guide to Economic Thought: An Introduction to Comparative Schools of Thought in Economics*, Brookfield, VT: Edward Elgar.

Maitre, P. (2000) "Main Invisible et Non-intentionnalité chez A. Smith," *Revue d'Economie Politique*, 110(5): 725–738.

Malinvaud, E. (1977; 2nd edn 1985) *The Theory of Unemployment Reconsidered*, New York: Basil Blackwell.

——(1985) *The Theory of Unemployment Reconsidered*, 2nd edn, New York: Basil Blackwell.

Mandeville, B. (1924 [1729, 1732]) *The Fable of the Bees*, 2 vols, ed. Kaye, F.B., Oxford: Clarendon Press.

Mankiw, N.G. (1990) "A Quick Refresher Course in Macroeconomics," *Journal of Economic Literature*, 78: 1645–1660.

Mankiw, N.G. and Romer, D. (eds) (1991) *New Keynesian Economics*, 2 vols, Cambridge, MA: MIT Press.

Mansfield, E. (ed.) (1971) *Microeconomics: Selected Readings*, New York: W.W. Norton.

Mantzavinos, C. (2001) *Individuals, Institutions, and Markets*, New York: Cambridge University Press.

Mayer, T. (1995) *Doing Economic Research*, Brookfield, VT: Edward Elgar.

Meacci, F. (1998) *Italian Economists of the 20th Century*, Northampton, MA: Edward Elgar.

Medema, S.G. (2002) "The Legal-Economic Tangle: Legal Realism, Institutionalism, and Chicago Law and Economics," manuscript, December edn.

Medema, S.G. and Samuels, W.J. (eds) (1996; paperback edn 1998) *The Foundations of Research in Economics: How Do Economists Do Economics?*, Brookfield, VT: Edward Elgar Publishing Ltd.

——(1997) "Ronald Coase and Coasean Economics: Some Questions, Conjectures and Implications," in Samuels, W.J., Medema, S.G. and Schmid, A.A. *The Economy as a Process of Valuation*, Lyme, NH: Edward Elgar.

——(eds) (1998) *The Foundations of Research in Economics: How Do Economists Do Economics?*, paperback edn, Brookfield, VT: Edward Elgar Publishing Ltd.

——(2001) *Historians of Economics and Economic Thought: The Construction of Disciplinary Memory*, New York: Routledge.

Meek, R.L., and Skinner, A. (1977) "The Development of Adam Smith's Ideas on the Division of Labour," in Meek, R.L. *Smith, Marx & After*, London: Chapman & Hall (reprinted with "very few amendments of substance" from *Economic Journal*, 83: 1094–1116).

Melman, S. (1975) "The Impact of Economics on Technology," *Journal of Economic Issues*, 9: 59–72.

Menand, L. (2001) *The Metaphysical Club*, New York: Farrar, Straus and Giroux.

Miller, P.J. (ed.) (1994) *The Rational Expectations Revolution: Readings from the Front Line*, Cambridge, MA: MIT Press.

Miller, T.P. (1995) "Francis Hutcheson and the Civic Humanist Tradition," in Hook, A. and Sher, R.B. (eds) *The Glasgow Enlightenment*, East Lothian: Tuckwell Press and Eighteenth-Century Scottish Studies Society.

Minowitz, P. (1993) *Profits, Priests, and Princes: Adam Smith's Emancipation of Economics from Politics and Religion*, Stanford, CA: Stanford University Press.

Mirowski, P. (1989) *More Heat than Light*, New York: Cambridge University Press.

——(ed.) (1994) *Natural Images in Economic Thought: "Markets Read in Tooth and Claw"*, New York: Cambridge University Press.

——(2002) *Machine Dreams: Economics Becomes a Cyborg Science*, New York: Cambridge University Press.

Mises, L. von. (1949) *Human Action: A Treatise on Economics*, New Haven, CT: Yale University Press.

Mitchell, W.C. (ed.) (1936) *What Veblen Taught*, New York: Viking.

——(1949) *Lecture Notes on Types of Economic Theory*, 2 vols, New York: Augustus C. Kelley.

Mohr, E. (ed.) (1999) *The Transfer of Economic Knowledge*, Northampton, MA: Edward Elgar.

Montes, L. (2001) *Smith and Newton: Some Methodological Issues Concerning General Economic Equilibrium Theory*, manuscript.

Morgan, M.S. (1990) *The History of Econometric Ideas*, New York: Cambridge University Press.

Morgan, M.S. and Rutherford, M. (eds) (1998) *From Interwar Pluralism to Postwar Neoclassicism*, Durham, NC: Duke University Press.

Mosely, F. (ed.) (1995) *Heterodox Economic Theories: True or False?*, Brookfield, VT: Edward Elgar.

Mueller, M.G. (ed.) (1966) *Readings in Macroeconomics*, New York: Holt, Rinehart and Winston.

Muller, J.Z. (1993) *Adam Smith in His Time and Ours: Designing the Decent Society*, New York: Free Press.

Nadeau, R. (1998) "Spontaneous Order," in Davis, J.B., Hands, D.W. and Mäki, U. (eds) *The Handbook of Economic Methodology*, Northampton, MA: Edward Elgar.

Nagel, E. (1961) *The Structure of Science: Problems in the Logic of Scientific Explanation*, New York: Harcourt, Brace & World.

Nakano-Matsushima, S. (2001) "Mandeville's 'Vice' as a Cognitive Process: A Neglected Mechanism for the Development of the Division of Labor," manuscript, 20 July edn.

Napoleoni, C. (1963) *Economic Thought of the Twentieth Century*, ed. and trans. Cigno, A., New York: John Wiley.

——(1972) *Economic Thought of the Twentieth Century*, expanded and trans. edn, ed. and trans. Cigno, A., New York: John Wiley.

——(1975) *Smith Ricardo Marx*, New York: John Wiley & Sons.

Nasar, S. (1998) *A Beautiful Mind*, New York: Simon & Schuster.

Natanson, M. (ed.) (1963) *Philosophy of the Social Sciences*, New York: Random House.

Nathan, R.P. (2000) *Social Science in Government: The Role of Policy Researchers*, New York: Rockefeller Institute Press.

Neff, F.A. (1946) *Economic Doctrines*, Wichita, KA: McGuin.

——(1950) *Economic Doctrines*, 2nd edn, New York: McGraw-Hill.

Negishi, T. (1989) *History of Economic Theory*, Amsterdam: North-Holland.

——(1994) *The History of Economics*, vol. 2, Brookfield, VT: Edward Elgar.

Neill, R. (1991) *A History of Canadian Economic Thought*, New York: Routledge.

Nelson, R.H. (2001) *Economics as Religion: From Samuelson to Chicago and Beyond*, University Park, PA: Pennsylvania State University Press.

Newman, P. (ed.) (1998) *The New Palgrave Dictionary of Economics and the Law*, 3 vols, New York: Stockton Press.

Newman, P.C. (1952) *The Development of Economic Thought*, New York: Prentice-Hall.

Newman, P.C., Gayer, A.D. and Spencer, M.H. (eds) (1954) *Source Readings in Economic Thought*, New York: Norton.

Niehans, J. (1990) *A History of Economic Theory: Classic Contributions 1720–1980*, Baltimore, MD: Johns Hopkins University Press.

Nisticò, S. and Tosato, D. (eds) (2002) *Competing Economic Theories*, New York: Routledge.

North, D. (1990) *Institutions, Institutional Change and Economic Performance*, Cambridge: Cambridge University Press.

O'Hara, P.A. (ed.) (2000) *Encyclopedia of Political Economy*, London: Routledge.

Oakley, A. (1994) *Classical Economic Man*, Brookfield, VT: Edward Elgar.

——(1999) *The Revival of Modern Austrian Economics: A Critical Assessment of its Subjectivist Origins*, Northampton, MA: Edward Elgar.

Ogus, A.I. (1995) "Law and Economics in the United Kingdom: Past, Present, and Future," *Journal of Law and Society*, 22(1): 26–34.

Olson, R. (ed.) (1971) *Science as Metaphor*, Belmont, CA: Wadsworth.

Oman, C.P. and Wignaraja, G. (1991) *The Postwar Evolution of Development Thinking*, New York: St. Martin's Press.

Oser, J. (1963) *The Evolution of Economic Thought*, New York: Harcourt, Brace & World.

——(1970) *The Evolution of Economic Thought*, 2nd edn, New York: Harcourt, Brace & World.

Oser, J. and Blanchfield, W.C. (1975) *The Evolution of Economic Thought*, 3rd edn, New York: Harcourt Brace Jovanovich.

Oser, J. and Brue, S.L. (1994) *The Evolution of Economic Thought*, 5th edn, authored by Brue, S.L., Fort Worth, TX: Dryden Press.

Ostrander, F.T. (2004) "Notes on Frank H. Knight's Course, History of Economic Thought, Economics 302, University of Chicago, 1933–34," *Research in the History of Economic Thought and Methodology*, 22(B).

——(2005a) "Notes on Frank H. Knight's Course, Economic Theory, Economics 301, University of Chicago, 1933–34," *Research in the History of Economic Thought and Methodology*, 23(B).

——(2005b) "Notes on Frank H. Knight's Course, Current Tendencies, Economics 303, University of Chicago, 1933–34," *Research in the History of Economic Thought and Methodology*, 23(B).

——(2005c) "Notes on Frank H. Knight's Course, Economics from an Institutional Standpoint, Economics 305, University of Chicago, 1933–34," *Research in the History of Economic Thought and Methodology*, 23(B).

——(2005d) "Notes on Henry C. Simons's Course, Public Finance, Economics 360, University of Chicago, 1933–34," *Research in the History of Economic Thought and Methodology*, 23(B).

Pack, S.J. (1991) *Capitalism as a Moral System*, Brookfield, VT: Edward Elgar.

Palgrave, R.H. Inglis (ed.) (1894–1899) *Dictionary of Political Economy*, 3 vols, New York: Macmillan.

Papandreou, A.G. (1958) *Economics as a Science*, Chicago, IL: J.B. Lippincott.

Patterson, S.H. (1932) *Readings in the History of Economic Thought*, New York: McGraw-Hill.

Paul, R.A. (1991) "Freud's Anthropology: A Reading of the 'Cultural Books'," in Neu, J. (ed.) *The Cambridge Companion to Freud*, New York: Cambridge University Press.

Peck, H.W. (1935) *Economic Thought and its Institutional Background*, New York: Farrar & Rinehart.

Peirce, C.S. (1957) *Essays in the Philosophy of Science*, ed. Vincent Tomas, New York: Liberal Arts Press.

Perelman, M. (1989) "Adam Smith and Dependent Social Relations," *History of Political Economy*, 21: 503–520.

Perlman, M. (1996) *The Character of Economic Thought, Economic Characters and Economic Institutions: Selected Essays*, Ann Arbor, MI: University of Michigan Press.

Perlman, M. and McCann, C.R., Jr. (1998) *The Pillars of Economic Understanding: Ideas and Traditions*, Ann Arbor, MI: University of Michigan Press.

Perry, G.L. and Tobin, J. (eds) (2000) *Economic Events, Ideas, and Policies: The 1960s and After*, Washington: Brookings Institution.

Phelps, E.S. (1990) *Seven Schools of Macroeconomic Thought*, Oxford: Clarendon Press.

Pocock, J. (1983) "Cambridge Paradigms and Scotch Philosophers," in Hont, I. and Ignatieff, M. (eds) *Wealth and Virtue*, Cambridge: Cambridge University Press.

Poovey, M. (1998) *A History of the Modern Fact: Problems of Knowledge in the Sciences of Wealth and Society*, Chicago, IL: University of Chicago Press.

Popper, K. (1965) *Conjectures and Refutations: The Growth of Scientific Knowledge*, New York: Harper & Row.

Porta, P.L. (1994) "The Present as History in Economic Analysis," *History of Economic Ideas* 2(2): 165–172. A summary of the article is found in Salanti, A. (ed.) (1990) *History of Economic Thought: How and Why?*, Bergamo: Quaderni del Dipartimento di Scienze Economiche, 12: 31–34.

Porter, T.M. (1986) *The Rise of Statistical Thinking, 1820–1900*, Princeton, NJ: Princeton University Press.

Potts, J. (2000) *The New Evolutionary Microeconomics*, Cheltenham: Edward Elgar.

Powell, W.W. and DiMaggio, P. (1991) *The New Institutionalism in Organizational Analysis*, Chicago: University of Chicago Press.

Pownall, T. (1776) *A Letter from Governor Pownall to Adam Smith, L.L.D. F.R.S. being an examination of several points of doctrine, laid down in his "Inquiry into the Nature and Causes of the Wealth of Nations"*, London.

Presley, J.R. and O'Brien, D.P. (eds) (1981) *Pioneers of Modern Economics in Britain*, vol. 1, London: Macmillan.

Presley, J.R. and Greenaway, D. (eds) (1989) *Pioneers of Modern Economics in Britain*, vol. 2, New York: St. Martin's Press.

Pressman, S. (1999) *Fifty Major Economists*, New York: Routledge.

Pribram, K. (1983) *A History of Economic Reasoning*, Baltimore, MD: Johns Hopkins University Press.

Pufendorf, S. (1927 [1673]) *De Officio Hominis et Civis Juxta Legen Naturalem Libri Duo*, trans. F.G. Moore, New York and Oxford: Oxford University Press.

Ramstad, Y. (1986) "A Pragmatist's Quest for Holistic Knowledge: The Scientific Methodology of John R. Commons," *Journal of Economic Issues*, 20: 1067–1105.

Ranadive, K.R. (1977) "The Wealth of Nations—The Vision and the Conceptualization," *Indian Economic Journal*, 24(3): 2295–2332. Reprinted in Wood, J.C. (ed.) (1984) *Adam Smith: Critical Assessments*, London: Croom Helm.

Raphael, D.D. (1997) "Smith," in Raphael, D.D., Winch, D. and Skidelsky, R. *Three Great Economists*, New York: Oxford University Press.

Rashid, S. (1990) "Adam Smith's Acknowledgements: Neo-Plagiarism and the Wealth of Nations," *Journal of Libertarian Studies*, 9(2): 1–24.

——(1992) "Adam Smith and Neo-plagiarism: A Reply," *Journal of Libertarian Studies*, 10 (Fall): 81–87.

Reder, M.W. (2003) "Economics and Religion: A Troubling Interface," *Research in the History of Economic Thought and Methodology*, 21(A): 213–238.

Reisman, D.A. (1977) *Richard Titmuss: Welfare and Society*, London: Heinemann.

——(1980) *Galbraith and Market Capitalism*, New York: St. Martin's Press.

——(1990a) *Alfred Marshall's Mission*, New York: St. Martin's Press.

——(1990b) *Theories of Collective Action: Downs, Olson, and Hirsch*, New York: St. Martin's Press.

——(1997) *Anthony Crosland: the Mixed Economy*, New York: St. Martin's Press.

Rich, D.Z. (1986) *Contemporary Economics: A Unifying Approach*, New York: Praeger.

Rima, I.H. (1967) *Development of Economic Analysis*, Homewood, IL: Irwin.

——(1972) *Development of Economic Analysis*, revised edn, Homewood, IL: Irwin.

——(1978) *Development of Economic Analysis*, 3rd edn, Homewood, IL: Irwin.

——(1986) *Development of Economic Analysis*, 4th edn, Homewood, IL: Irwin.

——(1991) *Development of Economic Analysis*, 5th edn, Homewood, IL: Irwin.

——(2001) *Development of Economic Analysis*, 6th edn, Homewood, IL: Irwin.

Rizzello, S. (1999) *The Economics of the Mind*, Northampton, MA: Edward Elgar.

Robbins, L. (1970) *The Evolution of Modern Economic Theory and Other Papers on the History of Economic Thought*, Chicago, IL: Aldine.

Robinson, J.H. (1921) *The Mind in the Making*, New York: Harpers.

Rogin, L. (1956) *The Meaning and Validity of Economic Theory: A Historical Approach*, New York: Harpers.

Roll, E. (1938) *A History of Economic Thought*, New York: Prentice-Hall.

——(1940) *A History of Economic Thought*, reprint edn, New York: Prentice-Hall.

——(1942) *A History of Economic Thought*, revised and enlarged 2nd edn, New York: Prentice-Hall; 4th edition, Homewood,: IL Irwin.

——(1946) *A History of Economic Thought*, reprint edn, New York: Prentice-Hall.

——(1956) *A History of Economic Thought*, 3rd edn, New York: Prentice-Hall.

——(1974) *A History of Economic Thought*, revised and enlarged 4th edn, Homewood IL: Prentice-Hall.

Rosenberg, A. (1992) "What is the Cognitive Status of Economic Theory?," in Backhouse, R.E. (ed.) *New Directions in Economic Methodology*, London: Routledge.

Rosenof, T. (1997) *Economics in the Long Run: New Deal Theorists and Their Legacies, 1933–1993*, Chapel Hill, NC: University of North Carolina Press.

Rostow, W.W. (1990) *Theorists of Economic Growth from David Hume to the Present: With a Perspective on the Next Century*, New York: Oxford University Press.

Rothbard, M.N. (1995a) *Economic Thought Before Adam Smith: An Austrian Perspective on the History of Economic Thought*, vol. 1, Brookfield, VT: Edward Elgar.

——(1995b) *Classical Economics: An Austrian Perspective on the History of Economic Thought*, vol. 2, Brookfield, VT: Edward Elgar.

Rothbard, M.N. (2000) "Freedom, Inequality, Primitivism and the Division of Labor," Auburn, AL: Ludwig von Mises Institute. Online at: http://www.mises.org/fipandol.asp

Routh, G. (1975) *The Origin of Economic Ideas*, White Plains, NY: International Arts and Sciences Press

——(1989) *The Origin of Economic Ideas*, 2nd edn, Dobbs Ferry, NY: Sheridan House.

Rubinstein, A. (2000) *Economics and Language*, New York: Cambridge University Press.

Rukstad, M.G. (1986) *Macroeconomic Decision Making in the World Economy: Text and Cases*, Chicago, IL: Dryden Press.

Rutherford, M. (2002) "Chicago Economics and Institutionalism," manuscript.

Rutherford, M. and Samuels, W.J. (eds) (1997) *Classics in Institutional Economics: The Founders, 1890–1945, vols 1 and 2, Thorstein Bunde Veblen*, London: Pickering & Chatto.

Salvemini, G. (1939) *Historian and Scientist; An Essay on the Nature of History and the Social Sciences*, Cambridge: Harvard University Press.

Samuels, W.J. (1973) "Adam Smith and the Economy as a System of Power," *Review of Social Economy*, 31: 123–137; *Indian Economic Journal*, 20: 363–381. Reprinted in Wood, J.C. (ed.) (1984) *Adam Smith: Critical Assessments*, Kent: Croom Helm.

——(1974a) *Pareto on Policy*, New York: Elsevier.

——(1974b) Review of Dorfman, J. (ed.) *Thorstein Veblen: Essays, Reviews, and Reports*, Clifton, NJ: Augustus M. Kelley, 1973, *Journal of Economic Issues*, 8: 957–963.

——(ed.) (1976) *The Chicago School of Political Economy*, East Lansing: Division of Research, Graduate School of Business Administration, Michigan State University.

——(1977) "The Political Economy of Adam Smith," *Ethics*, 87: 189–207. Reprinted in Wood, J.C. (ed.) (1984) *Adam Smith: Critical Assessments*, London: Croom Helm; and Samuels, W.J. (1992) *Essays in the History of Mainstream Political Economy*, London: Macmillan; New York: New York University Press.

——(ed.) (1979) *The Economy as a System of Power*, 2 vols, New Brunswick, NJ: Transaction.

——(1980) "Problems of Marginal Cost Pricing in Public Utilities," *Public Utilities Fortnightly*, 105 (31 January): 21–24.

——(ed.) (1983) "The Craft of the Historian of Economic Thought," *Research in the History of Economic Thought and Methodology*, 1.

——(ed.) (1988) *Institutional Economics*, 3 vols, Aldershot: Edward Elgar.

——(ed.) (1990a) *Economics as Discourse: An Analysis of the Language of Economists*, Boston: Kluwer.

——(1990b) "The Self-Referentiability of Thorstein Veblen's Theory of the Preconceptions of Economic Science," *Journal of Economic Issues*, 24: 695–718.

——(1992a) *Essays on the Economic Role of Government: Fundamentals*, New York: New York University Press.

——(ed.) (1992b) *New Horizons in Economic Thought: Appraisals of Leading Economists*, Aldershot: Edward Elgar.

——(1992c) "Legal Realism and the Burden of Symbolism: The Correspondence of Thurman Arnold," in *Essays in the History of Heterodox Political Economy*, New York: New York University Press. Reprinted from *Law and Society Review*, 13: 997–1011.

——(1993a) "In (Limited but Affirmative) Defence of Nihilism," *Review of Political Economy*, 5: 236–244.

——(1993b) "Adam Smith as Social Constructivist and Dialectician: Aspects of Intergenerational Intellectual Relations," *History of Economic Ideas*, 1: 171–192.

——(ed.) (1993c) *The Chicago School of Political Economy*, reprinted with a new introduction, New Brunswick, NJ: Transaction Books.

——(1994) "The Roles of Theory in Economics," in Klein, P.A. (ed.) *The Role of Theory*, Boston, MA: Kluwer.

——(1996a) "Reader's Guide to John R. Commons, 'Legal Foundations of Capitalism'," *Research in the History of Economic Thought and Methodology*, Archival Supplement 5: 1–61.

——(ed.) (1996b) *American Economists of the Late Twentieth Century*, Brookfield, VT: Edward Elgar.

——(gen. ed.) (1998) *European Economists of the Early 20th Century, vol. 1: Studies of Neglected Continental Thinkers of Belgium, France, The Netherlands, and Scandinavia*, Northampton, MA: Edward Elgar.

——(1999a) "The Problem of 'Do Not Quote or Cite Without Permission'," *Journal of the History of Economic Thought*, 21(2): 187–190.

——(1999b) "Hayek from the Perspective of an Institutionalist Historian of Economic Thought: An Interpretive Essay," *Journal Des Economistes et Des Etudes Humaines*, 9 (June–September): 279–290.

——(2000) "Selective Perception and the Social Construction of Econometrics," *History of Economic Ideas, 7*(3): 103–109.

——(2001a) "Some Problems in the Use of Language in Economics," *Review of Political Economy*, 13(1): 91–100.

——(2001b) "The Canon in Economics," in Forget, E.L. and Peart, S. (eds) *Reflections on the Classical Canon in Economics: Essays in Honor of Samuel Hollander*, New York: Routledge.

——(2002a) "Introduction to the Problem of the History of the Interwar Period," *Research in the History of Economic Thought and Methodology*, 18(A): 139–147.

——(gen. ed.) (2002b) *European Economists of the Early 20th Century, vol. 2: Studies of Neglected Continental Thinkers of Germany and Italy*, Northampton, MA: Edward Elgar.

——(2003) "Institutional Economics: Retrospect and Prospect,"*Research in the History of Economic Thought and Methodology*, Archival Supplement 21(C): 191–250.

——(2004) "F. Taylor Ostrander: A Brief Biography," *Research in the History of Economic Thought and Methodology*, Archival Supplement 22(B).

Samuels, W.J. and Medema, S.G. (1996) *The Foundations of Research in Economics: How Do Economists Do Economics?*, Brookfield, VT: Edward Elgar.

Samuels, W.J. and Mercuro, N. (eds) (1999) *The Fundamental Interrelationship Between Government and Property*, Stamford, CT: JAI Press.

Samuels, W.J. and Tool, M.R. (eds) (1989a) *State, Society, and Corporate Power*, 2nd edn, New Brunswick, NJ: Transaction.

——(eds) (1989b) *The Economy as a System of Power*, 2nd edn, New Brunswick, NJ: Transaction.

Samuels, W.J., Biddle, J.E. and Davis, J.B. (eds) (2003) *The Blackwell Companion to the History of Economic Thought*, Malden, MA: Blackwell.

Samuels, W.J., Hodgson, G.M. and Tool, M.R. (eds) (1994) *The Elgar Companion to Institutional and Evolutionary Economics*, 2 vols, Brookfield, VT: Edward Elgar.

Samuelson, P.A. (1954) "The Pure Theory of Public Expenditure," *Review of Economics and Statistics*, 36: 387–389.

——(1955) "Diagrammatic Exposition of a Theory of Public Expenditure," *Review of Economics and Statistics*, 37: 350–356.

Sandelin, B. (ed.) (1991) *The History of Swedish Economic Thought*, New York: Routledge.

Sandelin, B., Trautwein, H.M. and Wundrak, R. (2002) *A Short History of Economic Thought*, Stockholm: SNS Förlag.

Schlesinger, A.M., Jr. (2000) *A Life in the Twentieth Century*, Boston: Houghton Mifflin.

Schliesser, E. (2002) "Indispensable Hume: From Isaac Newton's Natural Philosophy to Adam Smith's 'Science of Man'," unpublished thesis, University of Chicago.

Schumpeter, J.A. (1954) *History of Economic Analysis*, New York: Oxford University Press.

——(1967 [1912]) *Economic Doctrine and Method*, New York: Oxford University Press.

Scott, W.A. (1933) *The Development of Economics*, New York: D. Appleton-Century.

Screpanti, E. and Zamagni, S. (1993) *An Outline of the History of Economic Thought*, New York: Oxford University Press.

Seidman, R.B. (1973) "Contract Law, the Free Market, and State Intervention: A Jurisprudential Perspective," *Journal of Economic Issues*, 7: 553–576.

Seligman, B.B. (1962) *Main Currents in Modern Economics*, New York: Free Press.

——(1990) *Main Currents in Modern Economics*, reprint edn, New Brunswick, NJ: Transaction.

Seligman, E.R.A. (ed.) (1937) *Encyclopaedia of the Social Sciences*, 15 vols, New York: Macmillan.

Shackle, G.L.S. (1967) *The Years of High Theory*, New York: Cambridge University Press.

Shackleton, J.R. (ed.) (1990) *New Thinking in Economics*, Brookfield, VT: Edward Elgar.

Shackleton, J.R. and Locksley, G. (eds) (1981) *Twelve Contemporary Economists*, New York: John Wiley.

Shaftesbury, A.A. (1964) *Characteristics of men, manners, opinions, times*, ed. and annotated John M. Robertson, introduction by Stanley Green.

Shapiro, M.J. (1993) *Reading "Adam Smith": Desire, History and Value*, Newbury Park, CA: Sage.

Shell, M. (1978) *The Economy as Literature*, Baltimore, MD: Johns Hopkins University Press.

——(1980) "Introduction," in Smith, A. *The Wealth of Nations*, New York: Penguin.

Shughart, W.F. and Razzolini, L. (eds) (2001) *The Elgar Companion to Public Choice*, Northampton, MA: Edward Elgar.

Sievers, A.M. (1962) *Revolution, Evolution, and the Economic Order*, Englewood Cliffs, NJ: Prentice-Hall.

Silk, L. (1976) *The Economists*, New York: Free Press.

Sills, D.L. (ed.) (1968) *International Encyclopedia of the Social Sciences*, 19 vols, New York: Macmillan.

Skinner, A.S. (1979) *A System of Social Science*, Oxford: Clarendon Press.

Skousen, M. (2001) *The Making of Modern Economics*, Armonk, NY: M.E. Sharpe.

Smith, A. (1976a) *The Theory of Moral Sentiments*, New York: Oxford University Press.

——(1976b) *An Inquiry into the Nature and Causes of the Wealth of Nations*, 2 vols, New York: Oxford University Press.

——(1978) *Lectures on Jurisprudence*, New York: Oxford University Press.

——(1980) *Essays on Philosophical Subjects*, New York: Oxford University Press.

——(1983) *Lectures on Rhetoric and Belles Lettres*, ed. J. C. Bryce, Oxford: Clarendon Press.

Smith, C. (2000) "Force of Habit: Hostility and Condescension Toward Religion in the University," *Christianity Today*, 8(5). Available online at: http://www.christianity-today.com/bc/2002/005/13.20.html

Soule, G.H. (1952) *Ideas of the Great Economists*, New York: Viking.

Sowell, T. (1987) "Thorstein Veblen," in Eatwell, J., Milgate, M. and Newman, P. (eds) *The New Palgrave: A Dictionary of Economics*, New York: Stockton Press.

Spann, Othmar (1972) *The History of Economics*, New York: Arno Press.

Spengler, J.J. (1970) "Notes on the International Transmission of Economic Ideas," *History of Political Economy*, 2(1): 133–151.

——(1974) "Was 1922–1972 a Golden Age in the History of Economics?," *Journal of Economic Issues*, 8(3): 525–553.

Spiegel, H.W. (1952) *The Development of Economic Thought*, New York: Wiley.

——(1971) *The Growth of Economic Thought*, Englewood Cliffs, NJ: Prentice-Hall.

——(1983) *The Growth of Economic Thought*, revised and expanded 2nd edn, Englewood Cliffs, NJ: Prentice-Hall.

——(1991) *The Growth of Economic Thought*, 3rd edn, Durham, NC: Duke University Press.

Spiegel, H.W. and Samuels, W.J. (eds) (1984) *Contemporary Economists in Perspective*, 2 vols, Greenwich, CT: JAI Press.

Staley, C.E. (1989) *A History of Economic Thought from Aristotle to Arrow*, Boston: Basil Blackwell.

Stark, W. (1943) *The Ideal Foundations of Economic Thought*, London: Kegan Paul, Trench & Co.

Stein, H. (1969) *The Fiscal Revolution in America*, Chicago: University of Chicago Press.

Stevenson, L. and Haberman, D.L. (1998) *Ten Theories of Human Nature*, 3rd edn, New York: Oxford University Press.

Stewart, D. (1980 [1794]) "Account of the Life and Writings of Adam Smith LL.D.," in Smith, A, *Essays on Philosophical Subjects*, ed. Wightman, W.P.D. and Bryce, J.C., Oxford: Clarendon Press.

Stigler, G.J. (1948) *Production and Distribution Theories: The Formative Period*, New York: Macmillan.

——(1949) *Five Lectures on Economic Problems*, London: Longmans, Green.

——(1952) *The Theory of Price*, revised edition, New York: Macmillan.

——(1965) *Essays in the History of Economics*, Chicago, IL: University of Chicago Press.

——(1966) *The Theory of Price*, 3rd edition, New York: Macmillan.

——(1982) *The Economist as Preacher and Other Essays*, Chicago, IL: University of Chicago Press.

Stigler, G.J. and Friedland, C. (1975) "The Citation Practices of Doctorates in Economics," *Journal of Political Economy*, 83: 477–507.

Stigler, S.M. (1986) *The History of Statistics: The Measurement of Uncertainty before 1900*, Cambridge, MA: Harvard University Press.

Stiglitz, J.E. (1991) "The Invisible Hand and Modern Welfare Economics," NBER Working Paper No. 3641, Cambridge, MA: National Bureau of Economic Research.

Still, J. and Warton, M. (1990) "Introduction," in Warton, M. and Still, J. (eds) *Intertextuality: Theories and Practices*, Manchester: Manchester University Press.

Subrahmanian, N. (1973) *Historiography*, Maurdai: Koodal Publishers.

Suppe, F. (ed.) (1977) *The Structure of Scientific Theories*, 2nd edn, Urbana, IL: University of Illinois Press.

Suranyi-Unger, T. (1932) *Economics in the Twentieth Century: The History of Its International Development*, New York: Norton.

Sutton, J. (2000) *Marshall's Tendencies: What Can Economists Know?*, Cambridge, MA: MIT Press.

Sweezy, P.M. (1953) *The Present as History*, New York: Monthly Review Press.

Szenberg, M. (1992) *Eminent Economists: Their Life Philosophies*, New York: Cambridge University Press.

——(1998) *Passion and Craft: Economists at Work*, Ann Arbor, MI: University of Michigan Press.

Taussig, F.W. (1989 [1915]) *Inventors and Money-Makers*, New Brunswick, NJ: Transaction.

Taylor, O.H. (1960) *A History of Economic Thought*, New York: McGraw-Hill.

Thompson, N. (2002) *Left in the Wilderness: The Political Economy of British Democratic Socialism since 1979*, Chesham: Acumen Publishing.

Thorn, R.S. (ed.) (1966) *Monetary Theory and Policy: Major Contributions to Contemporary Thought*, New York: Random House.

Tilman, R. (1973) "Thorstein Veblen: Incrementalist and Utopian," *American Journal of Economics and Sociology*, 32: 155–169.

——(1987) "Grace Jaffé and Richard Ely on Thorstein Veblen: An Unknown Chapter in American Economic Thought," *History of Political Economy*, 19(1): 141–162.

——(1992) *Thorstein Veblen and His Critics, 1891–1963*, Princeton, NJ: Princeton University Press.

——(ed.) (1993) *A Veblen Treasury*, Armonk, NY: M.E. Sharpe.

——(1999) "Thorstein Veblen and the Disinterest of Neoclassical Economists in Wasteful Consumption," *Journal of Politics, Culture and Society*, 13 (Winter): 207–224.

——(2001) *Ideology and Utopia in the Social Philosophy of the Libertarian Economists*, Westport, CT: Greenwood.

Tribe, K. (1977) *Richard Titmuss: Welfare and Society*, London: Heinemann.

——(1980) *Galbraith and Market Capitalism*, New York: New York University Press.

——(1990a) *Theories of Collective Action: Downs, Olson, and Hirsch*, New York: St. Martin's Press.

——(1990b) *The Political Economy of James Buchanan*, Basingstoke: Macmillan.

——(1997a) *Economic Careers: Economics and Economists in Britain, 1930–1970*, London: Routledge.

——(1997b) *Anthony Crosland: The Mixed Economy*, New York: St. Martin's Press.

——(1999) "Adam Smith: Critical Theorist?," *Journal of Economic Literature*, 37: 609–632.

Trigilia, C. (2002) *Economic Sociology: State, Market, and Society in Modern Capitalism*, New York: Blackwell.

Ugur, M. (ed.) (2002) *An Open Economy Macroeconomics Reader*, New York: Routledge.

Vaggi, G. and Groenewegen, P. (2003) *A Concise History of Economic Thought: From Mercantilism to Monetarism*, New York: Palgrave Macmillan.

van Daal, J. and Heertje, A. (1992) *Economic Thought in the Netherlands: 1650–1950*, Brookfield, VT: Avebury.

Veblen, T. (1892) "The Price of Wheat Since 1867," *Journal of Political Economy*, 1(1): 68–103.

——(1893) "The Food Supply and the Price of Wheat," *Journal of Political Economy*, 1(3): 365–379.

——(1898) "Why Is Economics Not an Evolutionary Science," *Quarterly Journal of Economics*, 12: 373–397. Reprinted in Veblen, T. (1919) *The Place of Science in Modern Civilisation*, New York: Viking; and in Rutherford, M. and Samuels, W.J. (eds) (1997) *Classics in Institutional Economics: The Founders, 1890–1945, vols 1 and 2, Thorstein Bunde Veblen*, London: Pickering & Chatto.

——(1904) *The Theory of Business Enterprise*, New York: Scribner's.

——(1917) *The Nature of Peace*, New York: Macmillan.

——(1919) *The Place of Science in Modern Civilisation*, New York: Viking.

——(1990) *The Place of Science in Modern Civilisation*, reprint edn, New Brunswick, NJ: Transaction.

——(1998) *The Nature of Peace*, reprint edn, New Brunswick, NJ: Transaction.

Walsh, V. and Gram, H. (1980) *Classical and Neoclassical Theories of General Equilibrium*, New York: Oxford University Press.

Warschauer, M. (2002) *Technology and Social Inclusion: Rethinking the Digital Divide*, Cambridge, MA: MIT Press.

Warsh, D. (1993) *Economic Principals: Masters and Mavericks of Modern Economics*, New York: Free Press.

Waterman, A.M.C. (1998) "Economics as Theology: Adam Smith's Wealth of Nations," manuscript.

Weinsheimer, J.C. (1993) *Eighteenth-Century Hermeneutics: Philosophy of Interpretation in England form Locke to Burke*, New Haven and London: Yale University Press.

Weintraub, E.R. (1985) *General Equilibrium Analysis: Studies in Appraisal*, New York: Cambridge University Press.

——(1991) *Stabilizing Dynamics: Constructing Economic Knowledge*, New York: Cambridge University Press.

——(1992) *Toward a History of Game Theory*, Durham, NC: Duke University Press.

——(2002) *How Economics Became a Mathematical Science*, Durham, NC: Duke University Press.

Weintraub, S. (ed.) (1977) *Modern Economic Thought*, Philadelphia, PA: University of Pennsylvania Press.

Werhane, P.H. (1991) *Adam Smith and His Legacy for Modern Capitalism*, New York: Oxford University Press.

West, E.G. (1969) "The Political Economy of Alienation: Karl Marx and Adam Smith," *Oxford Economic Papers*, 21(3): 1–23. Reprinted in Wood, J.C. (ed.) (1984) *Adam Smith: Critical Assessments*, London: Croom Helm.

——(1990) *Adam Smith and Modern Economics*, Brookfield, VT: Edward Elgar.

Whittaker, E. (1940) *A History of Economic Ideas*, London: Longmans, Green.

——(1960) *Schools and Streams of Economic Thought*, Chicago, IL: Rand McNally.

Wilber, C.K. and Harrison, R.S. (1978) "The Methodological Basis of Institutional Economics: Pattern Model, Storytelling and Holism," *Journal of Economic Issues*, 12: 61–89.

Williams, P.L. (1978) *The Emergence of the Theory of the Firm: From Adam Smith to Alfred Marshall*, New York: St. Martin's Press.

Williamson, O.E. (1985) *The Economic Institutions of Capitalism: Firms, Markets, Relational Contracting*, New York: Free Press.

Winch, D. (1969) *Economics and Policy: A Historical Study*, London: Hodder & Stoughton.

——(1996) *Riches and Poverty: An Intellectual History of Political Economy in Britain, 1750–1834*, New York: Cambridge University Press.

Wittgenstein, L. (1958) *Philosophical Investigations*, 3rd edn, New York: Macmillan.

Yamamoto, K. (2003) "Aquisition of Lexical Paraphrases form Text," unpublished paper, ATYR Spoken Language Translation Research Laboratories, Kyoto, Japan.

Yonay, Y.P. (1998) *The Struggle Over the Soul of Economics: Institutionalist and Neoclassical Economics in America between the Wars*, Princeton, NJ: Princeton University Press.

Young, J.T. (1997) *Economics as a Moral Science: The Political Economy of Adam Smith*, Lyme, NH: Edward Elgar.

——(forthcoming) *Adam Smith and the Physiocrats: Contrasting Views of the Law of Nature*.

Ziliak, S.T. (forthcoming) "Freedom to Exchange and the Rhetoric of Economic Correctness," *Research in the History of Economic Thought and Methodology*.

Zimmerman, K.F. (ed.) (2002) *Frontiers in Economics*, New York: Springer.

Zweig, F. (1950) *Economic Ideas: A Study of Historical Perspectives*, New York: Prentice-Hall.

Subject Index

Index of Names